GCSE
Chemistry

No doubt about it, GCSE Chemistry is a tough subject. Not to worry —
this CGP book has it covered, from facts and theory to practical skills.

What's more, we've included exam-style practice in every topic, *and*
put in a full set of practice papers to help you sharpen up your exam skills.

There are fully-worked answers at the back too, so it's easy to check how
you're doing and find out how to pick up the best marks possible!

How to access your free Online Edition

This book includes a free Online Edition to read on your PC, Mac or tablet.
You'll just need to go to **cgpbooks.co.uk/extras** and enter this code:

0948 7869 1922 2949

By the way, this code only works for one person. If somebody else has used
this book before you, they might have already claimed the Online Edition.

Complete
Revision & Practice
<u>Everything</u> you need to pass the exams!

Contents

Throughout this book you'll see grade stamps like these: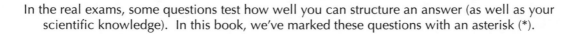

These grade stamps help to show how difficult the questions are.
Remember — to get a top grade you need to be able to answer **all** the questions, not just the hardest ones.

In the real exams, some questions test how well you can structure an answer (as well as your
scientific knowledge). In this book, we've marked these questions with an asterisk (*).

Published by CGP

Editors: Alex Billings, Charlotte Burrows, Charles Kitts, Christopher Lindle, Ciara McGlade, Ethan Starmer-Jones and Hayley Thompson.

Contributor: Paddy Gannon.

From original material by Richard Parsons.

With thanks to Barrie Crowther, Emily Forsberg, Emily Garrett, Emily Howe, Glenn Rogers and Karen Wells for the proofreading.

With thanks to Jan Greenway for the copyright research.

Contains public sector information published by the Health and Safety Executive and licensed under the Open Government Licence. http://www.nationalarchives.gov.uk/doc/open-government-licence/version/3/.

Graphs to show trend in Atmospheric CO_2 Concentration and global temperature on pages 166 and 167 based on data by EPICA community members 2004 and Siegenthaler et al 2005.

ISBN: 978 1 78294 881 0

Printed by Elanders Ltd, Newcastle upon Tyne.
Clipart from Corel®

What to Expect in the Exams

Before you get cracking with your <u>revision</u> and <u>exam practice</u>, here's a <u>handy guide</u> to what you'll have to face in the exams — and the <u>special features</u> of this book that we've included especially to <u>help you</u>. You're welcome.

1. **Topics** are Covered in **Different Papers**

For GCSE Chemistry, you'll sit <u>two exam papers</u> at the <u>end</u> of your course.

Paper	Time	No. of marks	Topics Assessed
1	1 hr 45 mins	100	1, 2, 3, 4 and 5
2	1 hr 45 mins	100	1, 6, 7, 8 and 9

2. There are **Different Question Types**

In each exam, you'll be expected to answer a mixture of <u>multiple-choice</u> questions, <u>calculations</u>, <u>short answer</u> questions, and two <u>longer, open response</u> questions.

We've marked open response questions in this book with an asterisk (*).

For <u>open response</u> questions, you'll be marked on the <u>structure</u> of your answer, not just its <u>scientific content</u>. So...

Fortunately, we've included loads of <u>questions</u> in this book, as well as a <u>set of practice papers</u> to give you the <u>best possible preparation</u> for the exams.

<u>Always</u> make sure:

- Your answer is <u>clear</u> and has a <u>logical structure</u>.
- The points you make <u>link together</u> and form a sensible <u>line of reasoning</u> (if appropriate for the question).
- You include <u>detailed, relevant information</u>.

3. You'll be Tested on Your **Maths...**

At least <u>20% of the total marks</u> for GCSE Chemistry will come from questions that test your <u>maths skills</u>. For these questions, always remember to:

EXAMPLE:

Look out for these <u>worked examples</u> in this book — they show you maths skills you'll need in the exam.

- Show your <u>working</u> — you could get marks for this, even if your final answer's wrong.
- Check that you're using the right <u>units</u>.
- Make sure your answer is given to an appropriate number of <u>significant figures</u>.

4. ...and on Your **Practical Skills**

Whenever one of the <u>core practicals</u> crops up in this book, it's marked up with stamps like these...

...and there's a whole section on Practical Skills on pages 194-199.

- GCSE Chemistry contains <u>8 mandatory core practicals</u> that you'll do during the course. You can be asked about these, and the practical skills involved in them, in the exams.
- At least <u>15% of the total marks</u> will be for questions that test your understanding of the practical activities and practical skills.
- For example, you might be asked to comment on the <u>design</u> of an experiment (the <u>apparatus</u> and <u>method</u>), make <u>predictions</u>, <u>analyse</u> or <u>interpret results</u>... Pretty much anything to do with planning and carrying out the investigations.

5. You'll Need to Know About **Working Scientifically**

<u>Working Scientifically</u> is all about how science is applied in the outside world by <u>real scientists</u>.

For example, you might be asked about ways that scientists <u>communicate</u> an idea to get their point across without being <u>biased</u>, or about the <u>limitations</u> of a scientific theory.

Working Scientifically is covered on pages 2-16.

You need to think about the <u>situation</u> that you've been given and use all your <u>scientific savvy</u> to answer the question. Always <u>read the question</u> and any <u>data</u> you've been given really carefully <u>before</u> you start writing your answer.

The Scientific Method

This section isn't about how to 'do' science — but it does show you the way most scientists work.

Scientists Come Up With **Hypotheses** — Then **Test** Them

1) Scientists try to explain things. They start by observing something they don't understand.

2) They then come up with a hypothesis — a possible explanation for what they've observed.

3) The next step is to test whether the hypothesis might be right or not. This involves making a prediction based on the hypothesis and testing it by gathering evidence (i.e. data) from investigations. If evidence from experiments backs up a prediction, you're a step closer to figuring out if the hypothesis is true.

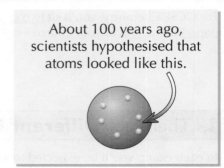
About 100 years ago, scientists hypothesised that atoms looked like this.

Several Scientists Will **Test** a Hypothesis

1) Normally, scientists share their findings in peer-reviewed journals, or at conferences.

2) Peer-review is where other scientists check results and scientific explanations to make sure they're 'scientific' (e.g. that experiments have been done in a sensible way) before they're published. It helps to detect false claims, but it doesn't mean that findings are correct — just that they're not wrong in any obvious way.

3) Once other scientists have found out about a hypothesis, they'll start basing their own predictions on it and carry out their own experiments. They'll also try to reproduce the original experiments to check the results — and if all the experiments in the world back up the hypothesis, then scientists start to think the hypothesis is true.

4) However, if a scientist does an experiment that doesn't fit with the hypothesis (and other scientists can reproduce the results) then the hypothesis may need to be modified or scrapped altogether.

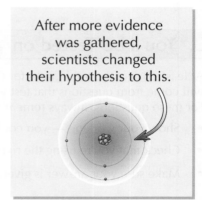
After more evidence was gathered, scientists changed their hypothesis to this.

If **All** the **Evidence** Supports a Hypothesis, It's **Accepted** — For Now

1) Accepted hypotheses are often referred to as theories. Our currently accepted theories are the ones that have survived this 'trial by evidence' — they've been tested many times over the years and survived.

2) However, theories never become totally indisputable fact. If new evidence comes along that can't be explained using the existing theory, then the hypothesising and testing is likely to start all over again.

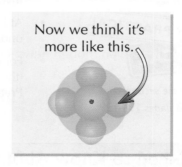
Now we think it's more like this.

Scientific models are constantly being refined...

The scientific method has been developed over time. Aristotle (a Greek philosopher) was the first person to realise that theories need to be based on observations. Muslim scholars then introduced the ideas of creating a hypothesis, testing it, and repeating work to check results.

Models and Communication

Once scientists have made a <u>new discovery</u>, they <u>don't</u> just keep it to themselves. Oh no. Time to learn about how scientific discoveries are <u>communicated</u>, and the <u>models</u> that are used to represent theories.

Theories Can Involve **Different Types** of **Models**

1) A <u>representational model</u> is a <u>simplified description</u> or <u>picture</u> of what's going on in real life. Like all models, it can be used to <u>explain observations</u> and <u>make predictions</u>. E.g. the Bohr model of an atom is a simplified way of showing the arrangement of electrons in an atom (see p.24). It can be used to explain trends down groups in the periodic table.

Scientists test models by carrying out experiments to check that the predictions made by the model happen as expected.

2) <u>Computational models</u> use computers to make <u>simulations</u> of complex real-life processes, such as climate change. They're used when there are a <u>lot</u> of different <u>variables</u> (factors that change) to consider, and because you can easily <u>change their design</u> to take into account <u>new data</u>.

3) All models have <u>limitations</u> on what they can explain or predict. E.g. <u>ball and stick models</u> (a type of spatial model) can be used to show how ions are arranged in an ionic compound. One of their limitations is that they <u>don't show</u> the <u>relative sizes</u> of the ions (see p.37).

Scientific Discoveries are **Communicated** to the **General Public**

Some scientific discoveries show that people should <u>change their habits</u>, or they might provide ideas that could be <u>developed</u> into new <u>technology</u>. So scientists need to <u>tell the world</u> about their discoveries.

Technologies are being developed that make use of <u>fullerenes</u> (see p.43). These include <u>drug delivery systems</u> for use in medicine. Information about these systems needs to be communicated to <u>doctors</u> so they can <u>use</u> them, and to <u>patients</u>, so they can make <u>informed decisions</u> about their <u>treatment</u>.

Scientific **Evidence** can be **Presented** in a **Biased Way**

1) Scientific discoveries that are reported in the <u>media</u> (e.g. newspapers or television) <u>aren't</u> peer-reviewed.

2) This means that, even though news stories are often <u>based</u> on data that has been peer-reviewed, the data might be <u>presented</u> in a way that is <u>over-simplified</u> or <u>inaccurate</u>, making it open to <u>misinterpretation</u>.

3) People who want to make a point can sometimes <u>present data</u> in a <u>biased way</u> (sometimes <u>without knowing</u> they're doing it). For example, a scientist might overemphasise a relationship in the data, or a newspaper article might describe details of data <u>supporting</u> an idea without giving any evidence <u>against</u> it.

Companies can present biased data to help sell products...

Sometimes a company may only want you to see half of the story so they present the data in a <u>biased way</u>. For example, a pharmaceutical company may want to encourage you to buy their drugs by telling you about all the <u>positives</u>, but not report the results of any <u>unfavourable studies</u>.

Issues Created by Science

Science has helped us <u>make progress</u> in loads of areas, from medicine to space travel.
But science still has its <u>issues</u>. And it <u>can't answer everything</u>, as you're about to find out.

Scientific Developments are Great, but they can Raise Issues

Scientific <u>knowledge is increased</u> by doing experiments. And this knowledge leads to <u>scientific developments</u>, e.g. new technologies or new advice. These developments can create <u>issues</u> though.
For example:

> <u>Economic issues:</u> Society <u>can't</u> always <u>afford</u> to do things scientists recommend (e.g. investing in alternative energy sources) without <u>cutting back elsewhere</u>.

> <u>Social issues:</u> Decisions based on scientific evidence affect <u>people</u> — e.g. should fossil fuels be taxed more highly? Would the effect on people's lifestyles be <u>acceptable</u>?

> <u>Personal issues:</u> Some decisions will affect <u>individuals</u>. For example, someone might support <u>alternative energy</u>, but object if a <u>wind farm</u> is built next to their house.

> <u>Environmental issues:</u> <u>Human activity</u> often affects the <u>natural environment</u>. For example, building a <u>dam</u> to produce electricity will change the <u>local habitat</u> so some species might be displaced. But it will also reduce our need for <u>fossil fuels</u>, so will help to reduce <u>climate change</u>.

Science Can't Answer Every Question — Especially Ethical Ones

1) We don't <u>understand everything</u>. We're always finding out <u>more</u>, but we'll never know <u>all</u> the answers.

2) In order to answer scientific questions, scientists need <u>data</u> to provide <u>evidence</u> for their hypotheses.

3) Some questions can't be answered <u>yet</u> because the data <u>can't</u> currently be <u>collected</u>, or because there's <u>not enough</u> data to <u>support</u> a theory.

4) <u>Eventually</u>, as we get <u>more evidence</u>, we'll answer some of the questions that <u>currently</u> can't be answered, e.g. what the impact of global warming on sea levels will be. But there will always be the "<u>Should we be doing this at all?</u>"-type questions that experiments <u>can't</u> help us to answer...

> Think about <u>new drugs which can be taken to boost your 'brain power'</u>.
> - Some people think they're <u>good</u> as they could improve concentration or memory. New drugs could let people think in ways beyond the powers of normal brains.
> - Other people say they're <u>bad</u> — they could give some people an <u>unfair advantage</u> in exams. And people might be <u>pressured</u> into taking them so that they could work more <u>effectively</u>, and for <u>longer hours</u>.

There are often issues with new scientific developments...

The trouble is, there's often <u>no clear right answer</u> where these issues are concerned. Different people have <u>different views</u>, depending on their priorities. These issues are full of <u>grey areas</u>.

Risk

Scientific discoveries are often great, but they can prove risky. With dangers all around, you've got to be aware of hazards — this includes how likely they are to cause harm and how serious the effects may be.

Nothing is Completely Risk-Free

1) A hazard is something that could potentially cause harm.

2) All hazards have a risk attached to them — this is the chance that the hazard will cause harm.

3) The risks of some things seem pretty obvious, or we've known about them for a while, like the risk of causing acid rain by polluting the atmosphere, or of having a car accident when you're travelling in a car.

4) New technology arising from scientific advances can bring new risks, e.g. scientists are unsure whether nanoparticles that are being used in cosmetics and suncream might be harming the cells in our bodies. These risks need to be considered alongside the benefits of the technology, e.g. improved sun protection.

5) You can estimate the size of a risk based on how many times something happens in a big sample (e.g. 100 000 people) over a given period (e.g. a year). For example, you could assess the risk of a driver crashing by recording how many people in a group of 100 000 drivers crashed their cars over a year.

6) To make decisions about activities that involve hazards, we need to take into account the chance of the hazard causing harm, and how serious the consequences would be if it did. If an activity involves a hazard that's very likely to cause harm, with serious consequences if it does, that activity is considered high risk.

People Make Their Own Decisions About Risk

1) Not all risks have the same consequences, e.g. if you chop veg with a sharp knife you risk cutting your finger, but if you go scuba-diving you risk death. You're much more likely to cut your finger during half an hour of chopping than to die during half an hour of scuba-diving. But most people are happier to accept a higher probability of an accident if the consequences are short-lived and fairly minor.

2) People tend to be more willing to accept a risk if they choose to do something (e.g. go scuba diving), compared to having the risk imposed on them (e.g. having a nuclear power station built next door).

3) People's perception of risk (how risky they think something is) isn't always accurate. They tend to view familiar activities as low-risk and unfamiliar activities as high-risk — even if that's not the case. For example, cycling on roads is often high-risk, but many people are happy to do it because it's a familiar activity. Air travel is actually pretty safe, but a lot of people perceive it as high-risk.

4) People may over-estimate the risk of things with long-term or invisible effects, e.g. ionising radiation.

The pros and cons of new technology must be weighed up...

The world's a dangerous place and it's impossible to rule out the chance of an accident altogether. But if you can recognise hazards and take steps to reduce the risks, you're more likely to stay safe.

Designing Investigations

Dig out your lab coat and dust off your badly-scratched safety goggles... it's <u>investigation time</u>.

Evidence Can **Support** or **Disprove** a **Hypothesis**

1) Scientists <u>observe</u> things and come up with <u>hypotheses</u> to test them (see p.2).
You need to be able to do the same. For example:

> <u>Observation</u>: People with big feet have spots. <u>Hypothesis</u>: Having big feet causes spots.

2) To <u>determine</u> whether or not a hypothesis is <u>right</u>, you need to do an <u>investigation</u> to gather evidence. To do this, you need to use your hypothesis to make a <u>prediction</u> — something you think <u>will happen</u> that you can test. E.g. people who have bigger feet will have more spots.

Investigations include experiments and studies.

3) Investigations are used to see if there are <u>patterns</u> or <u>relationships</u> between <u>two variables</u>, e.g. to see if there's a pattern or relationship between the variables 'number of spots' and 'size of feet'.

Evidence Needs to be **Repeatable**, **Reproducible** and **Valid**

1) <u>Repeatable</u> means that if the <u>same person</u> does an experiment again using the <u>same methods</u> and equipment, they'll get <u>similar results</u>.

2) <u>Reproducible</u> means that if <u>someone else</u> does the experiment, or a <u>different</u> method or piece of equipment is used, the results will still be <u>similar</u>.

3) If data is <u>repeatable</u> and <u>reproducible</u>, it's <u>reliable</u> and scientists are more likely to <u>have confidence</u> in it.

4) <u>Valid results</u> are both repeatable and reproducible AND they <u>answer the original question</u>. They come from experiments that were designed to be a <u>fair test</u>...

Make an Investigation a **Fair Test** By **Controlling the Variables**

1) In a lab experiment you usually <u>change one variable</u> and <u>measure</u> how it affects <u>another variable</u>.

2) To make it a fair test, <u>everything else</u> that could affect the results should <u>stay the same</u> — otherwise you can't tell if the thing you're changing is causing the results or not.

3) The variable you <u>CHANGE</u> is called the <u>INDEPENDENT</u> variable.

4) The variable you <u>MEASURE</u> when you change the independent variable is the <u>DEPENDENT</u> variable.

5) The variables that you <u>KEEP THE SAME</u> are called <u>CONTROL</u> variables.

> You could find how <u>temperature</u> affects <u>reaction rate</u> by measuring the <u>volume of gas</u> formed over time. The <u>independent variable</u> is the <u>temperature</u>. The <u>dependent variable</u> is the <u>volume of gas</u> produced. <u>Control variables</u> include the <u>concentration</u> and <u>amounts</u> of reactants, the <u>time period</u> you measure, etc.

6) Because you can't always control all the variables, you often need to use a <u>control experiment</u>. This is an experiment that's kept under the <u>same conditions</u> as the rest of the investigation, but <u>doesn't</u> have anything <u>done</u> to it. This is so that you can see what happens when you don't change anything at all.

Designing Investigations

The **Bigger** the **Sample Size** the **Better**

1) Data based on <u>small samples</u> isn't as good as data based on large samples. A sample should <u>represent</u> the <u>whole population</u> (i.e. it should share as many of the characteristics in the population as possible) — a small sample can't do that as well. It's also harder to spot <u>anomalies</u> if your sample size is too small.

2) The <u>bigger</u> the sample size the <u>better</u>, but scientists have to be <u>realistic</u> when choosing how big. For example, if you were studying the effects of a chemical used to sterilise water on the people drinking it, it'd be great to study <u>everyone</u> who was drinking the water (a huge sample), but it'd take ages and cost a bomb. It's more realistic to study a thousand people, with a mixture of ages, gender, and race.

Data Should be **Repeatable**, **Reproducible**, **Accurate** and **Precise**

1) To <u>check repeatability</u> you need to <u>repeat</u> the readings and check that the results are similar. You need to repeat each reading at least <u>three times</u>.

2) To make sure your results are <u>reproducible</u> you can cross check them by taking a <u>second set of readings</u> with <u>another instrument</u> (or a <u>different observer</u>).

3) Your data also needs to be <u>accurate</u>. Really accurate results are those that are <u>really close</u> to the <u>true answer</u>. The accuracy of your results usually depends on your <u>method</u> — you need to make sure you're measuring the right thing and that you don't <u>miss anything</u> that should be included in the measurements.
E.g. estimating the <u>amount of gas</u> released from a reaction by <u>counting the bubbles</u> isn't very accurate because you might <u>miss</u> some of the bubbles and they might have different <u>volumes</u>. It's <u>more accurate</u> to measure the volume of gas released using a <u>gas syringe</u> (see p.194).

4) Your data also needs to be <u>precise</u>. Precise results are ones where the data is <u>all really close</u> to the <u>mean</u> (average) of your repeated results (i.e. not spread out).

Repeat	Data set 1	Data set 2
1	12	11
2	14	17
3	13	14
Mean	<u>13</u>	<u>14</u>

Data set 1 is more precise than data set 2.

Your **Equipment** has to be **Right for the Job**

1) The measuring equipment you use has to be <u>sensitive enough</u> to measure the changes you're looking for. For example, if you need to measure changes of 1 cm³ you need to use a <u>measuring cylinder</u> or <u>burette</u> that can measure in <u>1 cm³</u> steps — it'd be no good trying with one that only measures 10 cm³ steps.

2) The <u>smallest change</u> a measuring instrument can <u>detect</u> is called its <u>resolution</u>. E.g. some mass balances have a resolution of 1 g, some have a resolution of 0.1 g, and some are even more sensitive.

3) Also, equipment needs to be <u>calibrated</u> by measuring a known value. If there's a <u>difference</u> between the <u>measured</u> and <u>known value</u>, you can use this to <u>correct</u> the inaccuracy of the equipment.

Designing Investigations

You Need to Look out for **Errors** and **Anomalous Results**

1) The results of your experiment will always <u>vary a bit</u> because of <u>random errors</u> — unpredictable differences caused by things like <u>human errors</u> in <u>measuring</u>. E.g. the errors you make when you take a reading from a burette are <u>random</u>. You have to <u>estimate</u> or <u>round</u> the level when it's between two marks — so sometimes your figure will be a bit above the real one, and sometimes it will be a bit below.

2) You can <u>reduce</u> the effect of random errors by taking <u>repeat readings</u> and finding the <u>mean</u>. This will make your results <u>more precise</u>.

3) If a measurement is wrong by the <u>same amount every time</u>, it's called a <u>systematic error</u>. For example, if you measured from the very end of your ruler instead of from the 0 cm mark every time, all your measurements would be a bit small. Repeating the experiment in the exact same way and calculating a mean <u>won't</u> correct a systematic error.

If there's no systematic error, then doing repeats and calculating a mean can make your results more accurate.

4) Just to make things more complicated, if a systematic error is caused by using <u>equipment</u> that <u>isn't zeroed properly</u>, it's called a <u>zero error</u>. For example, if a mass balance always reads 1 gram before you put anything on it, all your measurements will be 1 gram too heavy.

5) You can <u>compensate</u> for some systematic errors if you know about them, e.g. if a mass balance always reads 1 gram before you put anything on it, you can subtract 1 gram from all your results.

6) Sometimes you get a result that <u>doesn't fit in</u> with the rest at all. This is called an <u>anomalous result</u>. You should investigate it and try to <u>work out what happened</u>. If you can work out what happened (e.g. you measured something wrong) you can <u>ignore</u> it when processing your results.

Investigations Can be **Hazardous**

1) <u>Hazards</u> from science experiments might include:

- <u>Microorganisms</u>, e.g. some bacteria can make you ill.
- <u>Chemicals</u>, e.g. sulfuric acid can burn your skin and alcohols catch fire easily.
- <u>Fire</u>, e.g. an unattended Bunsen burner is a fire hazard.
- <u>Electricity</u>, e.g. faulty electrical equipment could give you a shock.

You can find out about potential hazards by looking in textbooks, doing some internet research, or asking your teacher.

2) Part of planning an investigation is making sure that it's <u>safe</u>.

3) You should always make sure that you <u>identify</u> all the hazards that you might encounter. Then you should think of ways of <u>reducing the risks</u> from the hazards you've identified. For example:

- If you're working with <u>sulfuric acid</u>, always wear gloves and safety goggles. This will reduce the risk of the acid coming into contact with your skin and eyes.
- If you're using a <u>Bunsen burner</u>, stand it on a heat proof mat. This will reduce the risk of starting a fire.

Designing an investigation is an involved process...

Collecting <u>data</u> is what investigations are all about. Designing a good investigation is really important to make sure that any data collected is <u>accurate</u>, <u>precise</u>, <u>repeatable</u> and <u>reproducible</u>.

Processing Data

Processing your data means doing some <u>calculations</u> with it to make it <u>more useful</u>.

Data Needs to be **Organised**

1) <u>Tables</u> are dead useful for <u>organising data</u>.

2) When you draw a table <u>use a ruler</u> and make sure <u>each column</u> has a <u>heading</u> (including the <u>units</u>).

There are **Different Ways** of **Processing Your Data**

1) When you've done repeats of an experiment you should always calculate the <u>mean</u> (average). To do this <u>add together</u> all the data values and <u>divide</u> by the total number of values in the sample.

2) You might also need to calculate the <u>range</u> (how spread out the data is). To do this find the <u>largest</u> number and <u>subtract</u> the <u>smallest</u> number from it.

Ignore anomalous results when calculating the mean and the range.

3) The <u>mode</u> is the <u>most common</u> result in your data set.

4) The <u>median</u> is the 'middle' value. You find it by arranging all your data in <u>numerical order</u>, and then seeing which value's in the middle. If there's two, you take the <u>mean</u> of them.

 **EXAMPLE:** **The results of an experiment to find the mass of gas lost from two reactions are shown below. Calculate the mean and the range for the mass of gas lost in each reaction.**

Test tube	Repeat 1 (g)	Repeat 2 (g)	Repeat 3 (g)	Mean (g)	Range (g)
A	28	37	32	(28 + 37 + 32) ÷ 3 = 32	37 − 28 = 9
B	47	51	60	(47 + 51 + 60) ÷ 3 = 53	60 − 47 = 13

Round to the **Lowest Number** of **Significant Figures**

The <u>first significant figure</u> of a number is the first digit that's <u>not zero</u>. The second and third significant figures come <u>straight after</u> (even if they're zeros). You should be aware of significant figures in calculations.

1) In <u>any</u> calculation where you need to round, you should round the answer to the <u>lowest number of significant figures</u> (s.f.) given.

2) Remember to write down <u>how many</u> significant figures you've rounded to after your answer.

3) If your calculation has multiple steps, <u>only</u> round the <u>final</u> answer, or it won't be as accurate.

 **EXAMPLE:** **The volume of one mole of gas is 24.0 dm³ at room temperature and pressure. How many moles are there in 4.6 dm³ of gas under the same conditions?**

No. of moles of gas = 4.6 dm³ ÷ 24.0 dm³ = 0.19166... = 0.19 mol (2 s.f.)

2 s.f.   3 s.f.

Final answer should be rounded to 2 s.f.

 EXAM TIP

Don't forget your calculator...

In the exam you could be given some <u>data</u> and be expected to <u>process it</u> in some way. Make sure you keep an eye on <u>significant figures</u> in your answers and <u>always write down your working</u>.

Presenting Data

Once you've processed your data, e.g. by calculating the mean, you can present your results in a nice <u>chart</u> or <u>graph</u>. This will help you to <u>spot any patterns</u> in your data.

Bar Charts Can be Used to Show Different Types of Data

Bar charts can be used to display:

1) <u>Categoric</u> data (comes in distinct categories, e.g. compound colour, group number).

2) <u>Discrete</u> data (the data can be counted in chunks, where there's no in-between value, e.g. number of protons is discrete because you can't have half a proton).

3) <u>Continuous</u> data (numerical data that can have any value in a range, e.g. length or temperature).

There are some <u>golden rules</u> you need to follow for <u>drawing</u> bar charts:

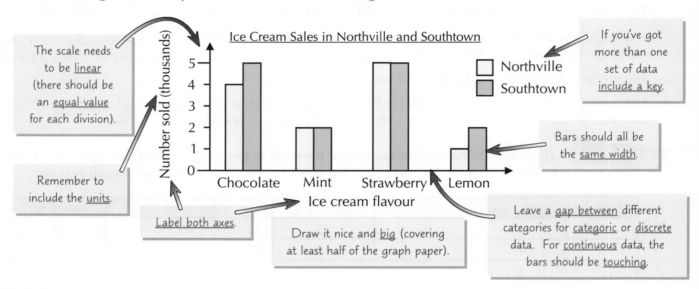

The scale needs to be <u>linear</u> (there should be an <u>equal value</u> for each division).

Remember to include the <u>units</u>.

<u>Label both axes</u>.

Draw it nice and <u>big</u> (covering at least half of the graph paper).

If you've got more than one set of data <u>include a key</u>.

Bars should all be the <u>same width</u>.

Leave a <u>gap between</u> different categories for <u>categoric</u> or <u>discrete</u> data. For <u>continuous</u> data, the bars should be <u>touching</u>.

Graphs Can be Used to Plot Continuous Data

1) If both variables are <u>continuous</u> you should use a <u>graph</u> to display the data.

2) Here are the <u>rules</u> for plotting points on a graph:

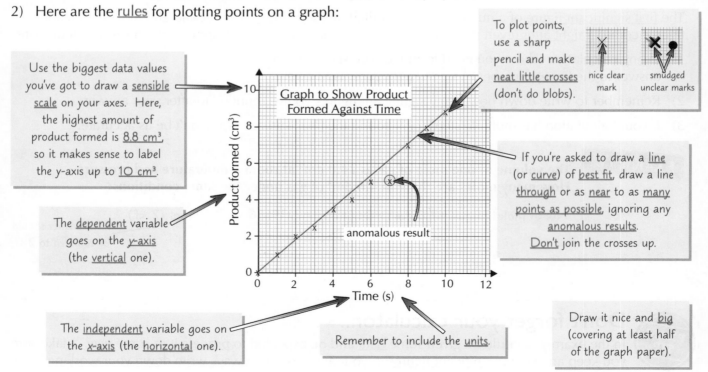

Use the biggest data values you've got to draw a <u>sensible</u> <u>scale</u> on your axes. Here, the highest amount of product formed is <u>8.8 cm³</u>, so it makes sense to label the y-axis up to <u>10 cm³</u>.

The <u>dependent</u> variable goes on the <u>y-axis</u> (the <u>vertical</u> one).

The <u>independent</u> variable goes on the <u>x-axis</u> (the <u>horizontal</u> one).

Remember to include the <u>units</u>.

To plot points, use a sharp pencil and make <u>neat little crosses</u> (don't do blobs).

If you're asked to draw a <u>line</u> (or <u>curve</u>) of <u>best fit</u>, draw a line <u>through</u> or as <u>near</u> to as <u>many points as possible</u>, ignoring any <u>anomalous results</u>. <u>Don't</u> join the crosses up.

Draw it nice and <u>big</u> (covering at least half of the graph paper).

More on Graphs

Graphs aren't just fun to plot, they're also really useful for showing <u>trends</u> in your data.

Graphs Can Give You a Lot of Information About Your Data

1) The <u>gradient</u> (slope) of a graph tells you how quickly the <u>dependent variable</u> changes if you change the <u>independent variable</u>.

You can use this method to calculate any rates from a graph, not just the rate of a reaction. Just remember that a rate is how much something changes over time, so x needs to be the time.

$$\text{gradient} = \frac{\text{change in } y}{\text{change in } x}$$

The <u>graph</u> below shows the <u>volume of gas</u> produced in a reaction against <u>time</u>. The graph is <u>linear</u> (it's a straight line graph), so you can simply calculate the <u>gradient</u> of the line to find out the <u>rate of reaction</u>.

1) To calculate the gradient, pick <u>two points</u> on the line that are easy to read and a <u>good distance</u> apart.

2) <u>Draw a line down</u> from one of the points and a <u>line across</u> from the other to make a <u>triangle</u>. The line drawn down the side of the triangle is the <u>change in y</u> and the line across the bottom is the <u>change in x</u>.

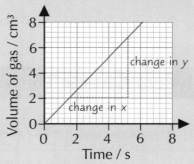

Change in y = 6.8 − 2.0 = 4.8 cm³   Change in x = 5.2 − 1.6 = 3.6 s

Rate = gradient = $\frac{\text{change in } y}{\text{change in } x} = \frac{4.8 \text{ cm}^3}{3.6 \text{ s}} = \underline{1.3 \text{ cm}^3\text{s}^{-1}}$

The units of the gradient are (units of y)/(units of x). cm³ s⁻¹ can also be written as cm³/s.

2) If you've got a <u>curved graph</u>, you can find the rate at any point by drawing a <u>tangent</u> — a straight line that touches a <u>single point</u> on a curve. You can then find the gradient of the tangent in the usual way, to give you the rate at that <u>point</u> (see page 142 for more on calculating gradients).

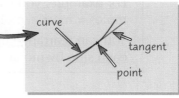

3) The <u>intercept</u> of a graph is where the line of best fit crosses one of the <u>axes</u>. The <u>x-intercept</u> is where the line of best fit crosses the x-axis and the <u>y-intercept</u> is where it crosses the <u>y-axis</u>.

Graphs Show the Relationship Between Two Variables

1) You can get <u>three</u> types of <u>correlation</u> (relationship) between variables:

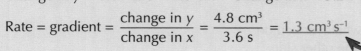

POSITIVE correlation: as one variable <u>increases</u> the other <u>increases</u>.

INVERSE (negative) correlation: as one variable <u>increases</u> the other <u>decreases</u>.

NO correlation: <u>no relationship</u> between the two variables.

2) Just because there's correlation, it doesn't mean the change in one variable is <u>causing</u> the change in the other — there might be <u>other factors</u> involved (see page 14).

Units and Equations

Graphs and maths skills are all very well, but the numbers don't mean much if you don't get the <u>units</u> right.

S.I. Units Are Used All Round the World

1) It wouldn't be all that useful if I defined volume in terms of <u>bath tubs</u>, you defined it in terms of <u>egg-cups</u> and my pal Fred defined it in terms of <u>balloons</u> — we'd never be able to compare our data.

2) To stop this happening, scientists have come up with a set of <u>standard units</u>, called S.I. units, that all scientists use to measure their data. Here are some S.I. units you'll see in chemistry:

Quantity	S.I. Base Unit
mass	kilogram, kg
length	metre, m
time	second, s
amount of substance	mole, mol

Always Check The Values Used in Equations Have the Right Units

1) Equations (sometimes called formulas) show <u>relationships</u> between <u>variables</u>.

2) To <u>rearrange</u> an equation, make sure that whatever you do to <u>one side</u> of the equation you also do to the <u>other side</u>.

> For example, you can find the <u>number of moles</u> of something using the equation:
> moles = mass ÷ molar mass.
> You can <u>rearrange</u> this equation to find the <u>mass</u> by <u>multiplying</u> <u>each side</u> by molar mass to give: mass = moles × molar mass.

3) To use an equation, you need to know the values of <u>all but one</u> of the variables. <u>Substitute</u> the values you do know into the formula, and do the calculation to work out the final variable.

4) Always make sure the values you put into an equation have the <u>right units</u>. For example, you might have done a titration experiment to work out the concentration of a solution. The volume of the solution will probably have been measured in cm^3, but the equation to find concentration uses volume in dm^3. So you'll have to <u>convert</u> your volume from cm^3 to dm^3 before you put it into the equation.

5) To make sure your units are <u>correct</u>, it can help to write down the <u>units</u> on each line of your <u>calculation</u>.

S.I. units help scientists to compare data...

You can only really <u>compare</u> things if they're in the <u>same units</u>. E.g. if the concentration of an acid was measured in $mol\ dm^{-3}$ and another acid in $g\ cm^{-3}$, it'd be hard to compare them.

Converting Units

You can <u>convert units</u> using <u>scaling prefixes</u>. This can save you from having to write a lot of 0's...

Scaling Prefixes Can Be Used for Large and Small Quantities

1) Quantities come in a huge <u>range</u> of sizes. For example, the volume of a swimming pool might be around 2 000 000 000 cm^3, while the volume of a cup is around 250 cm^3.

2) To make the size of numbers more <u>manageable</u>, larger or smaller units are used. These are the <u>S.I. base units</u> (e.g. metres) with a <u>prefix</u> in front:

Prefix	tera (T)	giga (G)	mega (M)	kilo (k)	deci (d)	centi (c)	milli (m)	micro (μ)	nano (n)
Multiple of Unit	10^{12}	10^9	1 000 000 (10^6)	1000	0.1	0.01	0.001	0.000001 (10^{-6})	10^{-9}

3) These <u>prefixes</u> tell you <u>how much bigger</u> or <u>smaller</u> a unit is than the base unit. So one <u>kilo</u>metre is <u>one thousand</u> metres.

4) To <u>swap</u> from one unit to another, all you need to know is what number you have to divide or multiply by to get from the original unit to the new unit — this is called the <u>conversion factor</u>.

The conversion factor is the number of times the smaller unit goes into the larger unit.

- To go from a <u>bigger unit</u> (like m) to a <u>smaller unit</u> (like cm), you <u>multiply</u> by the conversion factor.
- To go from a <u>smaller unit</u> (like g) to a <u>bigger unit</u> (like kg), you <u>divide</u> by the conversion factor.

5) Here are some conversions that'll be useful for GCSE chemistry:

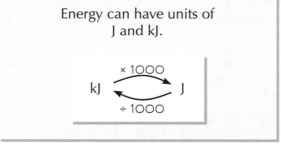

Energy can have units of J and kJ.

Mass can have units of kg and g.

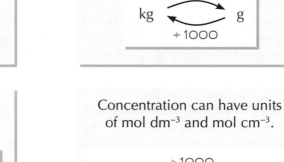

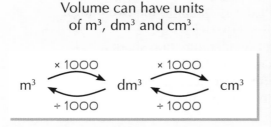

Volume can have units of m^3, dm^3 and cm^3.

Concentration can have units of mol dm^{-3} and mol cm^{-3}.

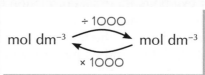

To convert from bigger units to smaller units...

...<u>multiply</u> by the <u>conversion factor</u>, and to convert from <u>smaller units</u> to <u>bigger units</u>, <u>divide</u> by the <u>conversion factor</u>. Don't go getting this the wrong way round or you'll get some odd answers.

Drawing Conclusions

Once you've carried out an experiment and processed your data, it's time to work out <u>what your data shows</u>.

You Can **Only Conclude** What the Data Shows and **No More**

1) Drawing conclusions might seem pretty straightforward — you just <u>look at your data</u> and <u>say what pattern or relationship you see</u> between the dependent and independent variables.

The table on the right shows the rate of a reaction in the presence of two <u>different</u> catalysts:	Catalyst	Rate of Reaction / cm³ s⁻¹	<u>CONCLUSION</u>: Catalyst <u>B</u> makes <u>this reaction</u> go faster than catalyst A.
	A	13.5	
	B	19.5	
	No catalyst	5.5	

2) But you've got to be really careful that your conclusion <u>matches the data</u> you've got and <u>doesn't go any further</u>.

You <u>can't</u> conclude that catalyst B increases the rate of <u>any other reaction</u> more than catalyst A — the results might be completely different.

3) You also need to be able to <u>use your results</u> to <u>justify your conclusion</u> (i.e. back up your conclusion with some specific data).

The rate of this reaction was <u>6 cm³ s⁻¹ faster</u> using catalyst B compared with catalyst A.

4) When writing a conclusion you need to <u>refer back</u> to the original hypothesis and say whether the data <u>supports it</u> or not:

The hypothesis for this experiment might have been that catalyst B would make the reaction go <u>quicker</u> than catalyst A. If so, the data <u>supports</u> the hypothesis.

Correlation **DOES NOT** Mean **Cause**

If two things are correlated (i.e. there's a relationship between them) it <u>doesn't</u> necessarily mean a change in one variable is <u>causing</u> the change in the other — this is <u>REALLY IMPORTANT</u> — <u>DON'T FORGET IT</u>. There are <u>three possible reasons</u> for a correlation:

1) <u>CHANCE</u>: It might seem strange, but two things can show a correlation purely due to <u>chance</u>.

> For example, one study might find a correlation between people's hair colour and how good they are at frisbee. But other scientists <u>don't</u> get a correlation when they investigate it — the results of the first study are just a <u>fluke</u>.

2) <u>LINKED BY A 3RD VARIABLE</u>: A lot of the time it may <u>look</u> as if a change in one variable is causing a change in the other, but it <u>isn't</u> — a <u>third variable links</u> the two things.

> For example, there's a correlation between <u>water temperature</u> and <u>shark attacks</u>. This isn't because warmer water makes sharks crazy. Instead, they're linked by a third variable — the <u>number of people swimming</u> (more people swim when the water's hotter, and with more people in the water you get more shark attacks).

3) <u>CAUSE</u>: Sometimes a change in one variable does <u>cause</u> a change in the other. You can only conclude that a correlation is due to cause when you've <u>controlled all the variables</u> that could affect the result.

> For example, there's a correlation between <u>smoking</u> and <u>lung cancer</u>. This is because chemicals in tobacco smoke cause lung cancer. This conclusion was only made once <u>other variables</u> (such as age and exposure to other things that cause cancer) had been <u>controlled</u> and shown <u>not</u> to affect people's risk of getting lung cancer.

Uncertainty

Uncertainty is how sure you can really be about your data. There's a little bit of maths to do, and also a formula to learn. But don't worry too much — it's no more than a simple bit of subtraction and division.

Uncertainty is the Amount of Error Your Measurements Might Have

1) When you repeat a measurement, you often get a slightly different figure each time you do it due to random error (see page 8). This means that each result has some uncertainty to it.

2) The measurements you make will also have some uncertainty in them due to limits in the resolution of the equipment you use (see page 7).

3) This all means that the mean of a set of results will also have some uncertainty to it. You can calculate the uncertainty of a mean result using the equation:

$$\text{uncertainty} = \frac{\text{range}}{2}$$

The range is the largest value minus the smallest value (see p.9).

4) The larger the range, the less precise your results are and the more uncertainty there will be in your results. Uncertainties are shown using the '±' symbol.

EXAMPLE:

The table below shows the results of a titration experiment to determine the volume of 0.5 mol dm⁻³ sodium hydroxide solution needed to neutralise 25 cm³ of a solution of hydrochloric acid with unknown concentration. Calculate the uncertainty of the mean.

1) First work out the range:

Range = 20.10 − 19.80
      = 0.30 cm³

Repeat	1	2	3	mean
Volume of sodium hydroxide / cm³	20.10	19.80	20.00	19.97

2) Use the range to find the uncertainty:

Uncertainty = range ÷ 2 = 0.30 ÷ 2 = 0.15 cm³
So the uncertainty of the mean = 19.97 ± 0.15 cm³

5) Measuring a greater amount of something helps to reduce uncertainty.

> For example, in a rate of reaction experiment, measuring the amount of product formed over a longer period compared to a shorter period will reduce the uncertainty in your results.

The smaller the uncertainty, the more precise your results...

Remember that equation for uncertainty. You never know when you might need it — you could be expected to use it in the exams. You need to make sure all the data is in the same units though. For example, if you had some measurements in metres, and some in centimetres, you'd need to convert them all into either metres or centimetres before you set about calculating uncertainty.

Evaluations

Hurrah! The end of another investigation. Well, now you have to work out all the things you did wrong. That's what evaluations are all about I'm afraid. Best get cracking with this page...

Evaluations — Describe How Investigations Could be Improved

An evaluation is a critical analysis of the whole investigation.

1) You should comment on the method — was it valid?
   Did you control all the other variables to make it a fair test?

2) Comment on the quality of the results — was there enough evidence to reach a valid conclusion? Were the results repeatable, reproducible, accurate and precise?

3) Were there any anomalous results? If there were none then say so.
   If there were any, try to explain them — were they caused by errors in measurement?
   Were there any other variables that could have affected the results?
   You should comment on the level of uncertainty in your results too.

4) All this analysis will allow you to say how confident you are that your conclusion is right.

5) Then you can suggest any changes to the method that would improve the quality of the results, so that you could have more confidence in your conclusion. For example, you might suggest changing the way you controlled a variable, or increasing the number of measurements you took. Taking more measurements at narrower intervals could give you a more accurate result. For example:

> Enzymes have an optimum temperature (a temperature at which they work best).
> Say you do an experiment to find an enzyme's optimum temperature and take measurements at 10 °C, 20 °C, 30 °C, 40 °C and 50 °C. The results of this experiment tell you the optimum is 40 °C. You could then repeat the experiment, taking more measurements around 40 °C to a get a more accurate value for the optimum.

6) You could also make more predictions based on your conclusion, then further experiments could be carried out to test them.

When suggesting improvements to the investigation, always make sure that you say why you think this would make the results better.

Always look for ways to improve your investigations

So there you have it — Working Scientifically. Make sure you know this stuff like the back of your hand. It's not just in the lab, when you're carrying out your groundbreaking investigations, that you'll need to know how to work scientifically. You can be asked about it in the exams as well. So swot up...

Chemical Equations

Chemical equations are used to show what is happening to substances involved in chemical reactions. They tell us what atoms are involved and how the substances change during a reaction.

Chemical Changes are Shown Using Chemical Equations

One way to show a chemical reaction is to write a word equation. It's not as quick as using chemical symbols and you can't tell straight away what's happened to each of the atoms, but it's dead easy.

> Here's an example — you're told that methane burns in oxygen giving carbon dioxide and water:
>
> methane + oxygen $\rightarrow$ carbon dioxide + water
>
> The molecules on the left-hand side of the equation are called the reactants (because they react with each other).
>
> The molecules on the right-hand side are called the products (because they've been produced from the reactants).

Symbol Equations Show the Atoms on Both Sides

Chemical changes can be shown in a kind of shorthand using symbol equations. Symbol equations just show the symbols or formulas of the reactants and products...

magnesium + oxygen   magnesium oxide

$$2Mg + O_2 \longrightarrow 2MgO$$

You'll have spotted that there's a '2' in front of the Mg and the MgO. The reason for this is explained on the next page.

Symbol Equations Need to be Balanced

1) There must always be the same number of atoms on both sides — they can't just disappear.

2) You balance the equation by putting numbers in front of the formulas where needed.

3) Take this equation for reacting sulfuric acid (H_2SO_4) with sodium hydroxide (NaOH) to get sodium sulfate (Na_2SO_4) and water (H_2O):

$$H_2SO_4 + NaOH \rightarrow Na_2SO_4 + H_2O$$

The formulas for all of the compounds are correct but the numbers of some atoms don't match up on both sides. E.g. there are 3 Hs on the left, but only 2 on the right. You can't change formulas like H_2SO_4 to H_2SO_5. You can only put numbers in front of them.

4) The equation needs balancing — this is covered on the next page.

Chemical equations form the basis of chemistry...

... so you're going to come across them an awful lot in this book. Remember, the reactants on the left-hand side of the equation react to form the products shown on the right-hand side. What's more, atoms can't be created or destroyed, so there needs to be the same number of each type on the left and right.

Chemical Equations

Here's how to **Balance** an **Equation**

The more you <u>practise</u>, the <u>quicker</u> you get, but all you do is this:

- Find an element that <u>doesn't balance</u> and <u>pencil in a number</u> to try and sort it out.
- <u>See where it gets you</u>. It may create <u>another imbalance</u>, but if so, pencil in <u>another number</u> and see where that gets you.
- Carry on chasing <u>unbalanced</u> elements and it'll <u>sort itself out</u> pretty quickly.

EXAMPLE:

In the equation on the previous page there aren't enough H atoms on the RHS (Right-Hand Side).

1) The only thing you can do about that is make it $2H_2O$ instead of just H_2O:

$$H_2SO_4 + NaOH \rightarrow Na_2SO_4 + 2H_2O$$

2) But that now causes too many H atoms and O atoms on the RHS, so to balance that up you could try putting $2NaOH$ on the LHS (Left-Hand Side):

$$H_2SO_4 + 2NaOH \rightarrow Na_2SO_4 + 2H_2O$$

3) And suddenly there it is. <u>Everything balances</u>. And you'll notice the Na just sorted itself out.

State Symbols Tell You the **State** of a Substance in an **Equation**

You saw on the previous page how a chemical reaction can be shown using a <u>word equation</u> or <u>symbol equation</u>. Symbol equations can also include <u>state symbols</u> next to each substance — they tell you what <u>physical state</u> the reactants and products are in:

> (s) — solid   (l) — liquid   (g) — gas   (aq) — aqueous

'Aqueous' means 'dissolved in water'.

Here are a <u>couple</u> of examples:

> <u>Aqueous</u> hydrogen chloride reacts with <u>solid</u> calcium carbonate to form <u>aqueous</u> calcium chloride, <u>liquid</u> water and carbon dioxide <u>gas</u>:
> $$2HCl_{(aq)} + CaCO_{3(s)} \rightarrow CaCl_{2(aq)} + H_2O_{(l)} + CO_{2(g)}$$

> Chlorine gas reacts with <u>aqueous</u> potassium iodide to form <u>aqueous</u> potassium chloride and <u>solid</u> iodine:
> $$Cl_{2(g)} + 2KI_{(aq)} \rightarrow 2KCl_{(aq)} + I_{2(s)}$$

Getting good at balancing equations takes patience and practice

Remember, a number <u>in front</u> of a formula applies to the <u>entire formula</u> — so $3Na_2SO_4$ means three lots of Na_2SO_4. The little numbers <u>within or at the end</u> of a formula only apply to the <u>atom</u> or <u>brackets</u> immediately before. So the 4 in Na_2SO_4 means there are 4 Os, but there's just 1 S, not 4.

Chemical Equations Involving Ions

Chemical reactions can also involve ions — charged atoms or molecules.

Learn the Formulas of Some Simple Compounds and Ions

1) Here are the chemical formulas of some common molecules. They crop up all the time.

- Water — H_2O
- Ammonia — NH_3
- Carbon dioxide — CO_2
- Hydrogen — H_2
- Chlorine — Cl_2
- Oxygen — O_2

2) You also need to be able to recall the formulas of certain ions.

3) For single atoms, you can use the periodic table to work out what charges their ions will form (see page 33).

Ions form when atoms, or groups of atoms, gain or lose electrons to form charged particles (see page 33).

4) For ions made up of groups of atoms, it's not so simple. You just have to learn these ones.

- Ammonium — NH_4^+
- Hydroxide — OH^-
- Nitrate — NO_3^-
- Carbonate — CO_3^{2-}
- Sulfate — SO_4^{2-}

Ionic Equations Show Just the Useful Bits of Reactions

1) You can also write an ionic equation for any reaction involving ions that happens in solution.

2) In an ionic equation, only the reacting particles (and the products they form) are included.

3) To write an ionic equation, all you need to do is look at the balanced symbol equation and take out any aqueous ions that are present on both sides of the equation.

 **EXAMPLE:** Write the ionic equation for the following reaction:
$$CaCl_{2\,(aq)} + 2NaOH_{(aq)} \rightarrow Ca(OH)_{2\,(s)} + 2NaCl_{(aq)}$$

You should make sure your symbol equation is balanced before you start trying to write the ionic equation (see the previous page for more on how to balance symbol equations).

1) Anything that's ionic (i.e. made of ions — see page 36) and aqueous will break up into its ions in solution. So, write out the equation showing all the aqueous ions separately.

$$Ca^{2+}_{(aq)} + 2Cl^-_{(aq)} + 2Na^+_{(aq)} + 2OH^-_{(aq)} \rightarrow Ca(OH)_{2\,(s)} + 2Na^+_{(aq)} + 2Cl^-_{(aq)}$$

2) To get to the ionic equation, cross out anything that's the same on both sides of the equation — here, that's the Na^+ and Cl^- ions.

$$Ca^{2+}_{(aq)} + \cancel{2Cl^-_{(aq)}} + \cancel{2Na^+_{(aq)}} + 2OH^-_{(aq)} \rightarrow Ca(OH)_{2\,(s)} + \cancel{2Na^+_{(aq)}} + \cancel{2Cl^-_{(aq)}}$$

$$Ca^{2+}_{(aq)} + 2OH^-_{(aq)} \rightarrow Ca(OH)_{2\,(s)}$$

The overall charge should be the same on both sides.
Here, charge on RHS = 0 and charge on LHS = (2+) + (2 × 1−) = 0.

Ionic equations show ionic substances reacting in a solution...

Make sure you learn all the molecules and ions on this page — it'll come in handy when you need to figure out how to write or balance equations. It's really important that you know what charges the different ions have too, as this will affect how they bond with other ions.

Hazards and Risk

Chemistry's a <u>risky business</u> — you'll sometimes have to handle some really <u>dangerous</u> chemicals...

You Need to Learn the Common Hazard Symbols

1) A <u>hazard</u> is anything that has the potential to cause harm or damage. The <u>risk</u> associated with that hazard is the <u>probability</u> of someone (or something) being harmed if they are exposed to the hazard.

2) Lots of the chemicals you'll meet in chemistry can be <u>bad for you</u> or <u>dangerous</u> in some way. That's why the chemical containers will normally have <u>symbols</u> on them to tell you what the dangers are.

3) Understanding these symbols means you'll be able to use suitable <u>safe-working procedures</u> in the lab.

Oxidising
<u>Provides oxygen</u> which allows other materials to <u>burn more fiercely</u>.
<u>Example:</u>
Liquid oxygen.

Environmental Hazard
<u>Harmful</u> to <u>organisms</u> and to the <u>environment</u>.
<u>Example:</u> Mercury.

Toxic
<u>Can cause death</u> by, e.g., being swallowed, breathed in, absorbed through the skin.
<u>Example:</u>
Hydrogen cyanide.

Harmful
Can cause irritation, <u>reddening</u> or <u>blistering of the skin</u>.
<u>Example:</u> Bleach.

Highly Flammable
<u>Catches fire</u> easily.
<u>Example:</u> Petrol.

Corrosive
<u>Destroys materials</u>, including <u>living tissues</u> (e.g. eyes and skin).
<u>Example:</u> Concentrated sulfuric acid.

You must pay attention to the hazard symbols on chemicals...

<u>Hazard symbols</u> are there for a reason — to make you <u>aware of the dangers</u> associated with the chemicals you're handling so you can take sensible precautions when using them. Make sure you know what each symbol <u>means</u>, so that you're prepared if you come across them in a practical.

Hazards and Risk

Experiments Involve **Risks** and **Hazards**

1) Many chemistry experiments have <u>risks</u> associated with them.
   These can include:

   - Risks associated with the <u>equipment</u> you're using
     (e.g. the risk of burning from an electric heater).
   - Risks associated with <u>chemicals</u> (see previous page).

2) When you <u>plan</u> an experiment, you need to <u>identify all the hazards</u>
   and what the risk is from each hazard. This includes:

   - Working out <u>how likely</u> it is that something could go wrong.
   - <u>How serious</u> it would be if it did.

3) You then need to think of ways to <u>reduce</u> these risks.
   This procedure is called a <u>risk assessment</u>.

   1) <u>Example</u>:
   A student is going to react a solution of sodium hydroxide
   with hydrochloric acid to form a metal salt and water.
   Identify any hazards in this experiment, and
   suggest how the student could reduce the risk.

   2) <u>Hazards</u>:
   Sodium hydroxide and hydrochloric acid are <u>harmful</u> at
   low concentrations and <u>corrosive</u> at high concentrations.
   Harmful substances can cause blistering or reddening
   of the skin, but corrosive substances are much <u>more
   dangerous</u> if they come into contact with your skin or eyes.

   3) <u>Suggestions to reduce the risk</u>:
   To <u>reduce the risks</u> posed by these hazards, the student should try to
   use <u>low concentrations</u> of the substances if possible, and <u>wear gloves</u>,
   a <u>lab coat</u> and <u>goggles</u> when handling the chemicals.

Risk assessments help to keep you safe during an experiment

There are <u>two parts</u> to a risk assessment — <u>identifying</u> all of the <u>hazards</u>, and finding ways to <u>reduce the
risks</u>. As well as thinking about how the chemicals that you're using might be <u>hazardous</u>, you also have to
think of other things that might be <u>risky</u> during an experiment, e.g. a Bunsen burner or glass equipment.

Warm-Up and Exam Questions

Right, that's enough learning for a bit. Time to test your knowledge with some questions.

Warm-Up Questions

1) Balance the equation: $Fe + Cl_2 \rightarrow FeCl_3$

2) Hydrogen and oxygen molecules are formed in a reaction where water splits apart.
   For this reaction: a) State the word equation.   b) Give a balanced symbol equation.

3) Write the ionic equation for the following reaction: $HNO_{3\,(aq)} + NaOH_{\,(aq)} \rightarrow NaNO_{3\,(aq)} + H_2O_{\,(l)}$

4) A student is carrying out an experiment using two chemicals. Chemical A is corrosive while chemical B is highly flammable. Suggest appropriate safety precautions the student could take to minimise the risks associated with the chemicals.

Exam Questions

1   Sodium hydroxide reacts with hydrochloric acid to make sodium chloride and water.

   (a)   Write a word equation for this reaction.

   [1 mark]

   (b)   The sodium hydroxide is in solution. Which state symbol would be used
   in a chemical equation to indicate that a substance is in solution?

   [1 mark]

2   Methane (CH_4) burns in oxygen to make carbon dioxide and water.

   (a)   State the names of the reactants in this reaction.

   [1 mark]

   (b)   State the names of the products in this reaction.

   [1 mark]

   (c)   Complete and balance the symbol equation for the reaction below.

   ....CH_4 + ... $\rightarrow$ ....CO_2 + ...H_2O

   [2 marks]

3   Sulfuric acid (H_2SO_4) reacts with ammonia to form ammonium sulfate, $(NH_4)_2SO_4$.

   (a)   Complete and balance the symbol equation below.

   ....H_2SO_4 + ... $\rightarrow$ ....$(NH_4)_2SO_4$

   [2 marks]

   (b)   In the balanced equation, how many atoms are there in the reactants?

   [1 mark]

   (c)   How many hydrogen atoms are present in ammonium sulfate?

   [1 mark]

The History of the Atom

Atoms are the <u>tiny particles</u> of <u>matter</u> (stuff that has a mass) which makes up <u>everything</u> in the universe. The next couple of pages are all about how <u>scientists</u> came to understand the atom as we do today.

The Theory of **Atomic Structure** Has **Changed** Over Time

At the start of the 19th century <u>John Dalton</u> described atoms as <u>solid spheres</u>, and said that different spheres made up the different <u>elements</u>.

In 1897 <u>J J Thomson</u> concluded from his experiments that atoms <u>weren't</u> solid spheres. His measurements of <u>charge</u> and <u>mass</u> showed that an atom must contain even smaller, negatively charged particles — <u>electrons</u>.

The 'solid sphere' idea of atomic structure had to be changed. The new theory was known as the '<u>plum pudding model</u>'.

The plum pudding model showed the atom as a <u>ball</u> of <u>positive charge</u> with <u>electrons</u> stuck in it.

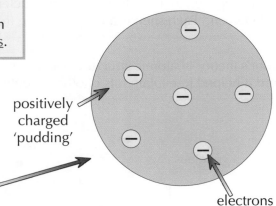

positively charged 'pudding'

electrons

Rutherford Showed that the **Plum Pudding Model** Was Wrong

1) In 1909, Ernest <u>Rutherford</u> and his students, Hans <u>Geiger</u> and Ernest <u>Marsden</u>, conducted the famous <u>gold foil experiment</u>. They fired positively charged <u>alpha particles</u> at an extremely thin sheet of gold.

2) From the plum pudding model, they were <u>expecting</u> the particles to <u>pass straight through</u> the sheet or be <u>slightly deflected</u> at most. This was because the positive charge of each atom was thought to be very <u>spread out</u> through the 'pudding' of the atom. But, whilst most of the particles <u>did</u> go <u>straight through</u> the gold sheet, some were deflected <u>more than expected</u>, and a small number were <u>deflected backwards</u>. So the plum pudding model <u>couldn't</u> be right.

3) Rutherford came up with an idea to explain this new evidence — the <u>nuclear model</u> of the atom. In this, there's a tiny, positively charged <u>nucleus</u> at the centre, where most of the <u>mass</u> is concentrated. A 'cloud' of negative electrons surrounds this nucleus — so most of the atom is <u>empty space</u>. When alpha particles came near the <u>concentrated</u>, <u>positive charge</u> of the <u>nucleus</u>, they were <u>deflected</u>. If they were fired directly at the nucleus, they were deflected <u>backwards</u>. Otherwise, they passed through the empty space.

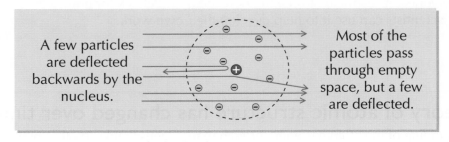

A few particles are deflected backwards by the nucleus.

Most of the particles pass through empty space, but a few are deflected.

The History of the Atom

The Refined **Bohr Model** Explains a Lot

1) Scientists realised that electrons in a 'cloud' around the nucleus of an atom, as Rutherford described, would be attracted to the nucleus, causing the atom to <u>collapse</u>.

2) Niels Bohr proposed a new model of the atom where all the electrons were contained in <u>shells</u>.

3) Bohr proposed that electrons <u>orbit</u> the nucleus in <u>fixed shells</u> and aren't anywhere in between. Each shell is a <u>fixed distance</u> from the <u>nucleus</u> and has a <u>fixed energy</u>.

4) Bohr's theory of atomic structure was supported by many <u>experiments</u> and it helped to explain lots of other scientists' <u>observations</u> at the time.

The Bohr model of the atom is pretty close to our currently accepted version of the atom (see next page).

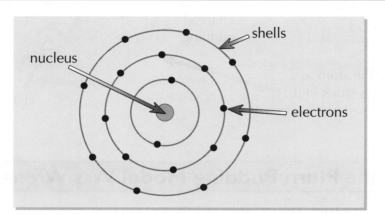

Scientific **Theories** Have to be Backed Up by **Evidence**

1) So, our current model of the atom is <u>completely different</u> to what people thought the atom looked like in the past. These different ideas were <u>accepted</u> because they fitted the <u>evidence</u> available at the time.

2) As scientists did more <u>experiments</u>, new evidence was found and our theory of the <u>structure</u> of the atom was <u>modified</u> to fit it. This is nearly always the way <u>scientific knowledge</u> develops — new evidence prompts people to come up with new, <u>improved ideas</u>. These ideas can be used to make <u>predictions</u> which, if proved correct, are a pretty good indication that the ideas are <u>right</u>.

3) Scientists also put their ideas and research up for <u>peer review</u>. This means everyone gets a chance to see the new ideas and check for errors, and then other scientists can use it to help <u>develop</u> their own work.

The theory of atomic structure has changed over time...

Our understanding of the atom has gone through <u>many stages</u> thanks to other people's work being built upon with <u>new evidence</u> and <u>new predictions</u> made. A fine example of the scientific method.

The Atom

All substances are made of <u>atoms</u>. They're really <u>tiny</u> — too small to see, even with a microscope.

Atoms Contain **Protons**, **Neutrons** and **Electrons**

The atom is made up of three <u>subatomic particles</u> — protons, neutrons and electrons.

- <u>Protons</u> are <u>heavy</u> and <u>positively charged</u>.
- <u>Neutrons</u> are <u>heavy</u> and <u>neutral</u>.
- <u>Electrons</u> have <u>hardly any mass</u> and are <u>negatively charged</u>.

Particle	Relative Mass	Relative Charge
Proton	1	+1
Neutron	1	0
Electron	0.0005	−1

Relative mass (measured in atomic mass units) measures mass on a scale where the mass of a proton or neutron is 1.

The **Nucleus**

1) It's in the <u>middle</u> of the atom.

2) It contains <u>protons</u> and <u>neutrons</u>.

3) It has a <u>positive charge</u> because of the protons.

4) Almost the <u>whole</u> mass of the atom is <u>concentrated</u> in the nucleus.

5) Compared to the overall size of the atom, the nucleus is <u>tiny</u>.

The **Electrons**

1) Electrons move <u>around</u> the nucleus in electron <u>shells</u>.

2) They're <u>negatively charged</u>.

3) They're <u>tiny</u>, but their shells cover <u>a lot of space</u>.

4) The <u>size</u> of their shells determines the size of the atom. Atoms have a radius (known as the atomic radius) of about 10^{-10} m.

5) Electrons have a <u>tiny</u> mass (so small that it's sometimes given as zero).

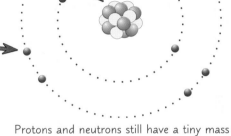

Protons and neutrons still have a tiny mass — they're just heavy compared to electrons.

In an Atom the Number of Protons **Equals** the Number of Electrons

1) Atoms are <u>neutral</u> — they have <u>no charge</u> overall (unlike ions).

An ion is an atom or group of atoms that has lost or gained electrons.

2) This is because they have the <u>same number</u> of <u>protons</u> as <u>electrons</u>.

3) The <u>charge</u> on the electrons is the <u>same</u> size as the charge on the <u>protons</u>, but <u>opposite</u> — so the charges <u>cancel out</u>.

4) In an ion, the number of protons <u>doesn't equal</u> the number of <u>electrons</u>. This means it has an <u>overall charge</u>. For example, an ion with a <u>2− charge</u> has <u>two more</u> electrons than protons.

Atomic Number and **Mass Number** Describe an Atom

1) The <u>nuclear symbol</u> of an atom tells you its <u>atomic (proton) number</u> and <u>mass number</u>.

2) The <u>atomic number</u> tells you how many <u>protons</u> an atom has. Every atom of an element has the <u>same number of protons</u>.

3) For a <u>neutral</u> atom, the number of protons equals the number of electrons, so the number of electrons equals the <u>atomic number</u>.

4) The <u>mass number</u> tells you the <u>total number</u> of <u>protons and neutrons</u> in the atom.

5) To work out the number of <u>neutrons</u> in an atom, just subtract the <u>atomic number</u> from the <u>mass number</u>.

Nuclear symbol for sodium

Mass number → 23

Atomic number → 11

Na

Element symbol

Electrons orbit around a nucleus containing protons and neutrons

Make sure you learn the <u>relative masses</u> and <u>relative charges</u> of the different parts of the atom.

Warm-Up and Exam Questions

Right, time to test whether you know more about the atom than Niels Bohr himself.
Yes, that's right, it's question time...

Warm-Up Questions

1) Draw and label a diagram to show the Bohr model of the atom.
2) State the relative charge and relative mass of an electron.
3) What does the mass number tell you about an atom?
4) A certain neutral atom of potassium has an atomic number of 19 and a mass number of 39.
   Give the number of electrons, protons and neutrons in the atom.

Exam Questions

1 This question is about atomic structure.

(a) Use your knowledge to complete **Figure 1**.

Name of particle	Relative charge
Proton	....
Neutron	....

Figure 1

[2 marks]

(b) Where are protons and neutrons found in an atom?

[1 mark]

(c) An atom has 8 electrons. How many protons does the atom have?

[1 mark]

(d) What is the relative mass of a proton?

[1 mark]

2 **Figure 2** gives some information about nitrogen.

Element	Number of protons	Mass number
nitrogen	7	14

Figure 2

(a) How many neutrons does nitrogen have?

[1 mark]

(b) Describe how the information in **Figure 2** can be used to work out the atomic number of nitrogen.

[1 mark]

3* Describe how the theory of atomic structure has changed throughout history.
Your answer should include the models of the atom proposed by John Dalton,
J J Thomson, Ernest Rutherford and Niels Bohr, and the current accepted model.

[6 marks]

Isotopes and Relative Atomic Masses

Atoms were reasonably straightforward, weren't they? Think again. Here come <u>isotopes</u> to confuse everything.

Isotopes are the Same Except for Extra Neutrons

1) <u>Isotopes</u> are defined as:

> <u>Different forms</u> of the <u>same element</u>, which have the <u>SAME number of PROTONS</u> but a <u>DIFFERENT number of NEUTRONS</u>.

2) So isotopes have the <u>same atomic number</u> but <u>different mass numbers</u>.

3) A very popular example of a pair of isotopes are <u>carbon-12</u> and <u>carbon-13</u>.

Remember that the number of protons in an atom is unique to each element. For example, every carbon atom will have 6 protons.

Carbon-12

6 PROTONS
6 ELECTRONS
6 NEUTRONS

$^{12}_{6}C$

Remember — the number of neutrons is just the mass number minus the atomic number.

Carbon-13

6 PROTONS
6 ELECTRONS
7 NEUTRONS

$^{13}_{6}C$

Relative Atomic Mass Takes Isotopes into Account

1) In the periodic table, the elements all have <u>two</u> numbers next to them. The <u>bigger one</u> is the <u>relative atomic mass</u> (A_r) of the element.

> The <u>relative atomic mass</u> of an element is the <u>average mass</u> of <u>one atom</u> of the element, compared to $^1/_{12}$ of the <u>mass</u> of <u>one atom</u> of <u>carbon-12</u>.

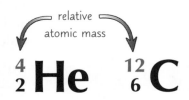

relative atomic mass

$^{4}_{2}He$ $^{12}_{6}C$

2) If an element only has <u>one isotope</u>, its A_r will be the same as its <u>mass number</u> (see page 25).

3) If an element has <u>more than one</u> isotope, its A_r is the <u>average</u> of the <u>mass numbers</u> of <u>all the different isotopes</u>, taking into account <u>how much</u> there is of each one. So, it might not be a whole number.

> For example, chlorine has two stable isotopes, <u>chlorine-35</u> and <u>chlorine-37</u>. There's <u>quite a lot</u> of chlorine-35 around and <u>not so much</u> chlorine-37 — so chlorine's A_r works out as <u>35.5</u>.

Isotopes and Relative Atomic Masses

A_r Can Be Worked Out from **Isotopic Abundances**

1) Different isotopes of an element occur in different quantities, or <u>isotopic abundances</u>.

2) You need to know how to <u>calculate</u> the <u>relative atomic mass</u> of an element from its <u>isotopic abundances</u>.

3) To work out the relative atomic mass of an element, you need to find the <u>average mass</u> of <u>all its atoms</u>. Here's how...

- <u>Multiply</u> each <u>relative isotopic mass</u> by its <u>isotopic abundance</u>.
- <u>Add up</u> the results.
- <u>Divide</u> by the <u>sum</u> of the <u>abundances</u>. (If the abundances are given as percentages, this will be 100.)

 **EXAMPLE:**

Boron has two isotopes, boron-10 and boron-11.
Given that the relative abundances or boron-10 and boron-11
are 4 and 16 respectively, work out the relative atomic mass of boron.

1) Multiply each <u>relative isotopic mass</u> by its <u>relative abundance</u>, then add up the results.

2) Divide this by the <u>sum</u> of the <u>isotopic abundances</u>.

$(10 \times 4) + (11 \times 16) = 216$

$216 \div (16 + 4) = 10.8$

 **EXAMPLE:**

Copper has two stable isotopes, copper-63 and copper-65.
Cu-63 has an abundance of 69.2% and Cu-65 has an abundance of 30.8%.
Calculate the relative atomic mass of copper to 1 decimal place.

$(63 \times 69.2) + (65 \times 30.8) = 6361.6$

$6361.6 \div 100 = 63.616 = 63.6$ (to 1 d.p.)

 **EXAMPLE:**

Magnesium has three stable isotopes, Mg-24, Mg-25 and Mg-26.
Mg-24 has an abundance of 79%, Mg-25 has an abundance of 10%
and Mg-26 has an abundance of 11%.
Calculate the relative atomic mass of magnesium to 1 decimal place.

$(24 \times 79) + (25 \times 10) + (26 \times 11) = 2432$

$2432 \div 100 = 24.32 = 24.3$ (to 1 d.p.)

Relative atomic mass is the average atomic mass of an element

Relative atomic mass takes into account all isotopes of an element — this is <u>different</u> to the <u>mass number</u>, which is the <u>mass</u> of a <u>specific isotope</u> of an element. It's easy to get them muddled up, but fortunately for you, there's a handy way to remember it — relative atomic mass has the symbol <u>A_r</u> and is an <u>average</u> mass. See, easy when you know how...

The Periodic Table

We haven't always known as much about chemistry as we do now. Early chemists looked to try and understand <u>patterns</u> in the elements' properties to get a bit of understanding.

Dmitri Mendeleev Made the First Proper Periodic Table

1) In <u>1869</u>, <u>Dmitri Mendeleev</u> arranged the 50 or so elements known at the time into a <u>Table of Elements</u>.

<u>Mendeleev's Table of the Elements</u>

```
H
Li Be                              B  C  N  O  F
Na Mg                              Al Si P  S  Cl
K  Ca *  Ti V  Cr Mn Fe Co Ni Cu Zn *  *  As Se Br
Rb Sr Y  Zr Nb Mo *  Ru Rh Pd Ag Cd In Sn Sb Te I
Cs Ba *  *  Ta W  *  Os Ir Pt Au Hg Tl Pb Bi
```

2) He began by sorting the elements into groups, based on their <u>properties</u> (and the properties of their <u>compounds</u>).

3) As he did this, he realised that if he put the elements in order of <u>atomic mass</u>, a pattern appeared — he could put elements with <u>similar chemical properties</u> in <u>columns</u>.

4) A few elements, however, seemed to end up in the <u>wrong columns</u>. In some cases this was because the atomic mass Mendeleev had was wrong (due to the presence of <u>isotopes</u>) — but some elements just didn't quite fit the pattern. Wherever this happened, he <u>switched</u> the order of the elements to keep those with the same properties in the same columns.

5) To keep elements with similar properties together, Mendeleev also had to leave some <u>gaps</u> (shown by the *s in the table above). He used the properties of the other elements in the columns with the gaps to <u>predict</u> the properties of <u>undiscovered elements</u>. When they were found and they <u>fitted the pattern</u>, it helped to confirm his ideas. For example, Mendeleev predicted the chemical and physical properties of an element he called <u>ekasilicon</u>, which we know today as <u>germanium</u>.

Mendeleev used chemical properties to sort the elements...

...and this meant that he was able to put them into <u>groups</u> and then into <u>columns</u> according to their atomic mass. His arrangement wasn't perfect, but the basic idea wasn't too far away from the periodic table we know today (see next page) which was made possible by sorting elements by their atomic number.

The Periodic Table

Mendeleev got fairly close to producing something that you might <u>recognise</u> as a periodic table. The big breakthrough came when the <u>structure</u> of the <u>atom</u> was understood a bit better.

The Periodic Table Helps you to See Patterns in Properties

1) Once <u>protons</u> and <u>electrons</u> were discovered, the <u>atomic number</u> (see p.25) of each element could be found, based on the number of protons in its nucleus. The <u>modern</u> periodic table (see below) shows the elements in order of ascending <u>atomic number</u> — and they fit the same <u>patterns</u> that Mendeleev worked out.

Remember, Mendeleev tried to order elements according to their atomic mass (not atomic number), which is why he sometimes had to swap them around to make them fit the patterns.

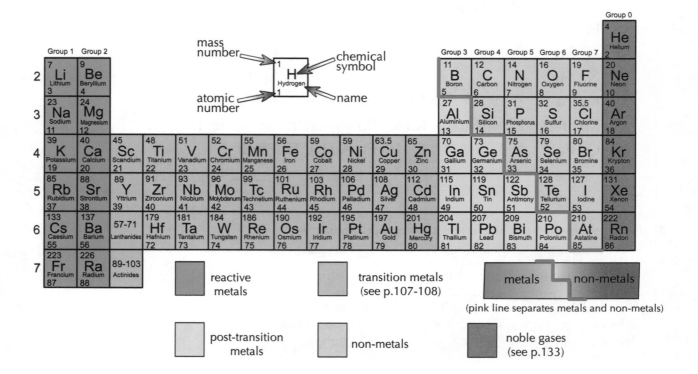

2) The periodic table is laid out so elements with <u>similar chemical properties</u> form <u>columns</u> called <u>groups</u>.

3) The <u>group</u> to which the element belongs <u>corresponds</u> to the <u>number of electrons</u> it has in its <u>outer shell</u>. E.g. <u>Group 1</u> elements have <u>1</u> outer shell electron, <u>Group 7</u> elements have <u>7</u>, etc. <u>Group 0</u> elements are the exception — they have <u>full</u> outer shells of <u>8</u> electrons (or 2 in the case of helium).

4) The rows are called <u>periods</u>. Each new period represents another full <u>shell</u> of electrons (see next page).

5) The period to which the element belongs corresponds to the <u>number of shells</u> of electrons it has.

The modern periodic table is vital for understanding chemistry

This is a good example of how science progresses. A scientist has a <u>basically good</u> (though incomplete) <u>hypothesis</u> (see page 2), and other scientists <u>question it</u> and <u>bring more evidence</u> to the table. The hypothesis may be <u>modified</u> or even <u>scrapped</u> to take account of available evidence. Only when all of the available evidence <u>supports</u> a hypothesis will it be <u>accepted</u>.

Electronic Configurations

The way in which electrons occupy 'shells' around the nucleus is responsible for lots of aspects of chemistry.

Electron Shell Rules:

1) Electrons always occupy <u>shells</u> (sometimes called <u>energy levels</u>).

2) The <u>lowest</u> energy levels are <u>always filled first</u> — these are the ones closest to the nucleus.

3) Only <u>a certain number</u> of electrons are allowed in each shell:

> 1st shell: 2   2nd shell: 8   3rd shell: 8

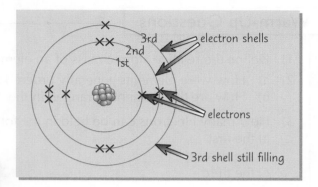

Working Out Electronic Configurations

The <u>electronic configurations</u> of the first <u>20</u> elements are shown in the diagram below.
They're not hard to work out. For a quick example, take nitrogen:

1) The periodic table tells you that the atomic number of nitrogen is <u>seven</u>. That means nitrogen has seven protons, so it must have <u>seven electrons</u>.

2) Follow the '<u>Electron Shell Rules</u>' above. The <u>first</u> shell can only take 2 electrons and the <u>second</u> shell can take a <u>maximum</u> of 8 electrons. So the electronic configuration of nitrogen must be <u>2.5</u>.

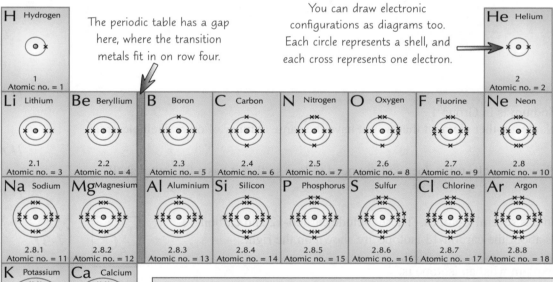

Example: To calculate the electronic configuration of argon, <u>follow the rules</u>. It's got 18 protons, so it <u>must</u> have 18 electrons. The first shell must have <u>2</u> electrons, the second shell must have <u>8</u>, and so the third shell must have <u>8</u> as well. It's as easy as <u>2.8.8</u>.

3) You can also work out the electronic configuration of an element from its <u>period</u> and <u>group</u>:

- The <u>number of shells</u> which contain electrons is the same as the <u>period</u> of the element.
- The <u>group number</u> tells you <u>how many electrons</u> occupy the <u>outer shell</u> of the element.

> Example: Sodium is in <u>period 3</u>, so it has <u>3</u> shells occupied. The first two shells must be full (2.8). It's in <u>Group 1</u>, so it has <u>1</u> electron in its outer shell. So its electronic configuration is <u>2.8.1</u>.

Warm-Up and Exam Questions

Well, that's a lot of information to take in... now it's time to see how much you can remember.

Warm-Up Questions

1) Define the relative atomic mass of an element.

2) a) How were elements generally ordered in Mendeleev's table of elements?
   b) How are the elements arranged in the modern periodic table?

3) How many electrons can be held in the following shells of an atom:
   a) the first
   b) the second
   c) the third

4) Give the electronic configuration of chlorine (atomic number = 17).

Exam Questions

1   Sodium has an atomic number of 11.

(a) Complete the dot and cross diagram to show
    the electron configuration of sodium.

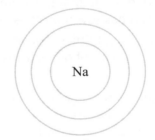

[1 mark]

(b) Sodium is in Group 1.
    Name another element that would have the same number of outer shell electrons.

[1 mark]

(c) How many electrons does sodium need to lose so that it has a full outer shell?

[1 mark]

2   Carbon has several isotopes. These include carbon-12 and carbon-13.
    Details about the carbon-13 isotope are shown on the right. $^{13}_{6}C$

(a) Explain what an isotope is.

[3 marks]

(b) Give the number of protons, neutrons and electrons that carbon-13 contains.

[3 marks]

(c) Details of element **X** are shown on the right. $^{13}_{7}X$
    Explain how you can tell that element **X** is not an isotope of carbon.

[1 mark]

(d) There are two isotopes of element **X**. One isotope has a mass number of 13 and a percentage
    abundance of 79%. The other isotope has a mass number of 14 and a percentage abundance of 21%.
    Use this information to calculate the relative atomic mass of element **X**. Give your answer to 1 d.p.

[4 marks]

Ions

Some atoms are keen on getting rid of some of their <u>electrons</u>. Others want more. That's <u>ions</u> for you...

Simple Ions Form When Atoms Lose or Gain **Electrons**

1) <u>Ions</u> are <u>charged</u> particles — they can be <u>single atoms</u> (e.g. Na⁺) or <u>groups of atoms</u> (e.g. NO_3^-).

2) When <u>atoms</u> lose or gain electrons to form ions, all they're trying to do is get a <u>full outer shell</u> (also called a "<u>stable electronic structure</u>"). Atoms like full outer shells — it's atom heaven.

3) <u>Negative ions</u> (anions) form when atoms <u>gain electrons</u> — they have more electrons than protons.
<u>Positive ions</u> (cations) form when atoms <u>lose electrons</u> — they have more protons than electrons.

4) The <u>number</u> of electrons lost or gained is the same as the <u>charge</u> on the ion. E.g. If 2 electrons are <u>lost</u> the charge is 2+. If 3 electrons are <u>gained</u> the charge is 3−.

You calculate the number of protons and neutrons in an ion in the same way as for an atom (see page 25).

- F⁻ has a <u>single negative charge</u>, so it must have one more electron than protons.
  F has an atomic number of 9, so it has 9 protons. So F⁻ must have 9 + 1 = <u>10 electrons</u>.
- Fe^{2+} has a <u>2+ charge</u>, so it must have two more protons than electrons.
  Fe has an atomic number of 26, so it has 26 protons. So Fe^{2+} must have 26 − 2 = <u>24 electrons</u>.

Groups **1 & 2** and **6 & 7** are the Most Likely to Form **Ions**

1) The elements that <u>most readily</u> form ions are those in <u>Groups 1, 2, 6 and 7</u>.

2) <u>Group 1 and 2 elements</u> are <u>metals</u> and they <u>lose</u> electrons to form <u>positive ions</u> (<u>cations</u>).

3) <u>Group 6 and 7 elements</u> are <u>non-metals</u>. They <u>gain</u> electrons to form <u>negative ions</u> (<u>anions</u>).

4) Elements in the same <u>group</u> all have the same number of <u>outer electrons</u>. So they have to <u>lose or gain</u> the same number to get a full outer shell. And this means that they form ions with the <u>same charges</u>.

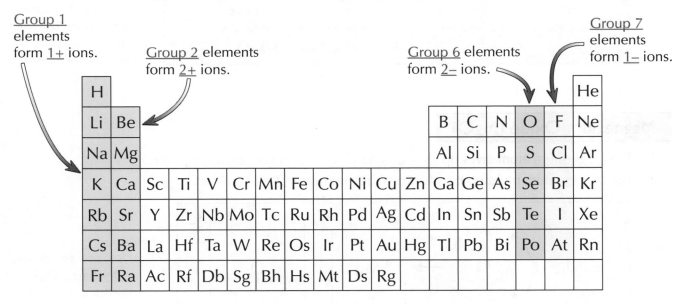

<u>Group 1</u> elements form <u>1+</u> ions.

<u>Group 2</u> elements form <u>2+</u> ions.

<u>Group 6</u> elements form <u>2−</u> ions.

<u>Group 7</u> elements form <u>1−</u> ions.

Ions are formed from the loss or gain of electrons...

Here's a way to remember what anions are: <u>an</u>ions are <u>n</u>egatively charged and are formed by gaining electrons. Then you just have to remember that <u>cat</u>ions are the <u>opposite</u> of anions — i.e. they're <u>positively charged</u> and formed by <u>losing</u> electrons.

Ionic Bonding

Time to find out how particles bond together to form compounds (bet you can't wait). There are three types of bonding you need to know about — ionic, covalent and metallic. First up, it's ionic bonds.

Ionic Bonding — **Transfer** of Electrons

1) When a metal and a non-metal react together, the metal atom loses electrons to form a positive ion (cation) and the non-metal gains these electrons to form a negative ion (anion).

2) These oppositely charged ions are strongly attracted to one another by electrostatic forces.

3) This attraction is called an ionic bond.

Dot and Cross Diagrams Show How Ionic Compounds Form

Dot and cross diagrams show the arrangement of electrons in an atom or ion. Each electron is represented by a dot or a cross. So these diagrams can show which atom the electrons in an ion originally came from.

Sodium Chloride (NaCl)

1) The sodium atom gives up its outer electron, becoming an Na^+ ion.

2) The chlorine atom picks up the electron, becoming a Cl^- (chloride) ion.

Remember, you can work out how many electrons an atom will gain or lose from its group number.

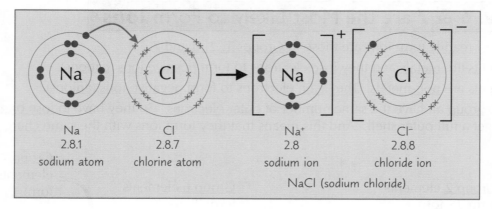

Na
2.8.1
sodium atom

Cl
2.8.7
chlorine atom

Na⁺
2.8
sodium ion

Cl⁻
2.8.8
chloride ion

NaCl (sodium chloride)

Here, the dots represent the Na electrons and the crosses represent the Cl electrons. All electrons are really identical, but this is a good way of following their movement.

Magnesium Oxide (MgO)

1) The magnesium atom gives up its two outer electrons, becoming an Mg^{2+} ion.

2) The oxygen atom picks up the electrons, becoming an O^{2-} (oxide) ion.

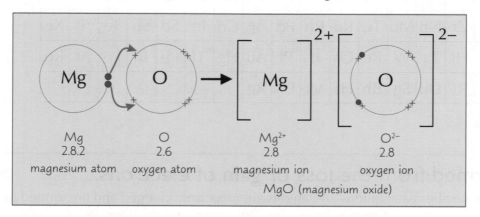

Mg
2.8.2
magnesium atom

O
2.6
oxygen atom

Mg²⁺
2.8
magnesium ion

O²⁻
2.8
oxygen ion

MgO (magnesium oxide)

Here we've only shown the outer shell of electrons on the dot and cross diagram — it makes it much simpler to see what's going on.

Ionic Bonding

Magnesium Chloride ($MgCl_2$)

1) The <u>magnesium</u> atom gives up its <u>two</u> outer electrons, becoming an <u>Mg^{2+}</u> ion.

2) The two <u>chlorine</u> atoms pick up <u>one electron each</u>, becoming <u>two Cl^-</u> (chloride) ions.

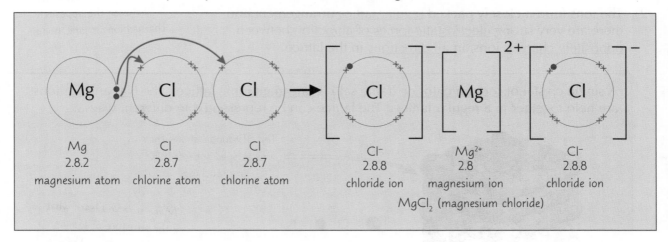

Sodium Oxide (Na_2O)

1) Two <u>sodium</u> atoms each give up their single outer electron, becoming <u>two Na^+</u> ions.

2) The <u>oxygen</u> atom picks up the <u>two</u> electrons, becoming an <u>O^{2-}</u> ion.

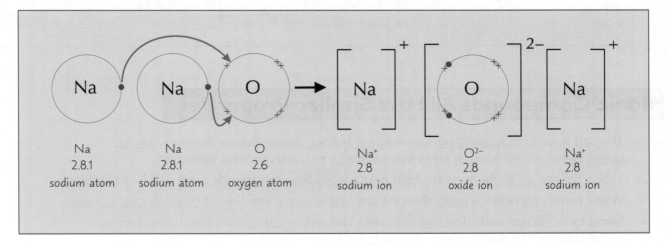

Dot and cross diagrams are useful for showing how ionic compounds are formed, but they have some <u>limitations</u> (see page 37).

Ionic bonding involves an electron transfer from one atom to another

<u>Metals</u> tend to <u>lose electrons</u> to form <u>positively charged ions</u>, and <u>non-metals</u> tend to <u>gain these electrons</u>. For example, it's <u>much easier</u> for a <u>magnesium atom</u> to <u>lose two</u> electrons than <u>gain six</u> electrons to form a compound, so this is what ends up happening. Make sure you can describe how different ionic compounds are formed using both <u>words</u> and <u>dot and cross diagrams</u>. It gets much easier with <u>practice</u>, I promise...

Ionic Compounds

An <u>ionic compound</u> is any compound that only contains <u>ionic bonds</u>...

Ionic Compounds Have a **Regular Lattice** Structure

1) <u>Ionic compounds</u> have a structure called a <u>giant ionic lattice</u>.
2) The ions form a closely packed <u>regular lattice</u> arrangement and there are very strong <u>electrostatic forces of attraction</u> between <u>oppositely charged</u> ions, in <u>all directions</u> in the lattice.

The electrostatic attraction between the oppositely charged ions is ionic bonding.

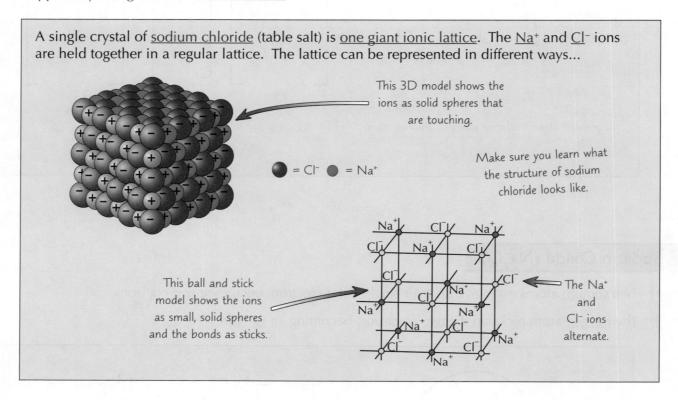

A single crystal of <u>sodium chloride</u> (table salt) is <u>one giant ionic lattice</u>. The Na^+ and Cl^- ions are held together in a regular lattice. The lattice can be represented in different ways...

This 3D model shows the ions as solid spheres that are touching.

$\bullet$ = Cl^- $\bullet$ = Na^+

Make sure you learn what the structure of sodium chloride looks like.

This ball and stick model shows the ions as small, solid spheres and the bonds as sticks.

The Na^+ and Cl^- ions alternate.

Ionic Compounds All Have **Similar Properties**

1) They all have <u>high melting points</u> and <u>high boiling points</u> due to the <u>many strong bonds</u> between the ions. It takes lots of <u>energy</u> to overcome this attraction.
2) When they're <u>solid</u>, the ions are held in place, so the compounds <u>can't</u> conduct electricity.
3) When ionic compounds <u>melt</u>, the ions are <u>free to move</u> and they'll <u>carry electric current</u>.
4) Some ionic compounds <u>dissolve</u> in water. The ions <u>separate</u> and are all <u>free to move</u> in the solution, so they'll <u>carry electric current</u>.

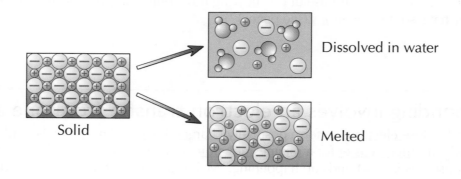

Solid

Dissolved in water

Melted

Ionic Compounds

You Can Work Out the **Formula** of an **Ionic Compound**

1) Ionic compounds (see page 36) are made up of a <u>positively charged</u> part and a <u>negatively charged</u> part.

2) The <u>overall charge</u> of <u>any ionic compound</u> is <u>zero</u>. So all the <u>negative charges</u> in the compound must <u>balance</u> all the <u>positive charges</u>.

3) You can use the charges on the <u>individual ions</u> present to work out the formula for the ionic compound.

4) You need to be able to write formulas using <u>chemical symbols</u>.

Ions with names ending in -ate (e.g. nitrate) are negative ions containing oxygen and at least one other element. Ions with names ending in -ide (e.g. chloride) are negative ions containing only one element (apart from hydroxide ions which are OH^-).

EXAMPLE: **What is the chemical formula of calcium nitrate?**

1) Write out the <u>formulas</u> of the calcium and nitrate ions.

Ca^{2+}, NO_3^-

2) The <u>overall charge</u> on the formula must be <u>zero</u>, so work out the ratio of Ca : NO_3 that gives an overall neutral charge.

To balance the 2+ charge on Ca^{2+}, you need two NO_3^- ions: $(+2) + (2 \times -1) = 0$. The formula is $Ca(NO_3)_2$

The brackets show you need two of the whole nitrate ion.

Models That Show Structures Have Some **Limitations**

It would be pretty tricky to draw out exactly what a substance looked like, so instead we use <u>models</u>. Each type of model has its own <u>advantages</u> and <u>disadvantages</u>...

1) <u>2D representations</u> (e.g. displayed formulas) of molecules are simple and great at showing what <u>atoms</u> something contains, and how the atoms are <u>connected</u>. They don't show the <u>shape</u> of the substance though, and they don't give you any idea about the <u>sizes</u> of the atoms.

2) <u>Dot and cross diagrams</u> (like those on pages 34, 35, 39 and 40) are useful for showing how compounds or molecules are formed and <u>where the electrons</u> in the bonds or ions <u>came from</u>. But they <u>don't</u> usually show you anything about the <u>size</u> of the atoms or ions or how they're <u>arranged</u>.

3) <u>3D models</u> of ionic solids show the <u>arrangement of ions</u>, but only show the outer layer of the substance.

<u>Ball and stick models</u> (like the one for NaCl on the previous page) show how the atoms in a substance are connected. You can draw them, or make them with plastic molecular model kits, or as computer models.

- They're great for helping to <u>visualise</u> structures, as they show the shape of the lattice or molecule in <u>3D</u>.

- They're <u>more realistic</u> than 2D drawings, but they're still a bit <u>misleading</u>. They make it look like there are <u>big gaps</u> between the atoms — in reality this is where the <u>electron clouds</u> interact.

- They also don't show the <u>correct scales</u> of the atoms or ions. The atoms and ions are actually different sizes, but this isn't shown well by ball and stick models.

It's easiest to make ball and stick models of small molecules. Here's one of ethanol (C_2H_5OH).

Ionic compounds form a giant lattice structure

As long as you can find the <u>charge</u> of the ions in an ionic compound, you can work out the <u>formula</u>. Try thinking of a few different positive and negative ions and how they might combine together to make ionic compounds, using the method shown in the example above.

Warm-Up and Exam Questions

That's all things ionic wrapped up (for now at least). Try your hand at these questions to make sure you've understood everything that's been covered over the last few pages.

Warm-Up Questions

1) What is an ion?
2) What is the charge on an ion formed from a Group 2 element?
3) Sodium chloride has a giant ionic structure. Explain why it has a high melting and boiling point.
4) Some ionic compounds conduct electricity when dissolved in water. Explain why.
5) What is the formula of the compound containing Al^{3+} and OH^- ions only?

Exam Questions

1 **Figure 1** shows the electronic structures of sodium and fluorine.

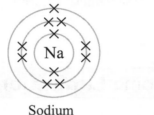

Sodium   Fluorine

Figure 1

(a) Describe what will happen when sodium and fluorine react, in terms of electrons.

[2 marks]

(b) When sodium and fluorine react they form an ionic compound.
Describe the structure of an ionic compound.

[3 marks]

2 When lithium reacts with oxygen it forms the ionic compound Li_2O.

(a) Name the compound formed.

[1 mark]

(b) Complete **Figure 2** below using arrows to show how the electrons are transferred when Li_2O is formed. Show the electron arrangements and the charges on the ions formed.

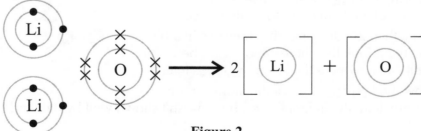

Figure 2   *[3 marks]*

(c) Explain why Li_2O conducts electricity when molten.

[2 marks]

(d) Lithium forms an ionic compound with chlorine.
What is the formula of this compound? Explain why this is.

[2 marks]

Covalent Bonding

These molecules might be <u>simple</u>, but you've still got to know about them...

Learn These Examples of Simple Molecular Substances

1) A covalent bond is a <u>strong bond</u> that forms when a <u>pair of electrons</u> is <u>shared</u> between <u>two atoms</u>.

2) <u>Simple molecular substances</u> are made up of molecules containing a <u>few atoms</u> joined together by <u>covalent bonds</u>. These dot and cross diagrams show six examples that you need to know about.

A covalent bond helps both of the atoms to make a full outer shell of electrons.

Hydrogen, H₂

Hydrogen atoms have just one electron. They <u>only need one more</u> to complete the first shell...

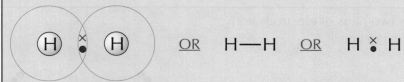

...so they often form <u>single covalent bonds</u>, either with other hydrogen atoms or with other elements, to achieve this.

Hydrogen chloride, HCl

This is very similar to H₂...

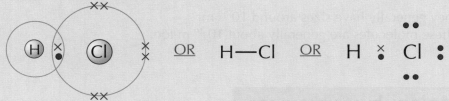

...again, both atoms only need <u>one more electron</u> to complete their outer shells.

Water, H₂O

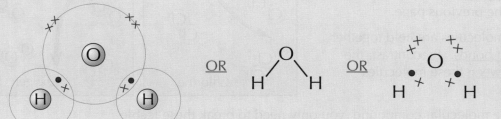

In <u>water molecules</u>, the oxygen shares a pair of electrons with two H atoms to form two <u>single covalent bonds</u>.

Methane, CH₄

Carbon has <u>four outer electrons</u>, which is <u>half</u> a full shell.

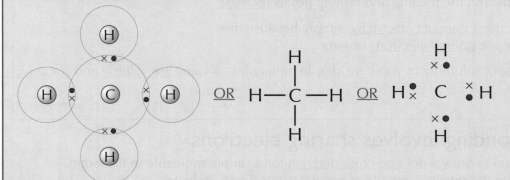

It can form <u>four covalent bonds</u> with <u>hydrogen</u> atoms to fill up its outer shell.

Covalent Bonding

Oxygen, O_2

An oxygen atom needs <u>two more electrons</u> to complete its outer shell.

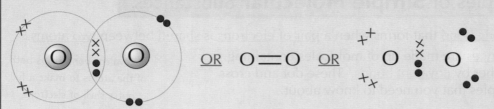

In <u>oxygen gas</u> each <u>oxygen atom</u> forms a <u>double covalent bond</u> (a bond made of <u>two shared electron pairs</u>) with another oxygen atom.

Carbon dioxide, CO_2

In <u>CO_2 molecules</u>, the carbon atom shares two pairs of electrons with two oxygen atoms to form two <u>double covalent bonds</u>.

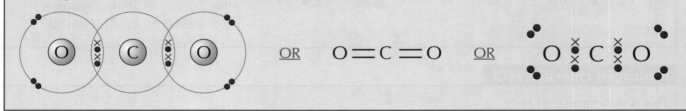

3) Simple molecules are tiny — they generally have sizes around 10^{-10} m.
   The bonds that form between these molecules are generally about 10^{-10} m too.

Properties of **Simple Molecular** Substances

1) Substances containing <u>covalent bonds</u> usually have <u>simple molecular structures</u>, like the examples shown above and on the previous page.

2) The atoms within the molecules are held together by <u>very strong covalent bonds</u>. By contrast, the forces of attraction <u>between</u> these molecules are <u>very weak</u>.

Weak intermolecular forces

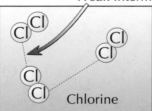

Chlorine

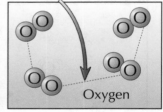

Oxygen

3) To melt or boil a simple molecular compound, you only need to break these <u>feeble intermolecular forces</u> and <u>not</u> the covalent bonds. So the melting and boiling points are <u>very low</u>, because the molecules are <u>easily parted</u> from each other.

4) Most molecular substances are <u>gases or liquids</u> at room temperature.

5) As molecules get <u>bigger</u>, the strength of the intermolecular forces <u>increases</u>, so <u>more energy</u> is needed to break them, and the melting and boiling points <u>increase</u>.

6) Molecular compounds <u>don't conduct electricity</u>, simply because they <u>aren't charged</u>, so there are <u>no free electrons</u> or ions.

7) There's no easy rule about solubility in water for simple molecules — some <u>are soluble</u> and some <u>aren't</u>.

EXAM TIP

Covalent bonding involves sharing electrons

You might be asked to draw a <u>dot and cross diagram</u> for a simple molecule in the exam. The ones shown on the previous couple of pages are good ones to learn.

Warm-Up and Exam Questions

The questions on this page are all about covalent bonding. Go through them and if you have any problems, make sure you look back at the relevant pages until you've got to grips with it all.

Warm-Up Questions

1) What is a covalent bond?
2) How many double covalent bonds does a molecule of carbon dioxide have?
3) What is the typical size of a simple molecule?
4) In which states are most simple molecular substances at room temperature?
5) Which forces are stronger in simple molecular substances
   — covalent bonds or intermolecular forces?
6) What forces need to be overcome to boil a simple molecular compound?

Exam Questions

1   Methane is a covalently bonded molecule with the formula CH_4.
     Complete the dot and cross diagram for the methane molecule.
     Show only the outer electrons.

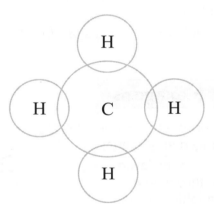

[2 marks]

2   Dot and cross diagrams can be used to show the position of electrons in covalent molecules.

   (a)   Draw a dot and cross diagram for hydrogen chloride (HCl). Only show the outer electrons.

[2 marks]

   (b)   Oxygen is in Group 6 of the periodic table.
          How many single bonds does it need to make to gain a full outer shell?

[1 mark]

3   Hydrogen chloride is a simple molecular substance.

   (a)   Explain why hydrogen chloride has poor electrical conductivity.

[1 mark]

   (b)   A molecule of hydrogen chloride has a stronger bond than a molecule of chlorine (Cl_2).
          However, hydrogen chloride boils at –85 °C, whereas chlorine boils at –34 °C.
          Suggest and explain why chlorine has a higher boiling point than hydrogen chloride.

[3 marks]

Giant Covalent Structures

Simple molecular substances aren't the only compounds held together by covalent bonds. <u>Giant covalent structures</u> are too. Here are some you need to know about for the <u>exam</u>.

Most **Giant Covalent** Structures Have Certain Properties

1) In giant covalent structures, <u>all</u> the atoms are <u>bonded</u> to <u>each other</u> by <u>strong</u> covalent bonds.
2) They have <u>very high</u> melting and boiling points as lots of energy is needed to break the covalent bonds.
3) They generally <u>don't</u> contain charged particles, so they <u>don't conduct electricity</u>. → *Apart from graphite and graphene.*
4) They <u>aren't</u> soluble in water.
5) The following examples are all <u>carbon-based giant covalent structures</u>.

Diamond is Very **Hard**

1) Diamond is made up of a network of carbon atoms that each form <u>four covalent bonds</u>.
2) The <u>strong covalent bonds</u> take lots of energy to break, so diamond has a <u>high melting point</u>.
3) The strong covalent bonds also hold the atoms in a <u>rigid lattice structure</u>, making diamond <u>really hard</u> — it's used to <u>strengthen cutting tools</u> (e.g. saw teeth and drill bits).
4) It <u>doesn't conduct electricity</u> because it has <u>no free electrons</u> or <u>ions</u>.

Graphite Contains **Sheets** of **Hexagons**

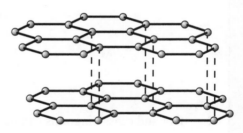

1) In graphite, each carbon atom only forms <u>three covalent bonds</u>, creating <u>sheets</u> of <u>carbon atoms</u> arranged in <u>hexagons</u>.
2) There <u>aren't</u> any covalent bonds <u>between</u> the layers — they're only held together <u>weakly</u>, so they're free to move over each other. This makes graphite <u>soft</u> and <u>slippery</u>, so it's ideal as a <u>lubricating material</u>.
3) Graphite's got a <u>high melting point</u> — the covalent bonds in the layers need <u>loads of energy</u> to break.
4) Only <u>three</u> out of each carbon's four outer electrons are used in bonds, so each carbon atom has <u>one</u> electron that's <u>delocalised</u> (free) and can move. So graphite <u>conducts electricity</u> and is often used to make <u>electrodes</u>.

Graphene is **One Layer** of **Graphite**

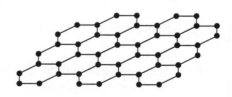

1) Graphene (a type of fullerene — see next page) is one layer of graphite.
2) It's a <u>sheet</u> of carbon atoms joined together in <u>hexagons</u>.
3) The sheet is just <u>one atom</u> thick, making it a <u>two-dimensional</u> compound.

Fullerenes and Polymers

Fullerenes and polymers are also made up of lots of covalently bonded atoms...

Fullerenes Form Spheres and Tubes

1) Fullerenes are molecules of carbon, shaped like closed tubes or hollow balls.

2) They're mainly made up of carbon atoms arranged in hexagons, but can also contain pentagons (rings of five carbons) or heptagons (rings of seven carbons).

3) Fullerenes can be used to 'cage' other molecules. The fullerene structure forms around another atom or molecule, which is then trapped inside. This could be used to deliver a drug directly to cells in the body.

4) Fullerenes have a huge surface area, so they could help make great industrial catalysts — individual catalyst molecules could be attached to the fullerenes (the bigger the surface area the better).

Catalysts speed up the rates of reactions without being used up (see page 147).

Nanotubes

1) Carbon nanotubes are also fullerenes. They're tiny cylinders of graphene — so they conduct electricity.

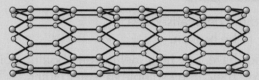

2) They also have a high tensile strength (they don't break when they're stretched), so can be used to strengthen materials without adding much weight.

3) For example, they can be used to strengthen sports equipment that needs to be strong but also lightweight (e.g. tennis rackets).

Buckminsterfullerene

Buckminsterfullerene has the molecular formula C_{60} and forms a hollow sphere made up of 20 hexagons and 12 pentagons. It's a stable molecule that forms soft brownish-black crystals.

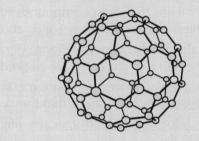

Polymers Are Made of Covalently Bonded Carbon Chains

1) Polymers are molecules made up of long chains of covalently bonded carbon atoms. A famous example is poly(ethene).

2) They're formed when lots of small molecules called monomers join together (see pages 177-179).

Poly(ethene)

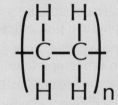

This is known as the repeat unit. The n shows that there are loads of these units joined, one after another.

Diamond, graphite and fullerenes contain exactly the same atoms

Apart from polymers, all of the giant covalent structures on the last two pages are made purely from carbon. The difference in properties between these structures is all down to the way the atoms are held together.

Topic 1 — Key Concepts in Chemistry

Metallic Bonding

Ever wondered what gives a <u>metal</u> its <u>properties</u>? It all comes down to <u>bonding</u>...

Metallic Bonding Involves Delocalised Electrons

1) <u>Metals</u> also consist of a <u>giant structure</u>.

2) The electrons in the <u>outer shell</u> of the metal atoms are <u>delocalised</u> (free to move around). There are strong forces of <u>electrostatic attraction</u> between the <u>positive metal ions</u> and the shared <u>negative electrons</u>.

3) These forces of attraction <u>hold</u> the <u>atoms</u> together in a <u>regular</u> structure and are known as <u>metallic bonding</u>. Metallic bonding is very <u>strong</u>.

4) Compounds that are held together by metallic bonding include metallic <u>elements</u> and <u>alloys</u> (see p.109).

5) It's the <u>delocalised electrons</u> in the metallic bonds which produce <u>all</u> the properties of metals.

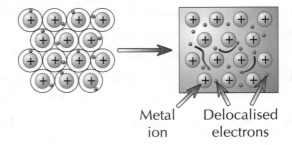

Metal ion   Delocalised electrons

Metals Have Certain Physical Properties

1) The electrostatic forces between the metal ions and the delocalised sea of electrons are very <u>strong</u>, so need <u>lots of energy</u> to be broken.

2) This means that most compounds with metallic bonds have very <u>high</u> melting and boiling points, so they're generally <u>shiny solids</u> at room temperature. They <u>aren't soluble</u> in water either.

3) Metals are also generally <u>more dense</u> than non-metals as the ions in the metallic structure are packed <u>close together</u>.

4) The <u>layers</u> of atoms in a pure metal can <u>slide over</u> each other (see page 109), making metals <u>malleable</u> — this means that they can be <u>hammered</u> or <u>rolled</u> into <u>flat sheets</u>.

5) The <u>delocalised electrons</u> carry electrical current through the material, so metals are good <u>conductors</u> of <u>electricity</u>.

Metals and Non-Metals Have Different Physical Properties

1) All metals have <u>metallic bonding</u> which causes them to have <u>similar</u> basic physical properties.

2) As non-metals <u>don't</u> have metallic bonding, they don't tend to exhibit the same properties as metals.

3) Non-metals form a variety of <u>different structures</u> so have a <u>range</u> of chemical and physical <u>properties</u>.

4) They tend to be <u>dull looking</u>, more <u>brittle</u>, have <u>lower boiling points</u> (they're not generally solids at room temperature), <u>don't</u> generally <u>conduct electricity</u> and often have a <u>lower density</u>.

The blue boxes show the metals in the periodic table (see p.30).

The white boxes show non-metals.

5) Metals and non-metals also have <u>different chemical properties</u>. Non-metals tend to <u>gain electrons</u> to form full outer shells — they are found on the top and right-hand side of the periodic table (see p.30) and their outer shells are generally <u>over half-filled</u>. Metals <u>lose electrons</u> to gain full outer shells — they're found at the bottom and left-hand side of the periodic table and their outer shells are generally <u>under half-filled</u>.

Metallic bonding is all about the delocalised electrons...

Delocalised electrons allow metals to be <u>good conductors</u> of <u>electricity</u> and have <u>high melting</u> and <u>boiling points</u>. You'll need to be able to <u>explain why</u> this is the case too...

Warm-Up and Exam Questions

You know the drill by now — have a crack at the questions on this page to see how much you really know. If you're struggling, take a look back over the last few pages and give it another read through...

Warm-Up Questions

1) Describe the differences in the hardness and electrical conductivity of diamond and graphite.
2) What are fullerenes?
3) What is a polymer?
4) Explain why most metals have a high melting point.

Exam Questions

1 Silicon carbide has a giant covalent structure and is a solid at room temperature.

(a) Explain, in terms of its bonding and structure, why silicon carbide has a high melting point.

[2 marks]

(b) Give **one** other example of a substance with a giant covalent structure.

[1 mark]

2 Copper is a metallic element. It can be used to make the wires in electrical circuits.

(a) State a property of copper that makes it suitable for use in electrical circuits, and explain why it has this property.

[2 marks]

(b) Explain why copper is also malleable.

[1 mark]

3 Graphite, diamond and fullerenes are entirely made from carbon but have different properties.

(a) Explain why the structure of graphite makes it a useful lubricant.

[2 marks]

(b) Explain why graphite is able to conduct electricity.

[1 mark]

(c) Using your knowledge of the structure of diamond, suggest why it is useful as a cutting tool.

[2 marks]

(d) **Figure 1** shows a fullerene.

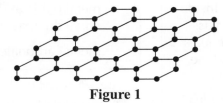

Figure 1

(i) Name the type of fullerene shown in **Figure 1**.

[1 mark]

(ii) Describe **one** property of fullerenes that makes them suitable for use in catalysts.

[1 mark]

Conservation of Mass

Conservation of mass is a really important concept in all of chemistry — so pay attention to this page...

In a Chemical Reaction, **Mass** is **Always Conserved**

1) During a chemical reaction no atoms are destroyed and no atoms are created.

2) This means there are the same number and types of atoms on each side of a reaction equation.

3) You can see this in action if you do a reaction in a closed system (this is a system where nothing can get in or out). The total mass of the system before and after doesn't change.

4) A good way of showing this is to do a precipitation reaction.

A precipitation reaction happens when two solutions react and an insoluble solid, called a precipitate, forms in the solution.

Example: Copper sulfate solution reacts with sodium hydroxide to form insoluble copper hydroxide and soluble sodium sulfate:

$$CuSO_{4(aq)} + 2NaOH_{(aq)} \rightarrow Cu(OH)_{2(s)} + Na_2SO_{4(aq)}$$

As no reactants or products can escape, the scales will read the same throughout the experiment.

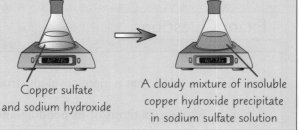

Copper sulfate and sodium hydroxide

A cloudy mixture of insoluble copper hydroxide precipitate in sodium sulfate solution

If the Mass **Seems to Change**, There's Usually a **Gas** Involved

In some experiments, you might observe a change of mass in an unsealed reaction vessel during a reaction. There are two reasons why this might happen:

1 If the mass increases, it's probably because at least one of the reactants is a gas that's found in air (e.g. oxygen) and the products are solids, liquids or aqueous.

- Before the reaction, the gas is floating around in the air. It's there, but it's not contained in the reaction vessel, so you can't measure its mass.

- When the gas reacts to form part of the product, it becomes contained inside the reaction vessel.

- So the total mass of the stuff inside the reaction vessel increases.

- For example, when a metal in an unsealed container reacts with oxygen from the air, the mass inside the container increases. The mass of the metal oxide produced equals the total mass of the metal and the oxygen that reacted from the air.

metal$_{(s)}$ + oxygen$_{(g)} \rightarrow$ metal oxide$_{(s)}$

2 If the mass decreases, it's probably because some, or all, of the reactants are solids, liquids or aqueous and at least one of the products is a gas.

- Before the reaction, any solid, liquid or aqueous reactants are contained in the reaction vessel.

- If the vessel isn't enclosed, then the gas can escape from the reaction vessel as it's formed. It's no longer contained in the reaction vessel, so you can't measure its mass.

- So the total mass of the stuff inside the reaction vessel decreases.

- For example, when a metal carbonate thermally decomposes in an unsealed container to form a metal oxide and carbon dioxide gas, the mass of the container will appear to decrease as the carbon dioxide escapes. But in reality, the mass of the metal oxide and the carbon dioxide produced will equal the mass of the metal carbonate that reacted.

metal carbonate$_{(s)} \rightarrow$ metal oxide$_{(s)}$ + carbon dioxide$_{(g)}$

A gas will expand to fill any container it's in. So if the reaction vessel isn't sealed the gas expands out from the vessel, and escapes into the air around. There's more about this on page 58.

The total mass of reactants is the same as the total mass of products

If the measured masses aren't the same, it's because the reaction hasn't occurred in a closed system.

Relative Masses and Chemical Formulas

You'll need to know how to work out <u>relative formula mass</u>, <u>empirical</u> and <u>molecular formulas</u> of substances...

Relative Formula Mass, M_r

You can find the relative atomic mass (A_r) of an element from the periodic table (see p.30). You'll be given the periodic table in the exam too, so there's no need to worry about remembering all the numbers.

The <u>relative formula mass</u>, M_r, of a compound is the relative atomic masses (A_r) of all the atoms in its formula <u>added together</u>.

EXAMPLE: Find the relative formula mass of:
a) **magnesium chloride, $MgCl_2$,**
b) **calcium hydroxide, $Ca(OH)_2$.**

a) Use the <u>periodic table</u> to find the <u>relative atomic masses</u> of magnesium and chlorine. Add up the relative atomic masses of all the atoms in the formula to get the relative formula mass.

$A_r(Mg) = 24$ $A_r(Cl) = 35.5$
$M_r(MgCl_2) = 24 + (2 \times 35.5)$
$= 24 + 71 = 95$
$M_r(MgCl_2) = 95$

b) The <u>small number 2</u> after the bracket in the formula $Ca(OH)_2$ means that <u>there's two of everything inside the brackets</u>.

$A_r(Ca) = 40$ $A_r(O) = 16$ $A_r(H) = 1$
$M_r(Ca(OH)_2) = 40 + [(16 + 1) \times 2]$
$= 40 + 34 = 74$
$M_r(Ca(OH)_2) = 74$

The M_r of a compound is equal to the <u>mass in grams</u> of <u>1 mole</u> (see next page) of the compound. So, 1 mole of magnesium chloride would weigh 95 g, and 1 mole of calcium hydroxide would weigh 74 g.

The **Empirical Formula** is the **Simplest Ratio** of Atoms

The <u>empirical formula</u> of a compound tells you the <u>smallest whole number ratio</u> of atoms in the compound.

EXAMPLE: Find the empirical formula of glucose, $C_6H_{12}O_6$.

The numbers in the <u>molecular formula</u> of <u>glucose</u> are <u>6</u>, <u>12</u> and <u>6</u>.
To simplify the ratio, divide them by the largest number that goes into 6, 12 and 6 <u>exactly</u> — that's <u>6</u>.

C: $6 \div 6 = 1$
H: $12 \div 6 = 2$
O: $6 \div 6 = 1$
The empirical formula of glucose is CH_2O.

You can use the <u>empirical formula</u> of a compound, together with its M_r, to find its molecular formula.

EXAMPLE: Compound X has the empirical formula C_2H_6N. The M_r of compound X is 88. Find the molecular formula of compound X.

1) Start by finding the M_r of the <u>empirical formula</u>. The A_r of carbon is <u>12</u>, the A_r of hydrogen is <u>1</u> and the A_r of nitrogen is <u>14</u>.

$M_r(C_2H_6N) = (2 \times A_r(C)) + (6 \times A_r(H)) + A_r(N)$
$= (2 \times 12) + (6 \times 1) + 14$
$= 24 + 6 + 14 = 44$

2) Divide the M_r of the compound by the M_r of the empirical formula.

$88 \div 44 = 2$

3) Now to get the <u>molecular formula</u>, you just <u>multiply</u> everything in the empirical formula by the result — in this case, by <u>2</u>.

C: $2 \times 2 = 4$ H: $6 \times 2 = 12$ N: $1 \times 2 = 2$
The molecular formula of compound X is $C_4H_{12}N_2$.

Empirical formulas are just simplified versions of molecular formulas

The <u>molecular formula</u> tells you the <u>actual number</u> of atoms of each element in <u>one molecule</u> of a compound. The <u>empirical formula</u> is <u>different</u> — it only gives you the <u>ratio</u> of atoms of each element.

Moles and Calculations

The mole seems like a strange old concept — it's difficult to see the relevance of the word "mole" to anything but a small burrowing animal. They're really important though, so make sure you're concentrating...

"The Mole" is the Name Given to a Certain Number of Particles

1) Just like a million is this many: 1 000 000, or a billion is this many: 1 000 000 000, a mole is an amount of particles (e.g. atoms, molecules or ions) equal to a number called Avogadro's constant, and it's this many: 602 000 000 000 000 000 000 000 or 6.02×10^{23}.

2) But why is Avogadro's constant useful? The answer is that when you get that number of atoms or molecules, of any element or compound, then, conveniently, they weigh exactly the same number of grams as the relative atomic mass, A_r, (or relative formula mass, M_r) of the element or compound.

One mole of atoms or molecules of any substance will have a mass in grams equal to the relative particle mass (A_r or M_r) for that substance.

3) Here are some examples:

Look back at the previous page if you've forgotten how to work out M_r.

Carbon has an A_r of 12.
So one mole of carbon weighs exactly 12 g.

Nitrogen gas, N_2, has an M_r of 28 (2×14).
So one mole of N_2 weighs exactly 28 g.

Hexane, C_6H_{14}, has an M_r of 86 ([6×12] + [14×1]).
So one mole of C_6H_{14} weighs exactly 86 g.

4) So 12 g of carbon, 28 g of nitrogen gas and 86 g of hexane all contain the same number of particles, namely one mole or 6.02×10^{23} particles.

A mole of a substance is 6.02×10^{23} particles of that substance

You'll need to make sure that you're crystal clear on moles before moving on, so you may need to read through this page a few times. Truth is, once you've got it, you've got it — it's a bit like riding a bike...

Moles and Calculations

Avogadro's Constant is Used to Calculate Numbers of Particles

You need to be able to work out the <u>number</u> of <u>molecules</u>, <u>atoms</u> or <u>ions</u> in a certain number of <u>moles</u>.

EXAMPLE: **How many atoms are there in 5 moles of oxygen gas?**

1) Multiply <u>Avogadro's constant</u> by the number of moles you have to find the number of particles.

$$6.02 \times 10^{23} \times 5 = 3.01 \times 10^{24}$$

2) There are two atoms in each molecule of oxygen gas, so <u>multiply</u> your answer by 2.

$$3.01 \times 10^{24} \times 2 = 6.02 \times 10^{24}$$

Give your answer in standard form (in terms of $\times 10^x$) to save you having to write out lots of 0's.

If you're asked for the number of particles in a given mass, you need to do some converting first. There's a <u>formula</u> you can use to find the number of moles in a certain mass of something.

$$\text{Number of Moles} = \frac{\text{Mass in g (of element or compound)}}{M_r \text{ (of compound) or } A_r \text{ (of element)}}$$

EXAMPLE: **How many magnesium atoms are there in 60 g of magnesium?** (A_r of Mg = 24)

1) Convert mass into moles using the equation.

$$\text{moles} = \text{mass} \div A_r$$
$$= 60 \div 24 = 2.5 \text{ moles}$$

2) Multiply the number of moles by <u>Avogadro's</u> <u>constant</u> to find the number of atoms.

$$6.02 \times 10^{23} \times 2.5$$
$$= 1.505 \times 10^{24}$$

If you need to get <u>from</u> a number of particles <u>to</u> a number of moles, you <u>divide</u> by 6.02×10^{23} instead.

You Need to be Able to Rearrange the Equation for Moles

1) Just being able to plug numbers into the equation <u>moles = mass $\div M_r$</u> isn't going to cut it in the exams. You need to be able to <u>rearrange</u> the formula to find out <u>other unknowns</u>, e.g. to find a mass if you've been given moles and M_r.

2) Putting an equation into a <u>formula triangle</u> makes rearranging equations straightforward. Here's the formula triangle that links moles, mass and relative formula mass.

$$\frac{\text{mass}}{\text{moles} \times M_r}$$

Or A_r.

3) To use a formula triangle, just cover the thing you want to find, and you're left with the expression you need to calculate it. The <u>line</u> through the triangle stands for <u>division</u>.

Moles and Calculations

EXAMPLE:

How many moles are there in 66 g of carbon dioxide?

M_r of carbon dioxide (CO_2) = 12 + (16 × 2) = 44

moles = mass ÷ M_r = 66 ÷ 44 = 1.5 moles

EXAMPLE:

What mass of carbon is there in 4 moles of carbon dioxide?

mass = moles × A_r(C)
= 4 × 12 = 48 g

Concentration is a Measure of How Crowded Things Are

1) The <u>more solute</u> (the solid you're dissolving) you dissolve in a given volume, the <u>more crowded</u> the particles are and the <u>more concentrated</u> the solution.

2) Concentration can be measured in <u>grams per dm^3</u> (<u>g dm^{-3}</u>) — so 1 gram of stuff dissolved in 1 dm^3 of solution has a concentration of <u>1 g dm^{-3}</u>.

3) Here's the formula for finding <u>concentration</u> from the <u>mass of solute</u>:

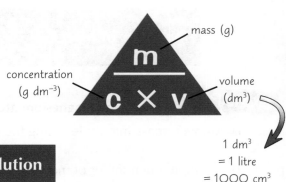

mass (g)

concentration (g dm^{-3})

volume (dm^3)

1 dm^3
= 1 litre
= 1000 cm^3

Concentration = Mass of solute ÷ Volume of solution

EXAMPLE:

25 g of copper sulfate is dissolved in 500 cm^3 of water. What's the concentration in g dm^{-3}?

1) Make sure the values are in the <u>right units</u>. The mass is already in g, but you need to convert the volume to dm^3.

1000 cm^3 = 1 dm^3, so
500 cm^3 = (500 ÷ 1000) dm^3 = 0.5 dm^3

2) Now just substitute the values into the formula:

concentration = 25 ÷ 0.5 = 50 g dm^{-3}

EXAMPLE:

What mass of sodium chloride is in 300 cm^3 of solution with a concentration of 12 g dm^{-3}?

1) Rearrange the formula so that mass is by itself.

mass = concentration × volume

2) Put the volume into the <u>right units</u>.

300 cm^3 = (300 ÷ 1000) dm^3 = 0.30 dm^3

3) Substitute the values into the rearranged formula.

mass = 12 × 0.30 = 3.6 g

Learn the formula triangles — they're really handy

Make sure you pay close attention to the <u>units</u> for any questions involving the formulas above. You might have to <u>convert</u> the units first. E.g. if you need to give a concentration in g dm^{-3}, make sure your mass value is in grams and your volume in dm^3 before doing the calculation.

Warm-Up and Exam Questions

Phew... that was heavy going. All that stands between you and a huge sigh of relief are these questions. Make sure you've understood everything on the last few pages though, or you may be in for a bumpy ride.

Warm-Up Questions

1) What is meant by the relative formula mass of a compound?
2) What is the empirical formula of a compound with the molecular formula $C_4H_8Cl_2$?
3) Write down the definition of a mole.
4) Calculate the number of moles in 90 g of water. M_r of water = 18.
5) 0.500 moles of substance X has a mass of 87.0 g. What is the relative formula mass of X?
6) What mass of sodium hydroxide is contained in 200 cm³ of a 55 g dm⁻³ solution?

Exam Questions

1   Which of the following is the M_r of calcium chloride ($CaCl_2$)?

    ☐ **A**   54

    ☐ **B**   75.5

    ☐ **C**   111

    ☐ **D**   71

[1 mark]

2   A student carries out the following reaction in an unsealed container:

$$2HCl_{(aq)} + MgCO_{3(s)} \rightarrow MgCl_{2(aq)} + H_2O_{(l)} + CO_{2(g)}$$

(a)   Calculate the relative formula mass of $MgCO_3$.

[1 mark]

(b)   Predict how the mass of the reaction vessel and its contents will change over the reaction. Explain your answer.

[3 marks]

3   A teacher decides to carry out the following reaction between solutions of potassium hydroxide and copper sulfate:

$$2KOH_{(aq)} + CuSO_{4(aq)} \rightarrow Cu(OH)_{2(s)} + K_2SO_{4(aq)}$$

(a)   The teacher uses 140 g of potassium hydroxide (KOH) in the reaction. Calculate, in grams, how much more KOH the teacher needs to have a 4 mole sample.

[3 marks]

(b)   1.25 moles of K_2SO_4 are produced in the experiment. Calculate the mass of K_2SO_4 produced.

[2 marks]

(c)   The teacher makes up a solution for another experiment by dissolving copper sulfate in 1500 ml of water. The concentration of copper ions in the solution is 12 g dm⁻³. Calculate the number of copper ions present in the solution.

[4 marks]

Calculating Empirical Formulas

You first met <u>empirical formulas</u> back on page 47, but now <u>they're back</u> and they mean business.

Empirical Formulas can be Calculated from Masses

You can work out the <u>empirical formula</u> of a compound from the masses of the elements it contains.

> **A sample of a hydrocarbon contains 36 g of carbon and 6 g of hydrogen. Work out the empirical formula of the hydrocarbon.**
>
> *Remember —*
> *moles =*
> *mass ÷ A_r.*
>
> 1) First work out how many <u>moles</u> of each <u>element</u> you have.
>
> $A_r(C) = 12$ moles of C = 36 ÷ 12 = 3 moles
> $A_r(H) = 1$ moles of H = 6 ÷ 1 = 6 moles
>
> 2) Work out the <u>smallest whole number ratio</u> between the moles of C and H atoms to get the <u>empirical formula</u>.
>
>   Ratio C:H = 3:6. Now divide both numbers by the smallest — here it's 3. So, the ratio C:H = 1:2. The empirical formula must be CH_2.

You can also find the empirical formula of a compound from the percentage of each element it contains (its percentage composition). The method for doing this is the same as the one above, but you divide the percentage (rather than the mass) of each element by its A_r.

You can Use Experiments to Find Empirical Formulas

Here's an <u>experiment</u> you could use to calculate the empirical formula of a metal oxide, e.g. magnesium oxide.

1) Get a <u>crucible</u> and heat it until it's red hot. (This will make sure it's <u>clean</u> and that there are no traces of <u>oil or water</u> lying around from a previous experiment.)

2) Leave the crucible to <u>cool</u>, then <u>weigh</u> it, along with its lid.

3) Add some clean <u>magnesium ribbon</u> to the crucible. <u>Reweigh</u> the crucible, lid and magnesium ribbon. The <u>mass of magnesium</u> you're using is this reading minus the initial reading for the mass of the crucible and lid.

4) <u>Heat</u> the crucible containing the magnesium. Put the lid on the crucible so as to <u>stop</u> any bits of solid from <u>escaping</u>, but leave a <u>small gap</u> to allow <u>oxygen</u> to enter the crucible.

5) Heat the crucible strongly for around <u>10 minutes</u>, or until all the magnesium ribbon has turned <u>white</u>.

6) Allow the crucible to <u>cool</u> and <u>reweigh</u> the crucible with the lid and its contents. The <u>mass</u> of <u>magnesium oxide</u> you have is this reading, minus the initial reading for the mass of the crucible and lid.

lid
crucible containing magnesium ribbon
gauze
tripod
HEAT

> **A student heats 1.08 g of magnesium ribbon in a crucible so it completely reacts to form magnesium oxide. The total mass of magnesium oxide formed was 1.80 g. Calculate the empirical formula of magnesium oxide.**
>
> 1) The extra mass in the magnesium oxide must have come from oxygen, so you can work out the <u>mass of oxygen</u>.
>
>   mass of O = 1.80 − 1.08 = 0.72 g
>
> 2) Work out the <u>number of moles</u> of <u>magnesium</u> and <u>oxygen atoms</u> involved in the reaction.
>
>   moles of Mg = 1.08 ÷ 24 = 0.045 moles
>   moles of O = 0.72 ÷ 16 = 0.045 moles
>
> 3) Work out the <u>lowest whole number ratio</u> between Mg and O by dividing the moles of both by the <u>smallest number</u>.
>
>   Mg = 0.045 ÷ 0.045 = 1
>   O = 0.045 ÷ 0.045 = 1
>
> This shows that the ratio between O and Mg in the formula is 1:1, so the empirical formula of the magnesium oxide must be MgO.

You can work out an empirical formula from experimental results...

Make sure you <u>fully understand</u> the example above — you may be asked <u>something similar</u> in the <u>exam</u>.

Limiting Reactants

Reactions don't go on forever — you need stuff in the reaction flask that can react.
Sooner or later one of the reactants <u>runs out</u> and the reaction <u>stops</u>.

Reactions **Stop** When **One** Reactant is **Used Up**

1) A reaction stops when all of one of the reactants is <u>used up</u>.
   Any other reactants are said to be in <u>excess</u>.

2) The reactant that's <u>used up</u> in a reaction is called the <u>limiting reactant</u> (because it limits the amount of product that's formed).

3) The amount of product formed is <u>directly proportional</u> to the amount of the <u>limiting reactant</u> used.

4) This is because if you add <u>more of the limiting reactant</u> there will be <u>more reactant particles</u> to take part in the reaction, which means <u>more product particles</u> are made (as long as the other reactants are in excess).

You can Calculate the Amount of **Product** from the **Limiting Reactant**

You can use a <u>balanced chemical equation</u> to work out the <u>mass of product formed</u> from a given <u>mass of a limiting reactant</u>. Here's how...

1) Write out the <u>balanced equation</u>.
2) <u>Work out relative formula masses</u> (M_r) of the reactant and product you're interested in.
3) Find out <u>how many moles</u> there are of the substance you <u>know</u> the mass of.
4) Use the balanced equation to work out <u>how many moles</u> there'll be of the other substance (i.e. how many moles of product will be made by this many moles of reactant).
5) Use the number of moles to calculate the <u>mass</u>.

You could also use this method to find the mass of a reactant needed to produce a known mass of a product.

EXAMPLE: **Calculate the mass of aluminium oxide, Al_2O_3, formed when 135 g of aluminium is burned in air.**

1) Write out the <u>balanced equation</u>:

$$4Al + 3O_2 \rightarrow 2Al_2O_3$$

2) Calculate the <u>relative formula masses</u> of the reactants and products you're interested in.

Al: 27 Al_2O_3: $(2 \times 27) + (3 \times 16) = 102$

3) <u>Calculate the number of moles</u> of aluminium in 135 g:

moles = mass ÷ M_r = 135 ÷ 27 = 5

4) Look at the <u>ratio</u> of moles in the equation:

4 moles of Al react to produce 2 moles of Al_2O_3 — half the number of moles are produced. So 5 moles of Al will react to produce 2.5 moles of Al_2O_3.

5) <u>Calculate the mass</u> of 2.5 moles of aluminium oxide:

mass = moles × M_r = 2.5 × 102 = 255 g

See the next page for another example on how to calculate masses using the chemical equation for a reaction.

Limiting Reactants

EXAMPLE:

Magnesium oxide, MgO, can be made by burning magnesium in air. What mass of magnesium is needed to make 100 g of magnesium oxide?

1) Write out the <u>balanced equation</u>.

$$2Mg + O_2 \rightarrow 2MgO$$

2) Work out the <u>relative formula masses</u> of the reactants and products you're interested in.

Mg: 24   MgO: 24 + 16 = 40

3) <u>Calculate the number of moles</u> of magnesium oxide in 100 g:

moles = mass ÷ M_r = 100 ÷ 40 = 2.5

4) Look at the <u>ratio</u> of moles in the equation:

2 moles of MgO are made from 2 moles of Mg. So 2.5 moles of MgO will be formed from 2.5 moles of Mg.

5) <u>Calculate the mass</u> of 2.5 moles of Mg.

mass = moles × M_r = 2.5 × 24 = 60 g

You Can Also Work Out **Limiting Reactants**

You can use a <u>balanced chemical equation</u> to work out the limiting reactant in a reaction.

EXAMPLE:

8.1 g of zinc oxide (ZnO) were put in a crucible with 0.30 g of carbon and heated until they reacted. Given that the balanced chemical equation for this reaction is: $2ZnO + C \rightarrow CO_2 + 2Zn$, work out the limiting reactant in this reaction.

1) Divide the mass of each substance by its M_r or A_r to find how many <u>moles</u> of each substance were reacted:

ZnO: $\frac{8.1}{81}$ = 0.10 mol

C: $\frac{0.30}{12}$ = 0.025 mol

This calculation uses a similar method to the one shown on the next page.

2) Divide by the <u>smallest number of moles</u>, which is 0.025:

ZnO: $\frac{0.10}{0.025}$ = 4.0

C: $\frac{0.025}{0.025}$ = 1.0

This is a neat way of making the smallest number of moles equal 1 — it often makes the other numbers a lot nicer too...

3) Compare the ratios between the moles of products with the balanced chemical equation.

In the balanced equation, ZnO and C react in a ratio of 2 : 1. Using the masses, there is a 4 : 1 ratio of ZnO to C. So, ZnO is in excess, and C must be the limiting reactant.

Practice makes perfect with these calculations...

The best thing to do is to <u>learn the method</u> for answering each type of question. Then you can follow the same process <u>every time</u> you <u>answer</u> one, and it'll become <u>second nature</u> in no time at all.

Balancing Equations Using Masses

You've already seen how to <u>balance equations</u> back on page 18. But, sometimes, you may have to balance equations given the <u>masses</u> of the reactants and products. Your good old friend the <u>mole</u> will come in handy.

You Can **Balance Equations** Using **Reacting Masses**

If you know the <u>masses</u> of the <u>reactants</u> and <u>products</u> that took part in a reaction, you can work out the <u>balanced symbol equation</u> for the reaction. Here are the steps you should take:

1) Divide the <u>mass</u> of each substance by its <u>relative formula mass</u> to find the <u>number of moles</u>.

   You may need to work out some unknown masses first (see below).

2) Divide the number of moles of each substance by the <u>smallest number of moles</u> in the reaction.

3) If needed, multiply all the numbers by the same amount to make them all <u>whole numbers</u>.

4) Write the <u>balanced symbol equation</u> for the reaction by putting these numbers in front of the formulas.

EXAMPLE:

Paula burns a metal, X, in oxygen. There is a single product, an oxide of the metal. Given that 25.4 g of X burns in 3.2 g of oxygen, write a balanced equation for this reaction. A_r of X = 63.5 and M_r of X oxide = 143.0.

1) Work out the <u>mass of metal oxide produced</u>. Because it's the only product, the mass of metal oxide produced must equal the <u>total mass of reactants</u>.

   This is because mass is always conserved in a chemical reaction (see p.46).

   25.4 + 3.2 = 28.6 g of X oxide

2) Divide the mass of each substance by its $\underline{M_r}$ or $\underline{A_r}$ to calculate how many <u>moles</u> of each substance reacted or were produced:

   X: $\frac{25.4}{63.5}$ = 0.40 mol O_2: $\frac{3.2}{32.0}$ = 0.10 mol   X oxide: $\frac{28.6}{143.0}$ = 0.20 mol

3) Divide by the <u>smallest number of moles</u>, which is 0.10:

   X: $\frac{0.40}{0.10}$ = 4.0 O_2: $\frac{0.10}{0.10}$ = 1.0   X oxide: $\frac{0.20}{0.10}$ = 2.0

   Remember, this step is used to make the smallest number of moles equal 1.

4) The numbers are all whole numbers, so you can write out the <u>balanced symbol equation</u> straight away.

   4X + O_2 → 2(X oxide)

5) The oxide of X must have a <u>chemical formula</u> containing X and O atoms. In order for the equation to balance, each molecule of X oxide must contain <u>one O atom</u> and <u>2 X atoms</u>.

   4X + O_2 → 2X_2O

Another handy method for balancing equations...

Remember, <u>moles</u> are a <u>measure</u> of the <u>number of particles</u> of a substance, but the <u>mass</u> of a substance depends on the M_r or A_r of <u>each particle</u>. You have to convert <u>mass</u> to <u>moles</u> when you're looking at the <u>ratios</u> in which particles react, because particles can have <u>very different masses</u> from each other — using moles allows you to <u>directly compare them</u>. If you just used their masses you could get the wrong answer.

Warm-Up and Exam Questions

It's nearly the end of Topic 1 but it's not quite done with yet. Before you start celebrating have a go at the questions on the last few pages of stuff. Don't skip over them — doing them now will help it all stick.

Warm-Up Questions

1) A 45.6 g sample of an oxide of nitrogen contains 13.9 g of nitrogen.
   What is the empirical formula of the nitrogen oxide?

2) Describe what a limiting reactant is.

3) In a reaction, suggest what happens to the amount of product formed
   if the amount of limiting reactant is halved?

Exam Questions

1   3.5 g of a metal, X, reacts completely with 4.0 g of oxygen to form 7.5 g of an oxide of the metal.
    A_r(metal X) = 7, M_r(oxygen) = 32, M_r(metal oxide) = 30.

   (a)   Calculate how many moles of each substance reacted or was produced.

   [2 marks]

   (b)   Use your answer to part **(a)** to write a balanced symbol equation for this reaction.

   [2 marks]

2   Sulfuric acid reacts with sodium hydrogen carbonate to produce aqueous sodium sulfate,
    water and carbon dioxide. The balanced equation for this reaction is:

   $$H_2SO_{4(aq)} + 2NaHCO_{3(s)} \rightarrow Na_2SO_{4(aq)} + 2H_2O_{(l)} + 2CO_{2(g)}$$

   A student reacted 6.0 g of solid $NaHCO_3$ with an excess of sulfuric acid (H_2SO_4).

   (a)   (i) Calculate the moles of Na_2SO_4 produced in this reaction.

   [3 marks]

   (ii) Calculate the mass of Na_2SO_4 produced in this reaction.

   [2 marks]

   (b)   The student repeated the experiment using double the amount of H_2SO_4.
         Explain why the mass of Na_2SO_4 produced in the reaction remained the same.

   [1 mark]

3   A student heats 2.4 g of iron oxide (Fe_2O_3) with 0.36 g of carbon until they reacted.
    The balanced chemical equation for the reaction is:

   $$2Fe_2O_3 + 3C \rightarrow 4Fe + 3CO_2$$

   (a)   Deduce which reactant was **not** in excess in this reaction.

   [4 marks]

   (b)   During a different experiment, the student heats some iron, Fe, in the presence of an unknown
         gas, Y_2. A single product forms, which is an ionic compound containing Fe and Y only.

         Given that during the reaction, the student heated 17.92 g of iron, and 52.00 g of product were
         formed, write a balanced equation for the reaction.
         A_r(Fe) = 56, M_r(product) = 162.5 and M_r(Y_2) = 71

   [4 marks]

Revision Summary for Topic 1

That wraps up Topic 1 — time to put yourself to the test and find out how much you really know.
- Try these questions and tick off each one when you get it right.
- When you've done all the questions under a heading and are completely happy with it, tick it off.

Chemical Equations, Risks and Hazards (p.17-21) ☐

1) What are the chemicals on the left-hand side of a chemical equation called? ☑
2) Write out the four state symbols used in chemical equations, and state what each one means. ☑
3) Write out the formulas, complete with charges, of the carbonate and sulfate ions. ☑
4) Sketch the following hazard symbols: a) toxic   b) harmful. ☑

Atoms, Isotopes, the Periodic Table and Electronic Configurations (p.23-31) ☐

5) Describe the main features of the plum pudding model of the atom. ☑
6) Name the three subatomic particles found in an atom, and state the relative mass of each. ☑
7) What can you say about the number of protons and electrons in a neutral atom? ☑
8) State what isotopes are, using an example to explain your answer. ☑
9) Describe why Dmitri Mendeleev had gaps in his version of the periodic table. ☑
10) What can you say about the number of electron shells in elements in the same period? ☑
11) What does the group number of an element in the periodic table tell you about its electronic structure? ☑

Types of Bonding and Structures (p.33-44) ☐

12) What charge will the ion of a Group 6 element have? ☑
13) Describe how ionic bonding occurs. ☑
14) Draw a dot and cross diagram to show how magnesium chloride forms. ☑
15) Outline the limitations associated with ball and stick models of molecules and compounds. ☑
16) Draw a dot and cross diagram to show the bonding in a molecule of:
    a) hydrogen   b) water ☑
17) Do simple molecular substances have high or low boiling points? ☑
18) Explain why hydrogen, H_2, doesn't conduct electricity. ☑
19) Describe the structures of the following substances:
    a) graphite   b) buckminsterfullerene ☑
20) Give three general properties of metals. ☑

Calculations and Moles (p.46-55) ☐

21) Why does the mass of a sealed system stay the same during a chemical reaction? ☑
22) State Avogadro's constant. ☑
23) What is the empirical formula of a compound? ☑
24) What equation links the number of moles with the mass and M_r of a substance? ☑
25) What equation links the concentration of a solution with its volume and the mass of solute used? ☑
26) What is the concentration, in g dm^{-3}, of a solution that contains 4 g of solute in 2 dm^3 of solvent? ☑
27) Outline an experiment you could use to work out the empirical formula of magnesium oxide. ☑
28) Describe how to balance an equation using the masses of the reactants and products in a reaction. ☑

States of Matter

All stuff is made of particles (molecules, ions or atoms). The forces between these particles can be weak or strong, depending on whether it's a solid, a liquid or a gas. Want to find out more? Then read on...

States of Matter Depend on the **Forces Between Particles**

1) There are three states of matter that you need to know about — solids, liquids and gases.
   You can model these three different states using the particle model.

2) In the particle model, each particle (it could be a molecule,
   an ion or an atom) is represented by a solid sphere.

3) The properties of each state of matter depend on the forces between the particles.

4) The forces between the particles can be weak or strong,
   depending on whether the substance is a solid, a liquid or a gas.

Solids

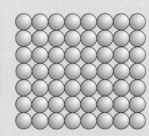

1) There are strong forces of attraction between particles, which
   hold them in fixed positions in a regular lattice arrangement.

2) The particles don't move from their positions,
   so all solids keep a definite shape and volume.

3) The particles in a solid don't have much energy.

4) They hardly move at all — in fact, they can only vibrate about
   their fixed positions. The hotter the solid becomes, the more
   they vibrate (causing solids to expand slightly when heated).

Liquids

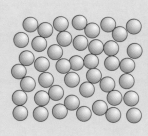

1) There is some force of attraction between the particles. They're
   free to move past each other, but they do tend to stick together.

2) Liquids don't keep a definite shape and will flow to fill the
   bottom of a container. But they do keep the same volume.

3) For any given substance, in the liquid state its particles will have more
   energy than in the solid state (but less energy than in the gas state).

4) The particles are constantly moving with random motion.
   The hotter the liquid gets, the faster they move.
   This causes liquids to expand slightly when heated.

Gases

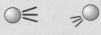

1) There's next to no force of attraction between the particles
   — they're free to move. They travel in straight lines and
   only interact when they collide.

2) Gases don't keep a definite shape or volume and will always
   fill any container. When particles bounce off the walls of a
   container they exert a pressure on the walls.

This means a
gas will escape
from a container
if it isn't airtight.

3) For any given substance, in the gas state its particles will
   have more energy that in the solid state or the liquid state.

4) The particles move constantly with random motion.
   The hotter the gas gets, the faster they move.
   Gases either expand when heated, or their pressure increases.

States of Matter

By adding or taking away energy from a substance, you can convert it from one physical state to another.

Heating or Cooling a Substance can Change its State

When a substance changes from one state of matter to another, it's a physical change. Physical changes are pretty easy to undo by heating or cooling.

The red arrows show heat being added. The blue arrows show heat being given out.

1) When a solid is heated, its particles gain more energy.

2) This makes the particles vibrate more, which weakens the forces that hold the solid together. This makes the solid expand.

3) At a certain temperature, called the melting point, the particles have enough energy to break free from their positions. This is called MELTING and the solid turns into a liquid.

4) When a liquid is heated, the particles get even more energy.

5) This energy makes the particles move faster, which weakens and breaks the bonds holding the liquid together.

6) At a certain temperature, called the boiling point, the particles have enough energy to break their bonds. This is BOILING (or evaporating). The liquid becomes a gas.

Solid

melting   freezing

Liquid

boiling (or evaporating)   condensing

Gas

12) At the melting point, so many bonds have formed between the particles that they're held in place. The liquid becomes a solid. This is FREEZING.

11) There's not enough energy to overcome the attraction between the particles, so more bonds form between them.

10) When a liquid cools, the particles have less energy, so move around less.

9) At the boiling point, so many bonds have formed between the gas particles that the gas becomes a liquid. This is called CONDENSING.

8) Bonds form between the particles.

7) As a gas cools, the particles no longer have enough energy to overcome the forces of attraction between them.

Solids can also change directly into a gas — this is called subliming.

States of Matter

Atoms are **Rearranged** During **Chemical Reactions**

1) <u>Chemical changes</u> are different to physical changes.

2) Chemical changes happen during <u>chemical reactions</u>, when bonds between atoms break and the atoms <u>change places</u>.

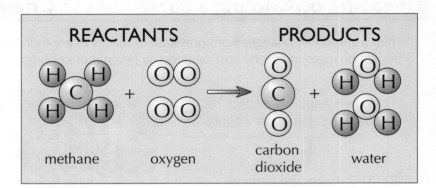

REACTANTS	PRODUCTS
methane oxygen	carbon dioxide water

3) The atoms from the substances you <u>start off</u> with (the <u>reactants</u>) are rearranged to form <u>different substances</u> (the <u>products</u>).

4) Compared to physical changes, chemical changes are often <u>hard to reverse</u>.

You Can Make **Predictions** about Substances from their **Properties**

You might be asked to <u>use data</u> to work out what <u>state</u> substances will be in under <u>certain conditions</u>.

EXAMPLE:

The table on the right gives information about the properties of four different substances.

Predict the state of substance D at 1000 °C.

Substance	Melting point / °C	Boiling point / °C
A	−218.4	−183.0
B	1535	2750
C	1410	2355
D	801	1413

1) The <u>melting point</u> of D is 801 °C and its <u>boiling point</u> is 1413 °C.
2) That means it's a solid <u>below 801 °C</u>, a gas <u>above 1413 °C</u>, and a liquid <u>in between</u>.
3) <u>1000 °C</u> is between 801 °C and 1413 °C, so... **D is a liquid at 1000 °C.**

Physical changes are reversible, chemical changes are less so...

Make sure you can describe what happens to particles, and the forces between them, as a substance is <u>heated</u> and <u>cooled</u>. Don't forget to learn the technical terms for each <u>state change</u> too.

Warm-Up and Exam Questions

Reckon you know all there is to know about this section so far? Have a go at these questions and see how you get on. If you get stuck on something, just flick back and give it another read through.

Warm-Up Questions

1) Put the three states of matter, solid, liquid and gas, in order of the strength of the forces between their particles, starting with the weakest.

2) What happens to the particles in a gas when it is heated?

3) What term is used to describe a change of state from:
   a) liquid to solid?   b) gas to liquid?   c) solid to liquid?   d) solid to gas?

Exam Questions

1   **Figure 1** shows a vessel in a distillery. The walls of the vessel are solid copper.

   (a) Describe the arrangement of particles in the solid copper walls of the vessel.

   [1 mark]

   (b) Inside the vessel, liquid ethanol is turned into ethanol gas. Explain the changes in arrangement, movement and energy of the ethanol particles when the liquid ethanol is heated to become a gas.

   [3 marks]

Figure 1

2   **Table 1** shows the melting and boiling points of three molecular substances.

Substance	Melting point (°C)	Boiling point (°C)
oxygen	−219	−183
chlorine	−101	−34
bromine	−7	59

Table 1

   (a) Predict the state of bromine at room temperature (25 °C).

   [1 mark]

   (b) Predict the state of chlorine at −29 °C.

   [1 mark]

3   This question is on states of matter.

   (a) Use your knowledge of how particles move to explain why gases fill their containers.

   [2 marks]

   (b) Use your knowledge of how particles move to explain why a liquid is able to flow but a solid is not.

   [2 marks]

Purity

Substances are often not <u>100% pure</u> — they might have <u>other stuff</u> that you can't see mixed in with them. The purity of a substance might need to be <u>checked</u> before, say, a drug is made from it.

Pure Substances Contain Only One Thing

1) In <u>everyday life</u>, the word '<u>pure</u>' is often used to mean 'clean' or 'natural'.

2) In <u>chemistry</u>, it's got a more <u>specific</u> meaning — a substance is <u>pure</u> if it's completely made up of a <u>single element or compound</u>.

3) If you've got <u>more than one</u> compound present, or different elements that aren't all part of a single compound, then you've got a <u>mixture</u>.

4) So, for example, <u>fresh air</u> might be thought of as nice and 'pure', but it's <u>chemically impure</u>, because it's a <u>mixture</u> of nitrogen, oxygen, argon, carbon dioxide, water vapour and various other gases.

5) Lots of <u>mixtures</u> are really <u>useful</u> — <u>alloys</u> (see page 109) are a great example. But sometimes chemists need to obtain a <u>pure sample</u> of a substance.

You Can Test for Purity Using Melting Points

1) Every <u>pure</u> substance has a <u>specific, sharp melting point</u> and <u>boiling point</u>. For example, pure ice melts at 0 °C, and pure water boils at 100 °C.

2) You can use this to test the <u>purity</u> of a sample of a substance, by comparing the <u>actual</u> melting point of the sample to the <u>expected value</u>.

3) If a substance is a <u>mixture</u> then it will melt gradually over a <u>range of temperatures</u>, rather than having a <u>sharp</u> melting point, like a pure substance.

4) <u>Impure</u> substances will melt over a range of temperatures, because they are effectively mixtures.

5) To measure the melting point of a substance, you can use <u>melting point apparatus</u>. This is a piece of kit that allows you to heat up a <u>small sample</u> of a solid <u>very slowly</u>, so you can observe and record the <u>exact temperature</u> that it melts at.

If you don't have melting point apparatus, you could use a water bath and a thermometer instead — but it's harder to control the temperature as exactly as when using this apparatus.

<u>Example</u>: Adil's teacher gives him samples of four <u>powdered solids</u>, labelled A, B, C and D. He uses <u>melting point apparatus</u> to determine the melting point of each of the solids. Adil's results are shown in the table below.

Solid	A	B	C	D
Melting point (°C)	82	72-79	101	63

Which of the four solids, A, B, C or D, was a mixture?

<u>Answer</u>: <u>B</u> — Adil's results show that solid B must be a <u>mixture</u>, because it melted over a <u>range of temperatures</u> (rather than melting at a specific temperature, as the other three solids did).

Pure substances are only made up of <u>one</u> element or compound...

...so their <u>melting</u> and <u>boiling</u> points are <u>specific</u>. There are many ways to <u>extract</u> a <u>pure substance</u> from a <u>mixture</u>. You'll learn about some of these techniques over the <u>next few pages</u>. Right, let's get cracking then.

Distillation

Distillation is used to separate mixtures which contain <u>liquids</u>. This first page looks at <u>simple</u> distillation.

Simple Distillation Separates Out Solutions

<u>Simple distillation</u> is used for separating out a <u>liquid</u> from a <u>solution</u>. Here's how to use simple distillation to get <u>pure water</u> from <u>seawater</u>:

1) Pour your sample of seawater into the <u>distillation flask</u>.

2) Set up the <u>apparatus</u> as shown in the diagram below. Connect the bottom end of the <u>condenser</u> to a cold tap using <u>rubber tubing</u>. Run <u>cold water</u> through the condenser to keep it cool.

3) Gradually heat the distillation flask. The part of the solution that has the lowest boiling point will <u>evaporate</u> — in this case, that's the water.

4) The water <u>vapour</u> passes into the condenser where it <u>cools</u> and <u>condenses</u> (turns back into a liquid). It then flows into the beaker where it is <u>collected</u>.

5) Eventually you'll end up with just the <u>salt</u> left in the flask.

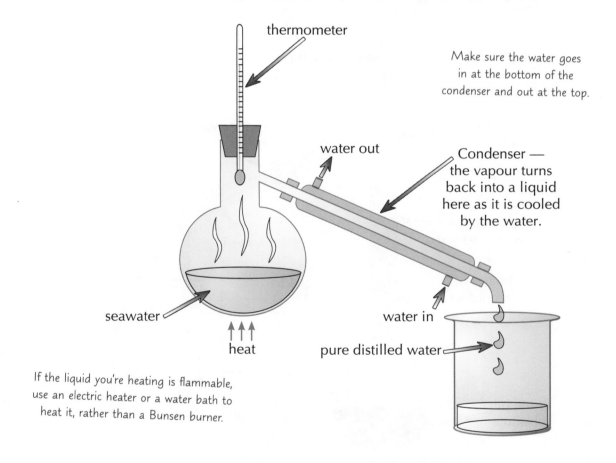

thermometer

Make sure the water goes in at the bottom of the condenser and out at the top.

water out

Condenser — the vapour turns back into a liquid here as it is cooled by the water.

seawater

heat

water in

pure distilled water

If the liquid you're heating is flammable, use an electric heater or a water bath to heat it, rather than a Bunsen burner.

The <u>problem</u> with simple distillation is that you can only use it to separate things with <u>very different</u> boiling points.

If you have a <u>mixture of liquids</u> with <u>similar boiling points</u>, you need another method to separate them out — like fractional distillation...

Distillation

Another type of distillation is <u>fractional distillation</u>. This is more complicated to carry out than simple distillation but it can separate out <u>mixtures of liquids</u> even if their <u>boiling points</u> are close together.

Fractional Distillation is Used to Separate a Mixture of Liquids

Here's a lab demonstration that can be used to model <u>fractional distillation of crude oil</u> at a <u>refinery</u>:

1) Put your <u>mixture</u> in a flask.

2) Attach a <u>fractionating column</u> and condenser above the flask as shown below.

3) Gradually heat the flask. The <u>different liquids</u> will all have <u>different boiling points</u> — so they will evaporate at <u>different temperatures</u>.

4) The liquid with the <u>lowest boiling point</u> evaporates first. When the temperature on the thermometer matches the boiling point of this liquid, it will reach the <u>top</u> of the column.

5) Liquids with <u>higher boiling points</u> might also start to evaporate. But the column is <u>cooler</u> towards the <u>top</u>, so they will only get part of the way up before <u>condensing</u> and running back down towards the flask.

6) When the first liquid has been collected, <u>raise the temperature</u> until the <u>next one</u> reaches the top.

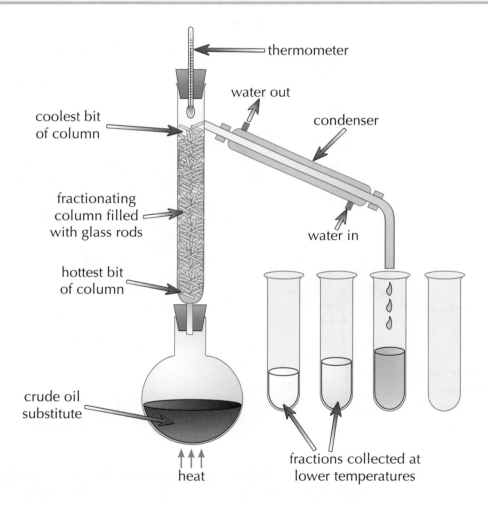

Fractional distillation is used in the lab and industry...

The <u>industrial method</u> for fractional distillation of crude oil <u>isn't quite as simple</u> as the one shown here. If you're desperate to find out what goes on in oil refineries, have a look at <u>page 155</u>.

Filtration and Crystallisation

If you've mixed a <u>solid</u> with a <u>liquid</u>, it should be pretty easy to <u>separate</u> them out again.
Which <u>method</u> you'll need to use depends on whether or not the solid can <u>dissolve</u> in the liquid.

Filtration is Used to Separate an Insoluble Solid from a Liquid

Filter paper folded
into a cone shape.

The solid is left in
the filter paper.

1) If the <u>product</u> of a reaction is an <u>insoluble solid</u>, you can use <u>filtration</u> to separate it out from the <u>liquid reaction mixture</u>.

2) It can be used in <u>purification</u> as well. For example, <u>solid impurities</u> can be separated out from a reaction mixture using <u>filtration</u>.

3) All you do is pop some <u>filter paper</u> into a <u>funnel</u> and pour your mixture into it. The liquid part of the mixture <u>runs through</u> the paper, leaving behind a <u>solid residue</u>.

Crystallisation Separates a Soluble Solid from a Solution

Here's how you <u>crystallise</u> a product...

evaporating
dish

1) Pour the solution into an <u>evaporating dish</u> and gently <u>heat</u> the solution. Some of the <u>water</u> will evaporate and the solution will get more <u>concentrated</u>.

2) Once some of the water has evaporated, <u>or</u> when you see crystals start to form (the <u>point of crystallisation</u>), remove the dish from the heat and leave the solution to <u>cool</u>.

3) The salt should start to form <u>crystals</u> as it becomes <u>insoluble</u> in the cold, highly concentrated solution.

4) <u>Filter</u> the crystals out of the solution, and leave them in a warm place to <u>dry</u>. You could also use a <u>drying oven</u> or a <u>desiccator</u> (a desiccator contains chemicals that remove water from the surroundings).

Choose the Right Purification Method

You might have to pick one of the <u>techniques</u> covered in this section to separate a mixture.
The best technique to use will depend on the <u>properties</u> of the <u>substances</u> in the mixture.

> <u>Example:</u>
> A <u>mixture</u> is composed of two substances, X and Y.
> <u>Substance X</u> is a <u>liquid</u> at room temperature, has a <u>melting point</u> of 5 °C and a <u>boiling point</u> of 60 °C.
> <u>Substance Y</u> is a <u>solid</u> at room temperature. It has a <u>melting point</u> of 745 °C and a <u>boiling point</u> of 1218 °C. Substance Y <u>dissolves completely</u> in substance X.
>
> Suggest a <u>purification method</u> you could use to obtain:
> a) A pure sample of substance X,   b) A pure sample of substance Y.
>
> <u>Answer:</u>
>
> a) To get X on its own, you need to <u>distil it</u> from the solution. You can use <u>simple distillation</u> here — there's no need for fractional distillation as there's only <u>one liquid</u> in the solution.
>   So, you could obtain a pure sample of substance X using simple distillation.
>
> b) To get a <u>soluble solid</u> out of a solution, you should use <u>crystallisation</u>.
>   In theory, if you <u>distilled</u> the mixture until all of substance X had evaporated off, you'd end up with just substance Y left in the flask. But there might be <u>traces</u> of substance X still hanging around — crystallisation's a better way of getting a <u>pure sample</u> of a solid from a solution.
>   So, you could obtain a pure sample of substance Y using crystallisation.

Crystallisation is for <u>s</u>oluble solids...

... and <u>f</u>iltration is for <u>i</u>nsoluble solids in a mixture. It's important to <u>remember</u> the <u>difference</u>.

Warm-Up and Exam Questions

So the last few pages have all been about mixtures and how to separate them.
Here are some questions to test whether you know your filtration from your distillation...

Warm-Up Questions

1) What is meant by a pure substance in chemistry?
2) What effect will impurities in a substance have on its boiling point?
3) Which technique could you use to separate a mixture of liquids with similar boiling points?
4) Name a separation technique that could be used to separate a soluble solid from a solution.

Exam Questions

1   Propan-1-ol, methanol and ethanol have boiling points of 97 °C, 65 °C and 78 °C respectively. **Grade 4-6**
    A student uses fractional distillation to separate a mixture of these compounds.
    State which liquid will be collected in the first fraction and explain why.

    [2 marks]

2   Lawn sand is a mixture of insoluble sharp sand and soluble ammonium sulfate fertiliser. **Grade 6-7**

    (a)   Describe how you would obtain pure, dry samples of the two components of lawn sand in the lab.

    [3 marks]

    (b)   A student separated 51.4 g of lawn sand into sharp sand and ammonium sulfate.
          After separation, the total mass of the two products was 52.6 g.
          Suggest a reason for the difference in mass.

    [1 mark]

3   **Table 1** gives the boiling points of three liquids. **Grade 6-7**

    (a)   State why simple distillation cannot be used to separate
          water from a solution of water and methanoic acid.

    [1 mark]

Liquid	Boiling point (°C)
Methanoic acid	101
Propanone	56
Water	100

Table 1

    (b)   The apparatus in **Figure 1** was used to separate
          a mixture of propanone and water.

          Complete the table using the options below.

          no liquid   water   propanone   both liquids

Temperature on thermometer	Contents of the flask	Contents of the beaker
30 °C	....	....
65 °C	....	....
110 °C	....	....

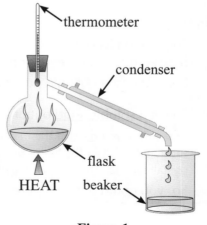

Figure 1

[3 marks]

Chromatography

Chromatography is a method used to separate a mixture of soluble substances and identify them.

Chromatography uses Two Phases

There are lots of different types of chromatography — but they all have two 'phases':

- A mobile phase — where the molecules can move. This is always a liquid or a gas.
- A stationary phase — where the molecules can't move. This can be a solid or a really thick liquid.

1) The components in the mixture separate out as the mobile phase moves over the stationary phase — they all end up in different places in the stationary phase.

2) This happens because each of the chemicals in a mixture will spend different amounts of time dissolved in the mobile phase and stuck to the stationary phase.

3) How fast a chemical moves through the stationary phase depends on how it 'distributes' itself between the two phases.

For each component in your mixture, you'll end up with one spot on your chromatogram (see next page for more on chromatograms).

In Paper Chromatography the Mobile Phase is a Solvent

In paper chromatography, the stationary phase is a piece of filter paper and the mobile phase is a solvent (e.g. water or ethanol). Here's the method for setting it up:

PRACTICAL

1) Draw a line near the bottom of the paper — this is the baseline.
(Use a pencil to do this — pencil marks are insoluble and won't move with the solvent as ink might.) Put a spot of the mixture to be separated on the line.

2) Put some of the solvent into a beaker.
Dip the bottom of the paper (but not the spot) into the solvent.

3) Put a watch glass on the top of the beaker to stop any solvent from evaporating away.

4) The solvent will start to move up the paper. When the chemicals in the mixture dissolve in the solvent, they will move up the paper too.

5) You will see the different chemicals in the sample separate out, forming spots at different places on the paper.
(If one of your components is insoluble in the mobile phase, it won't move — it'll stay as a spot on the baseline.)

6) Remove the paper from the beaker before the solvent reaches the top.
Mark the distance the solvent has moved (the solvent front) in pencil.

watch glass
solvent front
paper
spot of unknown substance
point of origin
solvent

There are a couple of extra things you should bear in mind too:

1) If any of the substances in a mixture are insoluble in one solvent (e.g. stay on the baseline), you could try re-running the experiment with the same mixture, but using a different solvent. You may find this separates out the components, allowing you to find their R_f values (see next page).

2) If you know that you have chemicals in your mixture that are colourless (e.g. amino acids), you might have to spray the chromatogram with a chemical called a locating agent to show where the spots are.

Chromatography separates the different dyes in inks

Make sure you use a pencil to draw your baseline. If you use a pen, all the components of the ink in the pen will get separated, along with the substance you're analysing, which will make your results very confusing. There's more on how you can analyse your results on the next page.

Interpreting Chromatograms

So, what use is <u>chromatography</u>, apart from making a pretty pattern of spots? Let's find out...

You can Calculate the R_f Value for Each Chemical

1) In <u>paper chromatography</u>, the piece of paper that you end up with is called a <u>chromatogram</u>.

2) You need to know how to work out the R_f <u>values</u> for the <u>spots</u> on a chromatogram.

3) An R_f value is the <u>ratio</u> between the distance travelled by the dissolved substance (the solute) and the distance travelled by the solvent.

4) You can find R_f values using the formula:

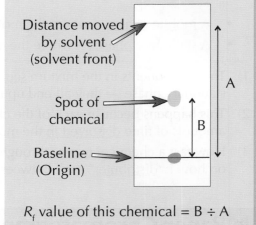

Distance moved by solvent (solvent front)

Spot of chemical

A

B

Baseline (Origin)

R_f value of this chemical = B ÷ A

$$R_f = \frac{\text{distance travelled by substance}}{\text{distance travelled by solvent}}$$

5) To find the distance travelled by the solute, measure from the <u>baseline</u> to the <u>centre of the spot</u>.

Different Substances Have Different R_f Values

1) The R_f <u>value</u> is controlled by the amount of time the molecules spend in each <u>phase</u>. This depends on <u>two things</u>:

- How <u>soluble</u> they are in the solvent.
- How <u>attracted</u> they are to the stationary phase.

2) Molecules with a <u>higher solubility</u> in the solvent (and which are <u>less attracted</u> to the paper) will spend more time in the <u>mobile phase</u> than the stationary phase — so they'll be carried <u>further</u> up the paper.

3) As a result, <u>different substances</u> will <u>separate out</u> on a chromatogram and have <u>different R_f values</u>.

There are Several Ways to Interpret a Chromatogram

1) Chromatography is often carried out to see if a certain substance is present in a mixture. You run a <u>pure sample</u> of a substance that you think might be in your mixture alongside a sample of the mixture itself. If the sample has the same R_f values as one of the spots, they're likely to be the <u>same</u>.

2) Chemists sometimes run samples of pure substances called <u>standard reference materials</u> (SRMs) next to a mixture to check the identities of its components. SRMs have controlled <u>concentrations and purities</u>.

3) You can also use chromatography to do a <u>purity test</u>. A <u>pure</u> substance <u>won't</u> be <u>separated</u> by <u>chromatography</u> — it'll move as <u>one blob</u> (while a <u>mixture</u> should give you <u>multiple blobs</u>).

You need to learn the formula for R_f

R_f values always lie <u>between 0 and 1</u>, as the <u>solvent</u> always <u>travels further</u> than any of the substances in the mixture. If you work out an R_f value to be outside this range, you know you've gone wrong somewhere (e.g. you may have written the fraction in the formula <u>upside-down</u>).

Combining Separation Techniques  PRACTICAL

You can <u>combine</u> separation techniques to analyse mixtures. Here's an example:

You can Use **Simple Distillation** and **Chromatography** to Analyse **Ink**

Here's one method of analysing the composition of an ink:

1) Ink is a mixture of different <u>dyes</u> dissolved in a <u>solvent</u>.

2) To work out what <u>solvent</u> the ink contains, you could try doing a <u>simple distillation</u>.

3) Simple distillation allows you to <u>evaporate</u> off the <u>solvent</u> and <u>collect it</u> — assuming that the solvent has the lowest boiling point of all the substances in the ink, it will <u>evaporate first</u>.

4) The <u>thermometer</u> in the distillation set-up will read the <u>boiling point</u> of the solvent when it's evaporating (and therefore when it's being collected).

5) You can use the boiling point of the solvent to try and determine what it is. For example, if the solvent in a certain ink evaporates at <u>100 °C</u>, it's quite likely to be <u>water</u>.

6) You could then carry out <u>paper chromatography</u> on a sample of the ink — this will separate out the different <u>dyes</u> in the ink, so that you can see <u>how many</u> there are.

7) You can compare the <u>R_f values</u> of the different spots on the chromatogram produced with <u>reference values</u> (or run further chromatography experiments with <u>pure</u> substances) to work out <u>what dyes are in the ink</u>.

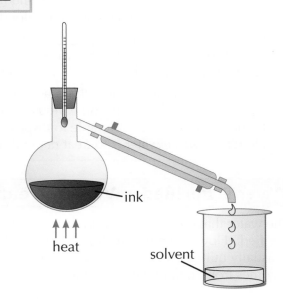

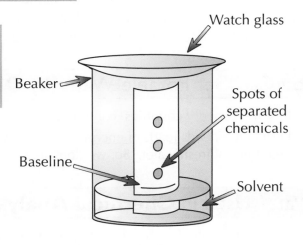

For full details on how to run distillation and chromatography experiments, look back at pages 63 and 67.

You're not just limited to using one separation technique...

Some mixtures are made up of <u>several components</u>, so you might need to use a <u>combination</u> of the methods covered in this section to get <u>all</u> the different components out. Make sure you <u>understand each step</u> of the experiment above — you may be <u>tested</u> on it in the <u>exam</u>.

Water Treatment

Water often needs to be purified to make it safe to drink...

There are a Variety of **Limited Water Resources** in the UK

In the UK, there are a number of sources of water which can be purified to provide us with potable water (water that is fit to drink). We get our water from:

1) SURFACE WATER: from lakes, rivers and reservoirs. In much of England and Wales, these sources start to run dry during the summer months.

2) GROUND WATER: from aquifers (rocks that trap water underground). In parts of south-east England, where surface water is very limited, as much as 70% of the domestic water supply comes from ground water.

3) WASTE WATER: from water that's been contaminated by a human process, e.g. as a by-product from some industrial processes. Treating waste water to make it potable is preferable to disposing of the water, which can be polluting. How easy waste water is to treat depends on the levels of contaminants in it.

Water is **Purified** in **Water Treatment Plants**

The water that comes out of your taps doesn't just come straight from the source — first it has to be purified. How much purification it needs will depend on the source. Ground water from aquifers is usually quite pure, but waste water and surface water needs a lot of treatment. But, wherever it comes from, before we can drink it most water will be purified using the following processes:

1) Filtration — a wire mesh screens out large twigs etc., and then gravel and sand beds filter out any other solid bits.

2) Sedimentation — iron sulfate or aluminium sulfate is added to the water, which makes fine particles clump together and settle at the bottom.

3) Chlorination — chlorine gas is bubbled through to kill harmful bacteria and other microbes.

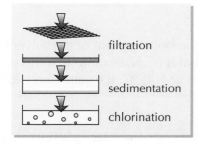

Some soluble impurities that are dissolved in the water are not removed as they can't be filtered out — these include the minerals which cause water hardness.

You Can Get Potable Water by **Distilling Sea Water**

1) In some very dry countries, e.g. Kuwait, sea water is distilled (see p.63) to produce drinking water.

2) Distillation needs loads of energy, so it's really expensive, especially if you're trying to produce large quantities of fresh water. So, we don't tend to use this method of producing potable water in the UK.

Water Used in **Chemical Analysis** must be **Pure**

1) Lots of chemistry involves carrying out experiments to work out what something is, or how it will react.

2) For experiments that involve mixing or dissolving something in water, you should use deionised water.

3) Deionised water is water that has had the ions (such as calcium, iron and copper ions) that are present in normal tap water removed.

4) These ions, although present in small amounts and harmless in tap water, can interfere with reactions. Using normal water could give your experiment a false result.

Water is purified in stages...

The big stuff (e.g. twigs and pebbles) is removed first, before smaller things such as microbes are dealt with.

Warm-Up and Exam Questions

Look, a chromatography question — those things are fun. Get your investigative hat on and get stuck in...

Warm-Up Questions

1) In paper chromatography, what is the stationary phase?
2) Why is a pencil used to draw the baseline on a chromatogram?
3) A mixture of two chemicals, A and B, is separated using paper chromatography.
   Chemical A is more soluble in the solvent than B is.
   Which chemical, A or B, will end up closer to the solvent front?
4) Outline how water is purified in a water treatment plant.
5) Name the process used to convert sea water to potable water.

Exam Questions

1   A student is making a solution to use in an experiment by dissolving pure, solid sodium iodide
    in water. Suggest why the student should not use tap water. State what he should use instead.

[2 marks]

PRACTICAL

2   A scientist used chromatography to analyse the composition of five inks. Four of the inks
    were unknown (**A – D**). The other was sunrise yellow. The results are shown in **Figure 1**.

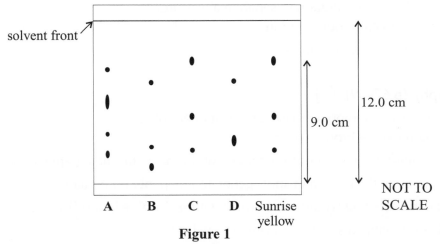

Figure 1

(a)   Explain how **Figure 1** shows that none of the inks are pure substances.

[1 mark]

(b)   Which ink definitely contains at least four different compounds?

[1 mark]

(c)   Which of the inks, **A-D**, could be the same as sunrise yellow? Explain your answer.

[2 marks]

(d)   Calculate the R_f value for the spot of chemical in sunrise yellow
      which is furthest up the chromatogram.

[2 marks]

(e)   State **one** technique you could use to identify the solvent in each of the inks.

[1 mark]

Revision Summary for Topic 2

That wraps up <u>Topic 2</u> — time to put yourself to the test and find out <u>how much you really know</u>.
- Try these questions and <u>tick off each one</u> when you <u>get it right</u>.
- When you've done <u>all the questions</u> under a heading and are <u>completely happy</u> with it, tick it off.

States of Matter and Changes of State (p.58-60) ☑

1) Name the three states of matter. ☑
2) Describe the arrangement of particles, and the forces between them, in a liquid. ☑
3) What happens to the forces between the particles in a solid as you melt it? ☑
4) What do you call the process of a substance changing from a liquid to a gas? ☑
5) What states of matter are you moving from and to if you are condensing a substance? ☑
6) Which are easier to reverse — chemical changes or physical changes? ☑

Purity (p.62) ☑

7) Explain why air isn't considered a pure substance, according to the scientific definition of pure. ☑
8) A substance melts over a range of temperatures. Is it likely to be a pure substance or a mixture? ☑

Distillation, Filtration and Crystallisation (p.63-65) ☑

9) Draw the apparatus you would use to carry out a simple distillation. ☑
10) What type of mixture would you separate using fractional distillation? ☑
11) Where is the hottest part of a fractionating column — at the top or at the bottom? ☑
12) a) When would you use filtration to separate a mixture?
    b) Describe how to carry out filtration. ☑
13) Describe how to carry out crystallisation. ☑

Chromatography (p.67-69) ☑

14) Explain what the terms 'mobile phase' and 'stationary phase'
    mean in the context of chromatography. ☑
15) What causes different substances to separate out during a chromatography experiment? ☑
16) What is the name of the pattern of spots generated by paper chromatography? ☑
17) Write out the formula you would use to work out the R_f value of a substance. ☑
18) How could you identify a substance from its R_f value? ☑

Water Treatment (p.70) ☑

19) Name three different sources of water that can be made potable. ☑
20) Name three processes that are used to make water potable. ☑
21) What is deionised water? ☑

Acids and Bases

You can test the pH of a solution using an <u>indicator</u> — and that means pretty <u>colours</u>...

The pH Scale Goes From 0 to 14

1) The pH scale is a measure of <u>how acidic or alkaline</u> a solution is. A <u>neutral</u> substance has <u>pH 7</u>.

2) An <u>acid</u> is a substance with a <u>pH</u> of <u>less than 7</u>. Acids form H^+ ions in water.

3) The higher the <u>concentration of hydrogen ions</u> in a solution, the <u>more acidic</u> it is, so the lower its pH will be. In other words, as the concentration of hydrogen ions <u>increases</u>, the <u>pH decreases</u>.

4) A <u>base</u> is a substance that reacts with an acid to produce a <u>salt</u> and <u>water</u>.

5) An <u>alkali</u> is a base that is <u>soluble</u> in water. All alkalis have a <u>pH</u> of <u>more than 7</u> and they form <u>OH^- ions</u> (otherwise known as <u>hydroxide ions</u>) in water.

6) In alkaline solutions, the higher the <u>concentration of OH^- ions</u>, the higher the pH.

You Can Measure the pH of a Solution

1) An <u>indicator</u> is a <u>dye</u> that <u>changes colour</u> depending on whether it's <u>above or below a certain pH</u>.

2) Indicators are simple to use — <u>add a few drops</u> to the solution you're testing, then compare the colour the solution goes to a <u>pH chart</u> for that indicator. E.g. here's the pH chart for <u>Universal indicator</u>.

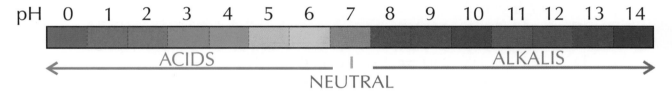

pH 0 1 2 3 4 5 6 7 8 9 10 11 12 13 14

ACIDS — NEUTRAL — ALKALIS

Some indicators that you need to know about are:
- litmus — is <u>red</u> in <u>acidic</u> solutions, <u>purple</u> in <u>neutral</u> solutions and <u>blue</u> in <u>alkaline</u> solutions.
- methyl orange — is <u>red</u> in <u>acidic solutions</u> and <u>yellow</u> in <u>neutral</u> and <u>alkaline</u> solutions.
- phenolphthalein — is colourless in acidic or neutral solutions and <u>pink</u> in <u>alkaline</u> solutions.

Acids and Bases Neutralise Each Other

1) The reaction between an acid and a base is called <u>neutralisation</u>. It produces a <u>salt</u> and <u>water</u>.

acid + base → salt + water   e.g.

$$HCl + NaOH \rightarrow NaCl + H_2O$$
acid   base   salt   water

2) Neutralisation reactions in <u>aqueous solution</u> can also be shown as an ionic equation (see p.19) in terms of <u>H^+</u> and <u>OH^- ions</u>:

$$H^+_{(aq)} + OH^-_{(aq)} \rightarrow H_2O_{(l)}$$

3) When an acid neutralises a base (or vice versa), the <u>products</u> are <u>neutral</u>, i.e. they have a <u>pH of 7</u>. At pH 7, the concentration of hydrogen ions is <u>equal to</u> the concentration of hydroxide ions.

Interesting fact — your skin is slightly acidic (pH 5.5)

When you mix an <u>acid</u> with an <u>alkali</u>, <u>hydrogen ions</u> from the acid react with <u>hydroxide ions</u> from the alkali to make <u>water</u>. The leftover bits of the acid and alkali make a <u>salt</u>.

Strong Acids, Weak Acids and their Reactions

Right then. More on <u>acids</u>. Brace yourself...

Acids **Produce Hydrogen Ions** in **Water**

All acids can <u>ionise</u> (or <u>dissociate</u>) in solution — that means splitting up to produce a <u>hydrogen ion</u>, H^+, and another ion. For example,

$$HCl \rightarrow H^+ + Cl^-$$
$$HNO_3 \rightarrow H^+ + NO_3^-$$

HCl and HNO_3 don't produce hydrogen ions until they meet water.

Acids Can be **Strong** or **Weak**

1) <u>Strong acids</u> (e.g. sulfuric, hydrochloric and nitric acids) <u>ionise almost completely</u> in water — a <u>large</u> proportion of the acid molecules dissociate to release H^+ ions. They tend to have low pHs (pH 0-2).

2) <u>Weak acids</u> (e.g. ethanoic, citric and carbonic acids) <u>do not fully ionise</u> in solution — only a <u>small</u> proportion of the acid molecules dissociate to release H^+ ions. Their pHs tend to be around 2-6.

3) The ionisation of a <u>weak</u> acid is a <u>reversible reaction</u>, which sets up an <u>equilibrium</u>. Since only a few of the acid particles release H^+ ions, the <u>equilibrium</u> lies well to the <u>left</u>.

<u>Strong acid</u>: $HCl \rightarrow H^+ + Cl^-$

<u>Weak acid</u>: $CH_3COOH \rightleftharpoons H^+ + CH_3COO^-$

For more on equilibria turn to page 102.

Don't Confuse **Strong** Acids with **Concentrated** Acids

1) Acid <u>strength</u> (i.e. strong or weak) tells you <u>what proportion</u> of the acid molecules <u>ionise</u> in water.

2) The <u>concentration</u> of an acid is different. Concentration measures <u>how much acid</u> there is in a litre (1 dm^3) of water. Concentration is basically how <u>watered down</u> your acid is.

3) An acid with a <u>large number</u> of <u>acid molecules</u> compared to the volume of water is said to be <u>concentrated</u>. An acid with a <u>small number</u> of acid molecules compared to the volume of water is said to be <u>dilute</u>.

Concentration is measured in $g\ dm^{-3}$ or $mol\ dm^{-3}$.

4) Note that concentration describes the <u>total number</u> of dissolved acid molecules — <u>not</u> the number of molecules that produce hydrogen ions.

5) The more grams (or moles) of acid per dm^3, the <u>more concentrated</u> the acid is.

6) So you can have a <u>dilute strong</u> acid, or a <u>concentrated weak</u> acid.

Strong Acids, Weak Acids and their Reactions

Changing the **Concentration** of an Acid Affects its pH

1) If the concentration of H^+ ions <u>increases</u> by a factor of <u>10</u>, the pH <u>decreases</u> by <u>1</u>.

2) So if the H^+ ion concentration <u>increases</u> by a factor of <u>100</u> (= 10 × 10), the pH <u>decreases</u> by <u>2</u> (= 1 + 1), and so on.

3) Decreasing the H^+ ion concentration has the opposite effect — a <u>decrease</u> by a factor of <u>10</u> in the H^+ concentration means an <u>increase</u> of <u>1</u> on the pH scale.

 **A solution with a hydrogen ion concentration of 0.001 mol dm^{-3} has a pH of 3. What would happen to the pH if you increased the hydrogen ion concentration to 0.01 mol dm^{-3}?**

The H^+ concentration has increased by a factor of 1O, so the pH would decrease by 1. So the new pH would be 3 − 1 = 2.

Acids React With **Metals** or **Metal Carbonates** to Form **Salts**

1) <u>Salts</u> are ionic compounds.

2) In general, <u>hydrochloric acid</u> produces <u>chloride</u> salts, <u>sulfuric acid</u> produces <u>sulfate salts</u> and <u>nitric acid</u> produces <u>nitrate salts</u>.

3) You need to know what happens when you react an <u>acid</u> with a <u>metal</u> or a <u>metal carbonate</u>:

Acid + Metal → Salt + Hydrogen

The reaction of nitric acid with metals can be more complicated — you get a nitrate salt, but instead of hydrogen gas, the other products are usually a mixture of water, NO and NO_2.

<u>Examples</u>: $2HCl + Mg \rightarrow MgCl_2 + H_2$ (Magnesium chloride)
$H_2SO_4 + Mg \rightarrow MgSO_4 + H_2$ (Magnesium sulfate)

1) You can <u>test for hydrogen</u> using a lighted splint.

2) Hydrogen makes a "<u>squeaky pop</u>" with a <u>lighted splint</u>.

3) The noise comes from the <u>hydrogen burning</u> with the <u>oxygen</u> in the air to form water.

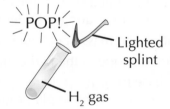

POP!

Lighted splint

H_2 gas

Acid + Metal Carbonate → Salt + Water + Carbon Dioxide

<u>Examples</u>:
$2HCl + Na_2CO_3 \rightarrow 2NaCl + H_2O + CO_2$ (Sodium chloride)
$H_2SO_4 + K_2CO_3 \rightarrow K_2SO_4 + H_2O + CO_2$ (Potassium sulfate)
$2HNO_3 + ZnCO_3 \rightarrow Zn(NO_3)_2 + H_2O + CO_2$ (Zinc nitrate)

1) You can test to see if a gas is <u>carbon dioxide</u> by bubbling it through <u>limewater</u>.

2) If the gas is carbon dioxide, the limewater will <u>turn cloudy</u>.

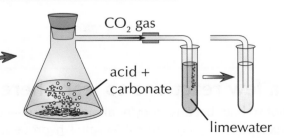

CO_2 gas

acid + carbonate

limewater

Topic 3 — Chemical Changes

Strong Acids, Weak Acids and their Reactions

Salts Also Form When Acids React with Bases

1) A salt is formed during a neutralisation reaction (a reaction between an acid and a base).

2) You need to be able to remember what happens when you add acids to various bases...

Acid + Metal Hydroxide → Salt + Water

Examples: $HCl + NaOH \rightarrow NaCl + H_2O$ (Sodium chloride)
$H_2SO_4 + Zn(OH)_2 \rightarrow ZnSO_4 + 2H_2O$ (Zinc sulfate)
$HNO_3 + KOH \rightarrow KNO_3 + H_2O$ (Potassium nitrate)

These are the same as the acid/base neutralisation reaction you met on page 73.

Acid + Metal Oxide → Salt + Water

Examples: $2HCl + CuO \rightarrow CuCl_2 + H_2O$ (Copper chloride)
$H_2SO_4 + ZnO \rightarrow ZnSO_4 + H_2O$ (Zinc sulfate)
$2HNO_3 + MgO \rightarrow Mg(NO_3)_2 + H_2O$ (Magnesium nitrate)

You Can Investigate How pH Changes in Neutralisation Reactions

Here's how to investigate the neutralisation reaction between calcium oxide (a base) and dilute hydrochloric acid.

You can do this experiment with calcium hydroxide too.

PRACTICAL

1) Start by measuring out a set volume of dilute hydrochloric acid into a conical flask. Use a pipette or a measuring cylinder for this (see page 194).

2) Measure out a fixed mass of calcium oxide using a mass balance.

3) Add the calcium oxide to the hydrochloric acid.

4) Wait for the base to completely react, then record the pH of the solution, using either a pH probe (see page 195) or Universal indicator paper. (You can use a glass rod to spot samples of the solution to the paper.)

5) Repeat steps 2 to 4 until all the acid has reacted. You'll know you've reached this point when you get unreacted calcium oxide sitting at the bottom of the flask.

6) You can then plot a graph to see how the pH changes with the mass of base added. You should find it looks a bit like this.

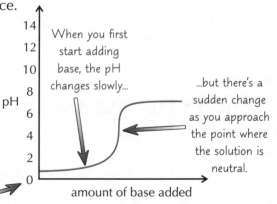

When you first start adding base, the pH changes slowly... ...but there's a sudden change as you approach the point where the solution is neutral.

Quite a few reactions to learn here...

...but it's not so bad, because they're all acid + base → salt + water (and sometimes carbon dioxide). The only exception is acid + metal → salt + hydrogen. Keep that in mind and you'll be laughing.

Warm-Up and Exam Questions

So you think you know everything there is to know about acids? Time to put yourself to the test.

Warm-Up Questions

1) What is a base?
2) What range of values can pH take?
3) What term is used to describe a solution with a pH of 7?
4) What's the difference between:
   a) a strong acid and a weak acid?   b) a dilute acid and a concentrated acid?
5) Name the two substances formed when hydrochloric acid reacts with sodium.
6) Write a balanced chemical equation for the reaction of sulfuric acid with calcium carbonate.
7) Describe the chemical test for carbon dioxide.

Exam Questions

1   A student had a sample of acid in a test tube. He gradually added some alkali to the acid. **Grade 4-6**

(a)   Name the type of ion that acids produce in aqueous solutions.

[1 mark]

(b)   What type of reaction took place in the student's experiment?

☐ thermal decomposition   ☐ neutralisation   ☐ redox   ☐ combustion

[1 mark]

PRACTICAL

2   Calcium hydroxide was added to a solution of dilute hydrochloric acid. **Grade 6-7**

(a)   Complete and balance the symbol equation given below for the reaction of hydrochloric acid with calcium hydroxide.

$$2HCl + Ca(OH)_2 \rightarrow \text{.......................} + \text{.......................}$$

[2 marks]

(b)   Universal indicator was used to indicate when the reaction was complete.
Dilute hydrochloric acid has a pH of around 1.
Describe the colour change you would expect to see as the acidic solution approached a neutral pH.

[2 marks]

In another experiment, the pH of the acid solution rose from 2 to 5
when the calcium hydroxide was added.

(c)   What factor would the hydrogen ion concentration of the solution have decreased by?

[1 mark]

(d)   Explain why the concentration of hydrogen ions decreases during the reaction.

[1 mark]

(e)   Calcium hydroxide is insoluble in water. What name is given to a soluble base?

[1 mark]

Making Insoluble Salts

Now it's time to learn which salts are <u>soluble</u> and which ones <u>are insoluble</u>.

The **Rules** of **Solubility**

Soluble things dissolve in water.
Insoluble things don't.

1) How you make a salt depends on whether it's <u>soluble</u> or <u>insoluble</u>.

2) You may need to work out if, when two solutions are mixed, a salt will form as a <u>precipitate</u> (i.e. it's an insoluble salt), or whether it will just form <u>in solution</u> (i.e. it's a soluble salt).

3) This table is a pretty fail-safe way of working out whether a substance is soluble in water or not.

Substance	Soluble or Insoluble?
common salts of sodium, potassium and ammonium	soluble
nitrates	soluble
common chlorides	soluble (except silver chloride and lead chloride)
common sulfates	soluble (except lead, barium and calcium sulfate)
common carbonates and hydroxides	insoluble (except for sodium, potassium and ammonium ones)

Making **Insoluble** Salts — **Precipitation** Reactions

1) To make a pure, dry sample of an <u>insoluble</u> salt, you can use a <u>precipitation reaction</u>. You just need to pick the right two <u>soluble salts</u> and <u>react</u> them together to get your <u>insoluble salt</u>.

2) E.g. to make <u>lead chloride</u> (insoluble), mix <u>lead nitrate</u> and <u>sodium chloride</u> (both soluble).

> lead nitrate + sodium chloride → lead chloride + sodium nitrate
>
> $Pb(NO_3)_{2\,(aq)} + 2NaCl_{(aq)} \rightarrow PbCl_{2\,(s)} + 2NaNO_{3\,(aq)}$

Method

1) Add 1 spatula of <u>lead nitrate</u> to a test tube. Add <u>water</u> to dissolve it. You should use deionised water to make sure there are no other ions about. <u>Shake it thoroughly</u> to ensure that all the lead nitrate has <u>dissolved</u>. Then, in a separate test tube, do the same with 1 spatula of <u>sodium chloride</u>.

2) Tip the <u>two solutions</u> into a small beaker, and give it a good stir to make sure it's all mixed together. The lead chloride should <u>precipitate</u> out.

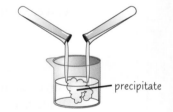
precipitate

3) Put a folded piece of <u>filter paper</u> into a <u>filter funnel</u>, and stick the funnel into a <u>conical flask</u>.

4) <u>Pour</u> the contents of the beaker into the middle of the filter paper. Make sure that the solution doesn't go above the filter paper — otherwise some of the solid could dribble down the side.

filter paper
filter funnel

5) <u>Swill out</u> the beaker with more deionised water, and tip this into the filter paper — to make sure you get <u>all the precipitate</u> from the beaker.

6) Rinse the contents of the filter paper with deionised water to make sure that <u>all the soluble sodium nitrate</u> has been washed away.

7) Then just scrape the <u>lead chloride</u> onto fresh filter paper and leave it to dry in an oven or a desiccator.

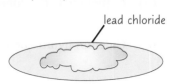
lead chloride

Making Soluble Salts

You met the technique for making <u>insoluble salts</u> on the previous page. Time to cover <u>soluble salts</u> now...

Making **Soluble Salts** — Use an **Acid** and an **Insoluble Base**

You can make a <u>soluble salt</u> by reacting an <u>acid</u> that contains one of the ions you want in the salt with an <u>insoluble base</u> that contains the other ion you need (often a <u>metal oxide</u> or <u>metal hydroxide</u>).

For some salts, you can use a <u>metal</u> instead of the base.

Method

1) Start by <u>heating the acid</u> in a <u>water bath</u> (see p.196) — this speeds up the reaction between the acid and the insoluble base. Do this in a <u>fume cupboard</u> to avoid releasing acid fumes into the room.

2) Then add the <u>base</u> to the <u>acid</u> — the base and acid will react to produce a <u>soluble salt</u> (and water). You will know when the base is in excess and all the acid has been neutralised because the excess solid will just <u>sink</u> to the bottom of the flask.

3) <u>Filter</u> off the <u>excess</u> solid to get a solution containing only the <u>salt</u> and <u>water</u>.

4) <u>Heat the solution gently</u>, using a Bunsen burner, to slowly <u>evaporate</u> off some of the water.

5) Leave the solution to cool and allow the salt to <u>crystallise</u> (see p.65).

6) Filter off the <u>solid salt</u> and leave it to <u>dry</u>.

filter paper

excess solid

filter funnel

salt and water

Example: You can add <u>copper oxide</u> to warm <u>sulfuric acid</u> to make a solution of <u>copper sulfate</u>:

$$CuO_{(s)} + H_2SO_{4\,(aq)} \rightarrow CuSO_{4\,(aq)} + H_2O_{(l)}$$

If you evaporate off some of the water and leave this solution to <u>crystallise</u>, you should get lovely <u>blue crystals</u> of <u>hydrated copper sulfate</u>, which you can <u>filter off</u> and <u>dry</u>.

Acid + insoluble base → soluble salt + water

It's important that you make sure the <u>base</u> is <u>in excess</u> in this experiment, so that you <u>don't have</u> any <u>leftover acid</u> in your product. That way, the <u>final solution</u> is simply a <u>soluble salt</u> and <u>water</u>.

Making Soluble Salts

You can Make Soluble Salts Using Acid/Alkali Reactions

1) Soluble salts (salts that dissolve in water) can be made by reacting an acid with an <u>alkali</u>.

2) But you can't tell whether the reaction has <u>finished</u> — there's no signal that all the acid has been neutralised. You also can't just add an <u>excess</u> of alkali to the acid, because the salt is <u>soluble</u> and would be contaminated with the excess alkali.

3) Instead, you need to work out <u>exactly</u> the right amount of alkali to <u>neutralise</u> the acid. For this, you need to do a <u>titration</u> using an <u>indicator</u>. Here's what you do...

Method

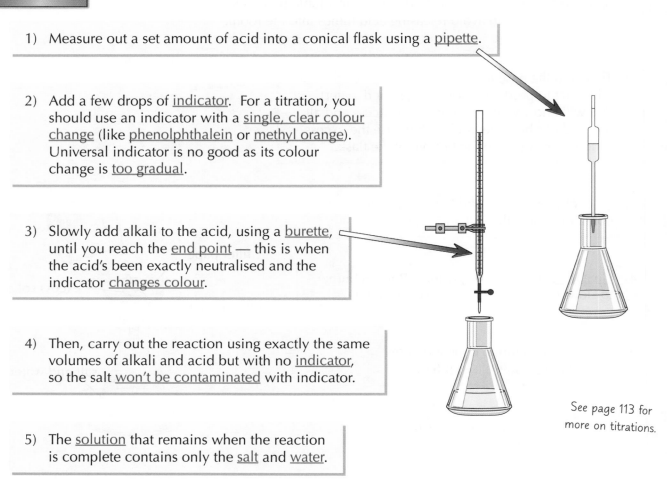

1) Measure out a set amount of acid into a conical flask using a <u>pipette</u>.

2) Add a few drops of <u>indicator</u>. For a titration, you should use an indicator with a <u>single, clear colour change</u> (like <u>phenolphthalein</u> or <u>methyl orange</u>). Universal indicator is no good as its colour change is <u>too gradual</u>.

3) Slowly add alkali to the acid, using a <u>burette</u>, until you reach the <u>end point</u> — this is when the acid's been exactly neutralised and the indicator <u>changes colour</u>.

4) Then, carry out the reaction using exactly the same volumes of alkali and acid but with no <u>indicator</u>, so the salt <u>won't be contaminated</u> with indicator.

5) The <u>solution</u> that remains when the reaction is complete contains only the <u>salt</u> and <u>water</u>.

See page 113 for more on titrations.

6) Slowly <u>evaporate</u> off some of the water and then leave the solution to crystallise (see page 65 for more on crystallisation). Filter off the solid and dry it — you'll be left with a <u>pure</u>, <u>dry</u> salt.

Titrations can be used to make sure the alkali isn't in excess

Alkalis are <u>soluble</u> in water, so it's hard to stop them from <u>contaminating</u> the soluble salt produced in the reaction. Fortunately, <u>titrations</u> can help you out — they allow you to <u>calculate</u> the <u>exact amount</u> of acid and alkali you need to add to <u>complete the reaction</u> without either of them being in excess. Splendid.

Warm-Up and Exam Questions

Salt, glorious salt. There were a lot of experimental methods crammed into the previous few pages, so make sure you can remember each of the steps and why they're important before tackling these questions.

Warm-Up Questions

1) State whether the following salts are soluble or insoluble:
   a) potassium chloride   b) copper carbonate   c) lead sulfate   d) ammonium hydroxide
2) Suggest two reactants you could use to form barium sulfate in a precipitation reaction.
3) Explain why a titration must be used to make a soluble salt by reacting an acid and an alkali.

Exam Questions

1   Lead nitrate and potassium chloride are both soluble salts.

Name the **two** products of the reaction between a solution of lead nitrate and a solution of potassium chloride. For each product, state whether it is soluble or insoluble in water.

[2 marks]

2   A student mixes calcium chloride and magnesium sulfate solutions in a beaker. The two solutions undergo the following reaction.

$$CaCl_{2\,(aq)} + MgSO_{4\,(aq)} \rightarrow CaSO_{4\,(s)} + MgCl_{2\,(aq)}$$

Describe a method that could be used to obtain a pure, dry sample of calcium sulfate ($CaSO_4$) from the products of the reaction.

[3 marks]

PRACTICAL

3   Copper sulfate is a soluble salt. It can be made by adding an excess of insoluble copper oxide to sulfuric acid until no further reaction occurs.

(a)   Give **one** observation that would indicate that the reaction is complete.

[1 mark]

(b)   Once the reaction is complete, the excess copper oxide can be separated from the copper sulfate solution using the apparatus shown in **Figure 1**. What is this method of separation called?

[1 mark]

(c)   Describe how you could produce solid copper sulfate from a solution of copper sulfate.

Figure 1

[3 marks]

4*   Sodium hydroxide solution and hydrochloric acid react to produce sodium chloride (a soluble salt).

Describe how you could produce a sample of pure, dry sodium chloride from sodium hydroxide solution and hydrochloric acid.

[6 marks]

Electrolysis

Now I hope you're sitting comfortably. We're about to embark on five pages on electrolysis.

Electrolysis Involves **Oxidation** and **Reduction**

1) Electrolysis is the breaking down of a substance using electricity. An electric current is passed through an electrolyte (a molten or dissolved ionic compound), causing it to decompose.

2) In electrolysis, oxidation (loss of electrons) and reduction (gain of electrons) occur.

See page 92 for more on oxidation and reduction.

3) The positive ions (cations) in the electrolyte move towards the cathode (negative electrode) and are reduced (gain electrons).

This creates a flow of charge through the electrolyte.

4) The negative ions (anions) in the electrolyte move towards the anode (positive electrode) and are oxidised (lose electrons).

5) As ions gain or lose electrons they form the uncharged substances and are discharged from the electrolyte.

Half Equations Show How **Electrons** are **Transferred** During **Reactions**

Half equations are really useful for showing what happens at each electrode during electrolysis. To write a half equation:

1) Put one of the things being oxidised or reduced on one side of an arrow, and the thing it gets oxidised or reduced to on the other.
2) Balance up the numbers of atoms just like in a normal equation.
3) Then add electrons (written e^-) on to one side to balance up the charges.

Examples: Sodium is losing one electron to become a sodium ion: $Na \rightarrow Na^+ + e^-$

Hydrogen ions are gaining electrons to become hydrogen: $2H^+ + 2e^- \rightarrow H_2$

The charges on each side of the equation should balance.

Electrolysis means splitting up an electrolyte with electricity

An electrolyte must be an ionic compound that is either molten or in solution. This is so that the ions are free to move towards the oppositely-charged electrode — the cathode for cations, and the anode for anions.

Electrochemical Cells

Right, now that you know what electrolysis is, it's time to find out how you set it all up.

Here's How to **Set Up** an **Electrochemical Cell**

1) An electrochemical cell is a circuit made up of the anode, cathode, electrolyte, a power source and the wires that connect the two electrodes.

2) You need to know how to set up an electrochemical cell. The method used depends on whether your electrolyte is a solution or a molten ionic substance.

You could put an ammeter or bulb in series with your circuit to check you've set it up correctly.

If Your **Electrolyte** is a **Solution**...

1) Get two inert (unreactive) electrodes, e.g. graphite or platinum electrodes.

2) Clean the surfaces of the electrodes using some emery paper (or sandpaper).

3) From this point on, be careful not to touch the surfaces of the electrodes with your hands — you could transfer grease back onto the strips.

4) Place both electrodes into a beaker filled with your electrolyte.

5) Connect the electrodes to a power supply using crocodile clips and wires. When you turn the power supply on, a current will flow through the cell.

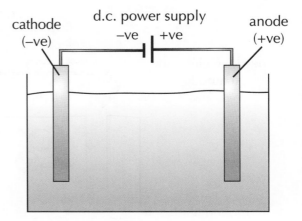

The voltage of the cell decreases as the electrolysis continues and the reactants get used up.

If Your **Electrolyte** is a **Molten Ionic Substance**...

1) Put your solid ionic substance (which will become your electrolyte) in a crucible.

2) Heat the crucible with a Bunsen burner until the solid's molten. You should do this in a fume cupboard to avoid releasing any toxic fumes into the room.

3) Once the solid's molten, dip two clean, inert electrodes into the electrolyte.

4) Then, connect the electrodes to a power supply using wires and clips — you should get a current flowing through the cell when you turn the power on.

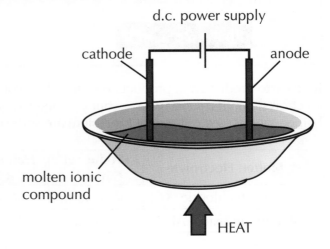

The electrodes should be clean before they're used in electrolysis

You can also do electrolysis with non-inert electrodes. Have a look at page 86 for more about this.

Electrolysis of Molten Substances

Time to cover what's <u>going on</u> at the <u>electrodes</u> themselves. First up, it's <u>molten ionic substances</u>...

Electrolysis of Molten Ionic Compounds Forms Elements

1) An <u>ionic solid can't</u> be electrolysed because the ions are in fixed positions and <u>can't move</u>.
2) <u>Molten ionic compounds can</u> be electrolysed because the ions can <u>move freely</u> and conduct electricity.
3) Positive <u>metal ions</u> are <u>reduced</u> to <u>metal atoms</u> at the cathode.
4) Negative <u>ions</u> are <u>oxidised</u> to atoms or molecules at the <u>anode</u>.
5) Molten ionic compounds are always broken up into their <u>elements</u>.

Example: Electrolysis of Molten Lead Bromide (PbBr$_2$)

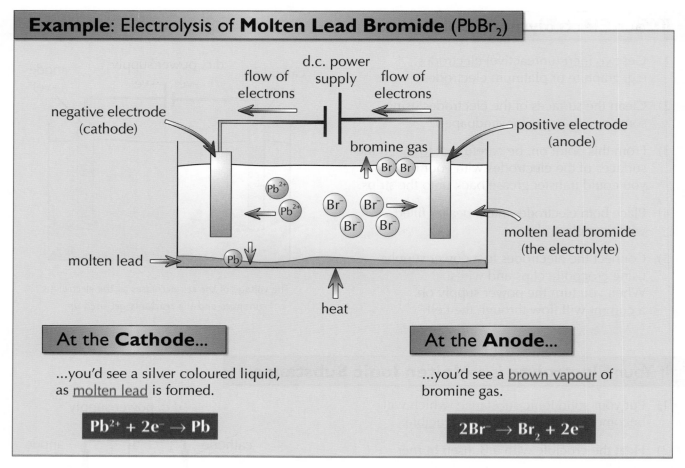

At the Cathode...

...you'd see a silver coloured liquid, as <u>molten lead</u> is formed.

$$Pb^{2+} + 2e^- \rightarrow Pb$$

At the Anode...

...you'd see a <u>brown vapour</u> of bromine gas.

$$2Br^- \rightarrow Br_2 + 2e^-$$

It's easy to predict what products you get when you electrolyse <u>molten</u> substances — but you need to get the <u>half equations</u> (see p.82) right too. Here are some examples:

See page 33 for predicting what ions different metals and non-metals form.

Molten Electrolyte	Product at Cathode	Half equation at Cathode	Product at Anode	Half equation at Anode
potassium chloride, KCl	potassium	$K^+ + e^- \rightarrow K$	chlorine	$2Cl^- \rightarrow Cl_2 + 2e^-$
aluminium oxide, Al$_2$O$_3$	aluminium	$Al^{3+} + 3e^- \rightarrow Al$	oxygen	$2O^{2-} \rightarrow O_2 + 4e^-$

Molten ionic compounds only have one source of ions

The <u>only ions</u> you need to worry about are those <u>present</u> in the ionic compound. As you'll find out on the next page, electrolysis of <u>aqueous solutions</u> is a little bit <u>harder</u> to get your head around, because you also have the <u>ions in water</u> to think about — so make sure you <u>fully understand</u> the stuff on this page before moving on.

Electrolysis of Aqueous Solutions

When carrying out electrolysis on an aqueous solution you have to factor in the ions in water.

Electrolysis of **Aqueous Solutions** is a Bit More Complicated

In aqueous solutions, as well as the ions from the ionic compound, there will be
hydrogen ions (H^+) and hydroxide ions (OH^-) from the water: $H_2O_{(l)} \rightleftharpoons H^+_{(aq)} + OH^-_{(aq)}$

Cathode

1) At the cathode, if H^+ ions and metal ions are present, hydrogen gas will be produced if the metal is more reactive than hydrogen (e.g. sodium).

2) If the metal is less reactive than hydrogen (e.g. copper or silver), then a solid layer of the pure metal will be produced instead.

Anode

1) At the anode, if OH^- and halide ions (Cl^-, Br^-, I^-) are present, molecules of chlorine, bromine or iodine will be formed.

2) If no halide ions are present, then oxygen will be formed.

You can use reactivity series to find out which metals are more or less reactive than hydrogen (see page 89).

Example: Electrolysis of **Sodium Chloride (NaCl) Solution**

1) A solution of sodium chloride (NaCl) contains four different ions: Na^+, Cl^-, OH^- and H^+.

2) Sodium metal is more reactive than hydrogen. So at the cathode, hydrogen gas is produced.

$$2H^+ + 2e^- \rightarrow H_2$$

3) Chloride ions are present in the solution. So at the anode chlorine gas is produced.

$$2Cl^- \rightarrow Cl_2 + 2e^-$$

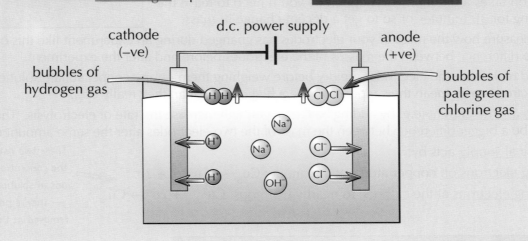

Here are some more examples of aqueous electrolytes and the products of their electrolysis:

Aqueous Electrolyte	Product at Cathode	Half equation at Cathode	Product at Anode	Half equation at Anode
copper chloride, $CuCl_2$	copper	$Cu^{2+} + 2e^- \rightarrow Cu$	chlorine	$2Cl^- \rightarrow Cl_2 + 2e^-$
sodium sulfate, Na_2SO_4	hydrogen	$2H^+ + 2e^- \rightarrow H_2$	oxygen	$4OH^- \rightarrow O_2 + 2H_2O + 4e^-$
water acidified with sulfuric acid, H_2O/H_2SO_4	hydrogen	$2H^+ + 2e^- \rightarrow H_2$	oxygen	$4OH^- \rightarrow O_2 + 2H_2O + 4e^-$

There are lots of ions to think about here...

EXAM TIP
In the exam, it might be a good idea to write out all of the ions in the solution, and then circle the ones that react at the electrodes. That way, you're less likely to forget any of the ions present.

PRACTICAL Electrolysis of Copper Sulfate

Electrolysis of **Copper Sulfate** with Inert Electrodes Produces **Oxygen**

1) A solution of copper sulfate ($CuSO_4$) contains four different ions: Cu^{2+}, SO_4^{2-}, H^+ and OH^-.

2) When you electrolyse copper sulfate solution with inert electrodes:

   - Copper is less reactive than hydrogen, so copper metal is produced at the cathode (you see a coating of copper on the electrode).

     $$Cu^{2+} + 2e^- \rightarrow Cu$$

   - There aren't any halide ions present, so oxygen and water are produced at the anode (you see bubbles of oxygen gas forming).

     $$4OH^- \rightarrow O_2 + 2H_2O + 4e^-$$

The method used to set up this electrochemical cell is on page 83.

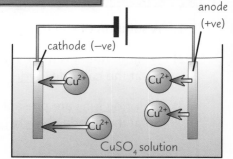

Non-Inert Electrodes Take Part in Electrolysis Reactions

1) If you set up an electrochemical cell in the same way as the one above, but using copper electrodes in a solution of copper sulfate instead of inert electrodes, the result is different.

2) As the reaction continues, the mass of the anode will decrease and the mass of the cathode will increase. This is because copper is transferred from the anode to the cathode.

3) The reaction takes a bit of time to happen — you'll need to leave the cell running for 30 minutes or so to get a decent change in mass.

4) You can measure how the mass of your electrodes has changed during an experiment like this one by finding the difference between the masses of the electrodes before and after the experiment.

5) You should make sure the electrodes are dry before weighing them — any copper sulfate solution on the electrodes may mean they appear to have a higher mass than they really do...

6) If you increase the current (e.g. by adding batteries) you will increase the rate of electrolysis. This means there will be a bigger difference between the mass of the two electrodes after the same amount of time.

7) The electrical supply acts by:
   - Pulling electrons off copper atoms at the anode: $Cu_{(s)} \rightarrow Cu^{2+}_{(aq)} + 2e^-$
   - Offering electrons at the cathode to nearby underline{Cu^{2+} ions}: $Cu^{2+}_{(aq)} + 2e^- \rightarrow Cu_{(s)}$

These two reactions mean the concentration of Cu^{2+} ions in solution is constant — they're produced and removed at the same rate.

Electrolysis Can be Used to **Purify Copper**

Copper can be extracted from its ore by reduction with carbon (see p.95), but copper made in this way is impure. Electrolysis is used to purify it — this method uses an electrochemical cell with copper electrodes:

When copper is underline{purified} using electrolysis, the anode starts off as a big lump of impure copper, the electrolyte is copper(II) sulfate solution (which contains Cu^{2+} ions) and the cathode starts off as a thin piece of pure copper. Here's what happens during the process:

1) The impure copper anode is oxidised, dissolving into the electrolyte to form copper ions:

   $$Cu \rightarrow Cu^{2+} + 2e^-$$

2) The copper ions are reduced at the pure copper cathode, and add to it as a layer of pure copper:

   $$Cu^{2+} + 2e^- \rightarrow Cu$$

3) Any impurities from the impure copper anode sink to the bottom of the cell, forming a sludge.

Warm-Up and Exam Questions

Time to test your mettle. Try and get through the following questions. If there's anything you're not quite sure about, have a look at the pages again until you can answer the questions without batting an eyelid.

Warm-Up Questions

1) a) Explain what is meant by "oxidation" in terms of the transfer of electrons.
   b) At which electrode does oxidation happen during electrolysis?
2) Describe how you would carry out an electrolysis where the electrolyte is a solution.
3) What products are made when molten zinc chloride is electrolysed?
4) What is formed at the anode during the electrolysis of an aqueous solution of sodium sulfate?
5) When you electrolyse copper sulfate solution with inert electrodes, what forms at the cathode?

Exam Questions

1   Aluminium is extracted by electrolysis of molten aluminium oxide (Al_2O_3).

   (a)   Complete the half equation below for the reaction that occurs at the negative electrode.

$$................ + 3e^- \rightarrow ....$$

[1 mark]

   (b)   Complete the half equation below for the reaction that occurs at the positive electrode.

$$................ \rightarrow .... + 4e^-$$

[1 mark]

   (c)   The positive electrode is made of carbon. Carbon is non-inert.
         Suggest why the positive electrode will need to be replaced over time.

[2 marks]

2   When sodium chloride solution is electrolysed, a gas is produced at each electrode.

   (a)   Name the gas produced at the negative electrode.

[1 mark]

   (b)   Give the half equation for the reaction at the negative electrode.

[1 mark]

   (c)   Name the gas produced at the positive electrode.

[1 mark]

   (d)   Give the half equation for the reaction at the positive electrode.

[1 mark]

   (e)   Explain why sodium hydroxide is left in solution at the end of the reaction.

[2 marks]

   (f)   If copper chloride solution is electrolysed, copper metal is produced
         at the negative electrode, instead of the gas named in part **(a)**. Explain why.

[1 mark]

Topic 3 — Chemical Changes

Revision Summary for Topic 3

That wraps up <u>Topic 3</u> — time to put yourself to the test and find out <u>how much you really know</u>.

- Try these questions and <u>tick off each one</u> when you <u>get it right</u>.
- When you've done <u>all the questions</u> under a heading and are <u>completely happy</u> with it, tick it off.

Acids and Bases (p.73-76) ☑

1) What pH value would a neutral substance have?

2) What is an alkali?

3) State what colours the following indicators are in acidic solutions:
   a) litmus
   b) methyl orange
   c) phenolphthalein

4) Write the ionic equation for a neutralisation reaction.

5) Sketch a pH curve to show how the pH changes when an excess of the base calcium hydroxide is added to hydrochloric acid.

6) Write an equation to show how ethanoic acid (CH_3COOH) acts as a weak acid.

7) If you increase the hydrogen ion concentration of a solution by a factor of 10, what will happen to the pH of the solution?

8) Write a chemical equation to show how hydrochloric acid reacts with copper oxide.

9) Describe a test you could carry out to test for hydrogen gas.

10) What would you expect to see if you bubbled carbon dioxide through limewater?

Making Salts (p.78-80) ☑

11) List three insoluble sulfates.

12) Name two soluble hydroxides.

13) Describe how you could make a pure sample of a soluble salt from an acid and an insoluble base.

14) Describe how you could make a pure sample of a soluble salt from an acid and an alkali.

Electrolysis (p.82-86) ☑

15) What is electrolysis?

16) Towards which electrode do the anions in an electrolyte move?

17) Describe how you would carry out an electrolysis where the electrolyte is a molten ionic compound.

18) At which electrode does the metal form during the electrolysis of a molten ionic compound?

19) Write a half equation to show what happens at the cathode in the electrolysis of copper chloride solution, $CuCl_2$.

20) Write a half equation to show what happens at the anode in the electrolysis of water acidified with sulfuric acid (H_2O/H_2SO_4).

21) Why do the masses of non-inert electrodes change during electrolysis?

22) Explain how electrolysis is used to purify copper.

The Reactivity Series

Reactivity series are lists of metals (sometimes with some carbon or hydrogen thrown in).
But they're not just any old lists in any old order. As the name suggests, they tell you all about reactivities.

If Something Gains Oxygen it's Oxidised

Oxidation can mean the reaction with, or addition of oxygen. Reduction can be the removal of oxygen.

> E.g. $Fe_2O_3 + 3CO \rightarrow 2Fe + 3CO_2$
> - Iron oxide is reduced to iron (as oxygen is removed).
> - Carbon monoxide is oxidised to carbon dioxide (as oxygen is added).

Reduction and oxidation can also be to do with electrons (see page 92).

Combustion reactions involve oxidation. They're always exothermic (see page 149).

> E.g. $CH_4 + 2O_2 \rightarrow CO_2 + 2H_2O$
> - Both the carbon and hydrogen are oxidised — they gain oxygen.
> - The oxygen molecules are reduced as the oxygen atoms get split up by the reaction.

The Reactivity Series Shows How Easily Metals Are Oxidised

1) A reactivity series is a table that lists metals in order of their reactivity.

2) As well as the metals, carbon is often included in reactivity series — a metal's position in the reactivity series compared to carbon dictates how it's extracted from its ore (see pages 95-96).

3) Hydrogen can be included in the reactivity series too — this shows the reactivity of metals with dilute acids (see next page).

4) Here's an example of a reactivity series:

If a metal is below hydrogen in the reactivity series, it's less reactive than hydrogen and won't react with dilute acids.

Because metals at the top of the reactivity series are less resistant to oxidation, they corrode easily. Metals at the bottom are more resistant to corrosion (see page 111 for more on corrosion).

least resistant to oxidation

most resistant to oxidation

The Reactivity Series	
Potassium	K
Sodium	Na
Calcium	Ca
Magnesium	Mg
Aluminium	Al
Carbon	C
Zinc	Zn
Iron	Fe
Hydrogen	H
Copper	Cu
Silver	Ag
Gold	Au

most reactive

least reactive

5) The metals at the top of the reactivity series are the most reactive — they easily lose their electrons to form cations (positive ions). They're also oxidised easily.

6) The metals at the bottom of the reactivity series are less reactive — they don't give up their electrons to form cations as easily. They're more resistant to oxidation than the metals higher up the reactivity series.

7) You can determine a metal's position in the reactivity series by reacting it with water and dilute acids (see p.90-91).

Metals at the top of a reactivity series are more reactive

Don't worry if you come across different reactivity series to the one shown above — they all work the same. The more reactive elements are at the top of the series and the less reactive ones are at the bottom.

Reactivity of Metals

Reactive metals tend to fizz around a bit when you drop them into acid.

How **Metals** React With **Acids** Tells You About Their **Reactivity**

1) The more easily a metal atom loses its outer electrons and forms a positive ion, the more reactive it will be.

2) Here's a classic experiment that you can do to show that some metals are more reactive than others. All you do is to place little pieces of various metals into dilute hydrochloric acid:

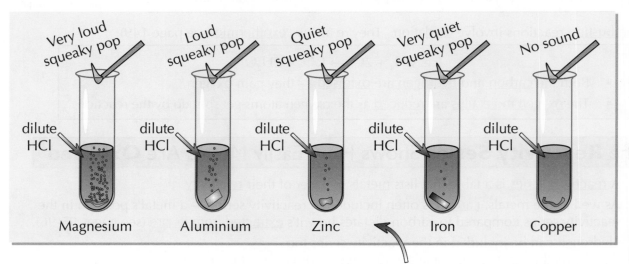

Very loud squeaky pop — dilute HCl — Magnesium

Loud squeaky pop — dilute HCl — Aluminium

Quiet squeaky pop — dilute HCl — Zinc

Very quiet squeaky pop — dilute HCl — Iron

No sound — dilute HCl — Copper

3) The more reactive the metal is, the faster the reaction with the acid will go (see page 75 for more on the reactions of metals with acids).

It's worth making sure the pieces of metal are a similar size and shape so as you can compare your results. Powdered metals will react much faster than lumps of metal as they've got a larger surface areas (see page 146).

4) Very reactive metals (e.g. magnesium) will fizz vigorously, less reactive metals (e.g. zinc) will bubble a bit, and unreactive metals (e.g. copper) will not react with dilute acids at all.

5) You can show that hydrogen is forming using the burning splint test (see page 75). The louder the squeaky pop, the more hydrogen has been made in the time period and the more reactive the metal is.

6) The speed of reaction is also indicated by the rate at which the bubbles of hydrogen are given off — the faster the bubbles form, the faster the reaction and the more reactive the metal.

You could also follow the rate of the reaction by using a gas syringe to measure the volume of gas given off at regular time intervals (see p.138) or using a thermometer to measure by how much the temperature changes (as the reaction of acids with metals is exothermic — see p.149).

PRACTICAL TIP

Always take care when carrying out experiments

It's a good idea to think about how you could minimise the possible risks before doing any practical work. For example, when carrying out the reaction above, you should wear goggles to protect yourself from any acid that might spit out of the test tube when you add the metal.

Reactivity of Metals

Some Metals React With Water

1) In a similar way to their reactions with acids, the reactions of metals with <u>water</u> also show the reactivity of metals.

2) This is the basic reaction:

   metal + water → metal hydroxide + hydrogen

3) Very reactive metals like <u>potassium</u>, <u>sodium</u>, <u>lithium</u> and <u>calcium</u> will all react <u>vigorously</u> with water.

squeaky pop

metal

water

bubbles of hydrogen gas

Less Reactive Metals Only React With Steam

1) Less reactive metals like <u>magnesium</u>, <u>zinc</u> and <u>iron</u> won't react much with cold water, but they will react with <u>steam</u>.

   less reactive metal + steam → metal oxide + hydrogen

2) You could show this in the lab using this <u>experiment</u>:

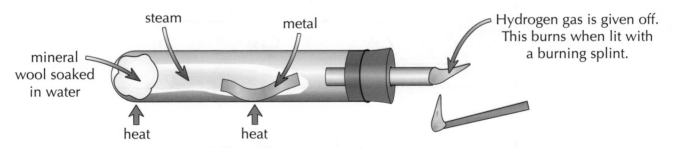

steam

metal

Hydrogen gas is given off. This burns when lit with a burning splint.

mineral wool soaked in water

heat

heat

3) <u>Copper</u> is so unreactive that it won't react with either water or steam.

Less reactive metals need a bit of encouragement to react with H_2O

Some metals lower down the reactivity series aren't reactive enough to react with liquid water — they'll only react if you give the water a bit more <u>energy</u> by heating it to form <u>steam</u>. Splendid.

Displacement Reactions

As well as by reacting metals with <u>dilute acids</u> and <u>water</u>, you can directly compare the reactivity of metals using <u>displacement reactions</u>. This involves reacting metals with <u>metal salt solutions</u>. Exciting stuff.

Displacement Reactions are Redox Reactions

1) As well as talking about <u>reduction</u> and <u>oxidation</u> in terms of the loss and gain of <u>oxygen</u> (as on page 89), you can also talk about them in terms of <u>electrons</u> (as in electrolysis).

2) <u>Oxidation</u> can be the <u>loss of electrons</u>, and <u>reduction</u> can be the <u>gain of electrons</u>.

> When dealing with electrons:
> <u>O</u>xidation <u>I</u>s <u>L</u>oss, <u>R</u>eduction <u>I</u>s <u>G</u>ain.

Remember it as OIL RIG.

3) Reduction and oxidation happen <u>simultaneously</u> — hence the name <u>redox</u> reactions.

4) <u>Displacement reactions</u> are examples of redox reactions.

5) In displacement reactions, a <u>more reactive element</u> reacts to take the place of a <u>less reactive element</u> in a compound. In metal displacement reactions, the more reactive metal loses electrons and the less reactive metal gains electrons.

6) So, during a displacement reaction, the <u>more reactive metal</u> is <u>oxidised</u>, and the <u>less reactive metal</u> is <u>reduced</u>. For example:

---

calcium + zinc sulfate → calcium sulfate + zinc

zinc is reduced

$$Ca \quad + \quad ZnSO_4 \quad \rightarrow \quad CaSO_4 \quad + \quad Zn$$

calcium is oxidised

---

aluminium + copper oxide → aluminium oxide + copper

copper is reduced

$$2Al \quad + \quad 3CuO \quad \rightarrow \quad Al_2O_3 \quad + \quad 3Cu$$

aluminium is oxidised

Remember OIL RIG — 'Oxidation is Loss, Reduction is Gain'

<u>OIL RIG</u> is a pretty handy way to remind yourself what goes on during a <u>redox reaction</u>. Make sure that you don't forget that redox reactions are all about the <u>transfer of electrons</u>.

Displacement Reactions

More Reactive Metals Displace Less Reactive Ones

1) If you put a <u>reactive metal</u> into a solution of a <u>less reactive metal salt</u>, the reactive metal will <u>replace</u> the <u>less reactive metal</u> in the salt.

<u>Example</u>: if you put an <u>iron nail</u> in a solution of <u>copper sulfate</u>, the more reactive iron will "<u>kick out</u>" the less reactive copper from the salt. You end up with <u>iron sulfate solution</u> and <u>copper metal</u>.

$$\text{copper sulfate} + \text{iron} \rightarrow \text{iron sulfate} + \text{copper}$$
$$CuSO_4 + Fe \rightarrow FeSO_4 + Cu$$

⟸ In this reaction, copper is reduced and iron is oxidised.

2) If you put a <u>less reactive metal</u> into a solution of a <u>more reactive metal salt</u>, <u>nothing</u> will happen.

<u>Example</u>: if you put a small piece of silver metal into a solution of <u>copper sulfate</u>, nothing will happen. The more reactive metal (copper) is already in the salt.

3) You can use displacement reactions to <u>work out</u> where in the reactivity series a metal should go.

<u>Example</u>: A student adds some <u>metals</u> to <u>metal salt solutions</u> and records whether any <u>reactions</u> happen. Use her table of results, below, to work out an <u>order of reactivity</u> for the metals.

	copper nitrate	magnesium chloride	zinc sulfate
copper	no reaction	no reaction	no reaction
magnesium	magnesium nitrate and copper formed	no reaction	magnesium sulfate and zinc formed
zinc	zinc nitrate and copper formed	no reaction	no reaction

- Magnesium <u>displaces</u> both <u>copper</u> and <u>zinc</u>, so it must be <u>more reactive</u> than both.
- Copper <u>is displaced by</u> both <u>magnesium</u> and <u>zinc</u>, so it must be <u>less reactive</u> than both.
- Zinc <u>can displace copper</u>, but <u>not magnesium</u>, so it must go between them.
- The <u>order of reactivity</u>, <u>from most to least</u>, is: <u>magnesium, zinc, copper</u>.

A displacement reaction is a type of redox reaction

In the exam, you could be given the <u>results</u> of some <u>displacement reactions</u> and asked to use them to work out the <u>order of reactivity</u> of the metals involved. It's worth getting to grips with how displacement reactions work — if you know your stuff it, could be easy marks in the exam.

Warm-Up and Exam Questions

Hoping to test your knowledge with some questions? You're in luck...

Warm-Up Questions

1) What determines the reactivity of a metal?
2) Gold is below magnesium in the reactivity series.
   Is gold more or less easily oxidised than magnesium?
3) Write the word equation for the reaction of a metal with water.
4) What is meant by the term reduction? Give your answer in terms of electrons.
5) State which species is being oxidised in this reaction: $Zn_{(s)} + CuCl_{2(aq)} \rightarrow ZnCl_{2(aq)} + Cu_{(s)}$

Exam Questions

1   **Figure 1** shows part of the reactivity series of metals.
    Hydrogen has also been included in this reactivity series.

    (a)   Name **one** metal from **Figure 1**
          that is more reactive than magnesium.

          [1 mark]

    (b)   Name **one** metal from **Figure 1**
          which would not react with dilute acid.

          [1 mark]

    (c)   A student adds a small piece of zinc to dilute acid.
          (i)   Name the gas produced during the reaction.

                [1 mark]

          (ii) The reaction produces bubbles of gas fairly slowly.
                Use this information to predict what would happen if
                the student repeated the experiment using iron.

                [2 marks]

Potassium K
Sodium Na
Calcium Ca
Magnesium Mg
Zinc Zn
Iron Fe
HYDROGEN H
Copper Cu

Figure 1

2   A student adds a piece of copper to some iron sulfate solution and a piece of iron to some copper
    sulfate solution. **Figure 2** shows what the test tubes looked like just after he added the metals.

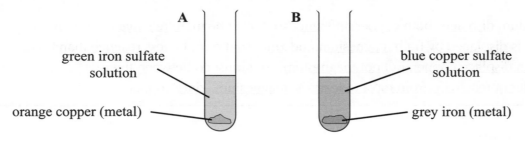

green iron sulfate
solution

orange copper (metal)

blue copper sulfate
solution

grey iron (metal)

Figure 2

Predict the appearance of the solutions in tubes **A** and **B** after 2 hours. Explain your answer.

[4 marks]

Extracting Metals Using Carbon

We get most of our metals by <u>extracting</u> them <u>from rocks</u> — read on to find out how...

Ores Contain Enough Metal to Make Extraction Worthwhile

1) A <u>metal ore</u> is a <u>rock</u> which contains <u>enough metal</u> to make it <u>economically worthwhile</u> extracting the metal from it. In many cases the ore is an <u>oxide</u> of the metal.

> <u>Example</u>: the main <u>aluminium ore</u> is called <u>bauxite</u>
> — it's aluminium oxide (Al_2O_3).

2) Most of the metals that we use are found in their <u>ores</u> in the <u>Earth's crust</u>. The ores are mined and the metals can then be <u>extracted</u> from the ores.

3) Some <u>unreactive metals</u>, such as gold and platinum, are present in the Earth's crust as <u>uncombined elements</u>. These metals can be mined straight out of the ground, but they usually need to be <u>refined</u> before they can be used.

Some Metals can be Extracted by Reduction with Carbon

1) A metal can be <u>extracted</u> from its ore chemically by <u>reduction</u> using <u>carbon</u>.

2) When an ore is reduced, <u>oxygen is removed</u> from it. For example:

Most of the time, you actually get a mixture of carbon dioxide (CO_2) and carbon monoxide (CO) when you reduce metal oxides with carbon.

$2Fe_2O_3$	+	$3C$	→	$4Fe$	+	$3CO_2$
iron oxide	+	carbon	→	iron	+	carbon dioxide

3) The position of the metal in the <u>reactivity series</u> determines whether it can be extracted by <u>reduction</u> with carbon.

See page 89 for more on the reactivity series.

- Metals <u>higher than carbon</u> in the reactivity series have to be extracted using <u>electrolysis</u> (see next page) which is expensive.
- Metals <u>below carbon</u> in the reactivity series can be extracted by <u>reduction</u> using <u>carbon</u>. For example, <u>iron oxide</u> is reduced in a <u>blast furnace</u> to make <u>iron</u>.
- This is because carbon <u>can only take</u> the <u>oxygen</u> away from metals which are <u>less reactive</u> than carbon <u>itself</u> is.

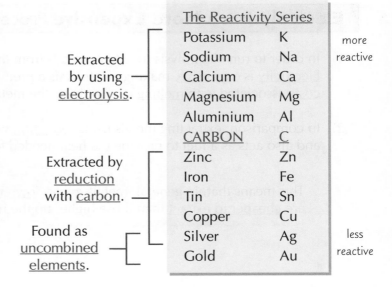

The Reactivity Series

Potassium	K	more reactive
Sodium	Na	
Calcium	Ca	
Magnesium	Mg	
Aluminium	Al	
CARBON	C	
Zinc	Zn	
Iron	Fe	
Tin	Sn	
Copper	Cu	
Silver	Ag	less reactive
Gold	Au	

Extracted by using electrolysis.

Extracted by reduction with carbon.

Found as uncombined elements.

Carbon can't reduce things that are above it in the reactivity series

Make sure you've got that reactivity series sorted in your head. If a metal's <u>below</u> carbon in the reactivity series, then it's <u>less reactive</u> than carbon and can be extracted from its ore by <u>reduction</u> using carbon.

Extracting Metals Using Electrolysis

Not all metals can be extracted from their ores by reduction with carbon — for some electrolysis is used.

Some Metals have to be Extracted by Electrolysis

1) Metals that are more reactive than carbon (see previous page) are extracted using electrolysis of molten compounds (see page 84 for more on this).

2) Once the metal ore is melted, an electric current is passed through it. The metal is discharged at the cathode and the non-metal at the anode.

The compounds have to be molten (i.e. liquid) so that the ions are free to move.

Example: Aluminium is extracted from its ore using electrolysis with carbon electrodes. Aluminium oxide (Al_2O_3) has a high melting point, so the ore is first dissolved in molten cryolite (an aluminium compound with a lower melting point than Al_2O_3) to lower the melting point. The ions in this molten mixture are free to move.

During electrolysis, aluminium is formed at the cathode:

$$Al^{3+} + 3e^- \rightarrow Al$$

Aluminium metal sinks to the bottom of the cell and is siphoned off.

Oxygen forms at the anode:

$$2O^{2-} \rightarrow O_2 + 4e^-$$

The overall equation is:

$$2Al_2O_{3(l)} \rightarrow 4Al_{(l)} + 3O_{2(g)}$$

Electrolysis is a More Expensive Process than Reduction with Carbon

1) In order to run electrolysis to extract metals from their ores, you need large amounts of electricity. Electricity is expensive, making electrolysis a pretty pricey process. There are also costs associated with melting or dissolving the metal ore so it can conduct electricity.

2) In comparison, extracting metals using reduction with carbon is much cheaper. Carbon is cheap, and also acts as a fuel to provide the heat needed for the reduction reaction to happen.

This means that, in general, metals lower down the reactivity series (less reactive metals) are cheaper to extract than those higher up the reactivity series (more reactive metals).

Electrolysis is used to extract reactive metals from their ores

Extracting aluminium by electrolysis is really handy, but it does have some downsides. In industry, the mixture of aluminium oxide and cryolite is heated to around 960 °C. This requires large amounts of energy, which often comes from burning fossil fuels and this contributes to global warming (see page 166 for more).

Biological Methods of Extracting Metals

So, metals can be extracted by reducing them with carbon, or by electrolysis. That's not all though —
there are some pretty nifty biological methods that can be used for extraction too.

There are **Biological Methods** to **Extract Metals**

1) The supply of some metal rich ores, e.g. copper ore, is limited.

We can also recycle metals to save resources (see page 98-99).

2) The demand for lots of metals is growing and this may lead to shortages in the future.

3) Scientists are looking into new ways of extracting metals from low-grade ores
   (ores that only contain small amounts of the metal) or from the waste that is
   currently produced when metals are extracted.

4) Examples of new methods to extract metals from their ores are bioleaching
   and phytoextraction. These are biological methods as they use living organisms.

Bioleaching

1) This uses bacteria to separate metals from their ores,
   e.g. copper can be separated from copper sulfide this way.
2) The bacteria get energy from the bonds between the atoms in
   the ore, separating out the metal from the ore in the process.
3) The leachate (the solution produced by the process) contains
   metal ions, which can be extracted, e.g. by electrolysis or
   displacement (see pages 92-93) with a more reactive metal.

This is a bacterial method of extracting metals.

Phytoextraction

1) This involves growing plants in soil that contains metal compounds.
2) The plants can't use or get rid of the metals so they gradually build up in the leaves.
3) The plants can be harvested, dried and burned in a furnace.
4) The ash contains metal compounds from which the metal can be
   extracted by electrolysis or displacement reactions.

5) Traditional methods of mining are pretty damaging to the environment (see page 99).
   These new methods of extraction have a much smaller impact, but the disadvantage is that they're slow.

EXAM TIP

Bioleaching and phytoextraction are biological methods

In the exam, you might be asked to evaluate the use of biological methods of extracting metals,
as an alternative to traditional methods of extraction. In general, biological methods are better for
the environment than traditional methods, but they take a lot longer to extract the desired metal.

Recycling and Life Cycle Assessments

Recycling's a hot topic. We don't have an infinite amount of materials, e.g. metals, to keep on making things from, so recycling's really important to make sure we don't run out of lots of important raw materials.

Recycling Conserves Resources and Energy

1) Extracting raw materials can take large amounts of energy, lots of which comes from burning fossil fuels.

2) Fossil fuels are running out (they're a non-renewable resource) so it's important to conserve them.
Not only this, but burning them contributes to acid rain and climate change (see pages 160 and 165-166).

3) Recycling materials saves energy as this process often only uses a small fraction
of the energy needed to extract and refine the material from scratch.

4) As there's a finite amount of many raw materials, e.g. metals, on Earth, recycling
conserves these resources too. Metals, like fossil fuels, are non-renewable.

5) It's particularly important to recycle materials that are rare.

Recycling Has Important Economic Benefits

1) As you saw above, extracting materials often requires more energy than just recycling them, and
energy doesn't come cheap. So recycling saves money.

2) It is particularly beneficial to the economy to recycle metals that are expensive to extract or buy.

3) Recycling is also a massive industry and creates lots of jobs. The materials
to be recycled need to be transported to and processed at recycling centres.
They then need to be reprocessed into new products which can be sold.

4) Jobs are created at every stage of this process — far more than are
created by simply disposing of waste by dumping it into landfill.

It's important to recycle — some resources are starting to run out...

If we increase the amount of products that we recycle, it'll reduce the amount of raw materials that need to be extracted. Recycling also saves money, as it generally uses less energy to recycle materials than to dig them up and process etc. That's the theory, at least. It's often harder to put into practice...

Recycling and Life Cycle Assessments

Recycling Protects the Environment

1) Extracting metals also impacts on the environment.
   Mines are damaging to the environment and destroy habitats
   — not to mention the fact that they're a bit of an eyesore.
   Recycling more metals means that we don't need so many mines.

2) Recycling materials also cuts down on the amount of rubbish that gets
   sent to landfill. Landfill takes up space and pollutes the surroundings.

Example: Recycling Aluminium

1) If you didn't recycle aluminium, you'd have to mine more aluminium
   ore — 4 tonnes for every 1 tonne of aluminium you need.

2) But mining makes a mess of the landscape (and these mines are often in rainforests).

3) The ore then needs to be transported, and the
   aluminium extracted (which uses loads of electricity).

4) It is also expensive to send the used aluminium to landfill.

5) So it's a complex calculation, but for every 1 kg of aluminium cans you recycle, you save:
   - 95% or so of the energy needed to mine and extract 'fresh' aluminium,
   - 4 kg of aluminium ore,   *In fact, aluminium's about the most*
   - a lot of waste.   *cost-effective metal to recycle.*

Life Cycle Assessments Show Total Environmental Costs

A life cycle assessment (LCA) looks at each stage of the life of a product —
from making the material from natural raw materials, to making the product
from the material, using the product and disposing of the product. It works
out the potential environmental impact of each stage.

*There's more on LCAs
on the next page.*

Recycling's great — it's useful in so many different ways...

The examiners might ask you to evaluate the benefits of metal recycling. Remember that recycling
doesn't just reduce the use of raw materials, it reduces the amount of energy used, the amount of
damage to the environment and the amount of waste produced. It also has economic benefits.

Recycling and Life Cycle Assessments

Life Cycle Assessments can be Split in to Different Stages

There are four main stages in a product's life that should be considered when carrying out an LCA.

Choice of material

1) Metals have to be mined and extracted from their ores. These processes need a lot of energy and cause a lot of pollution.

2) Raw materials for chemical manufacture often come from crude oil. Crude oil is a non-renewable resource, and supplies are decreasing. Also, obtaining crude oil from the ground and refining it into useful raw materials requires a lot of energy and generates pollution.

Manufacture

1) Manufacturing products uses a lot of energy and other resources.

2) It can also cause a lot of pollution, e.g. harmful fumes such as CO or HCl.

3) You also need to think about any waste products and how to dispose of them.

4) Some waste can be recycled and turned into other useful chemicals, reducing the amount that ends up polluting the environment.

5) Most chemical manufacture needs water. Businesses have to make sure they don't put polluted water back into the environment at the end of the process.

Product Use

Using the product can also damage the environment. For example:

1) Paint gives off toxic fumes.

2) Burning fuels releases greenhouse gases and other harmful substances.

3) Fertilisers can leach into streams and rivers and cause damage to ecosystems.

Disposal

1) Products are often disposed of in a landfill site at the end of their life.

2) This takes up space and can pollute land and water.

3) Products might be incinerated (burnt), which causes air pollution.

Some products can be disposed of by being recycled (see p.98-99).

EXAMPLE:

A company is carrying out a life cycle assessment to work out which car, A, B or C, it should make. Using the data in the table, explain which car the company should produce to minimise the environmental impact.

Car	CO_2 emissions (tonnes)	Waste solid produced (kg)	Water used (m^3)	Expected product lifespan (years)
A	17	10 720	8.2	11
B	21	5900	6.0	17
C	34	15 010	9.5	12

- Car A produces the least CO_2, but produces the second highest amount of waste solids and uses the second highest amount of water. It also has the shortest life span.

- Car B produces more CO_2 than car A, but produces by far the least waste solid, uses the least water and also has the longest life span. On balance, this looks a better choice than car A.

- Car C produces the most CO_2, the most waste solid, uses the most water, and has almost as short a life span as car A. This looks like the worst choice.

So, on balance, car B looks like the one that will have the least environmental impact.

LCAs look at the environmental impact of a product's entire life

Doing an LCA for a product is time consuming and expensive — there's a lot to take into account.

Warm-Up and Exam Questions

Time to have a go at some questions. If there's anything you're not quite sure about, have a look back at the relevant pages until you can answer the questions without batting an eyelid.

Warm-Up Questions

1) Explain why carbon can't be used to extract metals above it in the reactivity series.
2) List the main steps in the process of phytoextraction.
3) Give two economic benefits of recycling metals.
4) What are the four stages that need to be considered when conducting a life cycle assessment?

Exam Questions

1 Iron can be extracted by the reduction of iron(III) oxide (Fe_2O_3) with carbon (C), to produce iron and carbon dioxide.

    (a) Write a balanced symbol equation for this reaction.

[2 marks]

    (b) Explain why the iron(III) oxide is described as being reduced during this reaction.

[1 mark]

2 Aluminium is extracted by electrolysis of molten aluminium oxide (Al_2O_3).

    (a) The aluminium oxide is dissolved in molten cryolite. State why.

[1 mark]

    (b) Complete the half equation below for the reaction that occurs at the negative electrode.

$$\text{................} + 3e^- \rightarrow \text{.................}$$

[1 mark]

3 Copper needs to be extracted from its ore before it can be used.

    (a) Copper can be extracted biologically from low-grade ores using bacteria. Explain how the process works.

[3 marks]

    (b) Give **one** advantage and **one** disadvantage of using bioleaching rather than traditional methods of mining metals.

[2 marks]

4* **Figure 1** gives information about two types of carrier bag.

Use the information in **Figure 1** and your own knowledge to evaluate which type of bag has the smallest environmental impact over its lifetime.

[6 marks]

	Plastic Poly(ethene) Bag	Paper Bag
Raw Materials	Crude oil	Timber
Manufacture	The compounds needed to make the plastic are obtained from crude oil by fractional distillation, cracking and polymerisation.	Processing pulped timber uses lots of energy. Lots of waste is made.
Using the Product	Reusable, can be used for other things as well as shopping.	Usually single-use
Product Disposal	Recyclable but not biodegradable and will take up space in landfill and pollute land.	Biodegradable, non-toxic and can be recycled.

Figure 1

Dynamic Equilibrium

In a reversible reaction, both the forward and the backward reactions are happening at the same time.

Reversible Reactions can go Forwards and Backwards

A reversible reaction is one where the products can react with each other to produce the original reactants. In other words, it can go both ways.

$$A + B \rightleftharpoons C + D$$

The '$\rightleftharpoons$' shows that the reaction goes both ways.

The Haber process (see pages 121-122) is an example of a reversible reaction.
1) During the Haber process, nitrogen and hydrogen react to form ammonia: $N_2 + 3H_2 \rightleftharpoons 2NH_3$
   - The nitrogen (N_2) is obtained easily from the air, which is about 78% nitrogen.
   - The hydrogen (H_2) can be extracted from hydrocarbons from sources like natural gas and crude oil.
2) The Haber process is carried out at 450 °C, with a pressure of 200 atmospheres and an iron catalyst.

Reversible Reactions Will Reach Equilibrium

1) As the reactants (A and B) react, their concentrations fall — so the forward reaction will slow down. But as more and more of the products (C and D) are made and their concentrations rise, the backward reaction will speed up.

2) After a while the forward reaction will be going at exactly the same rate as the backward one — this is equilibrium.

See page 104 for more on concentrations and rate.

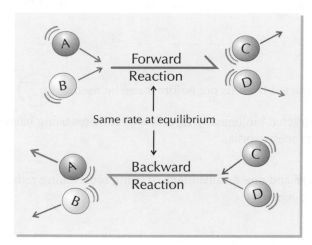
Same rate at equilibrium

3) At equilibrium both reactions are still happening, but there's no overall effect.

4) This is a dynamic equilibrium — the forward and backward reactions are both happening at the same time and at the same rate, and the concentrations of reactants and products have reached a balance and won't change.

5) Equilibrium can only be reached if the reversible reaction takes place in a 'closed system'. A closed system just means that none of the reactants or products can escape.

Dynamic equilibrium — lots of activity, but no overall effect

The idea of dynamic equilibrium is something that you need to get to grips with, as things will get more complicated over the next couple of pages. Have another read and make sure you've got the basics sorted.

Le Chatelier's Principle

This stuff might feel a bit complicated to start with, but it all comes down to one simple rule — whatever you do to a reversible reaction, the system will respond to try to undo your change. How contrary.

The **Position of Equilibrium** Can be on the **Right** or the **Left**

1) When a reaction's at equilibrium it doesn't mean that the amounts of reactants and products are equal.

2) Sometimes the equilibrium will lie to the right — this basically means "lots of the products and not much of the reactants" (i.e. the concentration of products is greater than the concentration of reactants).

3) Sometimes the equilibrium will lie to the left — this basically means "lots of the reactants but not much of the products" (the concentration of reactants is greater than the concentration of products).

4) The exact position of equilibrium depends on the conditions (as well as the reaction itself).

Three Things Can Change the **Position** of **Equilibrium**

1) Three things can change the position of equilibrium (which changes the amounts of products and reactants present at equilibrium).

2) These are temperature, pressure (for equilibria involving gases) and concentrations (of reactants or products).

The plural of equilibrium is 'equilibria'.

> Example: ammonium chloride $\rightleftharpoons$ ammonia + hydrogen chloride
>
> Heating this reaction moves the equilibrium to the right (more ammonia and hydrogen chloride) and cooling it moves it to the left (more ammonium chloride).

The **Equilibrium** Position Moves to **Minimise** Any Changes You Make

Le Chatelier's principle states that if there's a change in concentration, pressure or temperature in a reversible reaction, the equilibrium position will move to help counteract that change.

Temperature

All reactions are exothermic in one direction and endothermic in the other (see page 149).

1) If you decrease the temperature, the equilibrium will move in the exothermic direction to produce more heat.

2) If you increase the temperature, the equilibrium will move in the endothermic direction to absorb the extra heat.

> For example:
>
> $N_2 + 3H_2 \rightleftharpoons 2NH_3$
>
> This reaction is exothermic in the forward direction. If you decrease the temperature, the equilibrium will shift to the right (so you'll make more product).

Le Chatelier's Principle

Pressure

Changing pressure only affects equilibria involving <u>gases</u>.

1) If you <u>increase the pressure</u>, the equilibrium will move towards the side that has <u>fewer moles of gas</u> to <u>reduce</u> pressure.

2) If you <u>decrease the pressure</u>, the equilibrium will move towards the side that has <u>more moles of gas</u> to <u>increase</u> pressure.

<u>For example:</u>

$N_2 + 3H_2 \rightleftharpoons 2NH_3$

This reaction has <u>4 moles of gas</u> on the <u>left</u> and <u>2</u> on the <u>right</u>. If you <u>increase</u> the <u>pressure</u>, the equilibrium will shift to the <u>right</u> (so you'll make more product).

Concentration

1) If you <u>increase the concentration</u> of the <u>reactants</u>, the equilibrium will move to the <u>right</u> to <u>use up the reactants</u> (making <u>more products</u>).

2) If you <u>increase the concentration</u> of the <u>products</u>, the equilibrium will move to the <u>left</u> to <u>use up the products</u> (making <u>more reactants</u>).

3) <u>Decreasing</u> the concentration will have the <u>opposite effect</u>.

<u>For example:</u>

$N_2 + 3H_2 \rightleftharpoons 2NH_3$

If you <u>increase</u> the <u>concentration</u> of N_2 or H_2, the equilibrium will shift to the <u>right</u> to use up the extra reactants (so you'll make more product).

You Can **Predict** How the **Position of Equilibrium** Will Change

1) You can apply the rules above to any reversible reaction to work out how <u>changing the conditions</u> will affect the <u>equilibrium position</u>.

2) This has useful applications in <u>industry</u> — you can <u>increase yield</u> (see page 118) by changing the conditions to shift the equilibrium position to the <u>right</u> (towards the <u>products</u>).

 **EXAMPLE:**

The compound PCl_5 can be made using this reaction: $PCl_{3\,(g)} + Cl_{2\,(g)} \rightleftharpoons PCl_{5\,(g)}$
Explain what would happen to the equilibrium position and to the yield of PCl_5 if you increased the pressure that the reaction was being performed at.

According to Le Chatelier's Principle, if you increase the pressure, the position of equilibrium will move towards the side with fewer moles of gas to reduce the pressure. In this reaction there are 2 moles of gas in the reactants and 1 in the products.

The position of equilibrium will move to the right, since that is the side with fewer moles of gas. This shifts the equilibrium towards the products, so the yield of PCl_5 will increase.

 ## So, you do one thing, and the reaction does the other...

The best way to get your head around all this is to <u>practise it</u>. So find a reversible reaction, and then think about how <u>changing each condition</u> will affect the <u>position of equilibrium</u>.

Warm-Up and Exam Questions

Not long now 'til this section's over, but first there are some questions for you to tackle.

Warm-Up Questions

1) What can you say about forward and backward reaction rates at equilibrium?

2) Equilibrium can only be reached if the reaction takes place in a closed system. What is meant by a 'closed system'?

3) For the reaction, $N_{2(g)} + O_{2(g)} \rightleftharpoons 2NO_{(g)}$, how would changing the gas pressure affect the position of equilibrium?

4) For a reversible reaction, what is the effect on equilibrium of removing some of the reactants from the reaction mixture?

Exam Questions

1 In the reaction below, substances A and B react to form substances C and D.

$$2A + B \rightleftharpoons 2C + D$$

(a) State what the symbol $\rightleftharpoons$ indicates about the reaction of A and B.

[1 mark]

(b) State what is meant by the term **dynamic equilibrium**.

[1 mark]

2 This question is about how pressure affects the position of equilibrium.

Reaction 1: $N_2O_{4(g)} \rightleftharpoons 2NO_{2(g)}$

Reaction 2: $ClNO_{2(g)} + NO_{(g)} \rightleftharpoons NO_{2(g)} + ClNO_{(g)}$

(a) For Reaction 1, explain the effect of an **increase** in pressure on the amount of products at equilibrium.

[2 marks]

(b) For Reaction 2, explain the effect of a **decrease** in pressure on the amount of products at equilibrium.

[2 marks]

3 When calcium carbonate is heated to a high temperature in a closed system, an equilibrium is reached:

$$CaCO_{3(s)} \rightleftharpoons CaO_{(s)} + CO_{2(g)}$$

The forward reaction is endothermic.

(a) Explain whether the reverse reaction takes in or gives out energy.

[2 marks]

(b) Explain why changing the temperature of a reversible reaction always affects the position of the equilibrium.

[2 marks]

(c) For the reaction shown above, describe what would happen to the equilibrium position if the temperature was raised.

[1 mark]

Revision Summary for Topic 4

That's it for Topic 4 — there's just a page of questions standing between you and the end of the topic.
- Try these questions and tick off each one when you get it right.
- When you've done all the questions under a heading and are completely happy with it, tick it off.

The Reactions and Reactivity of Metals (p.89-93) ☑

1) Describe oxidation and reduction in terms of the addition and removal of oxygen. ☑
2) Identify which element is reduced in the following reaction: $CH_4 + 2O_2 \rightarrow CO_2 + 2H_2O$ ☑
3) In a reactivity series, where do you find the least reactive elements? ☑
4) True or false? The easier it is for a metal atom to form a positive ion, the more reactive it will be. ☑
5) You are given samples of four mystery metals and some dilute hydrochloric acid.
   Briefly describe how you could use these things to work out a reactivity series for the four metals. ☑
6) Describe oxidation in terms of electrons. ☑
7) What is a redox reaction? ☑
8) Describe what happens during a displacement reaction. ☑

Extracting Metals from their Ores (p.95-97) ☑

9) What is a metal ore and where are they usually found? ☑
10) Describe how metals less reactive than carbon are usually extracted from their ores. ☑
11) Name two biological methods that can be used to extract metals from low-grade ores. ☑

Conserving Resources (p.98-100) ☑

12) Explain how recycling metals helps to conserve energy. ☑
13) Give two ways in which recycling is better for the environment than disposing of waste in landfill. ☑
14) What is a life cycle assessment? ☑
15) Describe how the disposal of a product in landfill can affect the environment. ☑

Equilibria (p.102-104) ☑

16) Draw the symbol which shows that a reaction is reversible. ☑
17) If the position of equilibrium for a reversible reaction lies to the right,
    what does that tell you about the relative amounts of reactants and products present? ☑
18) State Le Chatelier's principle. ☑
19) Which of the following statements is true?
    a) Equilibrium can only be reached if a reversible reaction is taking place in an open system.
    b) If the forward reaction in a reversible reaction is exothermic,
       then the reverse reaction is endothermic.
    c) Increasing the pressure of a reversible reaction will cause the position
       of equilibrium to move towards the side that has more moles of gas. ☑
20) Describe what would happen to the equilibrium position of a reversible reaction
    if you increased the concentration of the reactants. ☑

Transition Metals

You'll find the transition metals sitting together slap bang in the middle of the periodic table. They've got plenty of different properties that you need to know about — so grab a cup of tea and a biscuit, and read on.

The **Transition Metals** Sit in the Middle of the Periodic Table

1) A lot of everyday metals are transition metals (e.g. copper, iron, zinc, gold, silver, platinum) — but there are loads of others as well.

2) If you get asked about a transition metal you've never heard of — don't panic. These 'new' transition metals will follow all the properties you've already learnt for the others.

Group 0

Group 1 Group 2

Group 3 Group 4 Group 5 Group 6 Group 7

The transition metals are right here in the middle of the periodic table.

45 Sc Scandium 21	48 Ti Titanium 22	51 V Vanadium 23	52 Cr Chromium 24	55 Mn Manganese 25	56 Fe Iron 26	59 Co Cobalt 27	59 Ni Nickel 28	63.5 Cu Copper 29	65 Zn Zinc 30
89 Y Yttrium 39	91 Zr Zirconium 40	93 Nb Niobium 41	96 Mo Molybdenum 42	98 Tc Technetium 43	101 Ru Ruthenium 44	103 Rh Rhodium 45	106 Pd Palladium 46	108 Ag Silver 47	112 Cd Cadmium 48
139 La Lanthanum 57	178 Hf Hafnium 72	181 Ta Tantalum 73	184 W Tungsten 74	186 Re Rhenium 75	190 Os Osmium 76	192 Ir Iridium 77	195 Pt Platinum 78	197 Au Gold 79	201 Hg Mercury 80
227 Ac Actinium 89	261 Rf Rutherfordium 104	262 Db Dubnium 105	266 Sg Seaborgium 106	264 Bh Bohrium 107	277 Hs Hassium 108	268 Mt Meitnerium 109	271 Ds Darmstadtium 110	272 Rg Roentgenium 111	

Transition metals can be called transition elements.

Transition Metals Have **Typical Metallic Properties**

1) The transition metals have all the typical properties of metals (see page 44) — they're relatively hard, strong, shiny and malleable materials that conduct heat and electricity well.

2) They have high melting points (with the exception of mercury, which is liquid at room temperature).

3) They also have high densities. For example, at room temperature, potassium (a Group 1 metal) has a density of 0.9 g cm^{-3}, while copper has a density of 9.0 g cm^{-3}, and iron has a density of 7.9 g cm^{-3}.

4) The properties of some transition metals make them really useful.

> Gold is used in jewellery because it's shiny and malleable, but it's also a great electrical conductor and really corrosion resistant, so it's used in some electronic components.

> Copper is used for water pipes because it's malleable and corrosion resistant. It's another good electrical conductor, so it's used in a lot of electrical wiring.

Transition metals are pretty useful elements...

Transition metals have similar properties to 'typical metals' but also have a few more unusual characteristics. These include forming coloured compounds and the ability to act as a catalyst (see next page for more).

Transition Metals

Transition Metals and Their Compounds Make Good **Catalysts**

A <u>catalyst</u> speeds up the <u>rate</u> of a reaction without being <u>changed</u>
or <u>used up</u> itself — see page 147 for more about catalysts.

> <u>Iron</u> is the catalyst used in the <u>Haber process</u>
> for making <u>ammonia</u> (see p.121).

> <u>Vanadium pentoxide</u> (V_2O_5) is the catalyst for
> making <u>sulfuric acid</u> in the <u>Contact process</u>.

Transition Metal Compounds are **Very Colourful**

1) The <u>compounds</u> of transition metals are <u>colourful</u>.
2) What colour they are depends on what <u>transition metal ion</u> they contain. For example:

> Compounds containing Fe^{2+}
> ions are usually <u>light green</u>.

> Compounds with Fe^{3+}
> ions are <u>orange/brown</u>
> (e.g. rust, see page 111).

> Compounds with Cu^{2+}
> ions are often <u>blue</u>.

*You don't need to learn all these colours —
they're just examples. Just be aware that
transition metals can form colourful compounds.*

| Titanium | Vanadium | Chromium | Manganese | Iron | Cobalt | Nickel | Copper |
| E.g. Ti^{3+} | E.g. V^{3+} | E.g. Cr^{2+} | E.g. Mn^{2+} | E.g. Fe^{3+} | E.g. Co^{2+} | E.g. Ni^{2+} | E.g. Cu^{2+} |

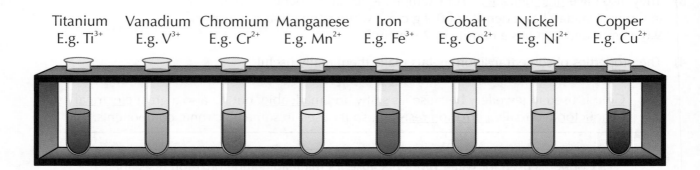

You can't get much more colourful than transition metal ions...

Transition metals are <u>everywhere</u>. They make good catalysts, iron's used to make steel for construction,
copper's used in electrical wiring, and you can even use their pretty compounds to colour stained glass.

Alloys

Pure metals often aren't quite right for certain jobs. But instead of just making do with what they've got, scientists mix stuff in with the metals to make them behave exactly how they need them to.

Alloys are Harder Than Pure Metals

1) Pure metals are malleable (easily shaped by hammering) because they have a regular arrangement of identical atoms. The layers of ions can slide over each other.

2) This means some metals aren't strong enough for certain uses, so alloys are used instead. Alloys are made by adding another element to a metal — that could be a non-metal or another metal.

3) Different elements have different sized atoms. So, for example, when an element such as carbon is added to pure iron, the smaller carbon atoms will upset the layers of pure iron atoms, making it more difficult for them to slide over each other. So alloys are stronger.

4) Many metals in use today are actually alloys. Because we understand about the properties of metals, alloys can be designed for specific uses.

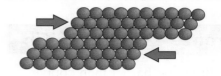

For more on the structure of metals have a look at p.44.

Pure Metals Don't Always Have the Properties Needed

1) For example, alloys of iron called steels are often used instead of pure iron. Steels are made by adding small amounts of carbon to the pure iron. Other metals are added as well to make alloy steels.

2) The properties of a steel are determined by the amount of carbon or other elements that are added.

3) In general, steels are harder and stronger than iron.

4) Iron on its own will rust (corrode) fairly quickly, but steel is much less likely to rust. A small amount of carbon makes a big difference.

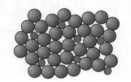

Type of Steel	Properties
Low carbon steel (0.1-0.3% carbon)	easily shaped
High carbon steel (0.22-2.5% carbon)	very strong, inflexible, brittle
Stainless steel (chromium added, and sometimes nickel)	corrosion-resistant, strong

A lot of things are made from steel — girders, bridges, engine parts, cutlery, washing machines, pans, ships, tools, cars etc.

Alloys are really important in industry

If the properties of a metal aren't quite right to a job, an alloy is often used instead. By mixing a metal with another element, the properties are changed. For example, the finished alloy can be a lot harder or less brittle — the mixture of elements can be varied to make an alloy with very specific properties.

Alloys

Steel isn't the only alloy around — there are plenty of other metals that are alloyed to change their properties.

There are Many **Alloys** Used in **Everyday Life**

Bronze = Copper + Tin

1) <u>Bronze</u> is harder than <u>copper</u>.
2) It's used to make medals, decorative ornaments and statues.

Brass = Copper + Zinc

1) <u>Brass</u> is more <u>malleable</u> than <u>bronze</u>.
2) It's used in situations where <u>lower friction</u> is required, such as in water taps and door fittings.

Gold Alloys are Used to Make Jewellery

1) Pure gold is very <u>soft</u> and <u>malleable</u>.
2) Metals such as <u>zinc</u>, <u>copper</u>, and <u>silver</u> are used to <u>strengthen</u> the gold.

> <u>Pure gold</u> is described as <u>24 carat</u>, so 18 carats means that 18 out of 24 parts of the alloy are pure gold. In other words, 18 carat gold is 75% gold. For example, an 18 carat gold ring with a mass of 20 g contains $20 \times (18 \div 24) = 15$ g of gold.

Aluminium Alloys are Used to Make Aircraft

1) Aluminium has a <u>low density</u> which is an important property in <u>aircraft</u> manufacture.
2) But <u>pure aluminium</u> is <u>not strong enough</u> for making aeroplanes, so it's alloyed with small amounts of other metals to increase its strength.

Magnalium = Aluminium + Magnesium

1) When it's made with small amounts of <u>magnesium</u> (about 5%), magnalium is <u>stronger</u>, <u>lighter</u> and <u>corrodes less easily</u> than pure aluminium.
2) This type of magnalium is used to make parts for <u>cars</u> and <u>aeroplanes</u>.
3) Magnalium with a <u>higher</u> magnesium content (about 50%) is used in <u>fireworks</u>, as it's <u>reactive</u> and burns <u>brightly</u>, like magnesium, but is <u>more stable</u> than pure magnesium.

The properties of an alloy depend on its composition

Memorising all the different alloys can be a right pain. <u>Cover</u> up the page, <u>scribble</u> down everything you can remember, and then <u>check</u> against the page again to see what you didn't get. <u>Repeat</u> this process until it's all sunk into your head. It'll be worth it come the exam...

Corrosion

Corrosion (e.g. rusting) is a process where something is slowly damaged or destroyed by a chemical process.

Rusting of Iron is a Redox Reaction

1) Metals can corrode in the presence of oxygen and water to form their metal oxides.

2) Corrosion of metals is caused by redox reactions. The metal loses electrons, so it's oxidised. Simultaneously, oxygen gains electrons when it reacts with the metal.

3) Rusting is the name for the corrosion of iron. Rusting only happens when the iron is in contact with both oxygen (from the air) and water.

Remember OIL RIG — Oxidation is Loss, Reduction is Gain (of electrons) — see p.92.

Experiments can show that both oxygen and water are needed for iron to rust.

- If you put an iron nail in a boiling tube with just water, it won't rust. Boiling the water beforehand will remove oxygen, and oil can be used to stop air getting in.

- If you put an iron nail in a boiling tube with just air, it won't rust. Calcium chloride can be used to absorb any water from the air.

- However, if you put an iron nail in a boiling tube with air and water, it will rust.

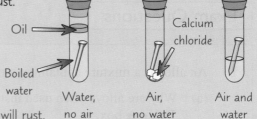

Water, no air   Air, no water   Air and water

There are Different Ways to Prevent Rusting

1) You can prevent rusting by coating the iron with a barrier. This keeps out the water, oxygen or both.

2) Painting is ideal for large and small structures. It can also be nice and colourful.

3) Oiling or greasing has to be used when moving parts are involved, like on bike chains.

4) You can also prevent rusting using sacrificial protection — this involves placing a more reactive metal with the iron. The water and oxygen react with this 'sacrificial' metal instead of with the object you're protecting.

5) Galvanising is an example of sacrificial protection, where a coat of zinc is put onto an iron object to prevent rusting. The zinc acts as sacrificial protection — it's more reactive than iron, so it'll lose electrons and corrode in preference to iron. The zinc also acts as a barrier.

Steel buckets and corrugated iron roofing are often galvanised.

Electroplating is Applying a Metal Coating to an Object

1) Electroplating is coating the surface of a metal with another metal using electrolysis.

2) The cathode is the object you're going to electroplate, the anode is the bar of metal you're using for the plating. Your electrolyte is a solution containing the metal ions of the metal you're plating.

3) Electroplating is really useful. Household objects like cutlery and cooking utensils are electroplated with metals to stop them corroding. The metals used for protection are unreactive and don't corrode easily.

4) Jewellery and decorative items are often electroplated with metals like gold or silver. This improves the appearance of the metals — making them look shiny and attractive.

Example: Electroplating silver onto a brass cup.
- The cathode is the brass cup and the anode is a bar of pure silver.
- The electrolyte is silver nitrate solution ($AgNO_3$).
- The silver ions from the electrolyte move towards the cathode and metal gets deposited on the brass cup. The anode keeps the silver ions in the solution 'topped up'.

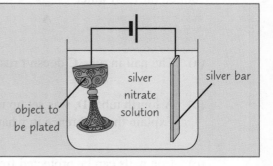

object to be plated   silver nitrate solution   silver bar

Cathode: $Ag^+ + e^- \rightarrow Ag$ Anode: $Ag \rightarrow Ag^+ + e^-$

Thankfully there are quite a few ways to prevent corrosion of metals

Paint, oil and grease have to be regularly re-applied to iron to stop it from rusting, which can get expensive.

Warm-Up and Exam Questions

Lots of information to learn on the previous few pages — here are some questions to test yourself on.

Warm-Up Questions

1) Give two typical properties of transition metals.
2) Which two metals is brass made from?
3) Explain why the rusting of metal is a redox reaction.

Exam Questions

1   An alloy is a mixture containing a metal and at least one other element.

(a)   Why are alloys often used instead of pure metals?
      Tick **one** box.

⬜   **A**   they are more plentiful

⬜   **B**   their properties make them more suitable for the application

⬜   **C**   they have a more regular structure

⬜   **D**   they are completely inert

[1 mark]

(b)   Magnalium is an alloy made up of two metals.
      (i)   Name the two metals that form magnalium.

[2 marks]

      (ii) State **one** use of magnalium. Explain why it is suitable for this use.

[2 marks]

2   In an experiment to investigate rusting, three iron nails were placed into separate boiling tubes for ten days. The experimental set-up is shown in **Figure 1**.

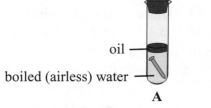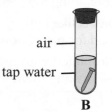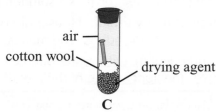

Figure 1

(a)   The nail in tube **C** doesn't rust. State which other tube would not contain a rusted nail.

[1 mark]

(b)   A fourth tube, **D**, was set up in the same way as tube **B** except the nail used was coated in paint. Explain the difference in what would happen to the nail in tube **D** compared with the nail in tube **B**.

[2 marks]

(c)   Iron nails can be protected from rusting by coating them with zinc. Explain how this method protects the nails from rust.

[3 marks]

Titrations

Titrations are a method of analysing the <u>concentrations</u> of solutions. They're pretty important.

Titrations are Used to Find Out Concentrations

Titrations allow you to find out <u>exactly</u> how much acid is needed to <u>neutralise</u> a given quantity of alkali (or vice versa).

1) Using a <u>pipette</u>, measure out a set volume of the <u>alkali</u> into a flask. Add a few drops of an <u>indicator</u> — usually <u>phenolphthalein</u> or <u>methyl orange</u> (see p.73).

You can't use Universal indicator — it changes colour gradually and you want a single colour change.

2) Fill a <u>burette</u> with a <u>standard solution</u> (a <u>known concentration</u>) of acid.

Keep the burette below eye level while you fill it — you don't want to be looking up if any acid spills.

3) Use the burette to add the acid to the alkali a bit at a time. <u>Swirl</u> the flask regularly. Go <u>slowly</u> (a drop at a time) when you think the alkali's almost neutralised.

To work out when this is, do a rough titration first. Don't worry about recording the exact end point first time, just note the approximate amount of acid you need, then go slowly as you get near this amount on the next runs. Doing your titration with your flask standing on a white tile will make the colour changes easier to see too.

4) The indicator <u>changes colour</u> when <u>all</u> the alkali has been <u>neutralised</u> — phenolphthalein is <u>pink</u> in <u>alkalis</u> but <u>colourless</u> in <u>acids</u>, and methyl orange is <u>yellow</u> in <u>alkalis</u> but <u>red</u> in <u>acids</u>.

5) <u>Record</u> the <u>volume</u> of acid used to <u>neutralise</u> the alkali (called the <u>titre</u>).

6) <u>Repeat</u> this process a few times, making sure you get <u>very similar</u> results each time. You can then take the <u>mean</u> (see p.9) of your results.

Here's the Apparatus You'll Use in a Titration:

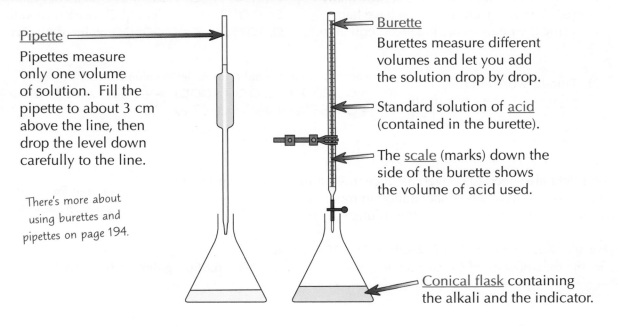

<u>Pipette</u>
Pipettes measure only one volume of solution. Fill the pipette to about 3 cm above the line, then drop the level down carefully to the line.

There's more about using burettes and pipettes on page 194.

<u>Burette</u>
Burettes measure different volumes and let you add the solution drop by drop.

Standard solution of <u>acid</u> (contained in the burette).

The <u>scale</u> (marks) down the side of the burette shows the volume of acid used.

<u>Conical flask</u> containing the alkali and the indicator.

 PRACTICAL TIP

Accuracy is everything...
When you're doing a <u>titration</u> you need to make sure that your results are as <u>accurate</u> as possible. To do this you need to a) go <u>slowly</u> as you reach the <u>end-point</u>, and b) do <u>repeats</u> and find a <u>mean</u>.

Titration Calculations

Once you've done the <u>practical</u> bit, you need to be able to carry out some <u>calculations</u> on your results.

You Can **Calculate Concentration** Using Your **Titration Results**

1) The <u>concentration</u> of a solution can be measured in <u>moles per dm³</u> — so 1 mole of a substance dissolved in 1 dm³ of solution has a concentration of <u>1 mole per dm³</u> (or 1 mol dm⁻³). (Concentration can also be measured in g dm⁻³ — see page 50 for more.)

2) The formula for <u>concentration</u> in <u>mol dm⁻³</u> is similar to the one for g dm⁻³:

> **concentration = number of moles ÷ volume of solution**

$$\frac{n}{c \times V}$$

moles (mol)

concentration (mol dm⁻³)   volume (dm³)

3) You can use the results of a <u>titration experiment</u> to calculate the concentration of the alkali when you know the concentration of the acid (or vice versa).

EXAMPLE:

It takes 25.0 cm³ of 0.100 mol dm⁻³ sulfuric acid to neutralise 30.0 cm³ of sodium hydroxide solution. The equation for this reaction is: $2NaOH + H_2SO_4 \rightarrow Na_2SO_4 + 2H_2O$ Find the concentration of the alkali in mol dm⁻³.

Convert the volume into dm³.
(1000 cm³ = 1 dm³)

1) Work out how many <u>moles</u> of acid you have, using the formula: moles = concentration × volume.

moles = 0.100 × (25.0 ÷ 1000)
= 0.00250 moles of H_2SO_4

2) Use the equation to work out how many <u>moles</u> of the alkali you must have had, using the ratios in the balanced equation.

1 mole of H_2SO_4 reacts with 2 moles of NaOH
So 0.00250 moles of H_2SO_4 must react with
0.00250 × 2 = 0.00500 moles of NaOH

3) Finally, work out the <u>concentration</u> of the alkali.

concentration = number of moles ÷ volume
= 0.00500 ÷ (30.0 ÷ 1000) —— *Again, convert the volume into dm³.*
= 0.1666... mol dm⁻³ = 0.167 mol dm⁻³

---

4) You might also need to convert a concentration in mol dm⁻³ into g dm⁻³. To do this, multiply the concentration in mol dm⁻³ by the <u>relative formula mass</u> of the solute.

To convert from g dm⁻³ to mol dm⁻³, divide by the M_r.

For the example above, M_r of NaOH = 23 + 16 + 1 = 40
So, the concentration of the solution in g dm⁻³ = 0.166... × 40 = 6.666... g dm⁻³ = 6.7 g dm⁻³.

Practise, practise, practise...

A lot of numbers to deal with here. The only way to get good at these titration calculations is by <u>practising</u> them, plain and simple. You can <u>check</u> your answer by doing the calculation in reverse — if you end up with the concentration that you're given in the question, you're onto a winner.

Calculations with Gases

With gases, it's easier to use volume instead of concentration. That's where the molar volume comes in.

Molar Volume is the Volume Occupied by One Mole of Gas

1) The volume occupied by one mole of a gas is known as the molar volume.
2) It usually has units of dm³ mol⁻¹ (dm³ per mole).
3) Here's the formula for calculating molar volume:

molar volume = gas volume ÷ number of moles

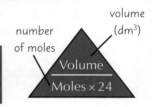

EXAMPLE: Under certain conditions, 0.050 moles of nitrogen gas, N_2, was found to occupy 1.4 dm³. What is the molar volume of nitrogen in dm³ mol⁻¹ under these conditions?

Substitute the moles and volume into the equation for the molar volume.

molar volume = volume ÷ number of moles
= 1.4 ÷ 0.050 = 28 dm³ mol⁻¹

Molar Volumes are the Same Under the Same Conditions

Avogadro's law states that under the same conditions, the same number of moles of different gases all occupy the same volume.

One mole of any gas always occupies 24 dm³ (= 24 000 cm³) at room temperature and pressure (RTP = 20 °C and 1 atmosphere).

So, at RTP, all gases have the same molar volume — 24 dm³ mol⁻¹.

In the exam, you'll be given the value of the molar volume at RTP if you need it.

EXAMPLE: What's the volume of 4.50 moles of chlorine at RTP?

1 mole = 24 dm³, so 4.50 moles = 4.50 × 24 dm³ = 108 dm³

EXAMPLE: How many moles are there in 8280 cm³ of hydrogen gas at RTP?

1) Make sure everything is in the right units.   1000 cm³ = 1 dm³
   You need to convert the volume into dm³.   So, 8280 cm³ = 8280 ÷ 1000 = 8.28 dm³

2) Rearrange the formula linking volume, number of moles and molar volume (24 dm³) to get number of moles on its own.   Number of moles = volume of gas ÷ 24

3) Substitute your values into the rearranged equation.   Number of moles = 8.28 ÷ 24 = 0.345 moles

You can use Avogadro's law with a balanced equation to work out the volume of gas a reaction will produce.

EXAMPLE: How much gas is produced when 11.5 g of sodium is reacted with excess water at RTP?

$$2Na_{(s)} + 2H_2O_{(l)} \rightarrow 2NaOH_{(aq)} + H_{2\,(g)}$$

1) Find the number of moles of Na used. A_r of Na = 23, so 11.5 g of Na = 11.5 ÷ 23 = 0.50 moles

2) Use the balanced equation to find the number of moles of H_2 this will produce.   From the equation, 2 moles of Na produce 1 mole of H_2, so 0.50 moles Na produces 0.50 ÷ 2 = 0.25 moles H_2.

3) Use the formula to find the volume of 0.25 moles of gas.   So the volume of H_2 = 0.25 × 24 = 6.0 dm³

Remember — one mole of any gas occupies 24 dm³ at RTP

Molar volumes can be tricky — but as long as you can use and rearrange the formula, all will be fine.

Warm-Up and Exam Questions

These pesky calculations can be quite tricky. Here are some questions to test yourself out on.
If you have any problems, have a look back through the topic.

Warm-Up Questions

1) What is the purpose of carrying out a titration?

2) How many moles of hydrochloric acid are there in 25 cm³ of a 0.1 mol dm⁻³ solution?

3) 2 moles of a gas occupies 45 dm³. Calculate the molar volume of the gas.

Exam Questions

1 In a titration, 30.4 cm³ of a solution of 1.00 mol dm⁻³ sodium hydroxide
   was required to neutralise 25.0 cm³ of a solution of sulfuric acid.

   (a) Calculate the number of moles of sodium hydroxide used in the titration.

   [1 mark]

   (b) Work out the number of moles of sulfuric acid used in the titration.
        The equation is: $2NaOH_{(aq)} + H_2SO_{4(aq)} \rightarrow Na_2SO_{4(aq)} + 2H_2O_{(l)}$

   [1 mark]

   (c) Calculate the concentration of the sulfuric acid solution in mol dm⁻³.

   [2 marks]

2 Calcium carbonate decomposes under heating to form calcium oxide and
   carbon dioxide. The balanced equation for this reaction is shown below:

$$CaCO_{3(s)} \rightarrow CaO_{(s)} + CO_{2(g)}$$

   25 g of CaCO₃ were heated by a student.
   Assuming that all the calcium carbonate decomposed, calculate the volume occupied at RTP by the
   quantity of CO₂ produced by this reaction. 1 mol of gas occupies 24 dm³ at RTP.
   (relative atomic masses: Ca = 40, O = 16, C = 12)

   [4 marks]

3 Jonah is concerned about the amount of acid in soft drinks. He decides to use a
   titration method to find the acid content of his favourite lemonade. He uses a solution
   of 0.10 mol dm⁻³ sodium hydroxide in titrations with 25 cm³ samples of the lemonade.
   His results are shown in the table.

Repeat	Initial burette reading / cm³	Final burette reading / cm³	Vol. of NaOH needed / cm³
1	0.0	9.4	9.4
2	9.4	18.4	9.0
3	18.4	27.4	9.0

   Jonah calculates that the average volume of 0.10 mol dm⁻³ NaOH needed is 9.0 cm³.
   The equation for the reaction in the titration can be written:
   $HA + NaOH \rightarrow NaA + H_2O$, where HA is the acid present in the lemonade.
   Calculate the concentration of acid HA present in the lemonade.

   [4 marks]

Atom Economy and Percentage Yield

It's important in <u>industrial reactions</u> that as much of the reactants as possible get turned into <u>useful products</u>. This depends on the <u>atom economy</u> and the <u>percentage yield</u> of the reaction.

Atom Economy is the % of Reactants Changed to Useful Products

1) A lot of reactions make <u>more than one product</u>. Some of them will be <u>useful</u>, but others will just be <u>waste</u>.

2) The <u>atom economy</u> of a reaction tells you what percentage of the <u>mass of the reactants</u> has been converted into your <u>desired product</u> when manufacturing a chemical. Here's the formula:

$$\text{Atom Economy} = \frac{\text{total } M_r \text{ of desired products}}{\text{total } M_r \text{ of all products}} \times 100$$

3) <u>100%</u> atom economy means that <u>all</u> the atoms in the reactants have been turned into <u>useful</u> (desired) <u>products</u>. The <u>higher</u> the atom economy the 'greener' the process.

 **EXAMPLE:**

Hydrogen gas can be made industrially by reacting natural gas (methane) with steam.
$$CH_{4\,(g)} + H_2O_{(g)} \rightarrow CO_{(g)} + 3H_{2\,(g)}$$
Calculate the atom economy of this reaction. Give your answer to 2 significant figures.

1) Identify the <u>desired product</u>.

The desired product is hydrogen gas (H_2).

2) Work out the total M_r of <u>all the products</u>.

M_r of all products = $M_r(CO) + [3 \times M_r(H_2)]$
$= (12 + 16) + [3 \times (2 \times 1)] = 28 + 6 = 34$

3) Then work out the total M_r of just the <u>desired products</u>.

M_r of desired products = $3 \times M_r(H_2) = 3 \times (2 \times 1) = 6$

4) Use the formula to calculate the <u>atom economy</u>.

Atom economy = $\dfrac{\text{total } M_r \text{ of desired products}}{\text{total } M_r \text{ of all products}} \times 100$

$= \dfrac{6}{34} \times 100 = 18\%$

So in this reaction, 82% of the starting materials are wasted.

 ## Atom economy is really important in industry

EXAM TIP
You might get asked about an <u>unfamiliar industrial reaction</u> in the exam. <u>Don't panic</u> — whatever example they give you, the same <u>theory</u> will apply when you're calculating the <u>atom economy</u>.

Atom Economy and Percentage Yield

High Atom Economy is Better for **Profits** and the **Environment**

1) Reactions with low atom economies use up resources very quickly. At the same time, they make lots of waste materials that have to be disposed of somehow. That tends to make these reactions unsustainable — the raw materials will run out and the waste has to go somewhere.

2) For the same reasons, low atom economy reactions aren't usually profitable. Raw materials can be expensive to buy and waste products can be expensive to remove and dispose of responsibly.

3) One way around the problem is to find a use for the waste products rather than just throwing them away. There's often more than one way to make the product you want — so the trick is to come up with a reaction that gives useful 'by-products' rather than useless ones.

4) Atom economy isn't the only factor to consider in industry. You also need to think about:

   - The percentage yield (see below) of the reaction — the higher the yield the better.
   - The rate of reaction (see page 137) — the rate of the reaction you're using must be fast enough to produce the amount of product you need in a sensible amount of time.
   - If the reaction's reversible (see page 102). To keep the yield of a reversible reaction high, you might need to alter the equilibrium position by changing reaction conditions (which can be expensive).

Percentage Yield Compares **Actual** and **Theoretical** Yield

1) The amount of product you get from a reaction is known as the yield. The more reactants you start with, the higher the actual yield will be — that's pretty obvious. But the percentage yield doesn't depend on the amount of reactants you started with — it's a percentage.

2) Percentage yield is given by the formula:

$$\text{Percentage yield} = \frac{\text{actual yield}}{\text{theoretical yield}} \times 100$$

The theoretical yield is sometimes called the predicted yield.

3) The theoretical yield of a reaction is the mass of product you'd make if all the reactants were converted to products. Theoretical yield can be calculated from the balanced reaction equation (see page 53).

4) Percentage yield is always somewhere between 0 and 100%. A 100% percentage yield means that you got all the product you expected to get. A 0% yield means that no product was made at all.

5) In a reaction with a low percentage yield, a lot of the reactants will be wasted. In industry it's important to use reactions with the highest yield possible to reduce waste and keep costs as low as possible.

Atom Economy and Percentage Yield

You Can **Calculate** the **Percentage Yield** of a Reaction

Percentage yield is often used to help work out <u>how efficient</u> an industrial reaction is.

 **EXAMPLE:**

In an industrial reaction, iron oxide reacts with carbon to make iron:

$$2Fe_2O_3 + 3C \rightarrow 4Fe + 3CO_2$$

Calculate the percentage yield if you started with 50 kg of iron oxide and produced 18.9 kg of iron.

1) Find the <u>relative formula mass</u> of iron oxide and the <u>relative atomic mass</u> of iron.

$M_r(Fe_2O_3) = (2 \times 56) + (3 \times 16) = 160$
$A_r(Fe) = 56$

Convert the mass to grams: 1 kg = 1000 g

2) Work out the number of <u>moles</u> of the reactant (iron oxide) you have.

moles of Fe_2O_3 = mass ÷ M_r
= $(50 \times 1000) \div 160$
= $50\,000 \div 160$ = 312.5 moles

3) Use the <u>balanced chemical equation</u> to work out how many moles of the desired product (iron) you should end up with.

The equation tells you that 2 moles of iron oxide produces 4 moles of iron. So 312.5 moles of iron oxide should produce $(312.5 \div 2) \times 4$ = 625 moles of iron.

4) Work out the <u>theoretical yield</u> of your desired product (iron) by converting this number of moles into mass.

mass = moles × A_r
= 625 × 56
= 35 000 g = 35 kg

Make sure your theoretical yield and your actual yield are in the same units.

5) Finally, pop the numbers into the formula to find the <u>percentage yield</u>.

percentage yield = $\dfrac{\text{actual yield}}{\text{theoretical yield}} \times 100$
= $\dfrac{18.9}{35} \times 100$ = 54%

Yields are Always **Less Than 100%**

In real life, you <u>never</u> get a 100% yield. There are a number of ways this can happen, for example:

- <u>Incomplete reactions</u> — if not all of the <u>reactants</u> are <u>converted</u> to product, the reaction is incomplete and the yield will be lower than expected.
- <u>Practical losses</u> — you always lose a bit when you transfer chemicals between containers. Imagine pouring a <u>liquid</u> into a new container — some is always left on the <u>inside surface</u> of the old container.
- <u>Unwanted reactions</u> — if unexpected reactions happen, the yield of the <u>intended product</u> goes down. These can be caused by <u>impurities</u> in the reactants, or sometimes by changes to the <u>reaction conditions</u>.

 MATHS TIP

Percentage yield is a measure of how successful a reaction is

Make sure you always <u>logic-check</u> your final answer when doing calculations. If you've ended up with a percentage yield of over 100%, something has gone wrong in your working.

Warm-Up and Exam Questions

Atom economy and percentage yield aren't too hard to calculate once you've had some practice.
So here are some questions to get you started...

Warm-Up Questions

1) What is the atom economy of the reaction shown? $2SO_2 + O_2 \rightarrow 2SO_3$
2) Why might a reaction with a low atom economy be unprofitable?
3) What is the formula for calculating the percentage yield of a reaction?
4) What is the percentage yield of a reaction which produced 4 g of product
   if the predicted yield was 5 g?

Exam Questions

1   Which one of the following statements about atom economy is true?
Tick **one** box.

[ ]   **A**   Reactions that only have one product have higher atom economies
than reactions that have two products.

[ ]   **B**   Reactions with a low atom economy tend to be better for
the environment than reactions with high atom economies.

[ ]   **C**   Reactions with low atom economies will generally produce
less waste than reactions with high atom economies.

[ ]   **D**   To calculate the atom economy of a reaction, you need to know the mass of
products you expected to form, and the mass of products that actually formed.

[1 mark]

2   Ethanol produced by the fermentation of sugar can be converted into ethene,
as shown below. The ethene can then be used to make polythene.

$$C_2H_6O_{(g)} \rightarrow C_2H_{4(g)} + H_2O_{(g)}$$

Calculate the atom economy of this reaction. (A_r values: C = 12, O = 16, H = 1)

[3 marks]

3*   Discuss the reasons why yields from chemical reactions are always less than 100%.

[6 marks]

4   A sample of copper was made by reducing 4.0 g of copper oxide with methane gas.
When the black copper oxide turned orange-red, the sample was scraped out into a beaker.
Sulfuric acid was added to dissolve any copper oxide that remained.
The sample was then filtered, washed and dried. 2.8 g of copper was obtained.
(A_r values: H = 1, Cu = 63.5, O = 16.) The equation for this reaction is:

$$CH_4 + 4CuO \rightarrow 4Cu + 2H_2O + CO_2$$

(a)   Use the equation to calculate the maximum mass of copper which could
be obtained from the reaction (the theoretical yield).

[3 marks]

(b)   Calculate the percentage yield of the reaction.

[2 marks]

The Haber Process

This is an <u>important industrial process</u>. It produces <u>ammonia</u> (NH_3), which is used to make <u>fertilisers</u>.

Nitrogen and Hydrogen are Needed to Make Ammonia

1) The <u>Haber process</u> produces <u>ammonia</u> using the following reaction:

$$\text{nitrogen} + \text{hydrogen} \rightleftharpoons \text{ammonia} \quad (+ \text{ heat})$$
$$N_{2(g)} \qquad 3H_{2(g)} \qquad\qquad 2NH_{3(g)}$$

You met the Haber process on page 102.

The reaction includes <u>nitrogen</u> and <u>hydrogen gases</u> being passed over an <u>iron catalyst</u> as shown below.

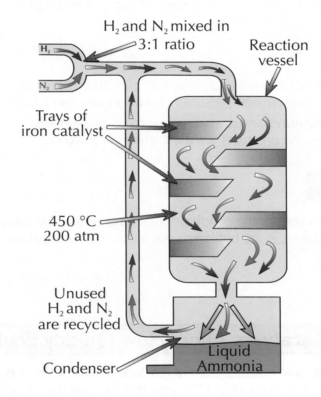

H_2 and N_2 mixed in 3:1 ratio

Reaction vessel

Trays of iron catalyst

450 °C 200 atm

Unused H_2 and N_2 are recycled

Condenser

Liquid Ammonia

2) <u>Higher pressures</u> favour the <u>forward</u> reaction (since there are four moles of gas on the left-hand side, for every two moles on the right — see the equation above).

3) So the pressure is set <u>as high as possible</u> to give the best yield (see page 118), without making the plant too expensive to build (e.g. it'd be too expensive to build a plant that'd stand pressures of over 1000 atmospheres). So, the operating pressure is <u>200 atmospheres</u>.

4) The <u>forward reaction</u> is <u>exothermic</u>, which means that <u>increasing</u> the <u>temperature</u> will actually move the equilibrium position the <u>wrong way</u> — away from ammonia and towards nitrogen and hydrogen. So the yield of ammonia would be greater at <u>lower temperatures</u>.

5) The trouble is, <u>lower temperatures</u> mean a <u>lower rate of reaction</u>. So in industry, the temperature is increased anyway, to get a much faster rate of reaction.

6) The 450 °C is a <u>compromise</u> between <u>maximum yield</u> and <u>speed of reaction</u>. It's better to wait just <u>20 seconds</u> for a <u>10% yield</u> than to have to wait <u>60 seconds</u> for a <u>20% yield</u>.

The Haber Process

Choosing the best reaction conditions for industrial processes like the Haber process can be a challenge.

The Conditions Used in **Industrial Processes** are a **Compromise**

You saw on the previous page how the conditions used in the Haber process are chosen. When you're designing an industrial process, there are a number of factors to consider:

Cost of Acquiring **Raw Materials**

1) The cost of extracting and refining the raw materials will affect whether the process is economically viable or not.

2) If the raw materials are too expensive to source, it may not be profitable to make the product.

Cost of **Energy**

1) Energy costs (costs associated with reaching and maintaining the conditions required for the reaction, e.g. temperature and pressure) also affect whether a reaction is profitable.

2) Generally, high temperatures and pressures cost more to maintain, so lower temperatures and pressures are used wherever possible.

Rate of **Reaction**

It's important to be able to control the conditions (the temperature, pressure and the presence of a catalyst) to maximise your yield, but keep your reaction running at an acceptable rate.

Conditions and **Catalysts** Affect How Quickly Equilibrium is Reached

1) The temperature, pressure and concentration of reactants also affect how quickly equilibrium is reached. If you increase the rate of reaction (see p.137), you also increase the rate at which you reach equilibrium.

2) So equilibrium is always reached faster using high temperatures, high pressures and high concentrations (but remember, depending on the reaction, using these conditions could decrease yield).

3) Catalysts are also useful in speeding up the how quickly equilibrium is reached.

> For example, in the Haber process, the iron catalyst makes the reaction go faster, so it reaches equilibrium faster too. But the catalyst doesn't affect the position of equilibrium, or the percentage yield.

Without the catalyst, the Haber process would have to be carried out at an even higher temperature in order to get a quick enough reaction — and that would reduce the % yield of ammonia even further. So the catalyst is very important.

The Haber process is a really important reaction

The Haber process is pretty hard stuff. It can take a while to get your head around <u>why</u> the conditions are chosen — have a good read over the last couple of pages to make sure you're happy with it before moving on. After all, it could end up being precious marks in the exam.

Fertilisers

There's a lot more to using <u>fertilisers</u> than making your garden look nice and pretty...

Fertilisers Help Plants Grow

1) The three main <u>essential</u> elements in fertilisers are <u>nitrogen</u>, <u>phosphorus</u> and <u>potassium</u>. Plants absorb these nutrients from the soil.

2) If plants don't get enough of these elements, their <u>growth</u> and <u>life processes</u> are affected.

3) Fertilisers <u>supply</u> these elements if they're missing from the soil, or provide <u>more</u> of them. This helps to increase the <u>crop yield</u>, as the crops can grow <u>faster</u> and <u>bigger</u>.

4) Ammonia fertilisers have some important <u>advantages</u> compared to <u>traditional fertilisers</u>, like manure. You can <u>control</u> the <u>compositions of chemicals</u> in them, as well as <u>how much</u> is made. Ammonia fertilisers are also <u>soluble</u>, so all the chemicals can <u>dissolve</u> down into the soil to reach the plants.

Ammonia is Used to Produce Nitrogen-Containing Compounds

1) Ammonia can be reacted with oxygen and water in a series of reactions to make <u>nitric acid</u>.

2) You can also react ammonia with acids, <u>including</u> nitric acid and phosphoric acid, to get <u>ammonium salts</u>.

3) For example, ammonia and nitric acid react together to produce the salt <u>ammonium nitrate</u> — a fertiliser:

$$NH_{3\,(aq)} + HNO_{3\,(aq)} \rightarrow NH_4NO_{3\,(aq)}$$

Different Methods are Used to Prepare Ammonium Sulfate

<u>Ammonium sulfate</u> is a fertiliser you can make in the lab. You'll need <u>ammonia</u> and <u>dilute sulfuric acid</u>. You can make most fertilisers using this <u>titration</u> method — just choose the right <u>acid</u> (nitric, sulfuric or phosphoric) and <u>alkali</u> (ammonia or potassium hydroxide) to get the <u>salt</u> you want.

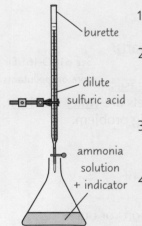

burette

dilute sulfuric acid

ammonia solution + indicator

1) Set up your apparatus as in the diagram. Add a few drops of <u>methyl orange indicator</u> to the ammonia — it'll turn <u>yellow</u>.   *See page 113 for more on titrations.*

2) <u>Slowly</u> add the dilute acid from the burette into the ammonia, until the yellow colour <u>just</u> changes to red. Gently swirl the flask as you add the acid. Go especially <u>slowly</u> when you get close to the end point. Methyl orange is <u>yellow</u> in <u>alkalis</u>, but <u>red</u> in <u>acids</u>, so this <u>colour change</u> means that <u>all</u> the ammonia is <u>neutralised</u> and you've got ammonium sulfate solution.

3) The ammonium sulfate solution isn't <u>pure</u> — it's still got <u>methyl orange</u> in it. To get <u>pure</u> ammonium sulfate crystals, you need to note <u>exactly</u> how much sulfuric acid it took to neutralise the ammonia, then repeat the titration using that volume of acid, but <u>no indicator</u>.

4) To get solid <u>ammonium sulfate crystals</u>, gently evaporate the solution (using a steam bath) until only a little bit is left. Leave it to <u>crystallise</u> then filter out the crystals and leave them to dry (see page 65).

1) The method above isn't used to make ammonium sulfate in <u>industry</u>. It's <u>impractical</u> to use burettes and steam baths for large quantities, and using crystallisation to get solid ammonium sulfate is <u>too slow</u>.

2) The industrial production of ammonium sulfate usually has <u>several stages</u>, as the ammonia and sulfuric acid have to be made from their <u>raw materials</u> first. <u>Ammonia</u> is made using the <u>Haber process</u> (see page 121), and <u>sulfuric acid</u> is produced using a process called the <u>Contact process</u>.

3) One industrial method uses a large reaction chamber filled with <u>ammonia gas</u>. Sulfuric acid is <u>sprayed</u> into the reaction chamber, where it reacts with the ammonia to produce ammonium sulfate powder.

Fertilisers are designed to give plants exactly what they need to grow

Yet another titration... It's pretty similar to the one you met back on page 113, so no need to panic.

Fuel Cells

Fuel cells are great — and the one you need to know about is particularly great in my opinion. The hydrogen-oxygen fuel cell uses hydrogen and oxygen to make electricity. Read on to find out more...

Fuel Cells Use Fuel and Oxygen to Produce Electrical Energy

1) Chemical cells produce a voltage across the cell, until all of one of the reactants has been used up.
2) A fuel cell is a type of chemical cell that's supplied with a fuel and oxygen and uses energy from the reaction between them to produce electrical energy efficiently.
3) There are a few different types of fuel cells, using different fuels and different electrolytes.

Hydrogen-Oxygen Fuel Cells use Hydrogen as a Fuel

1) The reaction between hydrogen and oxygen releases energy.
2) This is what happens in a hydrogen-oxygen fuel cell — you can produce a voltage (i.e. electrical energy) by reacting hydrogen and oxygen, and it doesn't produce any nasty pollutants, only nice clean water...
3) The overall reaction is:

$$\text{hydrogen} + \text{oxygen} \rightarrow \text{water}$$
$$2H_2 + O_2 \rightarrow 2H_2O$$

Hydrogen-Oxygen Fuel Cells Have Lots of Advantages

1) Hydrogen fuel cells are great — they're much more efficient than power stations or batteries at producing electricity. If you use the heat produced as well, their efficiency can be greater than 80%.
2) In a fuel cell, the electricity is generated directly from the reaction (so no turbines, generators, etc.).
3) Because there aren't a lot of stages to the process of generating electricity there are fewer places for energy to be lost as heat.
4) Unlike a car engine or a fossil fuel burning power station, there are no moving parts, so energy isn't lost through friction.

See p.160-161 for more on pollutants.

5) Fuel cell vehicles don't produce any conventional pollutants — no greenhouse gases, no nitrogen oxides, no sulfur dioxide, no carbon monoxide. The only by-products are water and heat. This would be a major advantage in cities, where air pollution from traffic is a big problem.

> This could mean no more smelly petrol and diesel cars, lorries and buses.
>
> It could also replace batteries — which are incredibly polluting to dispose of because they're usually made of highly toxic metal compounds.
>
> However, it's not likely to mean the end of either conventional power stations or our dependence on fossil fuels. That's because:
>
> - hydrogen is a gas so it takes up loads more space to store than liquid fuels like petrol.
> - it's very explosive so it's difficult to store safely.
> - the hydrogen fuel is often made either from hydrocarbons (from fossil fuels), or by electrolysis of water, which uses electricity (and that electricity's got to be generated somehow — usually this involves fossil fuels).

Hydrogen-oxygen fuel cells don't produce nasty pollutants

EXAM TIP You might be asked to evaluate whether a hydrogen-oxygen fuel cell would be useful for a given purpose in your exam, so make sure you've learned a few strengths and weaknesses of them.

Warm-Up and Exam Questions

So, now that you've gone over some stuff about making ammonia, fertilisers and fuel cells, don't just assume you're the bee's knees — test yourself with this lovely selection of questions.

Warm-Up Questions

1) a) What is the name given to the process which uses high temperature and pressure to convert nitrogen and hydrogen into ammonia?
   b) Name the catalyst used in the process described in a).

2) Write the formula of the salt produced in the reaction between ammonia and nitric acid.

3) What is a fuel cell?

Exam Questions

1 Farmers often use fertilisers.

(a) Fertilisers usually contain nitrogen. Name the **two** other elements they usually contain.

[2 marks]

(b) Explain why farmers apply fertilisers to their crops.

[2 marks]

2 Hydrogen-oxygen fuel cells use a chemical reaction to generate electricity.

(a) Write a balanced symbol equation to show the overall reaction in a hydrogen-oxygen fuel cell.

[2 marks]

(b) Describe **one** advantage and **one** disadvantage of using hydrogen fuel cells to power vehicles.

[2 marks]

3 Ammonia is made by combining two different gases at a pressure of 200 atm, a temperature of 450 °C and in the presence of a catalyst.

(a) Complete the balanced equation for the formation of ammonia.

.... + ... $\rightleftharpoons$ ..... NH_3

[2 marks]

(b) The forward reaction is exothermic. Explain what would happen to the yield of ammonia if the temperature was lowered.

[2 marks]

(c) Increasing the pressure increases the yield of the reaction. Suggest why a pressure greater than 200 atm isn't used.

[1 mark]

4* Describe a method for preparing pure crystals of ammonium sulfate in the laboratory using solutions of ammonia and sulfuric acid.

[6 marks]

Revision Summary for Topic 5

So, now you know everything there is to know about how useful chemistry can be in the real world. Okay, maybe not everything... But you should know enough to answer these questions.

- Try these questions and <u>tick off each one</u> when you <u>get it right</u>.
- When you've done <u>all the questions</u> under a heading and are <u>completely happy</u> with it, tick it off.

Transition Metals, Alloys and Corrosion (p.107-111) ☐

1) Give two examples of transition metals. ☑
2) a) Give two properties transition metals have in common with most other metals.
   b) Give two typical properties of transition metals that they don't share with most other metals. ☑
3) What is an alloy? ☑
4) Explain why alloys are usually stronger than pure metals. ☑
5) What element is added to iron to make steel? ☑
6) Give one use of: a) bronze,   b) brass. ☑
7) Give two conditions necessary for rusting to occur. ☑
8) Give two ways rusting can be prevented. ☑
9) Give the two main reasons why an object might be electroplated. ☑

Titrations and Calculations (p.113-119) ☐

10) Why is Universal indicator not used during titrations? ☑
11) At the start of a titration experiment, phenolphthalein was added to an acidic solution. What colour change would you see when the acid had been completely neutralised? ☑
12) What's the formula for calculating the concentration of a solution in mol dm^{-3}? ☑
13) What is the 'molar volume' of a gas? ☑
14) What volume does one mole of gas occupy at room temperature and pressure (RTP)? ☑
15) State the formula used to work out the atom economy of a reaction. ☑
16) Describe what is meant by the atom economy of a reaction. ☑
17) What does the term 'theoretical yield' mean? ☑
18) What does it mean if the percentage yield of a reaction is 100%? ☑

The Haber Process and Fertilisers (p.121-123) ☐

19) What chemical is manufactured using the Haber process? ☑
20) Explain why a temperature of 450 °C in the Haber process is a compromise between rate and yield. ☑
21) Suggest three conditions which cause equilibrium to be reached faster in the Haber process. ☑
22) Give two examples of compounds that are used as fertilisers. ☑
23) Briefly outline the main stages that are involved in the industrial production of ammonium sulfate. ☑

Fuel Cells (p.124) ☐

24) What is the only product of the reaction in a hydrogen-oxygen fuel cell? ☑
25) Hydrogen-oxygen fuel cells produce electricity in fewer stages than, for example, a power station. Explain how this makes them more efficient. ☑

Group 1 — Alkali Metals

You can predict how different elements will <u>react</u> from their position in the <u>periodic table</u> — elements in the <u>same group</u> will react in <u>similar ways</u>. Time to take a look at some of the groups, starting with <u>Group 1</u>...

Group 1 Metals are Known as the 'Alkali Metals'

The <u>Group 1</u> metals are lithium, sodium, potassium, rubidium, caesium and francium.

1) The alkali metals all have <u>one outer electron</u> — so they have <u>similar chemical properties</u>.

2) They all have the following <u>physical properties</u>:
   • <u>Low melting points</u> and <u>boiling points</u> (compared with other metals).
   • <u>Very soft</u> — they can be cut with a knife.

3) The alkali metals form <u>ionic</u> compounds. They lose their single outer electron <u>so easily</u> that sharing it is out of the question, so they <u>don't</u> form covalent bonds.

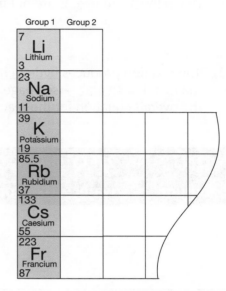

Group 1 Metals are **Very Reactive**

1) The Group 1 metals readily <u>lose</u> their single <u>outer electron</u> to form a <u>1+ ion</u> with a <u>stable electronic structure</u>.

2) The <u>more readily</u> a metal loses its outer electrons, the <u>more reactive</u> it is — so the Group 1 metals are very reactive.

3) As you go <u>down</u> Group 1, the alkali metals get <u>more reactive</u>. The <u>outer electron</u> is more easily <u>lost</u> because it's further from the nucleus (the <u>atomic radius</u> is <u>larger</u>) — so it's less strongly attracted to the nucleus and <u>less energy</u> is needed to remove it.

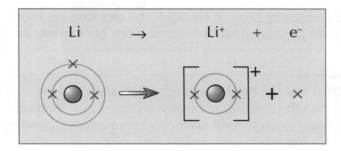

Alkali metals get more reactive as you go down the group

Remember, an alkali metal's reactivity comes from its ability to easily give up its outer shell electron — the more easily it does this, the more reactive it is. This explains why alkali metals at the bottom of the group are the most reactive — they lose their electrons much more easily than the metals at the top of the group.

Group 1 — Alkali Metals

You saw on the last page how the <u>reactivity</u> of the alkali metals <u>increases</u> as you move <u>down the group</u>. This <u>trend</u> is clearly shown in the reactions of the alkali metals with <u>water</u>. Read on to find out more.

Reactions with **Cold Water** Produce a **Hydroxide** and **Hydrogen**

1) When the <u>alkali metals</u> are put in <u>water</u>, they react <u>vigorously</u>.

2) The reaction produces <u>hydrogen gas</u> and a <u>hydroxide</u> of the metal (an <u>alkali</u> — see page 73). For example, here's the overall equation for the reaction of <u>sodium</u> with <u>water</u>:

squeaky pop

A squeaky pop shows H_2 gas is present — see p.75 for more.

$$2Na \quad + \quad 2H_2O \quad \rightarrow \quad 2NaOH \quad + \quad H_2$$
$$\text{sodium} \quad + \quad \text{water} \quad \rightarrow \quad \text{sodium hydroxide} \quad + \quad \text{hydrogen}$$

The same reaction happens with all of the alkali metals — make sure you can write balanced equations for them all.

You Can Make **Predictions** About the **Reactions** of Alkali Metals

1) The reactivity of Group 1 metals with water (and dilute acid) <u>increases</u> <u>down the group</u> because the outer electron is lost more easily in the reaction (see previous page). This results in the reaction becoming <u>more violent</u>:

- <u>Lithium</u> will <u>move</u> around the surface, <u>fizzing</u> furiously.
- <u>Sodium</u> and <u>potassium</u> do the same, but they also <u>melt</u> in the heat of the reaction. Potassium even gets hot enough to <u>ignite</u> the hydrogen gas being produced.

2) Because you know the <u>reactivity trend</u> in Group 1 (the elements get more reactive as you go down the group), you can make <u>predictions</u> about the reactions of elements further down the group.

<u>Example</u>: You may predict that the reactions of rubidium and caesium with water will be <u>more violent</u> than the reaction of potassium and water. And sure enough, <u>rubidium</u> and <u>caesium</u> react <u>violently</u> with water and tend to <u>explode</u> when they get wet...

REVISION TIP

All alkali metals react with water in a similar way

The reaction equations follow the same structure: metal + water → metal hydroxide + hydrogen. Make sure you know it and you'll be able to write the equation for any alkali metal and water.

Group 7 — Halogens

Here's a page on another periodic table group that you need to be familiar with — <u>the halogens</u>.

Group 7 Elements are Known as the 'Halogens'

<u>Group 7</u> is made up of the elements fluorine, chlorine, bromine, iodine and astatine.

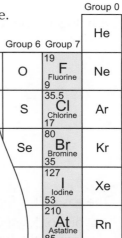

	Group 6	Group 7	Group 0
			He
	O	^{19} F Fluorine 9	Ne
	S	35.5 Cl Chlorine 17	Ar
	Se	80 Br Bromine 35	Kr
		127 I Iodine 53	Xe
		210 At Astatine 85	Rn

1) All Group 7 elements have <u>7 electrons in their outer shell</u> so they all have <u>similar chemical properties</u>.

2) The halogens exist as <u>diatomic molecules</u> (e.g. Cl_2, Br_2, I_2). Sharing one pair of electrons in a <u>covalent bond</u> (see page 39) gives both atoms a <u>full outer shell</u>.

3) As you go <u>down Group 7</u>, the <u>melting points</u> and <u>boiling points</u> of the halogens <u>increase</u>. This means that at <u>room temperature</u>:

<u>Chlorine</u> (Cl_2) is a fairly reactive, poisonous, <u>green gas</u>.

<u>Bromine</u> (Br_2) is a poisonous, <u>red-brown liquid</u> which gives off an <u>orange vapour</u>.

<u>Iodine</u> (I_2) is a <u>dark grey crystalline solid</u> which gives off a <u>purple vapour</u> when heated.

You Can Make **Predictions** About the **Properties** of Halogens

You can use the <u>trends in physical properties</u> from chlorine to iodine to <u>predict</u> the properties of halogens further down the group.

For example, you can see that the melting points <u>increase</u> down the group, and the colours of the halogens get <u>darker</u>, so you could predict that astatine (which comes below iodine) would be a <u>dark-coloured solid</u> at room temperature.

Test for **Chlorine** Using **Damp Blue Litmus Paper**

You can test to see if a gas is <u>chlorine</u> by holding a piece of <u>damp blue litmus paper</u> over it. Chlorine will <u>bleach</u> the litmus paper, turning it <u>white</u>. It may also turn <u>red</u> for a moment first — that's because a solution of chlorine is <u>acidic</u> (see p.73-76 for more on acids).

damp blue litmus paper

Halogens — one electron short of a full outer shell...

Halogens have seven electrons in their outer shell, so they need one more to complete it. That's why they all exist as diatomic molecules — they share one pair of their electrons to get a full outer shell.

Group 7 — Halogens

You need to know all about how the halogens <u>react</u>, so get reading this page...

Reactivity Decreases Going Down Group 7

1) A halogen atom only needs to <u>gain one electron</u> to form a <u>1– ion</u> with a <u>stable electronic structure</u>.

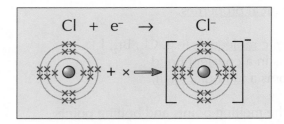

2) The <u>easier</u> it is for a halogen atom to <u>attract</u> an electron, the <u>more reactive</u> the halogen will be.

3) As you go <u>down</u> Group 7, the halogens become <u>less reactive</u> — it gets <u>harder</u> to attract the <u>extra</u> <u>electron</u> to fill the outer shell when it's <u>further away</u> from the nucleus (the <u>atomic radius</u> is <u>larger</u>).

The Halogens Can React With Metals and Hydrogen

1) The halogens will react vigorously with some metals to form <u>salts</u> called '<u>metal halides</u>'.

$2Na$	+	Cl_2	$\rightarrow$	$2NaCl$
sodium	+	chlorine	$\rightarrow$	sodium chloride

Metals lose electrons and form positive ions when they react.

2) Halogens <u>higher up</u> in Group 7 are <u>more</u> reactive because they can attract the <u>outer electron</u> of the metal <u>more easily</u>.

3) Halogens can also react with <u>hydrogen</u> to form <u>hydrogen halides</u>.

H_2	+	Cl_2	$\rightarrow$	$2HCl$
hydrogen	+	chlorine	$\rightarrow$	hydrogen chloride

4) Hydrogen halides are soluble, and they can <u>dissolve in water</u> to form <u>acidic solutions</u>. For example, HCl forms <u>hydrochloric acid</u> in water.

5) Since all halogens have the same number of electrons in their outer shells, they all have <u>similar reactions</u>. So you can use the reactions of <u>chlorine</u>, <u>bromine</u> and <u>iodine</u> to <u>predict</u> how <u>fluorine</u> and <u>astatine</u> will react.

Remember — halogens at the top of the group are the most reactive

The reactivity of a halogen depends on how easily it can attract an electron to get a full outer shell. Halogens at the top of the group are smaller, so can attract electrons more easily than those at the bottom.

Halogen Displacement Reactions

The halogens are competitive — the more reactive ones will push the less reactive ones out of a compound.

A More Reactive Halogen Will Displace a Less Reactive One

1) The elements in Group 7 take part in displacement reactions.

2) A displacement reaction is where a more reactive element 'pushes out' (displaces) a less reactive element from a compound.

3) The halogen displacement reactions are redox reactions. The halogens gain electrons (reduction) whilst halide ions lose electrons (oxidation).

Example: Chlorine Can Displace Bromine

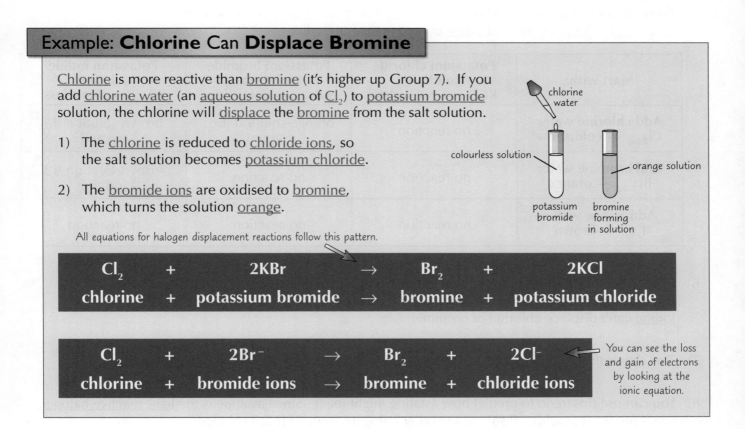

Chlorine is more reactive than bromine (it's higher up Group 7). If you add chlorine water (an aqueous solution of Cl_2) to potassium bromide solution, the chlorine will displace the bromine from the salt solution.

1) The chlorine is reduced to chloride ions, so the salt solution becomes potassium chloride.

2) The bromide ions are oxidised to bromine, which turns the solution orange.

chlorine water

colourless solution

orange solution

potassium bromide

bromine forming in solution

All equations for halogen displacement reactions follow this pattern.

$$Cl_2 + 2KBr \rightarrow Br_2 + 2KCl$$
chlorine + potassium bromide → bromine + potassium chloride

$$Cl_2 + 2Br^- \rightarrow Br_2 + 2Cl^-$$
chlorine + bromide ions → bromine + chloride ions

You can see the loss and gain of electrons by looking at the ionic equation.

Halogens higher up the group will displace the ones lower down

You need to be able to write balanced symbol and ionic equations for halogen displacement reactions. Luckily, since they all follow the same pattern, if you learn them for one reaction, you've learnt them all.

Halogen Displacement Reactions

A halide salt is made up of a <u>halide</u> and a <u>positive ion</u> (normally a <u>metal</u> or <u>hydrogen</u>). By adding halide salts to <u>halogens</u> and seeing which halogens <u>displace</u> the others, you can find out the halogens' <u>relative reactivities</u>.

Displacement Reactions Show Reactivity Trends

You can use <u>displacement reactions</u> to show the reactivity trend of the halogens.

1) Start by measuring out a small amount of a <u>halide salt solution</u> in a test tube.

2) Add a few drops of a <u>halogen solution</u> to it and shake the tube gently.

A halide salt that contains a metal can also be called a metal halide (see page 130).

3) If you see a <u>colour change</u>, then a reaction has happened — the halogen has displaced the halide ions from the salt. If no reaction happens, there <u>won't</u> be a colour change — the halogen is <u>less reactive</u> than the halide and so can't displace it.

4) Repeat the process using different combinations of halide salt and halogen.

5) The table below shows what should happen when you mix different combinations of <u>chlorine</u>, <u>bromine</u> and <u>iodine</u> water with solutions of the salts <u>potassium chloride</u>, <u>potassium bromide</u> and <u>potassium iodide</u>.

Start with:	Potassium chloride solution $KCl_{(aq)}$ — colourless	Potassium bromide solution $KBr_{(aq)}$ — colourless	Potassium iodide solution $KI_{(aq)}$ — colourless
Add chlorine water $Cl_{2\,(aq)}$ **— colourless**	no reaction	orange solution (Br_2) formed	brown solution (I_2) formed
Add bromine water $Br_{2\,(aq)}$ **— orange**	no reaction	no reaction	brown solution (I_2) formed
Add iodine water $I_{2\,(aq)}$ **— brown**	no reaction	no reaction	no reaction

6) <u>Chlorine</u> displaces both bromine and iodine from salt solutions.
<u>Bromine</u> can't displace chlorine, but it does displace iodine.
<u>Iodine</u> can't displace chlorine or bromine.

7) This shows the <u>reactivity trend</u> — the halogens get <u>less reactive</u> as you go <u>down</u> the group.

8) You can use this trend to predict how astatine might react. Since astatine is the <u>least reactive halogen</u>, you'd predict it <u>wouldn't displace</u> any other halogens from their salt solutions.

Chlorine can displace bromine and iodine...

...because it's more reactive than both of them. If you remember that halogens get less reactive as you go down the group, you can work out what will happen when you mix any halogen with any halide salt.

Group 0 — Noble Gases

The elements in Group 0 of the periodic table are known as the noble gases. 'Noble' here is just being used in the old chemistry sense of being unreactive — nothing to do with them being honourable or good.

Group 0 Elements are All Inert, Colourless Gases

Group 0 elements are called the noble gases. Group 0 is made up of the elements helium, neon, argon, krypton, xenon and radon.

1) All of the Group 0 elements are colourless gases at room temperature.

2) The noble gases are all monatomic — that just means that their gases are made up of single atoms (not molecules).

3) They're also more or less inert — this means they don't react with much at all. The reason for this is that they have a full outer shell of electrons. This means they don't easily give up or gain electrons.

4) As the noble gases are inert, they're non-flammable — they won't set on fire.

5) These properties make the gases pretty hard to observe — it took a long time for them to be discovered.

		Group 0
Group 6	Group 7	4 He Helium 2
O	F	20 Ne Neon 10
S	Cl	40 Ar Argon 18
	Br	84 Kr Krypton 36
	I	131 Xe Xenon 54
	At	222 Rn Radon 86

The Noble Gases have Many Everyday Uses...

1) Noble gases can be used to provide an inert atmosphere.

2) Argon does this in filament lamps (light bulbs). Since it's non-flammable, it stops the very hot filament from burning away. Flash photography uses the same principle — argon, krypton and xenon are used to stop the flash filament from burning up during the high temperature flashes.

3) Argon and helium can also be used to protect metals that are being welded. The inert atmosphere stops the hot metal reacting with oxygen.

4) Helium is used in airships and party balloons. Helium has a lower density than air — so it makes balloons float. It is also non-flammable, which makes it safer to use than hydrogen gas.

There are Patterns in the Properties of the Noble Gases

1) As with the other groups in the periodic table, there are also trends in the properties of the noble gases.

2) For example, boiling point, melting point and density all increase as you go down Group 0.

3) You could be given information about a particular property of the noble gases (or Group 7) and asked to use it to estimate the value of this property for a certain element. For example:

EXAMPLE:

Use the densities of helium (0.2 kg m^{-3}) and argon (1.8 kg m^{-3}) to predict the density of neon.

Neon comes between helium and argon in the group, so you can predict that its density will be roughly halfway between their densities:
$(0.2 + 1.8) \div 2 = 2.0 \div 2 = 1.0$

Neon should have a density of about 1.0 kg m^{-3}.

There are other methods you could use for these types of question, but don't worry — you'd get marks for any sensible answer.

4) You could be asked about how an element reacts too, so remember — elements in the same group react in similar ways because they all have the same number of electrons in their outer shells. And, to find out which group an element is in, all you need to do is look at the periodic table. Simple.

Make sure you include units with your answers in the exam

EXAM TIP

It's worth having a check to see if you've been asked to include units with your answer — even if you make a mistake in the calculation, you might still get a mark if you've included correct units.

Warm-Up and Exam Questions

These questions are all about the groups 1, 7 and 0 of the periodic table.
Treat the exam questions like the real thing — don't look back through the book until you've finished.

Warm-Up Questions

1) How many electrons do alkali metals have in their outer shells?
2) Do alkali metals get more or less reactive as you go down the group?
3) What happens to the boiling point of the halogens as you go down Group 7?
4) What is the product of a reaction between chlorine and sodium?
5) What is a displacement reaction?
6) Do halide ions have a positive or a negative charge?
7) In which group of the periodic table are the noble gases?

Exam Questions

1 **Figure 1** shows some of the physical properties of four of the halogens.

Halogen	Properties			
	Atomic number	Colour	Physical state at room temperature	Reactivity
Fluorine	9	yellow	gas	....
Chlorine	17	green	gas	....
Bromine	35	red-brown	liquid	....
Iodine	53	dark grey	solid	....

Figure 1

(a) **Figure 1** has a column for reactivity. Write an **X** in the row of the halogen with the **highest** reactivity and a **Y** in the row of the halogen with the **lowest** reactivity.

[2 marks]

(b) State the halogen in **Figure 1** with the highest melting point.

[1 mark]

2 The electronic configuration of a sodium atom is shown in **Figure 2**.

(a) State which group of the periodic table sodium belongs to.

[1 mark]

(b) Sodium chloride (NaCl) is an ionic compound formed from sodium cations and chloride anions.

Draw a diagram to show the electronic configuration of a sodium ion in sodium chloride. Clearly show the charge on the ion.

[2 marks]

Figure 2

Exam Questions

3   Chlorine is a Group 7 element.
Its electronic configuration is shown in **Figure 3**.

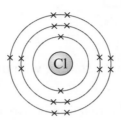

Figure 3

(a)   Describe a method of testing chlorine gas to confirm its identity.
Include in your answer the result you would expect to see if chlorine was present.

[2 marks]

When chlorine is bubbled through potassium iodide solution a reaction occurs.
The equation below shows the reaction.

$$Cl_{2(g)} \ + \ 2KI_{(aq)} \ \rightarrow \ I_{2(aq)} \ + \ 2KCl_{(aq)}$$

(b)   State what type of reaction this is.

[1 mark]

(c)   State the less reactive halogen in this reaction. Explain your answer.

[2 marks]

(d)   Chlorine gas can also react with potassium bromide.
Using your knowledge of Group 7 elements, predict the products of this reaction and their states.
Give an explanation for your answer.

[4 marks]

(e)   None of the elements in Group 0 will react with potassium iodide or potassium bromide.
Using your knowledge of the electronic structure of the Group 0 elements,
explain why no reaction occurs.

[2 marks]

4   Group 1 elements are metals.
They include lithium, sodium and potassium.

(a)   Explain why the Group 1 elements react vigorously with water.

[1 mark]

(b)   The Group 1 elements all react with water at a different rate. Explain why this is.

[3 marks]

(c)   (i)   Name the **two** products formed when potassium reacts with water.

[2 marks]

(ii) Write a balanced symbol equation for the reaction of potassium with water.

[2 marks]

Revision Summary for Topic 6

That wraps up Topic 6 — time to put yourself to the test and find out how much you really know.
- Try these questions and tick off each one when you get it right.
- When you've done all the questions under a heading and are completely happy with it, tick it off.

Group 1 — Alkali Metals (p.127-128) ☑

1) Give two properties of the Group 1 metals.
2) Explain why Group 1 metals are so reactive.
3) Put these alkali metals in order of reactivity, starting with the least reactive:
   potassium, caesium, lithium, sodium.
4) Write a balanced symbol equation for the reaction between potassium (K) and water.
5) What would you observe when reacting lithium with water?

Group 7 — Halogens (p.129-132) ☑

6) How many electrons do halogens have in their outer shells?
7) How many atoms are in each molecule of a halogen?
8) Describe the appearances and physical states of the following halogens
   at room temperature and pressure:
   a) chlorine,
   b) bromine,
   c) iodine.
9) Name the substance that is produced when potassium reacts with chlorine.
10) Why can halogen displacement reactions be described as redox reactions?
11) If chlorine water is added to potassium bromide solution, what colour will the solution turn?
12) Write a balanced symbol equation for the reaction between bromine (Br_2) and sodium (Na).

Group 0 — Noble Gases (p.133) ☑

13) At room temperature, what colour are the Group 0 gases?
14) Why is argon used in filament lamps?
15) Why are balloons filled with helium able to float in the air?
16) Does the boiling point of Group 0 elements increase or decrease going down the group?

Rates of Reaction

Reactions can be <u>fast</u> or <u>slow</u>. The following pages show a few ways you can <u>measure</u> the <u>rate of a reaction</u>.

The **Rate of Reaction** is **How Fast** the **Reaction Happens**

1) The <u>rate of a reaction</u> is how quickly a reaction happens.

2) It can be observed <u>either</u> by measuring how quickly the reactants are used up or how quickly the products are formed.

3) The <u>rate of a reaction</u> can be calculated using the following formula:

It's usually a lot easier to measure products forming.

$$\text{Rate of Reaction} = \frac{\text{amount of reactant used or amount of product formed}}{\text{time}}$$

You Can Do **Experiments** to Follow **Reaction Rates**

There are different ways that the rate of a reaction can be <u>measured</u>. Here's <u>one</u> example, and there are another <u>two</u> on the next page:

Precipitation

1) This method works for any reaction where mixing <u>two see-through solutions</u> produces a <u>precipitate</u>, which <u>clouds</u> the solution.

2) You <u>mix</u> the two reactant solutions and put the flask on a piece of paper that has a <u>mark</u> on it.

3) <u>Observe</u> the mark through the mixture and measure how long it takes for the mark to be <u>obscured</u>. The <u>faster</u> it disappears, the <u>faster</u> the reaction.

You can use this method to investigate how temperature affects the rate of the reaction between sodium thiosulfate and hydrochloric acid. See page 141.

4) The result is <u>subjective</u> — <u>different people</u> might not agree on <u>exactly</u> when the mark 'disappears'.

Make sure you use a method appropriate to your reaction

The method shown on this page only works if there's a <u>really obvious</u> change in the solution. If there's only a <u>small change</u> in colour, it <u>might not be possible</u> to observe and time the change.

Rates of Reaction

Change in Mass (Usually Gas Given Off)

1) You can measure the rate of a reaction that <u>produces a gas</u> using a <u>mass balance</u>.

2) As the gas is released, the <u>lost mass</u> is easily measured on the balance. The <u>quicker</u> the reading on the balance <u>drops</u>, the <u>faster</u> the reaction.

3) You know the reaction has <u>finished</u> when the reading on the balance <u>stops changing</u>.

4) You can use your results to plot a <u>graph</u> of <u>change in mass</u> against <u>time</u>.

5) This method does release the gas produced straight into the room — so if the gas is <u>harmful</u>, you must take <u>safety precautions</u>, e.g. do the experiment in a <u>fume cupboard</u>.

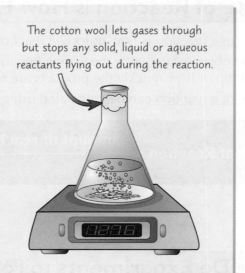

The cotton wool lets gases through but stops any solid, liquid or aqueous reactants flying out during the reaction.

The **Volume** of Gas Given Off

1) This involves the use of a <u>gas syringe</u> to measure the <u>volume</u> of gas given off.

2) The <u>more</u> gas given off during a set <u>time interval</u>, the <u>faster</u> the reaction.

3) You can tell the reaction has <u>finished</u> when <u>no more gas</u> is produced.

4) You can use your results to plot a graph of <u>gas volume</u> against <u>time elapsed</u>.

5) You need to be careful that you're using the <u>right size</u> gas syringe for your experiment though — if the reaction is too <u>vigorous</u>, you can blow the plunger out of the end of the syringe.

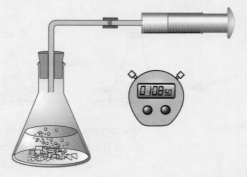

Each of these three methods has pros and cons

PRACTICAL TIP

The mass balance method is only accurate as long as the flask isn't <u>too hot</u>, otherwise the loss in mass that you see might be partly due to <u>evaporation</u> of liquid as well as being due to the loss of gas formed during the reaction. The first method (on the previous page) is <u>subjective</u> so it isn't very accurate, but if you're not producing a gas you can't use either of the other two.

Rate Experiments

You can use the three methods on the previous pages to measure the effects of different <u>factors</u> (<u>surface area</u>, <u>concentration</u> and <u>temperature</u>) on the rate of a reaction. The next few pages look at how.

You can Measure how **Surface Area** Affects **Rate**

Here's how you can carry out an experiment to measure the effect of <u>surface area</u> on <u>rate</u>, using marble chips and hydrochloric acid.

1) Set the apparatus up as shown in the diagram on the right.

2) Measure the <u>volume</u> of gas produced using a <u>gas syringe</u>. Take readings at <u>regular time intervals</u> and record the results in a table.

3) You can plot a <u>graph</u> of your results — <u>time</u> goes on the <u>x-axis</u> and volume goes on the <u>y-axis</u>.

4) <u>Repeat</u> the experiment with <u>exactly the same volume</u> and <u>concentration</u> of acid, and <u>exactly the same mass</u> of marble chips, but with the marble <u>more crunched up</u>.

5) Then <u>repeat</u> with the same mass of <u>powdered chalk</u>.

Marble and chalk are both made of calcium carbonate ($CaCO_3$).

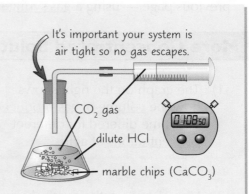

It's important your system is air tight so no gas escapes.

CO_2 gas

dilute HCl

marble chips ($CaCO_3$)

Finer Particles of **Solid** Mean a **Higher Rate**

1) The <u>sooner</u> a reaction finishes, the <u>faster</u> the reaction.

2) The <u>steeper</u> the gradient of the graph, the <u>faster</u> the rate of reaction. When the line becomes flat, <u>no more gas</u> is being produced and the reaction has <u>finished</u>.

3) Using <u>finer particles</u> means that the marble has a <u>larger surface area</u>.

4) <u>Lines 1 to 3</u> on the graph on the right show that the <u>finer</u> the particles are (and the <u>greater</u> the surface area of the solid reactants), the <u>sooner</u> the reaction finishes and so the <u>faster</u> the reaction.

5) <u>Line 4</u> shows the reaction if a <u>greater mass</u> of small marble chips is added. The <u>extra surface area</u> gives a <u>faster reaction</u> and there is also <u>more gas evolved</u> overall.

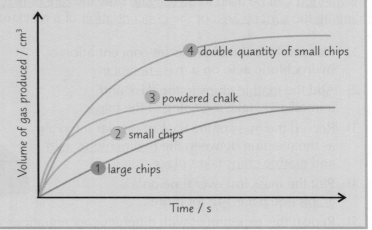

Volume of gas produced / cm³

4 double quantity of small chips

3 powdered chalk

2 small chips

1 large chips

Time / s

MATHS TIP

Increasing a reactant's surface area increases the reaction rate

The graph above shows how to <u>compare</u> rates of reactions when using solid reactants with different surface areas, but if you want to <u>calculate</u> a <u>numerical</u> value for the rate, you need to use a calculation. Take a look at p.142 for how to find the rate of reaction from a graph.

 **PRACTICAL** # Rate Experiments

Another important experiment — this time, how the <u>concentration</u> of a reactant can affect the <u>rate</u>.

Changing the **Concentration** of Acid Affects the **Rate** too

1) The reaction between marble chips and hydrochloric acid is also good for measuring how <u>changing the reactant concentration</u> affects reaction rate.

2) You can measure the <u>rate</u> of this reaction using the method shown on the previous page — using a <u>gas syringe</u> to measure the <u>volume</u> of gas released.

More Concentrated Solutions Mean a Higher Rate

1) The graph on the right shows how the <u>volume of gas produced</u> over time differed for different <u>concentrations</u> of acid.

2) <u>Lines 1 to 3</u> on the graph show that a <u>higher</u> concentration gives a <u>faster reaction</u>, with the reaction <u>finishing</u> sooner.

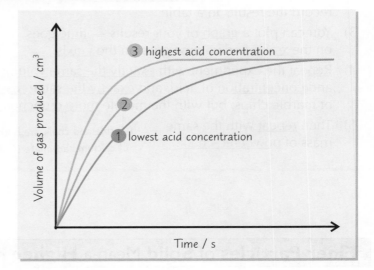

You Can Also Measure the **Change in Mass** During the Reaction

This <u>method</u> can be used to <u>investigate</u> how the <u>rate of reaction</u> is affected by <u>changing</u> the <u>surface area</u> or the <u>concentration</u> of a reactant.

1) Place a flask containing a set concentration of hydrochloric acid on a <u>mass balance</u>.

2) Add the <u>marble chips</u> to the flask and immediately take a reading of the <u>mass</u>.

3) Record the <u>mass</u> of the flask at regular intervals as the reaction between the <u>hydrochloric acid</u> and <u>marble chips</u> takes place.

4) Plot the mass lost over time on a <u>graph</u> (see page 142 for more).

5) Repeat this experiment with different <u>concentrations</u> of hydrochloric acid. Plot the mass lost over time for each concentration on the <u>same</u> graph, to allow <u>comparison</u> of the rates of each reaction.

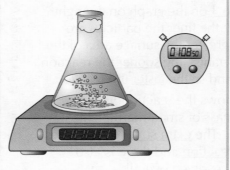

 PRACTICAL TIP ## The rate of the reaction is shown by how steep the slope is...

The <u>steeper</u> the slope, the <u>greater</u> the volume of gas produced in a set time, so the <u>faster</u> the <u>reaction rate</u>. Don't forget that you can also use the method involving a <u>mass balance</u> — then the graph would show the <u>mass lost</u> over time, instead of the <u>volume of gas released</u>.

Rate Experiments

That's right — another page, another <u>reaction rate experiment</u> to learn. This one's a <u>precipitation</u> reaction, which means using the method covered back on page 137. Have a flick back if you need to.

Reaction Rate is Also Affected by Temperature

1) You can see how <u>temperature</u> affects reaction <u>rate</u> by looking at the reaction between sodium thiosulfate and hydrochloric acid.

2) Sodium thiosulfate and hydrochloric acid are both <u>clear</u>, <u>colourless solutions</u>. They react together to form a <u>yellow precipitate</u> of <u>sulfur</u>.

3) You can use the amount of <u>time</u> that it takes for the coloured precipitate to form as a measure of the <u>rate</u> of this reaction.

4) You use a method like the one on page 137 to carry out this experiment.

You can find out how temperature affects the reaction rate on page 145.

- Measure out fixed volumes of <u>sodium thiosulfate</u> and <u>hydrochloric acid</u>, using a measuring cylinder.

- Use a <u>water bath</u> to <u>gently heat</u> both solutions to the desired temperature before you mix them.

- Mix the solutions in a conical flask. Place the flask over a black mark on a piece of paper which can be seen through the solution. Watch the <u>black mark</u> disappear through the <u>cloudy</u>, <u>yellow sulfur</u> and <u>time</u> how long it takes to go.

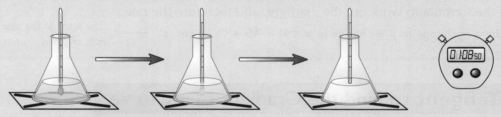

- The reaction can be repeated for solutions at <u>different temperatures</u>.

- The <u>depth</u> and <u>volumes</u> of liquid must be kept the same each time. The <u>concentrations</u> of the solutions must also be kept the same.

- You can use your results to measure what effect <u>changing the temperature</u> has on the <u>rate</u> of the reaction. The <u>shorter</u> the length of time taken for the mark to be obscured, the <u>faster</u> the rate.

Higher Temperatures Mean a Higher Rate

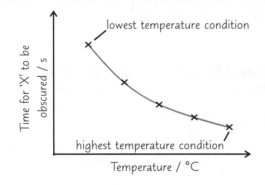

1) You can plot the <u>time taken</u> for the mark to disappear against the <u>temperature</u> of the reacting solutions.

2) If you look at the <u>graph</u>, you can see that the reactions that happened at <u>lower</u> temperatures took <u>longer</u> to obscure the mark, whereas the reactions happening at <u>higher</u> temperatures finished <u>sooner</u>.

3) So <u>increasing</u> the temperature <u>increases the rate</u> of the reaction.

How temperature, concentration and pressure affect the rate of a reaction can be explained using collision theory — see p.145-146.

Hotter mixtures have more energy and so react faster...

With all of these experiments, you need to make sure you're only changing <u>one thing</u> for each repeat. So for this one, you need to make sure only <u>temperature</u> is changed, and not, e.g. the <u>concentration</u> of HCl. That way you'll know that it's definitely the temperature affecting the <u>rate</u>.

Calculating Rates

You can work out rates of reaction using <u>graphs</u> — to do that, you need to know how to measure <u>gradients</u>...

Faster Rates of Reaction are Shown by Steeper Gradients

If you have a graph of <u>amount of product formed</u> (or <u>reactant used up</u>) against <u>time</u>, then the <u>gradient</u> (slope) of the graph will be equal to the rate of the reaction — the <u>steeper</u> the slope, the <u>faster</u> the rate.

The gradient of a <u>straight line</u> is given by the equation:

gradient = change in _y_ ÷ change in _x_

EXAMPLE: **Calculate the rate of the reaction shown on the graph below.**

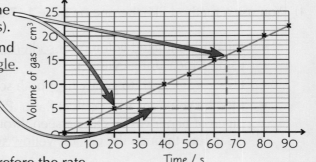

1) Find two <u>points on the line</u> that are <u>easy to read</u> the _x_ and _y_ values of (ones that pass through grid lines).

2) Draw a line straight <u>down</u> from the higher point and straight <u>across</u> from the lower one to make a <u>triangle</u>.

3) The <u>height</u> of your triangle = <u>change in _y_</u>
The <u>base</u> of your triangle = <u>change in _x_</u>

Change in _y_ = 16 − 5 = 11
Change in _x_ = 65 − 20 = 45

4) Use the formula to work out the <u>gradient</u>, and therefore the rate.

Gradient = change in _y_ ÷ change in _x_ = 11 ÷ 45 = 0.24 cm³ s⁻¹ ⎯⎯⎯ The units of the rate are just "units of _y_-axis ÷ units of _x_-axis".

Draw a Tangent to Find the Gradient of a Curve

1) If your graph (or part of it) is a <u>curve</u>, the gradient, and therefore <u>rate</u>, is different at different points along the curve.

2) To find the <u>gradient</u> of the graph at a certain point, you'll have to draw a <u>tangent</u> at that point.

3) A tangent is just a line that <u>touches the curve</u> and has the <u>same gradient</u> as the line at that point.

4) To draw a tangent, place a <u>ruler</u> on the line of best fit at the point you're interested in, so you can see the <u>whole curve</u>. Adjust the ruler so the space between the ruler and the curve is the same on both sides of the point. Draw a line <u>along the ruler</u> to make the <u>tangent</u>.

5) The rate at that point is then just the <u>gradient</u> of the <u>tangent</u>.

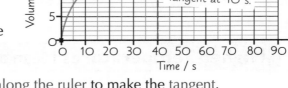

EXAMPLE: **The graph below shows the concentration of product formed, measured at regular intervals, during a chemical reaction. What is the rate of reaction at 3 minutes?**

1) Position a <u>ruler</u> on the graph at the point where you want to know the rate — here it's <u>3 minutes</u>.

2) Adjust the ruler until the <u>space</u> between the ruler and the curve is <u>equal</u> on <u>both sides</u> of the point.

3) Draw a line along the ruler to make the <u>tangent</u>. Extend the line <u>right across</u> the graph.

4) Pick <u>two points</u> on the line that are easy to read. Use them to calculate the <u>gradient</u> of the tangent in order to find the <u>rate</u>:

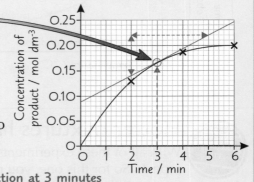

gradient = change in _y_ ÷ change in _x_
= (0.22 − 0.14) ÷ (5.0 − 2.0)
= 0.08 ÷ 3.0 = 0.027

So, the rate of reaction at 3 minutes was 0.027 mol dm⁻³ min⁻¹.

Warm-Up and Exam Questions

Make sure you take some time to do these questions before moving on — they'll help you pull together all of that information you've just learned about rate experiments, so that it really sticks.

Warm-Up Questions

1) What is meant by the rate of a reaction?

2) Reaction A forms more product than Reaction B over 30 seconds. Which reaction, A or B, has a higher rate?

3) What effect does increasing the surface area of a reactant have on the rate of a reaction?

4) What is the equation for calculating the gradient of a straight line on a graph?

Exam Questions

PRACTICAL

1   **Figure 1** shows one method of measuring the rate of a reaction which produces a gas.

(a)   What piece of apparatus necessary for measuring the rate of this reaction is missing from **Figure 1**?

[1 mark]

(b)   Name the piece of apparatus in **Figure 1** labelled **X**.

[1 mark]

(c)   Describe **one** other method of measuring the rate of a reaction which produces a gas.

[2 marks]

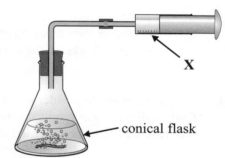

Figure 1

PRACTICAL

2   Set volumes of sodium thiosulfate and hydrochloric acid were reacted at different temperatures. The time taken for a black cross to be obscured by the sulfur precipitate was measured at each temperature. The results are shown in **Figure 2**.

(a)   Give **two** variables that should be kept constant in this experiment.

[2 marks]

(b)   Plot the results on a graph (with time on the *x*-axis) and draw a line of best fit.

[4 marks]

(c)   Describe the relationship illustrated by your graph.

[1 mark]

Temperature / °C	Time / s
55	6
36	11
24	17
16	27
9	40
5	51

Figure 2

(d)   Describe how the results would change if the experiment was repeated with a **lower** concentration of sodium thiosulfate.

[1 mark]

(e)   Suggest how you could assess if the results of the experiment are repeatable.

[2 marks]

Exam Questions

3   A teacher demonstrated an experiment to investigate the effect of concentration on the
     rate of a reaction. The teacher added 0.5 mol dm^{-3} hydrochloric acid (HCl) to 50 g
     of marble chips and measured the volume of gas produced at regular time intervals.
     The teacher then repeated the experiment using 1 mol dm^{-3} HCl and the same mass
     of marble chips of the same size. The results are shown in **Figure 3**.

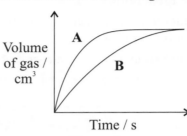

Figure 3

(a)   Identify which curve on **Figure 3**, **A** or **B**, shows the result of the experiment using 1 mol dm^{-3} HCl.

[1 mark]

(b)   The teacher made sure that the temperature of the reactants was the same in each repeat.
      Explain why the temperature needed to be controlled.

[1 mark]

(c)   The teacher then repeated experiment **A**, but with 50 g of powdered chalk instead of marble chips.
      On **Figure 3**, sketch the curve you would expect to see from this experiment. Label it **C**.

[1 mark]

4   Calcium carbonate powder was added to a conical flask containing dilute hydrochloric acid.
     Carbon dioxide was produced and collected in a gas syringe. The volume of gas released
     was recorded at 10 second intervals in **Figure 4**:

Time / s	0	10	20	30	40	50	60
Volume of CO_2 / cm^3	0	24	32	36	38	39	40

Figure 4

(a)   Calculate the rate of reaction between 0 and 60 seconds. Give your answer in cm^3 s^{-1}.

[1 mark]

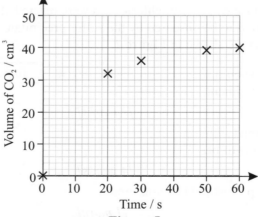

Figure 5

(b)   Two of the results listed in **Figure 4** are missing from **Figure 5**.
      Plot these missing points and draw a line of best fit on **Figure 5**.

[2 marks]

(c)   Use your graph to find the rate of the reaction 25 seconds after starting the experiment.
      Give your answer in cm^3 s^{-1}.

[4 marks]

Collision Theory

The rate of a reaction depends on: <u>temperature</u>, <u>concentration</u> (or <u>pressure</u> for gases) and the <u>size of the particles</u> (for solids). This is because these factors affect how particles in a reaction <u>collide</u> with each other.

Particles **Must Collide** with **Enough Energy** in Order to React

<u>Reaction rates</u> are explained by <u>collision theory</u>. It's simple really.

> <u>The rate of a chemical reaction</u> depends on:
> - The <u>collision frequency</u> of reacting particles (<u>how often they collide</u>). The <u>more</u> successful collisions there are, the <u>faster</u> the reaction is.
> - The <u>energy transferred</u> during a collision. The minimum energy that particles need to react when they collide is called the <u>activation energy</u>. Particles need to collide with <u>at least the activation energy</u> for the collision to be <u>successful</u>.

A successful collision is a collision that ends in the particles reacting to form products.

The **More Collisions**, the **Higher** the Rate of Reaction

1) Reactions happen if <u>particles collide</u> with enough <u>energy</u> to react.
2) So, if you <u>increase</u> the <u>number</u> of collisions or the <u>energy</u> with which the particles collide, the reaction happens <u>more quickly</u> (i.e. the rate increases).
3) <u>Temperature</u>, <u>concentration (or pressure)</u> and <u>surface area</u> all affect the <u>rate</u> of a reaction. First up is the effect of <u>temperature</u> on rate...

Increasing the **Temperature** Increases **Rate**

1) When the <u>temperature is increased</u> the particles <u>move faster</u>. If they move faster, they're going to have <u>more frequent collisions</u>.
2) Higher temperatures also increase the <u>energy</u> of the collisions, since the particles are moving <u>faster</u>. Reactions <u>only happen</u> if the particles collide with <u>enough energy</u>.
3) This means that at <u>higher</u> temperatures there will be more <u>successful collisions</u> (more particles will <u>collide</u> with <u>enough energy</u> to react). So <u>increasing</u> the temperature <u>increases</u> the rate of reaction.

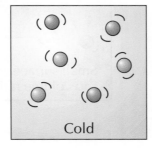

Cold

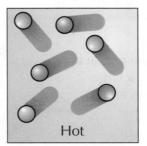

Hot

Just colliding isn't enough — there needs to be enough energy too...

<u>Collision theory</u> is the key to understanding how lots of factors can affect the <u>reaction rate</u>. Just think of how changing a particular factor might affect the <u>particles</u> in a reaction mixture and how they <u>bump</u> into each other. Then you can figure out whether the rate of the reaction is likely to be <u>increased</u> or <u>decreased</u>.

Collision Theory

Now for another <u>two factors</u> that affect the rate of a reaction — <u>concentration</u> (or <u>pressure</u>) and <u>surface area</u>.

Increasing **Concentration** (or **Pressure**) Increases **Rate**

1) If a <u>solution</u> is made more <u>concentrated</u> it means there are more particles of <u>reactant</u> in the same volume. This makes collisions <u>more likely</u>, so the reaction rate <u>increases</u>.

2) In a <u>gas</u>, increasing the <u>pressure</u> means that the particles are <u>more crowded</u>. This means that the frequency of <u>collisions</u> between particles will <u>increase</u> — so the rate of reaction will also <u>increase</u>.

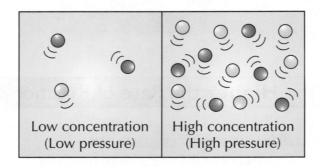

Low concentration
(Low pressure)

High concentration
(High pressure)

Smaller Solid Particles (or **More Surface Area**) Means a Higher **Rate**

1) If one reactant is a <u>solid</u>, breaking it into <u>smaller</u> pieces will <u>increase its surface area to volume ratio</u> (i.e. more of the solid will be exposed, compared to its overall volume).

2) The particles around it will have <u>more area to work on</u>, so the frequency of collisions will <u>increase</u>.

3) This means that the rate of reaction is faster for solids with a larger <u>surface area to volume</u> ratio.

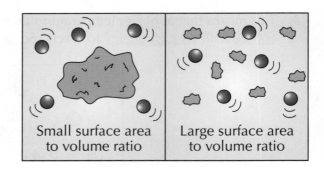

Small surface area
to volume ratio

Large surface area
to volume ratio

It's easier to learn stuff when you know the reasons for it

Once you've learnt everything off these two pages, the rates of reaction pages should start making a lot more sense to you. The concept's fairly simple — the more often particles bump into each other, and the harder they hit when they do, the faster the reaction happens.

Topic 7 — Rates of Reaction and Energy Changes

Catalysts

Catalysts are very important for commercial reasons — they increase reaction rate and reduce energy costs in industrial reactions. They're also important in living things — read on to find out more...

A **Catalyst Increases** the **Rate** of a Reaction

1) A catalyst is a substance which increases the rate of a reaction, without being chemically changed or used up in the reaction.

2) Using a catalyst won't change the products of the reaction — so the reaction equation will stay the same.

3) Because it isn't used up, you only need a tiny bit to catalyse large amounts of reactants.

4) Catalysts tend to be very fussy about which reactions they catalyse though — you can't just stick any old catalyst in a reaction and expect it to work.

5) Catalysts work by decreasing the activation energy (see page 145) needed for a reaction to occur.

6) They do this by providing an alternative reaction pathway that has a lower activation energy.

7) As a result, more of the particles have at least the minimum amount of energy needed for a reaction to occur when the particles collide.

8) You can see this if you look at a reaction profile.

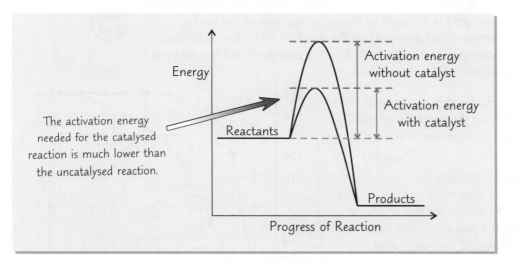

The activation energy needed for the catalysed reaction is much lower than the uncatalysed reaction.

Reaction profiles show the energy levels of the reactants and the products in a reaction. There are more reaction profiles on p.149-150.

Enzymes Control **Cell Reactions**

1) Enzymes are biological catalysts.

2) This means that they catalyse (speed up) the chemical reactions in living cells.

3) Reactions catalysed by enzymes include respiration, photosynthesis and protein synthesis.

- Enzymes from yeast cells are used in the fermentation process which is used to make alcoholic drinks.
- They catalyse the reaction that converts sugars (such as glucose) into ethanol and carbon dioxide.

There is more on fermentation and the production of ethanol on page 182-183.

Enzymes make sure reactions happen fast enough for us to stay alive

Some reactions take a very long time to happen by themselves, which isn't good for industrial reactions. Catalysts help to produce an acceptable amount of product in an acceptable length of time.

Warm-Up and Exam Questions

It's easy to think that you've understood something when you've just read through it. These questions should test whether you really understand the previous few pages, and get you ready for the next bit.

Warm-Up Questions

1) According to collision theory, what must happen in order for two particles to react?
2) Explain why breaking a reactant into smaller pieces can affect the rate of a reaction.
3) True or False? A catalyst is unchanged chemically during a reaction.
4) Explain why enzymes are considered biological catalysts.

Exam Questions

1   A student is investigating how the rate of the reaction between calcium carbonate and excess hydrochloric acid is affected by the concentration of the acid. She measured the volume of gas given off by the reaction when two different concentrations of hydrochloric acid were used — 0.2 mol dm^{-3} and 0.4 mol dm^{-3}. **Figure 1** shows the results of the experiment.

(a)   Suggest two variables that the student would have to keep the same for each run to make the experiment a fair test.

[2 marks]

(b)   Using **Figure 1**, calculate the difference in the volume of gas produced at 30 seconds for the reaction using 0.4 mol dm^{-3} acid and the reaction using 0.2 mol dm^{-3} acid.

[1 mark]

(c)   Using your knowledge of collision theory, explain the difference between the two curves shown in **Figure 1**.

[3 marks]

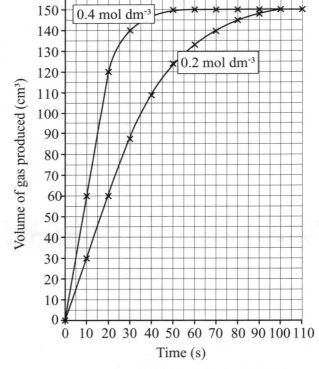

Figure 1

2*   Hydrogen gas and ethene gas react to form ethane. Nickel can be used as a catalyst for this reaction.

Using your knowledge of collision theory, explain how the rate of this reaction can be increased.

[6 marks]

Endothermic and Exothermic Reactions

Endothermic and exothermic reactions are all about taking in and giving out energy to the surroundings.

Reactions are Exothermic or Endothermic

An EXOTHERMIC reaction is one which gives out energy to the surroundings, usually in the form of heat and usually shown by a rise in temperature of the surroundings.

Combustion reactions (where something burns in oxygen — see page 156) are always exothermic.

An ENDOTHERMIC reaction is one which takes in energy from the surroundings, usually in the form of heat and usually shown by a fall in temperature of the surroundings.

Reaction Profiles Show if a Reaction's Exo- or Endothermic

Reaction profiles show the energy levels of the reactants and the products in a reaction. You can use them to work out if energy is released (exothermic) or taken in (endothermic).

1) This shows an exothermic reaction — the products are at a lower energy than the reactants.

2) The difference in height represents the energy given out in the reaction.

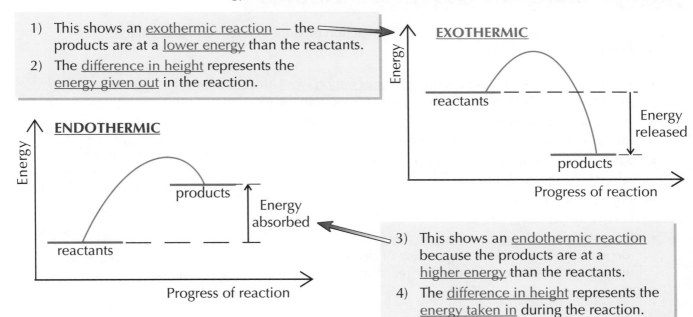

3) This shows an endothermic reaction because the products are at a higher energy than the reactants.

4) The difference in height represents the energy taken in during the reaction.

A reaction profile shows the energy levels during a reaction

Remember, "exo-" = exit, so an exothermic reaction is one that gives out energy — and endothermic just means the opposite. The diagrams above might seem a bit confusing — remember, it's the energy in the chemicals themselves, not in their surroundings, which is being measured. To help you remember them, why not draw them out and label them for yourself.

Endothermic and Exothermic Reactions

Sometimes it's not enough to just know if a reaction is <u>endothermic</u> or <u>exothermic</u>. You may also need to know <u>how much</u> energy is absorbed or released — you can do experiments to find this out.

Activation Energy is the Energy Needed to Start a Reaction

1) The <u>activation energy</u> is the <u>minimum</u> amount of energy needed for <u>bonds to break</u> (see page 152) and a reaction to start.

2) On a reaction profile, it's the energy difference between the <u>reactants</u> and the <u>highest point</u> on the curve.

3) It's a bit like having to <u>climb up</u> one side of a hill before you can ski/snowboard/sledge/fall down the <u>other side</u>.

4) If the <u>energy</u> input is <u>less than</u> the activation energy there <u>won't</u> be enough energy to <u>start</u> the reaction — so nothing will happen.

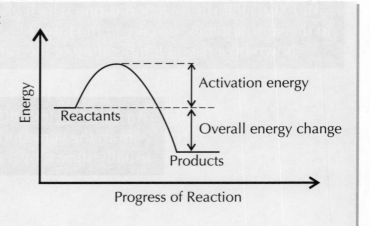

Temperature Changes can be Measured

You can follow the <u>change in temperature</u> of a reaction mixture as a reaction takes place. You can do this in the following way:

- Put a <u>polystyrene cup</u> into a large <u>beaker of cotton wool</u> (the cotton wool gives <u>insulation</u> to help limit energy transfer to or from the reaction mixture).
- Add a known volume of your <u>first reagent</u> to the cup.
- Measure the <u>initial temperature</u> of the solution.
- Add a measured mass/volume of your <u>second reagent</u> and <u>stir</u> the reaction mixture.
- Put a <u>lid</u> on the cup to reduce any energy lost by <u>evaporation</u>.
- Record the <u>maximum</u> or <u>minimum temperature</u> (depending on whether it's increasing or decreasing) that the mixture reaches during the reaction.
- Calculate the <u>temperature change</u>.

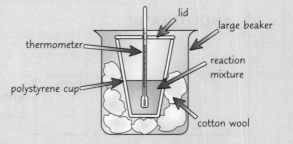

You can also use this method to see the effect that different variables have on the amount of energy transferred, e.g. the mass or concentration of the reactants.

Activation energy — the energy needed to get a reaction going

It's really important that the reaction mixture is <u>well insulated</u> in the method shown above. Without insulation, energy might <u>escape</u> or be transferred <u>to</u> the reaction mixture. This will affect what temperature change the thermometer records — insulation ensures that just the temperature change in the reaction <u>itself</u> is measured.

Endothermic and Exothermic Reactions

For certain types of reaction you can sometimes predict whether energy will be released or taken in. This page covers a few different types of reaction you should know about.

The **Change** in **Temperature** Depends on the **Reagents** Used

You can measure the temperature change for different types of reaction. Whether there's an increase or decrease in temperature depends on which reagents take part in the reaction.

Dissolving Salts in Water

1) You can measure the temperature change when dissolving salts in water by adding the salt to a polystyrene cup of water and measuring the change in temperature when the salt has dissolved.
2) Dissolving ammonium chloride decreases the temperature of the reaction mixture — it's endothermic.
3) Dissolving calcium chloride causes the temperature of the solution to rise — it's exothermic.

Neutralisation Reactions

1) In a neutralisation reaction (see page 73), an acid and a base react to form a salt and water. Most neutralisation reactions are exothermic, e.g. $HCl + NaOH \rightarrow NaCl + H_2O$
2) However, the neutralisation reaction between ethanoic acid and sodium carbonate is endothermic.

Displacement Reactions

1) In a displacement reaction (see page 92), a more reactive element displaces a less reactive element in a compound. These types of reactions are accompanied by a release of energy — they're exothermic.
2) Zinc powder and copper sulfate react in a displacement reaction forming zinc sulfate and copper.

Precipitation Reactions

1) Precipitates are insoluble solids which can sometimes form when two solutions are mixed together.
2) Precipitation reactions are exothermic. For example, the reaction between lead(II) nitrate solution and potassium iodide forming a lead iodide precipitate would result in an increase in the temperature of the surroundings.

You need to know about each type of reaction here...

Certain types of reaction, e.g. precipitation or displacement reactions, are always exothermic. For other types, e.g. dissolving salts, you need to be a bit more careful as it depends on the reagents used.

Bond Energies

Energy transfer in chemical reactions is all to do with <u>making and breaking bonds</u>.

There's more on energy transfer on page 149.

Energy Must Always be **Supplied** to **Break Bonds**

1) During a chemical reaction, <u>old bonds are broken</u> and <u>new bonds are formed</u>.

2) Energy must be <u>supplied</u> to break <u>existing bonds</u> — so bond breaking is an <u>endothermic</u> process.

3) Energy is <u>released</u> when new bonds are <u>formed</u> — so bond formation is an <u>exothermic</u> process.

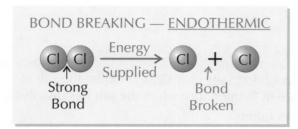

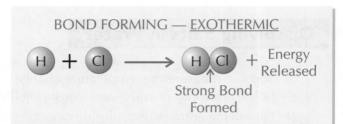

4) In <u>endothermic</u> reactions, the energy <u>used</u> to break bonds is <u>greater</u> than the energy <u>released</u> by forming them.

5) In <u>exothermic</u> reactions, the energy <u>released</u> by forming bonds is <u>greater</u> than the energy used to <u>break</u> 'em.

Bond Energy Calculations — Need to be Practised

1) <u>Every</u> chemical bond has a particular <u>bond energy</u> associated with it. This <u>bond energy</u> varies slightly depending on the <u>compound</u> the bond occurs in.

2) You can use these <u>known bond energies</u> to calculate the <u>overall energy change</u> for a reaction.

> **Overall Energy Change = Energy required to break bonds − Energy released by forming bonds**

3) A <u>positive</u> energy change means an <u>endothermic</u> reaction and a <u>negative</u> energy change means an <u>exothermic</u> reaction.

4) You need to <u>practise</u> a few of these, but the basic idea is really very simple...

Using the bond energy values below, calculate the energy change for the following reaction, where hydrogen and chlorine react to produce hydrogen chloride:

$$H\!-\!H + Cl\!-\!Cl \rightarrow 2H\!-\!Cl$$

H—H: 436 kJ mol⁻¹   Cl—Cl: 242 kJ mol⁻¹   H—Cl: 431 kJ mol⁻¹

1) Work out the energy required to break the <u>original bonds</u> in the reactants.

$(1 \times$ H—H$) + (1 \times$ Cl—Cl$) = 436 + 242$
$= 678$ kJ mol⁻¹

2) Work out the energy released by forming the <u>new bonds</u> in the products.

$(2 \times$ H—Cl$) = 2 \times 431$
$= 862$ kJ mol⁻¹

3) Work out the overall change.

In this reaction, the energy released by forming bonds is greater than the energy used to break them so the reaction is exothermic.

overall energy change = energy required to break bonds − energy released by forming bonds
$= 678 - 862 = -184$ kJ mol⁻¹

It's useful to draw out the molecules in full for these calculations...

... then you can count all the different types of bonds more easily. This might look hard now, but with a bit of practice you'll find it much easier, and it'll win you easy marks if you understand all the theory behind it.

Warm-Up and Exam Questions

Funny diagrams, a whole bunch of reactions, bond energy calculations — there's a lot to get your head around on the last few pages. Here are some questions so that you can check how you're getting on.

Warm-Up Questions

1) What is an exothermic reaction?
2) What is an endothermic reaction?
3) What is meant by the activation energy of a reaction?
4) Lead(II) nitrate reacts with potassium iodide to form a lead iodide precipitate. State the temperature change that this reaction results in.
5) Is energy released when bonds are formed or when bonds are broken?

Exam Questions

1   The diagrams in **Figure 1** represent the energy changes in four different chemical reactions.

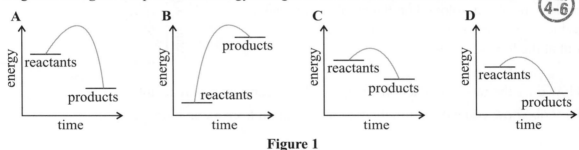

Figure 1

Write the letter of **one** diagram, **A**, **B**, **C** or **D**, which illustrates an endothermic reaction.

[1 mark]

2   A student places two beakers of ethanoic acid and dilute potassium hydroxide into a water bath until they are both 25 °C. He adds the ethanoic acid and then the potassium hydroxide to a polystyrene cup. After 1 minute the temperature of the mixture is 28.5 °C.

(a)   Is this reaction endothermic or exothermic? Explain your answer.

[2 marks]

(b)   The student put a lid on the polystyrene cup during the experiment. Suggest why this was done.

[1 mark]

3   When methane burns in air it produces carbon dioxide and water, as shown in **Figure 2**.
The bond energies for each bond in the molecules involved are shown in **Figure 3**.

$$H-\overset{\displaystyle H}{\underset{\displaystyle H}{C}}-H \; + \; 2\,O=O \; \rightarrow \; O=C=O \; + \; 2\,H-O-H$$

Figure 2

	Bond energies / kJ mol^{-1}
C – H	414
O = O	494
C = O	800
O – H	459

Figure 3

(a)   Which **two** types of bond are broken during the reaction shown in **Figure 2**?

[1 mark]

(b)   Calculate the overall energy change for the reaction shown in **Figure 2**.

[4 marks]

Revision Summary for Topic 7

That's one more topic down. Make sure you're happy before moving on, by giving these questions a go.
- Try these questions and <u>tick off each one</u> when you <u>get it right</u>.
- When you've done <u>all the questions</u> under a heading and are <u>completely happy</u> with it, tick it off.

Rates of Reaction (p.137-142) ☑

1) State the formula for calculating the rate of reaction. ☑

2) A student carries out a reaction which produces carbon dioxide gas. He collects the carbon dioxide in a gas syringe. How will he know when the reaction has finished? ☑

3) Draw a diagram of equipment you could use to measure the rate of reaction between hydrochloric acid and marble chips. ☑

4) Describe how you could investigate how the surface area of calcium carbonate affects the rate of reaction between calcium carbonate and hydrochloric acid. ☑

5) Excess hydrochloric acid is added to 25 g of marble chips. The carbon dioxide produced is captured in a gas syringe, and its volume is recorded over time. The experiment is repeated three times, at three different temperatures, and the results are plotted on the graph on the right. Which experiment, A, B or C, was carried out at the lowest temperature?

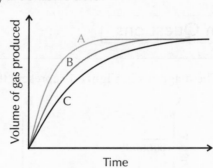

6) How does the rate of a reaction change with concentration of reactants? ☑

7) Describe how you would find the rate of a reaction from a curve on a graph. ☑

Collision Theory and Catalysts (p.145-147) ☐

8) What is the term for the minimum energy needed in a collision between reacting particles in order for a reaction to occur? ☑

9) In a gaseous reaction, why would a decrease in pressure result in a slower rate of reaction? ☑

10) What effect does a catalyst have on the activation energy needed for a reaction to take place? ☑

11) Explain why only a small amount of catalyst is needed for a reaction, even when starting with a large quantity of reactants. ☑

12) Give two examples of reactions catalysed by enzymes. ☑

Energy Changes in Chemical Reactions (p.149-152) ☐

13) What change in temperature would you expect to observe in an exothermic reaction? ☑

14) Describe how you could measure the temperature changes in a neutralisation reaction. ☑

15) Describe the temperature change that would take place in a displacement reaction. ☑

16) Is energy required for the breaking of bonds or the forming of bonds? ☑

17) What is the equation for calculating the overall energy change for a reaction? ☑

Fractional Distillation

Fossil fuels like coal, oil and gas are called non-renewable fuels — they take so long to make that they're being used up much faster than they're being formed. They're finite resources — one day they'll run out.

Crude Oil is Separated into Different Hydrocarbon Fractions

1) Crude oil is our main source of hydrocarbons and is used as a raw material (sometimes called a feedstock) to create lots of useful substances used in the petrochemical industry.

2) It's formed underground, over millions of years (at high temperatures and pressures), from the buried remains of plants and animals. It's a non-renewable (finite) resource, so one day it will run out.

3) Crude oil is a complex mixture of lots of different hydrocarbons — compounds which contain just carbon and hydrogen. The hydrocarbons found in crude oil have their carbon atoms arranged in either chains or rings and are mostly alkanes (hydrocarbons with the general formula C_nH_{2n+2}).

4) Crude oil can be separated out into fractions — simpler, more useful mixtures containing groups of hydrocarbons of similar lengths (i.e. they have similar numbers of carbon and hydrogen atoms). The fractions from crude oil, e.g. petrol, kerosene and diesel, are examples of non-renewable fossil fuels. (Methane, the main component of natural gas, is another non-renewable fossil fuel.)

5) The different fractions in crude oil are separated by fractional distillation. The oil is heated until most of it has turned into gas. The gases enter a fractionating column (and the liquid bit, bitumen, is drained off at the bottom).

> Natural gas is a mixture of gases which forms underground in a similar way to crude oil.

6) In the column there's a temperature gradient (i.e. it's hot at the bottom and gets cooler as you go up).

7) The longer hydrocarbons have higher boiling points. They turn back into liquids and drain out of the column early on, when they're near the bottom. The shorter hydrocarbons have lower boiling points. They turn to liquid and drain out much later on, near to the top of the column where it's cooler.

8) You end up with the crude oil mixture separated out into different fractions. Each fraction contains a mixture of hydrocarbons, mostly alkanes (see page 175) with similar boiling points.

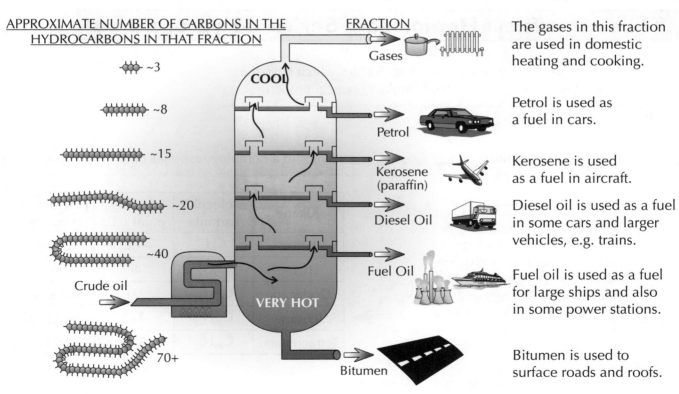

APPROXIMATE NUMBER OF CARBONS IN THE HYDROCARBONS IN THAT FRACTION

FRACTION

~3

~8

~15

~20

~40

Crude oil

70+

COOL

VERY HOT

Gases — The gases in this fraction are used in domestic heating and cooking.

Petrol — Petrol is used as a fuel in cars.

Kerosene (paraffin) — Kerosene is used as a fuel in aircraft.

Diesel Oil — Diesel oil is used as a fuel in some cars and larger vehicles, e.g. trains.

Fuel Oil — Fuel oil is used as a fuel for large ships and also in some power stations.

Bitumen — Bitumen is used to surface roads and roofs.

Each fraction has molecules of similar lengths and similar boiling points

Each fraction is used in a slightly different way — make sure you remember the different uses for each one.

Hydrocarbons

Time to look at hydrocarbons in more detail. First on the agenda — why hydrocarbons make good fuels.

Fuels Release Energy in Combustion Reactions

1) As you saw on the previous page, many hydrocarbons are used as fuels.

2) This is because the combustion reactions that happen when you burn them in oxygen give out lots of energy — the reactions are very exothermic (see page 149).

3) When you burn hydrocarbons in plenty of oxygen, the only products are carbon dioxide and water — this is called complete combustion.

Hydrocarbon + oxygen → carbon dioxide + water

E.g. C_3H_8 + $5O_2$ → $3CO_2$ + $4H_2O$

4) Incomplete combustion occurs when a hydrocarbon burns in a limited supply of oxygen (see page 160).

There are Different Homologous Series of Hydrocarbons

1) A homologous series is a family of molecules which have the same general formula and share similar chemical properties.

2) The molecular formulas of neighbouring compounds in a homologous series differ by a CH_2 unit.

3) The physical properties of compounds in a homologous series vary between the different molecules. For example, the bigger a molecule is, the higher the boiling point will be (see next page).

Alkane	Molecular formula	Boiling point (°C)	Fraction in crude oil
Methane	CH_4	−162	Gases
Ethane	C_2H_6	−89	Gases
Dodecane	$C_{12}H_{26}$	216	Kerosene
Icosane	$C_{20}H_{42}$	343	Diesel Oil
Tetracontane	$C_{40}H_{82}$	524	Fuel Oil

4) Alkanes and alkenes (see page 175) are two different homologous series of hydrocarbons.

Hydrocarbons

The <u>physical properties</u> of crude oil fractions all depend on how <u>big</u> the hydrocarbons in that fraction are.

Intermolecular Forces are Stronger Between Bigger Molecules

1) The <u>size</u> of a hydrocarbon determines which <u>fraction</u> of crude oil it will separate into (see page 155).
2) Each fraction contains hydrocarbons (mostly <u>alkanes</u>) with <u>similar</u> numbers of <u>carbon</u> atoms, so all of the molecules in a fraction will have <u>similar properties</u> and behave in similar ways.
3) The <u>physical properties</u> are determined by the <u>intermolecular forces</u> that hold the chains together.

Boiling Point

- The <u>intermolecular forces</u> of attraction break a lot more <u>easily</u> in <u>small</u> molecules than they do in bigger molecules. That's because the forces are much <u>stronger</u> between big molecules than they are between small molecules.
- It makes sense if you think about it — even if a big molecule can overcome the forces attracting it to another molecule at a <u>few points</u> along its length, it's still got lots of <u>other</u> places where the force is still strong enough to hold it in place.
- That's why <u>big</u> molecules have <u>higher boiling points</u> than small molecules do.

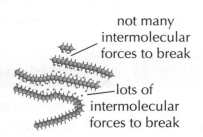

not many intermolecular forces to break

lots of intermolecular forces to break

Ease of Ignition

- <u>Shorter</u> hydrocarbons are <u>easy to ignite</u> because they have lower boiling points, so tend to be gases at room temperature.
- These gas molecules mix with <u>oxygen</u> in the air to produce a gas mixture which bursts into flames if it comes into contact with a <u>spark</u>.
- <u>Longer</u> hydrocarbons are usually <u>liquids</u> at room temperature. They have higher boiling points and are much <u>harder</u> to ignite.

Viscosity

- <u>Viscosity</u> measures how easily a substance <u>flows</u>.
- The <u>stronger</u> the force is between hydrocarbon molecules, the <u>harder</u> it is for the liquid to <u>flow</u>.
- Fractions containing <u>longer</u> hydrocarbons have a <u>higher viscosity</u> — they're <u>thick</u> like treacle.
- Fractions made up of <u>shorter</u> hydrocarbons have a <u>lower viscosity</u> and are much <u>runnier</u>.

The size of a hydrocarbon determines its properties

<u>Intermolecular forces</u> are <u>stronger</u> between <u>longer chain</u> hydrocarbons than shorter chain ones. You can remember the effects of this with the <u>three H's</u> — <u>longer</u> chain hydrocarbons have **h**igher <u>boiling points</u> and **h**igher <u>viscosity</u> and are **h**arder to <u>ignite</u> than <u>shorter</u> chain hydrocarbons.

Cracking

Crude oil fractions from fractional distillation are split into <u>smaller molecules</u> — this is called <u>cracking</u>. It's dead important — otherwise we might not have enough fuel for cars and planes and things.

Cracking is **Splitting Up** Long-Chain Hydrocarbons

1) <u>Cracking</u> turns long saturated (alkane) molecules into <u>smaller unsaturated</u> (<u>alkene</u>) and <u>alkane</u> molecules (which are much more <u>useful</u>).

2) It's a form of <u>thermal decomposition</u>, which is when one substance <u>breaks down</u> into at least two new ones when you <u>heat it</u>. This means breaking <u>strong covalent bonds</u>, so you need <u>lots of energy</u>. A <u>catalyst</u> is often added to speed things up.

3) A lot of the longer molecules produced from <u>fractional distillation</u> are <u>cracked</u> into smaller ones because there's <u>more demand</u> for products like <u>petrol</u> and <u>diesel</u> than for bitumen and fuel oil.

4) Cracking also produces lots of <u>alkene</u> molecules, which can be used to make <u>polymers</u> (mostly plastics).

Cracking Involves **Heat, Moderate Pressures** and a **Catalyst**

1) <u>Vaporised hydrocarbons</u> are passed over <u>powdered catalyst</u> at about <u>400 °C–700 °C</u> and <u>70 atm</u>.

2) <u>Aluminium oxide</u> is the <u>catalyst</u> used. The <u>long-chain</u> molecules <u>split apart</u> or "crack" on the <u>surface</u> of the bits of catalyst.

You don't need to remember the conditions used for cracking.

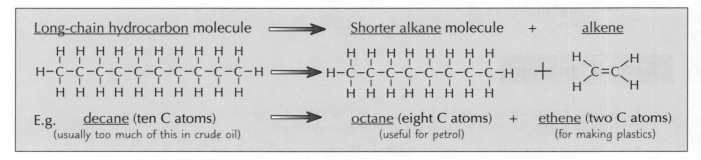

3) You can use the apparatus shown below to crack <u>alkanes</u> in the lab. During this reaction, the alkane is heated until it is <u>vaporised</u>. It then breaks down when it comes into contact with the catalyst, producing a mixture of <u>short-chain alkanes</u> and <u>alkenes</u>.

vaporised alkane

a mixture of shorter chain alkanes and alkenes

catalyst

Cracking Helps Match **Supply** and **Demand**

The examiner might give you a <u>table</u> like the one below to show the <u>supply</u> and <u>demand</u> for various fractions obtained from crude oil. You could be asked which fraction is <u>more likely to be cracked</u> to provide us with petrol and diesel oil (demand for petrol and diesel oil is greater than the amount in crude oil).

Fraction	Approx % in crude oil	Approx % demand
Gases	2	4
Petrol	16	27
Kerosene	13	8
Diesel Oil	19	23
Fuel Oil and Bitumen	50	38

OK, you could use the <u>kerosene fraction</u> to supply the extra <u>petrol</u> and the <u>fuel oil and bitumen fraction</u> to supply the extra <u>diesel oil</u>.

Or you could crack the <u>fuel oil and bitumen</u> to supply <u>both</u> the extra <u>petrol</u> and the extra <u>diesel oil</u>. This might be cleverer, as there's a lot more fuel oil/bitumen than kerosene.

Warm-Up and Exam Questions

Hydrocarbons contain only hydrogen and carbon atoms. This page contains only Warm-Up and Exam Questions. Time to get thinking.

Warm-Up Questions

1) What is each of the following used for?
   a) kerosene   b) diesel oil   c) bitumen

2) What two products are made by the complete combustion of a hydrocarbon?

3) Give an example of a homologous series found in crude oil.

4) Describe the relationship between the length of the molecules in a hydrocarbon and the ease with which it ignites.

Exam Question

1   Crude oil can be separated into a number of different compounds in a fractional distillation column. **Figure 1** shows a fractional distillation column.

FRACTIONS

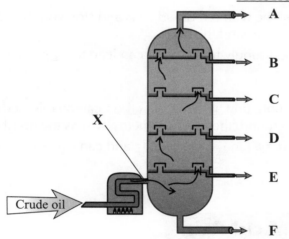

Figure 1

(a)   Which letter, **A-F**, represents the fraction with the shortest hydrocarbon molecules?

[1 mark]

(b)   Which letter, **A-F**, represents the fraction with the highest boiling point?

[1 mark]

(c)   Gaseous crude oil enters near the bottom of the fractional distillation column (point **X** in **Figure 1**). Explain why different fractions exit the column at different points and how this relates to their structure.

[3 marks]

Cracking is a process used to break longer chain molecules in crude oil down to shorter ones.

(d)   Why is cracking an important process in the petrochemical industry?

[1 mark]

(e)   Octane (C_8H_{18}) can be cracked to form two products. Complete the equation below for this reaction:

$$C_8H_{18} \rightarrow \text{.............} + 2C_3H_6$$

[1 mark]

Pollutants

You get lots of nasties like carbon monoxide, oxides of nitrogen and sulfur dioxide when you burn fossil fuels.

Incomplete Combustion Produces Carbon Monoxide and Soot

1) Complete combustion reactions of hydrocarbons produce only carbon dioxide and water (see page 156).

2) If there's not enough oxygen around for complete combustion, you get incomplete combustion. This can happen in some appliances, e.g. boilers, that use carbon compounds as fuels.

3) The products of incomplete combustion contain less oxygen than carbon dioxide.

4) As well as carbon dioxide and water, incomplete combustion produces carbon monoxide (CO), a toxic gas, and carbon in the form of soot.

- Carbon monoxide can combine with red blood cells and stop your blood from doing its proper job of carrying oxygen around the body.
- A lack of oxygen in the blood supply to the brain can lead to fainting, a coma or even death.

- During incomplete combustion, tiny particles of carbon can be released into the atmosphere. When they fall back to the ground, they deposit themselves as the horrible black dust we call soot.
- Soot makes buildings look dirty, reduces air quality and can cause or worsen respiratory problems.

Sulfur Dioxide Causes Acid Rain

1) When fossil fuels are burned, they release mostly CO_2 (a big cause of global warming, see page 166).

2) But they also release other harmful gases — especially sulfur dioxide and various nitrogen oxides.

3) The sulfur dioxide (SO_2) comes from sulfur impurities in the fossil fuels.

4) When sulfur dioxide mixes with clouds, it forms dilute sulfuric acid. This then falls as acid rain.

5) Acid rain causes lakes to become acidic and many plants and animals die as a result.

6) Acid rain kills trees, damages limestone buildings and stone statues, and can also make metal corrode.

Pollutants

Oxides of Nitrogen Are Also Pollutants

1) Nitrogen oxides are created from a reaction between the nitrogen and oxygen in the air, caused by the energy released by combustion reactions, for example, in the internal combustion engines of cars.

2) Nitrogen oxides are harmful pollutants — they can contribute to acid rain and, at ground level, can cause photochemical smog.

3) Photochemical smog is a type of air pollution that can cause breathing difficulties, headaches and tiredness.

Hydrogen can be Used as a Clean, Renewable Fuel

Hydrogen gas can also be used to power vehicles. It's often used as a fuel in fuel cells (see page 124).

Pros

1) Hydrogen is a very clean fuel. In a hydrogen fuel cell, hydrogen combines with oxygen to produce energy, and the only waste product is water — no nasty pollutants like carbon dioxide, toxic carbon monoxide or soot (which are produced when fossil fuels are burnt).

2) Hydrogen is obtained from water, which is a renewable resource, so it's not going to run out (unlike fossil fuels). Hydrogen can even be obtained from the water produced by the cell when it's used in fuel cells.

You get the hydrogen from the electrolysis of water.

Cons

1) You need a special, expensive engine.

2) Hydrogen gas needs to be manufactured, which is expensive and often uses energy from another source — this energy often comes from burning fossil fuels, which produces pollutants.

3) Hydrogen is hard to store and not widely available.

Fossil fuels are bad news — but we depend on them for many things

Make sure you know the different pollutants that are given out when fossil fuels are burnt, along with the negative effects that each of the pollutants has on us and the environment.

The Atmosphere

Scientists have looked at <u>evidence</u> from rocks, air bubbles in ice and fossils to see how our <u>atmosphere</u> has <u>changed</u> over many, many years. Here's one theory about how our atmosphere might have evolved.

Phase 1 — **Volcanoes** Gave Out **Steam** and **CO_2**

1) The Earth's surface was originally <u>molten</u> for many millions of years. There was almost no atmosphere.

2) Eventually the Earth's surface cooled and a <u>thin crust</u> formed, but <u>volcanoes</u> kept erupting, releasing gases from <u>inside the Earth</u>. This 'degassing' released mainly <u>carbon dioxide</u>, but also <u>steam</u>, <u>methane</u> and <u>ammonia</u>.

3) When things eventually settled down, the early atmosphere was <u>mostly CO_2</u> and water vapour. There was very little oxygen.

4) The water vapour later <u>condensed</u> to form the <u>oceans</u>.

Phase 2 — **Green Plants** Evolved and Produced **Oxygen**

1) A lot of the early CO_2 <u>dissolved</u> into the oceans.

2) <u>Nitrogen gas (N_2)</u> was then put into the atmosphere in two ways — it was formed by ammonia reacting with oxygen, and was released by denitrifying bacteria.

3) N_2 isn't very <u>reactive</u>. So the amount of N_2 in the atmosphere <u>increased</u>, because it was being <u>made</u> but not <u>broken down</u>.

4) Next, <u>green plants</u> evolved over most of the Earth. As they photosynthesised, they <u>removed CO_2</u> and <u>produced O_2</u>.

5) Thanks to the plants, the amount of O_2 in the air gradually <u>built up</u> and much of the CO_2 eventually got <u>locked up</u> in <u>fossil fuels</u> and <u>sedimentary rocks</u>.

Phase 3 — **Ozone Layer** Allows Evolution of **Complex Animals**

1) The build-up of <u>oxygen</u> in the atmosphere <u>killed off</u> early organisms that couldn't tolerate it.

2) But it did allow the <u>evolution</u> of more <u>complex</u> organisms that <u>made use</u> of the oxygen.

3) The oxygen also created the <u>ozone layer</u> (O_3), which <u>blocked</u> harmful rays from the Sun and <u>enabled</u> even <u>more complex</u> organisms to evolve.

4) There is virtually <u>no CO_2</u> left now, compared to how much there used to be.

Today's Atmosphere is Mainly **Nitrogen** and **Oxygen**

The atmosphere <u>today</u> is made up of:

- approximately <u>78% nitrogen</u> and approximately <u>21% oxygen</u>,

- small amounts of other gases (each making up <u>less than 1%</u> of the atmosphere), mainly carbon dioxide, noble gases and water vapour.

There's more about today's atmosphere on p.164-166.

Test for **Oxygen** Using a **Glowing Splint**

You can <u>test</u> for oxygen by checking if the gas will <u>relight</u> a <u>glowing splint</u>.

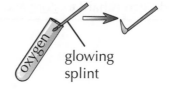

glowing splint

Before volcanic activity, the Earth didn't even have an atmosphere

One way scientists can get information about what Earth's <u>atmosphere</u> was like in the past is from <u>Antarctic ice cores</u>. Each year a layer of <u>ice</u> forms with tiny <u>bubbles of air</u> trapped in it. The <u>deeper</u> you go in the ice, the <u>older</u> the air. So analysing bubbles from different layers shows you how the atmosphere has <u>changed</u>.

Warm-Up and Exam Questions

There's lots of important information in this section on air pollution and the Earth's atmosphere. Answer these questions to see what you can remember and what you need to go over again.

Warm-Up Questions

1) What is meant by the incomplete combustion of hydrocarbons?

2) a) Name two pollutants that could be released as a result of the incomplete combustion of hydrocarbons, that wouldn't be released as a result of complete combustion.

   b) For each pollutant you named in part a), state one way in which it could affect human health.

3) State one advantage and one disadvantage of using hydrogen gas to fuel cars.

Exam Questions

1 Which of the following statements about nitrogen oxides is correct?

   ☐ **A**   Nitrogen oxides are produced by car batteries.

   ☐ **B**   Nitrogen oxides are produced in the internal combustion engines of cars.

   ☐ **C**   Using hydrogen as a fuel increases the amount of nitrogen oxides in the atmosphere.

   ☐ **D**   Nitrogen oxides react with carbon dioxide in the air to produce acid rain.

[1 mark]

2 Burning fossil fuels can produce pollutants like sulfur dioxide. Sulfur dioxide can cause acid rain.

(a) Explain why sulfur dioxide is produced when some fossil fuels are burned.

[1 mark]

(b) Describe how sulfur dioxide can cause acid rain.

[2 marks]

(c) Give **one** environmental problem caused by acid rain.

[1 mark]

3* Some information about the amounts of oxygen, carbon dioxide and water vapour in the Earth's atmosphere is shown in **Figure 1**.

Gas	Amount in atmosphere today (%)
Oxygen	21
Carbon dioxide	0.04
Water vapour	0.25

Figure 1

Describe the composition of the Earth's early atmosphere and explain the main changes that are thought to have occurred over the past 4 billion years to result in the amounts of oxygen, carbon dioxide and water vapour shown in **Figure 1**.

[6 marks]

The Greenhouse Effect

Some of the gases in the <u>atmosphere</u> are <u>greenhouse gases</u> — they help to <u>trap</u> the <u>Sun's energy</u>, which keeps the Earth nice and <u>warm</u>. Without them, the <u>average global temperature</u> would be over <u>30 °C cooler</u>. Brrr...

The **Greenhouse Effect** Helps to **Keep** the **Earth Warm**

1) <u>Greenhouse gases</u>, such as <u>carbon dioxide</u>, methane and water vapour, are present in small amounts in the Earth's atmosphere.

2) They act like an <u>insulating</u> layer, keeping the Earth <u>warm</u> — this is the <u>greenhouse effect</u>. Here's how it works...

The greenhouse effect is very important — it's what keeps the Earth warm enough for us to live on.

1) The <u>Sun</u> emits <u>short wavelength</u> electromagnetic radiation, which <u>passes through</u> the Earth's atmosphere as it isn't absorbed by greenhouse gases.

2) The short wavelength radiation reaches the <u>Earth's surface</u>, is <u>absorbed</u>, and then is <u>re-emitted</u> as <u>long wavelength</u>, infrared (IR) radiation.

3) This radiation is <u>absorbed</u> by <u>greenhouse gases</u> in the atmosphere.

4) The greenhouse gases then <u>re-radiate</u> it in all directions — including back towards Earth.

5) The IR radiation is <u>thermal radiation</u>, so it <u>warms</u> the surface of the <u>Earth</u>.

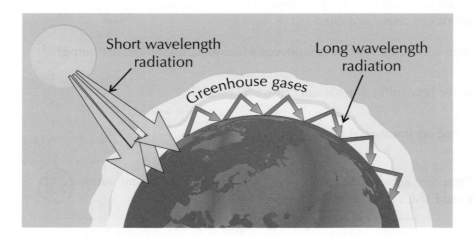

Short wavelength radiation

Long wavelength radiation

Greenhouse gases

If the <u>concentration</u> of <u>greenhouse gases</u> in the atmosphere <u>increases</u>, you get an <u>enhanced greenhouse effect</u>, which causes the Earth to get <u>warmer</u>.

Atmospheric greenhouse gases make the Earth a warmer place

There's a lot to get your <u>head around</u> here. The main thing to remember is that <u>greenhouse gases absorb</u> a lot of the <u>long wavelength IR radiation</u> from the <u>Earth's surface</u>. They <u>re-emit</u> this radiation in <u>all directions</u>, but as some is re-emitted <u>back towards Earth</u>, the gases have an <u>overall warming effect</u> on the <u>Earth's surface</u>.

Climate Change

The amount of <u>greenhouse gases</u> in the atmosphere is <u>increasing</u> — and it's mainly down to <u>human activity</u>.

Human Activity Affects the Atmospheric Carbon Dioxide Level

1) Over the <u>last 150 years</u> or so, the <u>human population</u> has <u>rapidly increased</u>.

2) This means that <u>more energy</u> is needed for lighting, heating, cooking, transport and so on.

3) People's <u>lifestyles</u> are changing too. More and more countries are becoming <u>industrialised</u> and <u>well-off</u>. This means the average <u>energy demand per person</u> is also increasing (since people have <u>more electrical gadgets</u>, more people have <u>cars</u> or <u>travel on planes</u>, etc.).

As the consumption of fossil fuels increases, so does the concentration of CO_2 in the atmosphere.

4) This increased energy consumption comes mainly from the <u>burning of fossil fuels</u>, which releases <u>more CO_2</u>.

5) More people also means more land is needed to build <u>houses</u> and grow <u>food</u>. This space is often made by <u>chopping down trees</u> — this is called <u>deforestation</u>. But plants are the main things <u>taking carbon dioxide out of the atmosphere</u> (as they photosynthesise) — so fewer plants means less carbon dioxide is <u>taken out</u> of the atmosphere.

6) The graph shows how CO_2 levels in the atmosphere have <u>risen</u> over the last 300 years.

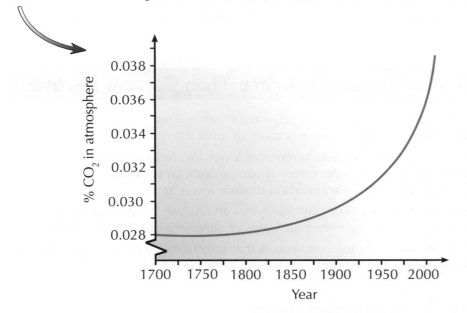

CO_2 is also added to the atmosphere through non-human activities, e.g. volcanoes erupting.

Livestock Farming Affects the Atmospheric Methane Level

1) The level of <u>carbon dioxide</u> in the atmosphere is <u>increasing</u>, but that's not the whole story...

2) The greenhouse gas <u>methane</u> is also causing problems. The concentration of methane has risen lots in recent years due to increased human activity.

3) Methane is produced in the <u>digestive processes</u> of certain <u>livestock</u> (e.g. cattle, goats and camels). So, the <u>more livestock we farm</u>, the <u>more methane</u> is produced.

4) Though it's currently only present in <u>tiny amounts</u> in our atmosphere, the increasing concentration of methane is an issue as it's a super-effective <u>greenhouse gas</u>.

Climate Change

Increasing Levels of Greenhouse Gases Cause Climate Change

1) Historically, <u>temperature change</u> at the Earth's surface is <u>correlated</u> to the level of <u>carbon dioxide</u> in the atmosphere. Recently, the average temperature at the Earth's surface has been <u>increasing</u> as the level of carbon dioxide has <u>increased</u>.

2) There's a <u>scientific consensus</u> that extra greenhouse gases from <u>human activity</u> have caused the average <u>temperature</u> of the Earth to <u>increase</u>, due to the enhanced greenhouse effect — see page 164. This effect is known as <u>global warming</u>.

3) Global warming is a type of <u>climate change</u> and causes other types of climate change, e.g. changing rainfall patterns. It could also cause severe <u>flooding</u> due to the polar ice caps melting. It's a BIG problem that could affect the whole world, so we need to deal with it seriously.

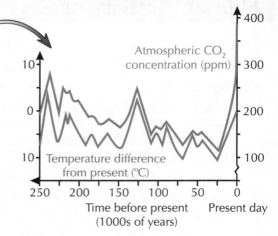

Most of the scientific community agree that global warming is <u>anthropogenic</u> (caused by humans). But some scientists believe that the current rises in global temperature are just <u>natural fluctuations</u> and that we don't have <u>enough data</u> to prove that global warming is caused by increasing CO_2 emissions or human activity.

Historical Data is Much Less Accurate Than Current Records

1) <u>Current global temperature</u> and <u>carbon dioxide levels</u> can be worked out pretty accurately as they're based on measurements taken all over the world.

2) Historical data is <u>less accurate</u> — less data was taken over fewer locations and the methods used to collect the data were less accurate. If you go back far enough, there are <u>no records</u> of global temperature and carbon dioxide levels at all...

3) But there are ways to <u>estimate past data</u>. For example, you can analyse <u>fossils</u>, <u>tree rings</u> or <u>gas bubbles</u> trapped in <u>ice sheets</u> to estimate past levels of atmospheric carbon dioxide.

4) The problem with using these kinds of measurements is that they're much <u>less precise</u> than current measurements made using <u>instrumental sampling</u>. They're also much <u>less representative</u> of global levels.

We Can Try to Use Less Fossil Fuels

1) In order to prevent or <u>slow down climate change</u>, we need to <u>cut down</u> on the amount of greenhouse gases we're releasing into the atmosphere.

2) To <u>reduce carbon dioxide emissions</u>, we can try to limit our own use of fossil fuels. This could be by doing things on a personal level, like <u>walking</u> or <u>cycling</u> instead of driving or <u>turning your central heating down</u>.

3) On a larger scale, the UK government has formed plans to encourage the public and industry to become more <u>energy efficient</u>, to create financial incentives to reduce CO_2 emissions, to use more renewable energy and to increase research into new energy sources.

People can get quite hot under the collar talking about all this...

That's because climate change could have a <u>massive impact</u> on many people's lives across the world. It's really important that we understand what <u>causes</u> it, as well as how to prevent any <u>damaging consequences</u>.

Warm-Up and Exam Questions

We're approaching the end of another topic. All that's standing between you and a well-earned break are a few questions on the greenhouse effect and climate change. Time to see how much you remember.

Warm-Up Questions

1) Carbon dioxide is a greenhouse gas.
   Name two more greenhouse gases present in the atmosphere.

2) What is the greenhouse effect?

3) Give a reason why the levels of atmospheric greenhouse gases will increase as a result of:
   a) deforestation,
   b) an increase in energy consumption,
   c) an increase in livestock farming.

4) What is global warming?

Exam Questions

1   **Figure 1** shows an estimate of how the atmospheric CO_2 concentration and the Earth's surface temperature have changed over the last 250 000 years.

   (a) Give **one** reason why historical data may be less accurate than data collected more recently.

   [1 mark]

   (b) In 1960, the atmospheric CO_2 concentration was 317 ppm. In 2010, it was 22.7% higher than in 1960.

   Calculate the atmospheric CO_2 concentration in 2010. Give your answer to three significant figures.

   [2 marks]

   (c) Give **one** conclusion that can be drawn from **Figure 1**.

   [1 mark]

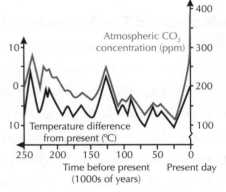

Figure 1

2   Carbon dioxide is a greenhouse gas.

   (a) Explain how carbon dioxide contributes to the greenhouse effect.

   [2 marks]

   The level of atmospheric carbon dioxide is increasing, which has enhanced the greenhouse effect. This has led to global warming.

   (b) State **two** effects that an increase in global temperature could have on the environment.

   [2 marks]

   (c) (i) Give **one** measure an individual could take to reduce their carbon dioxide emissions on a personal level.

   [1 mark]

   (ii) Give **one** way that governments can act to encourage reductions in carbon dioxide emissions.

   [1 mark]

Revision Summary for Topic 8

That wraps up <u>Topic 8</u> — time to put yourself to the test and find out <u>how much you really know</u>.
- Try these questions and <u>tick off each one</u> when you <u>get it right</u>.
- When you've done <u>all the questions</u> under a heading and are <u>completely happy</u> with it, tick it off.

Fractional Distillation, Hydrocarbons and Cracking (p.155-158) ☑

1) Name two applications of hydrocarbons. ☑
2) How is crude oil formed? ☑
3) Which elements are hydrocarbons made from? ☑
4) What is the purpose of fractional distillation? ☑
5) Do longer or shorter hydrocarbons drain out near the bottom of the fractional distillation column? ☑
6) What is the gas fraction used for? ☑
7) What is fuel oil used for? ☑
8) Give the word equation for the complete combustion of hydrocarbons. ☑
9) What is the definition of a homologous series? ☑
10) Explain why long hydrocarbons have a high boiling point. ☑
11) Are longer or shorter hydrocarbons associated with a low viscosity? ☑
12) What is cracking? ☑

Pollutants and The Atmosphere (p.160-162) ☑

13) Why does incomplete combustion of hydrocarbons occur? ☑
14) Why is carbon monoxide bad for human health? ☑
15) Name a gas that contributes to the production of acid rain. ☑
16) Give three problems associated with acid rain. ☑
17) Name the gases given out by volcanoes millions of years ago. ☑
18) How was nitrogen gas originally put into the atmosphere? ☑
19) How did the formation of the oceans affect the level of carbon dioxide in the Earth's atmosphere? ☑
20) How could you test an unknown gas to see if it was oxygen? ☑

The Greenhouse Effect and Climate Change (p.164-166) ☑

21) Give two reasons why the increasing human population has affected the level of atmospheric CO_2. ☑
22) How has human activity led to an increase in the concentration of methane in the atmosphere? ☑
23) How is global warming caused? ☑

Tests for Cations and Anions

So, tests for identifying ions in mystery compounds probably don't get your heart racing with excitement, but this section includes lots of different colours so just think of all the pretty revision notes you could make...

You Can Use **Flame Tests** to Identify **Metal Ions**

1) Compounds of some metals produce a characteristic colour when heated in a flame.

2) You can test for various metal ions by putting your substance in a flame and seeing what colour the flame goes.

- Lithium ions, Li^+, give a (crimson) red flame.
- Sodium ions, Na^+, give a yellow flame.
- Potassium ions, K^+, give a lilac flame.
- Calcium ions, Ca^{2+}, give an orange-red flame.
- Copper ions, Cu^{2+}, give a blue-green flame.

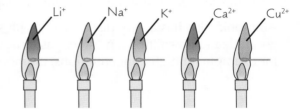

3) To carry out a flame test in the lab, first clean a nichrome wire loop by dipping it into hydrochloric acid and then rinsing it in distilled water.

4) Then dip the wire loop into a sample of the metal compound and put the loop in the clear blue part of a Bunsen flame (the hottest bit). Record what colour the flame goes.

This test only works if the mystery compound contains just one type of metal ion — otherwise you'll get a confusing mixture of colours.

Some **Metal Ions** Form a **Coloured Precipitate** with **NaOH**

This is also a test for metal ions, but it's slightly more complicated:

1) Many metal hydroxides are insoluble and precipitate out of solution when formed. Some of these hydroxides have a characteristic colour.

2) For this test, you add a few drops of sodium hydroxide solution to a solution of your mystery compound.

3) If a hydroxide precipitate forms, you can use its colour to tell which metal ion was in the compound.

Metal Ion	Colour of Precipitate	Ionic Equation
Aluminium, Al^{3+}	White at first. But then redissolves in excess NaOH to form a colourless solution.	$Al^{3+}_{(aq)} + 3OH^-_{(aq)} \rightarrow Al(OH)_{3(s)}$ Then: $Al(OH)_{3(s)} + OH^-_{(aq)} \rightarrow Al(OH)_4{}^-_{(aq)}$
Calcium, Ca^{2+}	White	$Ca^{2+}_{(aq)} + 2OH^-_{(aq)} \rightarrow Ca(OH)_{2(s)}$
Copper(II), Cu^{2+}	Blue	$Cu^{2+}_{(aq)} + 2OH^-_{(aq)} \rightarrow Cu(OH)_{2(s)}$
Iron(II), Fe^{2+}	Green	$Fe^{2+}_{(aq)} + 2OH^-_{(aq)} \rightarrow Fe(OH)_{2(s)}$
Iron(III), Fe^{3+}	Brown	$Fe^{3+}_{(aq)} + 3OH^-_{(aq)} \rightarrow Fe(OH)_{3(s)}$

There's more about ionic equations on page 19.

Flame tests are only useful for testing one type of ion at a time

Lots of ions and colours to learn here, so just take your time. It might help to come up with little ways of remembering the colours — like Li+ttle Red Riding Hood. Or Yellow BaNa+Na+s. It's fab.

 # Tests for Cations and Anions

Now that you're all warmed up, time for another page on <u>identifying ions</u> in mystery compounds.

Adding **NaOH** to **Ammonium Ions** Produces **Ammonia**

1) To work out whether a substance contains <u>ammonium ions</u> (NH_4^+), all you need to do is add some <u>sodium hydroxide</u> solution to a solution of your mystery substance and gently heat it. If ammonia gas is given off, it means that there are ammonium ions in your mystery substance.

2) You can test for <u>ammonia gas</u> by holding a piece of <u>damp red litmus paper</u> over it. If the mystery gas is ammonia, the litmus paper will <u>turn blue</u>.

3) Ammonia also has a very distinctive <u>strong smell</u>, but it's not a good idea to go sniffing a mystery gas to figure out what it is — for example, at high concentrations, ammonia is an <u>irritant</u> and <u>toxic</u>.

damp red litmus paper

Test for **Halide Ions** Using **Silver Nitrate Solution**

To test for <u>chloride</u> ions (Cl⁻), <u>bromide</u> ions (Br⁻) or <u>iodide</u> ions (I⁻), add some <u>dilute nitric acid</u> (HNO_3), followed by a few drops of <u>silver nitrate solution</u> ($AgNO_3$).

Nitric acid needs to be added first to get rid of any carbonate ions — they produce a pale precipitate with silver nitrate too, which would confuse the results. You can't use hydrochloric acid, because you'd be adding chloride ions.

$$Ag^+_{(aq)} + Cl^-_{(aq)} \longrightarrow AgCl_{(s)}$$ A <u>chloride</u> gives a <u>white precipitate</u> of <u>silver chloride</u>.

$$Ag^+_{(aq)} + Br^-_{(aq)} \longrightarrow AgBr_{(s)}$$ A <u>bromide</u> gives a <u>cream precipitate</u> of <u>silver bromide</u>.

$$Ag^+_{(aq)} + I^-_{(aq)} \longrightarrow AgI_{(s)}$$ An <u>iodide</u> gives a <u>yellow precipitate</u> of <u>silver iodide</u>.

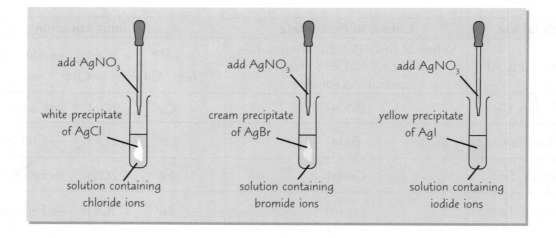

Halide ions can form coloured precipitates with silver nitrate

 There are a few tests to learn here, along with their results. That's quite a bit of information to take in, so don't just stare at the whole page till your eyes are swimming and you never ever want to see the word '<u>precipitate</u>' again. Just learn the tests <u>one by one</u> and you'll be absolutely fine.

Tests for Cations and Anions

There's a couple more tests for ions on this page. These ones both involve testing for <u>negative ions</u> (anions).

Test for **Carbonates** Using **Dilute Acid**

1) To test for <u>carbonate ions</u> (CO_3^{2-}) in solution, add some dilute <u>acid</u>.

2) If there are carbonate ions present, the mixture will <u>fizz</u> — this is because the carbonate will react with the acid to produce <u>carbon dioxide gas</u>:

The test for carbon dioxide is covered on page 75.

$$\text{carbonate ions + acid} \rightarrow \text{carbon dioxide + water}$$
$$CO_3^{2-} + 2H^+ \rightarrow CO_2 + H_2O$$

3) You can check to see if a gas is <u>carbon dioxide</u> by bubbling it through <u>limewater</u>. If it is carbon dioxide, the limewater turns <u>milky</u>.

Test for **Sulfate Ions** Using **Barium Chloride Solution**

1) To test for <u>sulfate ions</u> in solution, first add some <u>dilute hydrochloric acid</u> to the test sample — this stops any precipitation reactions not involving sulfate ions from taking place.

2) Then add some <u>barium chloride solution</u>. If there are sulfate ions in the solution, a <u>white precipitate</u> of barium sulfate will form:

$$\text{barium ions + sulfate ions} \rightarrow \text{barium sulfate}$$
$$Ba^{2+}_{(aq)} + SO_4^{2-}_{(aq)} \rightarrow BaSO_{4\,(s)}$$

The Test for Each Ion must be **Unique**

1) It's important that you know the <u>tests</u> for all the <u>ions</u> on this page, and the previous two pages for that matter.

2) Each test is <u>unique</u> — it gives certain results depending on the ions present. It would be no good if each test gave the <u>same response</u> for <u>different ions</u> — that way you'd have <u>no idea</u> of knowing what ions you actually had in a given sample.

Carbon dioxide turns limewater milky

Just because a solution bubbles when you add acid, doesn't mean that there are carbonate ions present — the gas produced might not be carbon dioxide. To make sure, it's best to bubble the gas through limewater. If it turns milky this indicates that the solution contains carbonate ions.

Flame Photometry

Flame photometry is a pretty fancy technique that can <u>accurately identify</u> different metal ions in solution and find their <u>concentrations</u>. And as a bonus, it produces some more lovely colours.

Every **Metal Ion** Gives a Characteristic **Line Spectrum**

1) Flame photometry is an <u>instrumental method</u> that allows you to <u>identify</u> ions in a dilute solution.

2) Each ion produces a unique <u>line spectrum</u> with different lines present in different places.

A line spectrum for an <u>ion</u> could look something like this:

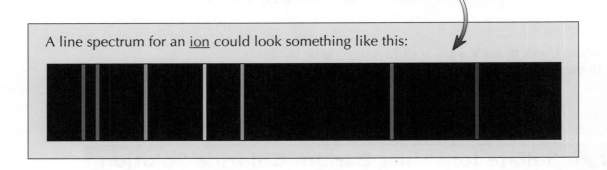

3) The <u>intensity</u> of the measured wavelength indicates the <u>concentration</u> of that ion in solution. You can work out concentration from intensity using a <u>calibration curve</u>. Here's how...

EXAMPLE: **Flame photometry was carried out on a sample, known to contain calcium ions. The measured wavelength known to be emitted by calcium ions had an emission intensity of 4.5. Use the calibration curve to work out the concentration of calcium ions in the sample.**

1) Find the intensity on <u>y-axis</u>.

2) Travel along <u>horizontally</u> from this point, until you reach the <u>curve</u>.

3) Draw a straight line <u>down</u> to the <u>x-axis</u> and read off <u>concentration</u>.

4) So the concentration of calcium ions in the sample is 0.25 mol dm^{-3}.

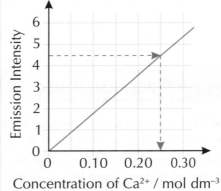

It's the same idea as a flame test, but you get more information

When you do a bog standard flame test for metal ions, you get a coloured flame. But determining what colour the flame is can be a bit <u>subjective</u>. Flame photometry produces a <u>line spectrum</u> instead. The pattern on the line spectrum is <u>unique</u> for every ion — and it's easy to tell the different patterns of lines apart just by comparing them. So it's a more accurate method of identifying an ion than a flame test.

Flame Photometry

Flame Photometry Works for Mixtures

Flame photometry can also be used to identify different ions in <u>mixtures</u>. This makes it more useful than <u>flame tests</u>, which only work for substances that contain a <u>single metal ion</u>.

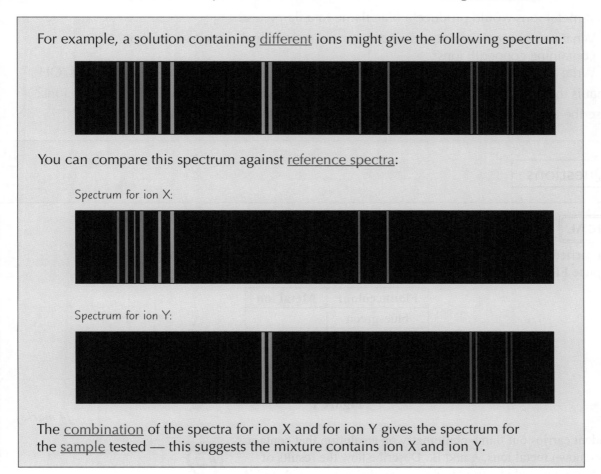

For example, a solution containing <u>different</u> ions might give the following spectrum:

You can compare this spectrum against <u>reference spectra</u>:

Spectrum for ion X:

Spectrum for ion Y:

The <u>combination</u> of the spectra for ion X and for ion Y gives the spectrum for the <u>sample</u> tested — this suggests the mixture contains ion X and ion Y.

Machines can Analyse Unknown Substances

Chemists often use <u>instrumental analysis</u> (i.e. tests that use machines), such as flame photometry, <u>instead</u> of conducting manual tests.

<u>Advantages of Using Machines</u>:
- <u>Very sensitive</u> — they can detect even the <u>tiniest amounts</u> of substances.
- <u>Very fast</u> and tests can be automated.
- <u>Very accurate</u> — they don't involve <u>human error</u>, like manual analysis does.

Unfortunately, machines can't do the exam for you...

<u>Instrumental analysis</u> is <u>fast</u> and it gives you results that are <u>accurate</u>, even if there's only a <u>tiny amount</u> of a substance present. For example, <u>flame photometry</u> is used in environmental monitoring to detect small amounts of any metals that may be present in samples of soil and water. It's a really powerful technique.

Warm-Up and Exam Questions

Now some questions to hone your skills. There are quite a few little details to learn for all those ion tests, plus all the flame photometry stuff, so make sure you've got it all before you move on.

Warm-Up Questions

1) What metal ions would produce a lilac flame in a flame test?
2) a) What colour precipitate forms when you add sodium hydroxide to a solution containing copper(II) ions?
   b) Write an ionic equation for the reaction between copper ions (Cu^{2+}) and hydroxide ions (OH^-).
3) What is the colour of the precipitate formed when silver nitrate is reacted with chloride ions?
4) Describe two advantages of using instrumental methods to identify ions.

Exam Questions

PRACTICAL

1   Kelly carried out flame tests on compounds of four different metal ions. Complete **Figure 1**, below, which shows her results.

Flame colour	Metal ion
blue-green	
	Li$^+$
yellow	
	Ca^{2+}

Figure 1

[4 marks]

2   A student carries out flame photometry on a solution that contains two unknown metal ions, A and B. Describe how the results of the experiment could be used to determine the identity of A and B.

[2 marks]

PRACTICAL

3   **Figure 2** shows the results of a series of chemical tests conducted on two unknown compounds, **X** and **Y**.

Test	Observation	
	Compound X	**Compound Y**
a few drops of sodium hydroxide solution	white precipitate	green precipitate
hydrochloric acid and barium chloride solution	white precipitate	no precipitate
nitric acid and silver nitrate solution	no precipitate	yellow precipitate

Figure 2

(a)   What is the chemical name of compound **Y**?

[2 marks]

(b)   A student says "From these results, I can be certain that compound **X** is calcium sulfate." State whether he is correct. Explain your answer.

[3 marks]

Alkanes and Alkenes

Alkanes and alkenes are dead useful. And all there is to them is some hydrogen and some carbon.

Alkanes are Saturated Hydrocarbons

1) A homologous series is a group of chemicals that have similar chemical structures.
2) Alkanes are a homologous series of hydrocarbons — they contain just carbon and hydrogen atoms.
3) Alkanes have the general formula C_nH_{2n+2}. E.g an alkane with 5 carbons has $(2 \times 5) + 2 = 12$ hydrogens.
4) Different alkanes have chains of different lengths. These are the first four alkanes:

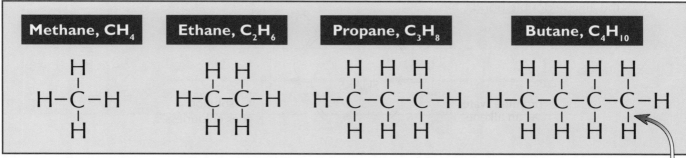

Methane, CH_4 **Ethane, C_2H_6** **Propane, C_3H_8** **Butane, C_4H_{10}**

5) The diagrams above show that all the atoms have formed bonds with as many other atoms as they can — this means they're saturated.

Carbon atoms tend to make four bonds, but hydrogen atoms can only make one.

Each straight line shows a covalent bond (page 39).

Alkenes Have a C=C Double Bond

1) A functional group is a group of atoms that determine how a molecule reacts. Members of a homologous series all contain the same functional group.
2) Alkenes are a homologous series of hydrocarbons with one C=C functional group. They have the general formula C_nH_{2n} — they have twice as many hydrogens as carbons.

This is a carbon-carbon double bond.

3) They are known as unsaturated because they can make more bonds — the double bond can open up, allowing the two carbon atoms to bond with other atoms.
4) The first three alkenes are ethene, propene, butene (see below).

Both but-1-ene and but-2-ene can just be called butene.

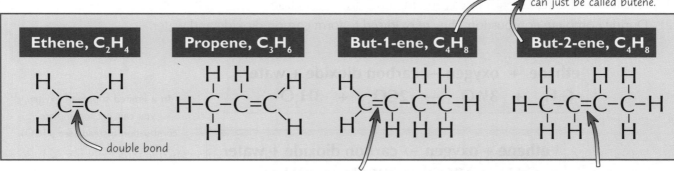

Ethene, C_2H_4 **Propene, C_3H_6** **But-1-ene, C_4H_8** **But-2-ene, C_4H_8**

double bond

In longer chains, the double bond can go at the end of the chain or in the middle.

REVISION TIP

Alkanes and alkenes are both types of hydrocarbon

Don't get confused between alkanes and alkenes. They may look (and sound) similar but that double bond makes a lot of difference, especially to their reactivities (see next page for more).

Alkanes and Alkenes

So now you're an expert on the structures of alkanes and alkenes, it's time to look at a couple of their <u>reactions</u>.

Alkenes Turn Bromine Water Colourless

You can test for an alkene using <u>bromine water</u>.

1) When shaken together, an alkene will <u>decolourise</u> bromine water, turning it from <u>orange</u> to <u>colourless</u>.

2) This is because an <u>addition reaction</u> takes place where bromine is <u>added</u> across the <u>alkene double bond</u>.

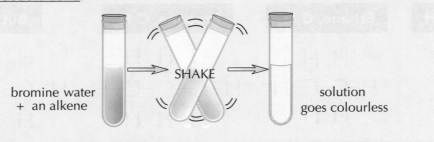

bromine water + an alkene → SHAKE → solution goes colourless

3) Alkanes <u>don't</u> react with bromine water as they don't contain double bonds.

Example

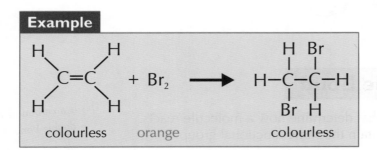

colourless   orange   colourless

Alkenes also react with steam in addition reactions.

Hydrocarbons are Oxidised in Combustion Reactions

1) Alkanes and alkenes <u>burn</u> in <u>oxygen</u> in <u>combustion reactions</u>.

2) During complete combustion, they're oxidised to form <u>carbon dioxide</u> and <u>water</u>.

ethane + oxygen → carbon dioxide + water
C_2H_6 + $3\frac{1}{2}O_2$ → $2CO_2$ + $3H_2O$

In a limited supply of oxygen, you can get incomplete combustion instead (see p.160).

ethene + oxygen → carbon dioxide + water
C_2H_4 + $3O_2$ → $2CO_2$ + $2H_2O$

A few more reactions to learn here

A really important test is using <u>bromine water</u> to test if you've got an alkane or an alkene. With the alkane, the bromine water will <u>stay orange</u>, whereas with an alkene the solution will <u>turn colourless</u>.

Addition Polymers

Polymers are made by joining lots of <u>little molecules</u> together in <u>long chains</u>.

Addition Polymers are Made From Unsaturated Monomers

1) <u>Polymers</u> are substances of <u>high average relative molecular mass</u> made by joining up lots of small repeating units called <u>monomers</u>.

2) The monomers that make up <u>addition polymers</u> have a <u>double covalent bond</u>.

3) Lots of <u>unsaturated monomer molecules</u> (<u>alkenes</u> — see page 175) can open up their <u>double bonds</u> and join together to form <u>polymer chains</u>. This is called <u>addition polymerisation</u>.

For example, lots of ethene molecules (C_2H_4) can react together to form <u>poly(ethene)</u> — $(C_2H_4)_n$:

<u>Many monomers</u>   <u>Polymer</u>

pressure and catalyst

The reaction can also be shown like this:

The 'n' represents 'any number' — it just means you start with lots of ethene molecules.

pressure and catalyst

Many single ethenes   poly(ethene)

This is a shorthand way of showing polymer chains. See the next page for how to draw them.

4) The <u>name</u> of the polymer comes from the <u>type of monomer</u> it's made from — you just put <u>brackets</u> around it and stick the word "<u>poly</u>" in front of it. So <u>propene</u> becomes <u>poly(propene)</u>, etc.

5) To get the <u>formula</u> of the polymer, you just put the formula of the <u>monomer</u> in brackets and put a little 'n' after it. So C_3H_6 becomes $(C_3H_6)_n$. Simple.

Addition polymerisation usually needs high pressure and a catalyst

The name of a polymer is determined by the monomers that were used to make it. So you can work out what monomers a polymer is made of from its name — e.g. poly(butene) is made up of butene monomers.

Addition Polymers

Polymers aren't usually drawn in diagrams as long chains — they're represented using <u>repeat units</u>.

You Can Draw the **Repeat Unit** of a **Polymer**

1) Drawing the <u>displayed formula</u> of an <u>addition polymer</u> from the displayed formula of its <u>monomer</u> is easy.

- Join the carbons together in a <u>row</u> with <u>no</u> double bonds between them.
- Stick a pair of <u>brackets</u> around the repeating bit, and put an '<u>n</u>' after it (to show that there are lots of monomers).
- You should also draw a bond from each of the two carbons in the chain that pass through the brackets — this shows the chain continues.

Chloroethene → Poly(chloroethene)

2) To get from the <u>displayed formula</u> of the <u>polymer</u> to the displayed formula of the <u>monomer</u>, just do the reverse.

Draw out the <u>repeating bit</u> of the polymer, get rid of the two bonds going out through the brackets and put a <u>double bond</u> between the <u>carbons</u>.

Propene → Poly(propene)

Properties of Polymers Make Them Suitable for Different Uses

1) <u>Poly(tetrafluoroethene)</u> (PTFE), <u>poly(chloroethene)</u> (PVC), <u>poly(ethene)</u> and <u>poly(propene)</u> are <u>addition polymers</u>.
2) Each polymer has its own set of <u>properties</u>.
3) The set of properties make them perfect for making certain things. Here are some examples...

The properties depend on the arrangement of polymer chains and the forces between them.

Polymer	Properties	Uses
Poly(ethene)	flexible, electrical insulator, cheap	plastic bags, bottles, wire insulation
Poly(propene)	flexible, strong, tough, mouldable	crates, furniture, ropes
Poly(chloroethene) (PVC)	tough, cheap	window frames, water pipes
Poly(tetrafluoroethene) (PTFE)	unreactive, tough, non-stick	non-stick pans, waterproof clothing

 Addition polymer carbon chains have no C=C bonds
Make sure you can recognise and draw polymers and their monomers by <u>practising lots of times</u>.

Condensation Polymers

Condensation polymers are a bit trickier than their addition polymer cousins. Ready? Here we go...

Polymers can be Made by **Condensation Polymerisation**

1) Condensation polymerisation usually involves two different types of monomer.
2) The monomers react together and bonds form between them, making polymer chains.
3) Each monomer has to contain at least two functional groups, one on each end of the molecule.
4) Each functional group can react with the functional group of another monomer, creating long chains of alternating monomers. For each new bond that forms, a small molecule (e.g. water) is lost.

Polyesters are **Condensation Polymers**

See p.182 and 185 for more on alcohols and carboxylic acids.

1) Polyesters form when dicarboxylic acid monomers and diol monomers react together.

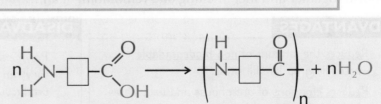

Dicarboxylic acid monomer   Diol monomer   The blocks represent the rest of each molecule.   Polyester   Water

2) The dicarboxylic acid monomers contain two carboxylic acid (-COOH) groups and the diol monomers contain two alcohol (-OH) groups.
3) When the carboxylic acid group reacts with the alcohol group, it forms an ester link.
4) Polyesters are condensation polymers — each time an ester link is formed, a molecule of water is lost.

There are Many Important **Naturally Occurring Polymers**

Not all polymers are synthetic (man-made). There are also many polymers that occur naturally — some of which are vital for keeping us alive, such as DNA and proteins.

1) DNA is a complex molecule that contains genetic information.
2) It contains two strands and each strand is made up of nucleotide monomers that bond together in a polymerisation reaction.
3) DNA is made from four different monomers called nucleotides.

1) Amino acid monomers form polymers known as proteins via condensation polymerisation.
2) Proteins have many important uses in the human body, e.g. in enzymes (see page 147).

Amino acid monomer   Protein

1) Carbohydrates are molecules containing carbon, oxygen and hydrogen, used by living things to produce energy.
2) Starch and cellulose are large, complex carbohydrates, which are made up of many smaller units of carbohydrates, known as sugars, joined together in a long chain.

Water can be released when condensation polymers are made...

This happens when an ester link is formed between a carboxylic acid and an alcohol to produce a polyester.

Disposing of Polymers

It's easy to throw away old plastic bottles and plastic packaging without giving much thought — but we need to start thinking about the <u>impact</u> on the <u>environment</u> today and the <u>availability</u> of plastics in the future.

Polymers are Made From Crude Oil

1) <u>Plastics</u> are a type of <u>polymer</u> which are made from <u>crude oil</u>.
   Crude oil is a <u>finite</u> resource — eventually, it will all get used up and run out.

2) The more we use up our crude oil resources, the more <u>expensive</u> crude oil will become — this will then <u>increase the price</u> of crude oil products.

3) Crude oil isn't just used to make <u>plastics</u> — we need it for lots of different things, such as petrol for cars and heating our homes. As resources dry up, we will face the dilemma of how to use the remaining oil. One way we can help delay this problem is by <u>recycling</u> our polymers.

The Disposal of Polymers Comes with Many Problems

In the UK, over <u>2 million</u> tonnes of plastic waste are generated each year.
It's important to find ways to get rid of this waste while <u>minimising environmental damage</u>.

<u>Disposal of Polymers in Landfill Sites:</u>

1) A lot of plastics get dumped in <u>landfill sites</u>. This is usually when different polymers are too <u>difficult</u> or <u>expensive</u> to <u>separate</u> and recycle.

2) Lots of <u>valuable land</u> is quickly getting used up for use as landfill sites.

3) Most polymers are <u>non-biodegradable</u> — they're not broken down by microorganisms. This means that they will sit in landfill for years and years and years and years...

<u>Disposal of Polymers by Combustion:</u>

1) <u>Burning plastics</u> produces a lot of <u>energy</u> and this can be used to <u>generate electricity</u>. But there are downsides to burning plastics, too...

2) If not carefully controlled, <u>toxic gases</u> can be released from the combustion of plastics. For example, when polymers that contain chlorine (such as PVC) are burned, they produce HCl — this has to be removed.

3) <u>Carbon dioxide</u> is also produced and this contributes to <u>global warming</u>.

Recycling Polymers Has Both Pros and Cons

1) <u>Recycling</u> polymers is a great way to limit the amount of crude oil we're using and avoid the <u>environmental impact</u> of burning and landfills.

2) Unfortunately, recycling is not as <u>simple</u> as throwing all the plastic rubbish together and then melting and remoulding it all...

ADVANTAGES

- <u>Reduces</u> the amount of <u>non-biodegradable</u> waste filling up landfill sites.
- <u>Reduces emissions</u> of greenhouse and toxic gases which can be released from burning polymers.
- Recycling generally uses up <u>less water</u> and <u>energy resources</u> than when making new plastics.
- <u>Reduces</u> the amount of <u>crude oil</u> needed to produce more plastics.
- Recycling generally <u>saves money</u> and <u>creates jobs</u>.

DISADVANTAGES

- Polymers must be <u>separated</u> by type before they can be <u>melted</u> and <u>reformed</u> into a new product — this can be <u>difficult</u> and <u>expensive</u>.
- If polymers are <u>mixed</u> together, the <u>quality</u> of the final recycled polymer product could be <u>reduced</u>.
- Polymers can only be recycled a <u>finite</u> number of times. Over time, the <u>strength</u> of the polymer can decrease.
- Melting down polymers can release dangerous gases into the atmosphere. These are <u>harmful</u> to plants and animals.

Recycling polymers can save money and resources

So, if you didn't realise how important recycling polymers was, you should definitely know now. It's hard to imagine a life without plastics or petrol, but if we carry on the way we're going, it could soon become reality...

Warm-Up and Exam Questions

I'm sure you have everything on these pages learnt and understood. But just to check, try these questions.

Warm-Up Questions

1) What are alkanes?
2) Why is an alkene described as unsaturated?
3) Draw the product of the reaction between ethene and bromine.
4) Name the monomer that proteins are made of.

Exam Questions

1 Complete the table to show the missing information for the two alkenes given.

Name of alkene	Formula	Displayed formula
ethene		
	C_3H_6	

[4 marks]

2 Polyesters form through condensation reactions.

(a) Name the molecule released when an ester link is formed during a condensation reaction.

[1 mark]

(b) Give **two** types of monomer that react together to form a polyester.

[2 marks]

3 Propene can undergo an addition polymerisation reaction to form a polymer.

(a) Draw the bonds to complete the displayed formula of the polymer formed in this addition polymerisation reaction.

$$\left(\begin{array}{cc} H & H \\ C & C \\ CH_3 & H \end{array}\right)_n$$

[1 mark]

(b) Name the polymer formed in this reaction.

[1 mark]

4* When a product made from polymers comes to the end of its lifespan, it needs to be disposed of. One type of disposal is recycling, where polymers are melted down and remoulded into a new product.
Discuss the advantages and disadvantages of recycling polymers.

[6 marks]

Alcohols

This page is about different types of <u>alcohol</u> — and that's not just beer and wine.

Alcohols Have an '-OH' Functional Group and End in '-ol'

1) The <u>general formula</u> of an alcohol is: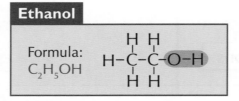
So an alcohol with 2 carbons has the formula C_2H_5OH.

2) All alcohols contain an <u>-OH functional group</u>. Here are the <u>first four</u> alcohols in the homologous series:

Methanol

Formula: CH_3OH

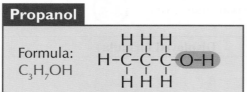

Ethanol

Formula: C_2H_5OH

Propanol

Formula: C_3H_7OH

Butanol

Formula: C_4H_9OH

3) The basic <u>naming</u> system is the same as for alkanes — but replace the final '-<u>e</u>' with '-<u>ol</u>'.

4) Don't write CH_4O instead of CH_3OH — it doesn't show the <u>functional -OH group</u>.

5) It is possible to get alcohols where the -OH group is attached to <u>different carbon atoms</u> in the carbon chain, or alcohols with <u>more than one</u> -OH group (like the ones that form condensation polymers on page 179).

You can Make Alkenes by Dehydrating Alcohols

If you heat a mixture of an <u>alcohol</u> and an <u>acid catalyst</u>, an <u>alkene</u> and <u>water</u> are formed in a <u>dehydration</u> reaction. For example:

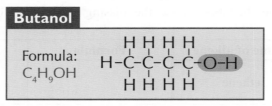

It's known as a dehydration reaction because a molecule of water is lost from the alcohol for each alkene molecule formed.

Ethanol can be Made by Fermentation

1) <u>Fermentation</u> is the process of using <u>yeast</u> to convert a type of <u>carbohydrate</u> called sugars into <u>alcohol</u>.

This is the formula for glucose — a common sugar.

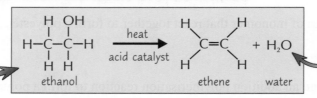

The products are ethanol and carbon dioxide.

2) The carbohydrate can come from any source, but the <u>sugar cane</u> and <u>sugar beet</u> plants are often used.

3) Yeast cells contain an <u>enzyme</u>. Enzymes are naturally occurring <u>catalysts</u> (see page 147) — they speed up reactions.

The general formula of alcohols is $C_nH_{2n+1}OH$

For the exam, make sure you learn the structures of the <u>first four alcohols</u>. You also need to be able to recognise alcohols from their <u>names</u> or <u>formulae</u>, but as long as you know the basic <u>naming system</u> (see p.175), it shouldn't be too hard to figure each one out.

Alcohols

You Can do **Fermentation** in the **Lab**

1) Here's how you would <u>make</u> a <u>solution of ethanol</u> by fermentation:

Ethanol is an alcohol (see previous page).

- Mix <u>yeast</u> and a solution of a <u>carbohydrate</u> (e.g. glucose) in a clean container. <u>Seal</u> the container and leave it in a <u>warm place</u>.

- Keep the mixture between <u>30 °C</u> and <u>40 °C</u> — fermentation happens <u>fastest</u> between these temperatures. At lower temperatures, the reaction slows down. If it's <u>too hot</u> the enzyme in the yeast <u>denatures</u> (is destroyed) and the reaction would stop.

- It's important to keep the mixture in <u>anaerobic conditions</u> (no oxygen). Oxygen converts the <u>ethanol</u> to <u>ethanoic acid</u> (which is what you get in <u>vinegar</u>.

- When the <u>concentration</u> of alcohol reaches about 10 to 20%, the fermentation reaction <u>stops</u>, because the yeast gets <u>killed off</u> by the alcohol.

- The yeast will fall to the <u>bottom</u> of the container — you can collect the <u>ethanol solution</u> from the <u>top</u>.

2) The fermented mixture can be <u>distilled</u> (see below) to produce more concentrated alcohol. Brandy is distilled from wine, whisky is distilled from fermented grain and vodka's distilled from fermented grain or potatoes.

3) Different types of alcoholic drink contain <u>different percentages</u> of ethanol. The typical ethanol concentration of <u>beer</u> is about <u>4%</u> whilst some <u>spirits</u> have a concentration of <u>40%</u>.

Fractional Distillation is Used to **Concentrate** Ethanol

1) A <u>dilute solution</u> of ethanol is produced by fermentation.

2) To make a concentration of ethanol above 20%, ethanol must be <u>concentrated</u> by <u>fractional distillation</u> of the fermentation mixture. Fractional distillation separates mixtures by heating them.

3) Ethanol has a <u>lower</u> boiling point than <u>water</u>. This means that when the fermentation mixture is heated, <u>ethanol evaporates</u> and the vapour rises up the fractionating column, while the <u>water</u> stays as a <u>liquid</u>.

4) A Liebig condenser is used to <u>condense</u> the ethanol vapour by cooling it. The concentrated ethanol can then be collected in a separate flask.

For more on the fractional distillation separation technique, see page 64.

thermometer
water out
fractionating column
Liebig condenser
water in
dilute ethanol solution
concentrated solution of ethanol
heat

Yeast enzymes can only work in a narrow range of temperatures...

...that's why it's really important to keep the temperature between 30 °C and 40 °C during fermentation.

Combustion of Alcohols

Time for another experiment. This one looks at how effectively different <u>alcohols</u> work as <u>fuels</u>.

Alcohols can be Used as Fuels

1) <u>Alcohols</u> can be used for <u>fuel</u> because when they're <u>burned</u>, they release <u>energy</u>.

2) Some countries that have little or no oil deposits but plenty of land and sunshine (e.g. Brazil) grow loads of <u>sugar cane</u>, which they <u>ferment</u> to form ethanol. This ethanol is then used to help fuel cars.

Alcohol can be Burned to Heat Up Water

Some alcohols are <u>better fuels</u> than others. To see which alcohol is best, you can do an experiment using different alcohols to heat up a specific volume of water.

1) Put some alcohol into a <u>spirit burner</u> and measure the <u>mass</u> of the burner and fuel using a <u>mass balance</u>.
   Alcohols are hazardous to humans — e.g. methanol is toxic and propanol is an irritant — so you should make sure you're wearing gloves and safety glasses.

2) Measure 100 cm³ <u>distilled water</u> into a <u>copper calorimeter</u> (use the same container for each experiment).

3) <u>Insulate</u> the calorimeter by using a <u>draught excluder</u>, then cover with an <u>insulating lid</u> after placing a <u>thermometer</u> inside. This helps to make sure that minimal energy is lost to the surroundings.

4) Take the <u>initial temperature</u> of the water then put the burner under the calorimeter and <u>light the wick</u>.
   Alcohol is highly flammable so direct contact with the flame should be avoided - just light the wick.

5) <u>Stir</u> the water throughout using the thermometer. When the heat from the burner has made the temperature of the water rise by <u>20 °C</u>, blow out the spirit burner.
   The apparatus will get hot during the experiment, so you should allow it to cool before touching it, or use tongs.

6) Immediately <u>reweigh</u> the burner and fuel.

7) <u>Repeat</u> the experiment using other alcohols but make sure that you keep all other variables the <u>same</u> for each experiment, including the:
   - <u>mass/volume</u> of water,
   - <u>height</u> of the container above the wick,
   - <u>length</u> of the wick / <u>height</u> of the flame,
   - number of <u>moles</u> of alcohol.

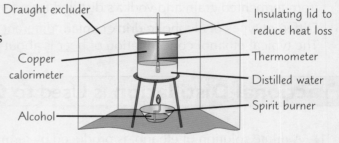

Less Alcohol Burned Means a Better Fuel

1) You can use the <u>results</u> from your experiment to <u>compare the efficiency of alcohols as fuels</u>.

2) An alcohol will be more <u>efficient</u> as a fuel compared to another alcohol if less fuel is needed to raise the temperature of the water by a given amount.

	Ethanol	Propanol	Butanol	Pentanol
Temperature rise (°C)	20	20	20	20
Mass of fuel used (g)	0.48	0.39	0.34	0.28

Less pentanol, $C_5H_{11}OH$, is needed to heat the water by 20 °C compared to the mass of ethanol, C_2H_5OH, needed.

3) These results show that the <u>longer the carbon chain</u> of the alcohol, the <u>more efficient</u> the fuel will be. So, pentanol is more efficient than butanol and butanol is more efficient than propanol.

Make sure you're only testing the effect of different alcohols

To keep it a fair test, it's important to keep all variables the same — only change the type of alcohol used. This ensures other variables don't affect the result, e.g how close the flame was to the water.

Carboxylic Acids

If you oxidise an <u>alcohol</u> from page 182, you end up with a <u>carboxylic acid</u>.
They may sound scary, but once you learn the basic structure, they aren't too bad at all.

You Can Make a **Carboxylic Acid** by **Oxidising** an **Alcohol**

1) When something's <u>oxidised</u>, it gains oxygen.

2) <u>Carboxylic acids</u> are made when <u>alcohols</u> are oxidised.
   You need an oxidising agent for this.

Oxidation can also describe the loss of electrons (see page 92).

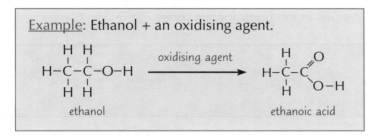

Example: Ethanol + an oxidising agent.

ethanol →(oxidising agent)→ ethanoic acid

Alcohols can only form carboxylic acids in this way if the -OH group is attached to a carbon that's only attached to one carbon itself.

3) Solutions of carboxylic acids have <u>properties</u> that they <u>share with other acids</u>. For example:

> • They <u>react</u> like other acids. E.g. they react with carbonates
>   to produce carbon dioxide, a salt and water.
> • When in solution, they can <u>ionise</u> and release <u>H^+ ions</u>,
>   which make the solution acidic (see p.73). Since they only
>   <u>partially ionise</u>, carboxylic acids are <u>weak acids</u> (see p.74).

4) The basic <u>naming</u> system for carboxylic acids is the same as for
   alkanes — but replace the final '<u>-e</u>' with '<u>-oic acid</u>'.

5) Carboxylic acids are another homologous series of molecules. They have the
   <u>general formula</u> $C_{n-1}H_{2n-1}COOH$ and they have a <u>-COOH functional group</u>.

6) Here are the <u>first four carboxylic acids</u> in the homologous series. They can each be
   formed by oxidising the alcohol which contains the same <u>total number of carbons</u>
   (i.e. methanol is oxidised to methanoic acid, ethanol is oxidised to ethanoic acid, and so on).

Methanoic acid

Formula:
HCOOH

Ethanoic acid

Formula:
CH_3COOH

Propanoic acid

Formula:
C_2H_5COOH

Butanoic acid

Formula:
C_3H_7COOH

7) Remember — members of a homologous series have similar reactions because they contain the same
   <u>functional group</u>. So if you know how a <u>certain molecule</u> in a homologous series reacts
   (e.g. ethanol forming ethanoic acid), you can <u>predict</u> how other molecules in that series react.

Warm-Up and Exam Questions

Time to test how much you know about alcohols and carboxylic acids...

Warm-Up Questions

1) What is the general formula of an alcohol?

2) a) Name the organism which can be used to produce ethanol by fermentation.
   b) State two conditions that are required for fermentation to occur.

3) Give the equation for the production of ethanol from glucose by fermentation.

4) Name the first four carboxylic acids in the homologous series.

Exam Questions

1 Which of the following structures, **A**, **B**, **C**, or **D** shows butanol?

A
$$H-\overset{\overset{\displaystyle H}{|}}{\underset{\underset{\displaystyle H}{|}}{C}}-\overset{\overset{\displaystyle H}{|}}{\underset{\underset{\displaystyle H}{|}}{C}}-\overset{\overset{\displaystyle H}{|}}{\underset{\underset{\displaystyle H}{|}}{C}}-O-H$$

B
$$H-\overset{\overset{\displaystyle H}{|}}{\underset{\underset{\displaystyle H}{|}}{C}}-\overset{\overset{\displaystyle H}{|}}{\underset{\underset{\displaystyle H}{|}}{C}}-\overset{\overset{\displaystyle H}{|}}{\underset{\underset{\displaystyle H}{|}}{C}}-C\overset{\displaystyle O}{\underset{\displaystyle OH}{}}$$

C
$$H-\overset{\overset{\displaystyle H}{|}}{\underset{\underset{\displaystyle H}{|}}{C}}-\overset{\overset{\displaystyle H}{|}}{\underset{\underset{\displaystyle H}{|}}{C}}-\overset{\overset{\displaystyle H}{|}}{\underset{\underset{\underset{\displaystyle H}{|}}{O}}{C}}-\overset{\overset{\displaystyle H}{|}}{\underset{\underset{\displaystyle H}{|}}{C}}-H$$

D
$$H-\overset{\overset{\displaystyle H}{|}}{\underset{\underset{\displaystyle H}{|}}{C}}-\overset{\overset{\displaystyle H}{|}}{\underset{\underset{\displaystyle H}{|}}{C}}=C\overset{\displaystyle H}{\underset{\displaystyle H}{}}$$

[1 mark]

2 Carboxylic acids are a widely used family of organic chemicals.

(a) Draw bonds and missing atoms to complete the displayed formula of ethanoic acid.

$$C-C$$

[1 mark]

(b) i) Name the alcohol that can be oxidised to produce propanoic acid.

[1 mark]

ii) What type of substance is required to convert an alcohol to a carboxylic acid?

[1 mark]

> **PRACTICAL**

3 Alcohols are an important group of organic chemicals. The most widely used alcohol is ethanol.

(a) Name the alcohol in this homologous series that contains one carbon atom.

[1 mark]

(b) Ethanol can be used as a fuel. It burns in oxygen to give carbon dioxide and water. Balance the symbol equation for this reaction.

$$......C_2H_5OH \ + \ ......O_2 \ \rightarrow \ ......CO_2 \ + \ ......H_2O$$

[1 mark]

(c)* Describe an experimental method that could be used to compare the efficiency of ethanol and pentanol as fuels.

[6 marks]

Nanoparticles

Time for some properly cutting-edge science now. Nanoparticles have loads of really useful properties and new uses for them are being developed all the time. They've got some pretty unique features...

Nanoparticles are Really Really Really Really Tiny

1) Really tiny particles, 1–100 nanometers across, are called 'nanoparticles' (1 nm = 0.000 000 001 m). Nanoparticles contain roughly a few hundred atoms — so they're bigger than atoms (atoms are around 0.1–0.5 nm) and simple molecules, but smaller than pretty much anything else.

2) Fullerenes are nanoparticles. The fullerenes include nanotubes (see page 43), tiny hollow carbon tubes. All those covalent bonds make carbon nanotubes very strong.

3) A nanoparticle has very different properties from the 'bulk' chemical that it's made from — e.g. fullerenes have different properties from big lumps of carbon.

For more on fullerenes, see page 43.

Nanoparticles Have a High Surface Area to Volume Ratio

1) As particles decrease in size, the size of their surface area increases in relation to their volume — so their surface area to volume ratio increases.

surface area to volume ratio = surface area ÷ volume

- Imagine splitting a cube up into mini-cubes, then splitting each mini-cube into mini-mini-cubes and so on.
- You end up with cubes that have a much larger combined surface area but the same volume as the original cube.
- So, each mini-mini-cube has a high surface area to volume ratio — that's why the surface area to volume ratio of nanoparticles is so much greater than the bulk material.

2) The high surface area to volume ratio gives nanoparticles different properties from larger particles. This is because a much greater proportion of their atoms are available to interact with substances they come into contact with.

Nanoparticles have a high surface area relative to their volume

"High surface area to volume ratio" sounds like a bit of a mouthful, but all it means is that the surface area of a nanoparticle is large compared to the amount of space that it takes up.

Nanoparticles

Nanoparticles Can **Modify** the Properties of **Materials**

Using nanoparticles is known as nanoscience. Many new uses of nanoparticles are being developed:

1) They have a huge surface area to volume ratio, so they can make good catalysts (see p.147). This is because reactions take place on the surface of catalysts, so the bigger the surface area, the more collisions there will be and so the faster the rate of reaction.

2) New cosmetics, e.g. sunscreens, have been made using nanoparticles. The small particles provide better protection but don't leave white marks on the skin.

3) Nanomedicine is a hot topic. The idea is that tiny fullerenes are absorbed more easily by the body than most particles. This means they could deliver drugs right into the cells where they're needed.

4) New lubricant coatings using fullerenes could be used in, e.g. artificial joints and gears.

5) Nanotubes conduct electricity, so they can be used in tiny electric circuits for computer chips.

6) Nanoparticles are added to plastics in sports equipment, e.g. tennis rackets, golf clubs and golf balls. They make the plastic much stronger and more durable, without adding much mass (hardly any at all).

7) Silver nanoparticles are added to the polymer fibres used to make surgical masks and wound dressings. This gives the fibres antibacterial properties.

The Effects of Nanoparticles on **Health** Aren't Fully **Understood**

1) Although nanoparticles are useful, the way they affect the body isn't fully understood, so it's important that any new products are tested thoroughly to minimise the risks.

The large surface area to volume ratio could be making them more toxic.

2) Some people are worried that products containing nanoparticles have been made available before any possible harmful effects on human health have been investigated properly — in other words, we don't know what the side effects or long-term impacts on health could be.

For example, some nanoparticles used in medicine don't break down easily so they could start to build up in cells. They could also cause problems such as lung inflammation if they're breathed in.

There are lots of possible uses for nanotechnology

EXAM TIP

You may be asked why nanoparticles are used for certain applications, given their properties. You might even be faced with a type of nanoparticle you're not familiar with. Don't panic, just read the question carefully and apply what you know about nanoparticles to the question.

Types of Materials

The <u>properties</u> of materials are all to do with the <u>bonding</u> in them. Look back at pages 34-44 for more about different types of bonding and how this affects something's properties. Now, more on properties.

There are Lots of **Different Types** of **Polymer**

Polymerisation reactions involving <u>different monomers</u> can be used to make a <u>wide range</u> of polymers. Different polymers have different <u>physical properties</u> — some are <u>stronger</u>, <u>stretchier</u>, more <u>easily moulded</u>, and so on. These physical properties make them suited for <u>different uses</u>:

See p.177-179 for more on polymers.

- <u>Strong, rigid</u> polymers such as <u>high-density poly(ethene)</u> are used to make water pipes.
- <u>Light, stretchy</u> polymers such as <u>low-density poly(ethene)</u> are used for plastic bags and squeezy bottles.
- <u>Poly(styrene) foam</u> is used in <u>packaging</u> to protect breakable things, and as a <u>thermal insulator</u>.
- <u>Heat-resistant</u> polymers such as <u>melamine</u> resin and <u>poly(propene)</u> are used to make <u>plastic kettles</u>.

Ceramics are **Stiff** but **Brittle**

Ceramics include glass, porcelain and bone china.

<u>Ceramics</u> are made by baking substances, such as clay, to produce a <u>brittle</u>, <u>stiff</u> material.

- <u>Clay</u> is a mineral formed from <u>weathered</u> and <u>decomposed rock</u>. It's <u>soft</u> when it's <u>dug up</u> out of the ground, which makes it <u>easy to mould</u> into different shapes required for pottery or bricks.
- It can be <u>hardened</u> by firing at very <u>high temperatures</u>. This makes it <u>ideal</u> as a <u>building</u> material — clay bricks can <u>withstand</u> the <u>weight</u> of lots <u>more bricks</u> on top of them.

- <u>Glass</u> is generally <u>transparent</u> and <u>strong</u>, can be <u>moulded</u> when hot and can be <u>brittle</u> when thin.
- The majority of glass made is <u>soda-lime glass</u> which is made by heating <u>limestone</u>, <u>sand</u> and <u>sodium carbonate</u> (soda) until they melt. When the mixture cools it comes out as <u>glass</u>.

Composites are Made of **Different Materials**

Composites, such as <u>fibreglass</u> and <u>concrete</u>, are made of one material (the reinforcement) <u>embedded</u> in another (the matrix/binder). The <u>properties</u> of a composite depend on the properties of the materials it is <u>made from</u>. For example:

<u>Carbon fibre</u> composites have been made using carbon atoms bonded together to make carbon fibres or carbon <u>nanotubes</u> (see p.43) held together in a polymer resin matrix. These polymers are expensive to make but are very <u>strong</u> and <u>light</u> making them ideal for use in aerospace and sports car manufacturing.

Metals are Good **Conductors**

Metals are generally very good at <u>conducting</u> both <u>heat</u> and <u>electricity</u>. They typically have a <u>high density</u> and are <u>malleable</u>. Metals can also be <u>mixed</u> with other elements to form <u>alloys</u>.

See p. 44 for more on metals and p.109 for more on alloys.

Getting the material right for a particular use is really important

You might have to pick the right material for a given use in your exam, so make sure you know the properties of the materials on this page. Give this a go to get it in your head — cover the page, scribble down everything you can remember, check to see how well you did, and repeat.

Materials and Their Uses

It's all very well making a material but it needs to be fit for purpose. You need to be able to understand <u>why</u> a certain material is used and <u>not</u> another material. For example, why a kettle is made of <u>metal</u> and not <u>wood</u>.

Different **Materials** are Suited to Different **Jobs**

What materials are used for depends on their <u>properties</u>. In the <u>exam</u> they might ask you to <u>interpret</u> <u>information</u> about the properties of materials and <u>assess</u> the <u>suitability</u> of these materials for different purposes.

Polymers

1) <u>Polymers</u> are really adaptable — for example, they're often <u>flexible</u>, so they can be bent without breaking, and can be <u>easily moulded</u> into almost any shape.

2) They're often <u>cheaper</u> than most other materials, and they also tend to be <u>less</u> <u>dense</u> than most metals or ceramics, so they're often used when designing products that need to have a low mass.

3) They're also <u>thermal</u> and <u>electrical insulators</u>.

4) Polymers can <u>degrade</u> and <u>break down</u> over time, so polymer products don't always last as long as those made from other materials.

Metals

1) <u>Metals</u> are <u>good conductors</u> of <u>heat</u> and <u>electricity</u> — which can be an advantage or a disadvantage, depending on what the material is needed for.

2) They're <u>malleable</u>, so like polymers they can be formed into a variety of shapes.

3) Some metals corrode easily, but products made from <u>corrosion resistant</u> metals can last for a very long time.

4) Metals are usually <u>less brittle</u> than either ceramics or polymers, so they're likely to <u>deform</u> but stay in one piece where other materials may <u>shatter</u>.

You should know all about the bonding in metals (see page 44) and polymers (see pages 177-179).

Composites

1) <u>Composites</u> have different properties depending on the <u>matrix/binder</u> and the <u>reinforcement</u>.

2) The combination of <u>component materials</u> used can be altered, so composites can be designed to have specific properties for a <u>specific purpose</u>.

3) The main <u>disadvantage</u> of composites is that they tend to be much more <u>expensive</u> to produce than other materials.

Lightweight composites are often used in aircraft manufacture.

Ceramics

1) <u>Ceramics</u>, like polymers, are <u>insulators</u> of heat and electricity.

2) They're much more <u>brittle</u> and <u>stiff</u> than most other materials, but they're also <u>strong</u> and <u>hard wearing</u>.

3) They don't <u>degrade</u> or <u>corrode</u> like other materials can, so they last a lot longer — that's why we still use glass in windows instead of clear plastic.

How a material is used will depend on its properties

A property that is desirable for one application may be a disadvantage in another — e.g. metals are used for kitchenware as they conduct heat well, but they'd be useless if you were trying to insulate your home.

Materials and Their Uses

Just one more page on materials. This one is all about deciding which material is <u>suitable</u> for a certain <u>use</u>.

Different Materials have Different Properties

Each type of material has a <u>different</u> set of <u>physical properties</u>. You can compare these properties to see what material would be <u>best</u> for making a certain product.

For example, the data below tells you that <u>HDPE</u> has a <u>low tensile strength</u> (it breaks easily) and is <u>less dense</u> than soda-lime glass, a carbon fibre composite and aluminium...

	HDPE	Soda-lime glass	Carbon fibre composite	Aluminium
Tensile strength (MPa)	37	19 – 77	1860	90
Density (g cm⁻³)	0.94 – 0.97	2.44	1.50	2.70

You Need to Be Able to Interpret Information about Materials

You can <u>use information</u> about the properties of materials (like the info in the table above) and <u>assess</u> their <u>suitability</u> for different uses.

EXAMPLE:

A company is investigating the best material to make a fencing sword. The sword needs to be strong and lightweight, and is intended to be sold mainly to beginners to the sport of fencing.

Using the data in the table, suggest which material from the table the company should use.

Material	Density (g cm⁻³)	Strength (MPa)	Cost
Steel	7.8	780	Low
Poly(propene)	0.94	48	Low
Copper	8.9	220	Medium
Carbon fibre	1.5	4100	High

Poly(propene) can be ruled out — it's cheap and light but a lot weaker than all the other options.

Copper's heavier, weaker and more expensive than steel, so it can't be the best option.

Carbon fibre is really strong and light, but it's also expensive.
This is a sword for beginners, so the price should be kept down.

Steel swords will have a fairly high strength relative to their weight and would be cheap to make.
So steel is the best material for the job.

As well as making sure a product is <u>fit for its purpose</u>, <u>life cycle assessment data</u> (see p.99-100) is also used to work out how <u>environmentally friendly</u> the manufacture, use and disposal of a product is.

You may need to interpret data for different materials

The best way to answer the type of question shown in the example above is to start by thinking about what properties the object should have. Then have a look at the information about the materials that you've been given and select the material which has the most suitable properties.

Warm-Up and Exam Questions

Phew, that was a lot of information to take in. By now you should be pretty confident in the different properties of nanoparticles, metals, polymers, ceramics and composites. Time for some questions...

Warm-Up Questions

1) How does the surface area to volume ratio change as particles get smaller?
2) Give two uses of nanoparticles.
3) What are ceramics?
4) Carbon-fibre is an example of a composite material. Name one other composite material.
5) Describe two of the main properties of polymers.

Exam Questions

1 Some people are concerned about the use of nanoparticles in medicines and cosmetics. Suggest one reason why some people are concerned about the use of nanoparticles and suggest what could be done to minimise the risks.

[2 marks]

2 When a company is choosing what materials to use to make a particular product, they will consider the properties, availability and cost of the materials that they could use. **Figure 1** shows some properties of two different materials.

Material	Density (g cm⁻³)	Strength (MPa)	Flexibility	Corrosion resistance	Cost
Steel	7.8	780	Low	Low	Low
Aluminium alloy	2.7	565	Low	High	Medium-high
Carbon-fibre composite	1.5	4100	Low	High	Very high
Polypropene plastic	0.9	48	High	High	Low

Figure 1

(a) Which of the materials in **Figure 1** would be most suitable for use in a garden chair? Explain your answer.

[3 marks]

(b) Many aeroplane parts need to withstand high forces, so they must be made from strong materials.

   (i) Using the information in **Figure 1**, explain why aluminium alloy is often used to make aeroplane parts instead of steel.

[2 marks]

   (ii) Carbon-fibre composites are less commonly used for aeroplane parts than aluminium alloys. Suggest one reason for this.

[1 mark]

Revision Summary for Topic 9

That wraps up <u>Topic 9</u> — time to try these questions to see if you've got this topic in the bag.
- Try these questions and <u>tick off each one</u> when you <u>get it right</u>.
- When you've done <u>all the questions</u> under a heading and are <u>completely happy</u> with it, tick it off.

Tests for Ions (p.169-173) ☑

1) What colour flame is produced when copper is heated in a flame? ☑
2) What gas will turn damp, red litmus paper blue? ☑
3) Describe how you would test a solution for carbonate ions. ☑
4) In flame photometry, what does the intensity of the light at the measured wavelength show? ☑

Alkanes and Alkenes (p.175-176) ☑

5) What are alkenes? ☑
6) Describe the colour change that occurs when an alkene is added to bromine water. ☑
7) Name the products that would be formed if an alkane was burned in a good supply of oxygen. ☑

Polymers (p.177-180) ☑

8) What functional group does a monomer need to form addition polymers? ☑
9) List three properties of poly(ethene). ☑
10) Draw the displayed formula of poly(ethene). ☑
11) Name the type of monomers that form DNA. ☑
12) What are plastics made from? ☑
13) Why do polymers need to be separated before they can be recycled? ☑

Alcohols and Carboxylic Acids (p.182-185) ☑

14) What is the chemical formula for butanol? ☑
15) Draw a diagram of the equipment you would use to concentrate a solution of dilute ethanol. ☑
16) Explain why it is important to insulate the copper calorimeter when carrying out an experiment comparing the efficiency of different alcohols as fuels. ☑
17) Which alcohol would be a more efficient fuel — methanol or propanol? ☑
18) Name the product formed when ethanol is oxidised. ☑
19) Name the carboxylic acid with the chemical formula C_2H_5COOH. ☑

Nanoparticles and Types of Materials (p.187-191) ☑

20) How big are nanoparticles? ☑
21) Explain why a high surface area to volume ratio gives nanoparticles different properties to larger particles. ☑
22) Why are nanoparticles good for making sunscreens? ☑
23) Give two properties of ceramics. ☑
24) Name a type of material that is a good electrical conductor. ☑
25) What is a composite? ☑

Taking Measurements

This section covers <u>practical skills</u> you'll need to know about for your course.

- You'll have to do <u>8 core practicals</u> (experiments). These are covered earlier in the book and they're <u>highlighted</u> with <u>practical stamps</u> like this one.

- The following pages of this section cover some <u>extra bits and bobs</u> you need to know about practical work. First up, using apparatus to take measurements...

Three Ways to Measure Liquids

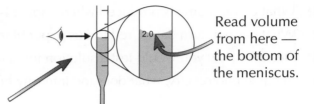

Read volume from here — the bottom of the meniscus.

There are a few methods you might use to measure the volume of a liquid. Whichever method you use, always read the volume from the <u>bottom of the meniscus</u> (the curved upper surface of the liquid) when it's at <u>eye level</u>.

<u>Pipettes</u> are long, narrow tubes that are used to suck up an <u>accurate</u> volume of liquid and <u>transfer</u> it to another container. A <u>pipette filler</u> attached to the end of the pipette is used so that you can <u>safely control</u> the amount of liquid you're drawing up. Pipettes are often <u>calibrated</u> to allow for the fact that the last drop of liquid stays in the pipette when the liquid is ejected. This reduces <u>transfer errors</u>.

pipette filler

<u>Burettes</u> measure from top to bottom (so when they're filled to the top of the scale, the scale reads zero). They have a tap at the bottom which you can use to release the liquid into another container (you can even release it drop by drop). To use a burette, take an <u>initial reading</u>, and once you've released as much liquid as you want, take a <u>final reading</u>. The <u>difference</u> between the readings tells you <u>how much</u> liquid you used.

Burettes are used a lot for titrations. There's loads more about titrations on page 113.

<u>Measuring cylinders</u> are the most common way to measure out a liquid. They come in all different <u>sizes</u>. Make sure you choose one that's the right size for the measurement you want to make. It's no good using a huge 1000 cm³ cylinder to measure out 2 cm³ of a liquid — the graduations will be too big, and you'll end up with <u>massive errors</u>. It'd be much better to use one that measures up to 10 cm³.

If you only want a couple of drops of liquid, and don't need it to be accurately measured, you can use a dropping pipette to transfer it. For example, this is how you'd add a couple of drops of indicator into a mixture.

Gas Syringes Measure Gas Volumes

1) Gases can be measured with a gas syringe.

2) They should be measured at <u>room temperature and pressure</u> as the <u>volume</u> of a gas <u>changes</u> with temperature and pressure.

3) You should also use a gas syringe that's the <u>right size</u> for the measurement you're making.

4) Before you use the syringe, you should make sure it's completely sealed and that the plunger moves smoothly.

Remember — burettes release liquid and pipettes suck it up

Pipettes, burettes and measuring cylinders may look quite similar from simple diagrams, but the differences between them are much more obvious when you use them in real life. The best kind of revision for these practical techniques is real <u>hands-on experience</u>.

Taking Measurements

Solids Should Be Measured Using a Balance

1) To weigh a solid, start by putting the <u>container</u> you're weighing your substance <u>into</u> on the <u>balance</u>.

2) Set the balance to exactly <u>zero</u> and then start weighing out your substance.

3) It's <u>no good</u> carefully weighing out your solid if it's not all transferred to your reaction vessel — the amount in the <u>reaction vessel</u> won't be the same as your measurement. Here are a couple of methods you can use to make sure that none gets left in your weighing container...

- If you're <u>dissolving</u> the solid in a solvent to make a <u>solution</u>, you could <u>wash</u> any remaining solid into the new container using the <u>solvent</u>. This way you know that <u>all</u> the solid you weighed has been transferred.

- You could set the balance to zero <u>before</u> you put your <u>weighing container</u> on the balance. Then <u>reweigh</u> the weighing container <u>after</u> you've transferred the solid. Use the <u>difference in mass</u> to work out <u>exactly</u> how much solid you added to your experiment.

You May Have to Measure the Time Taken for a Change

1) You should use a <u>stopwatch</u> to <u>time</u> experiments. These measure to the nearest <u>0.1 s</u> so are <u>sensitive</u>.

2) Always make sure you <u>start</u> and <u>stop</u> the stopwatch at exactly the right time. For example, if you're investigating the rate of an experiment, you should start timing at the <u>exact moment</u> you mix the reagents and start the reaction. If you're measuring the time taken for a precipitate to form, you should watch the reaction like a hawk so you can <u>stop</u> timing the moment it goes cloudy.

Measure pH to Find Out How Acidic or Alkaline a Solution Is

You need to be able to decide the best method for measuring pH, depending on what your experiment is.

1) <u>Indicators</u> are dyes that <u>change colour</u> depending on whether they're in an <u>acid</u> or an <u>alkali</u>. You use them by adding a couple of drops of the indicator to the solution you're interested in. They're useful for titration reactions, when you want to find the point at which a solution is neutralised.

2) <u>Universal indicator</u> is a <u>mixture</u> of indicators that changes colour <u>gradually</u> as pH changes. It doesn't show a <u>sudden</u> colour change. It's useful for <u>estimating</u> the pH of a solution based on its colour.

3) Indicators can be soaked into <u>paper</u> and strips of this paper can be used for testing pH. If you use a dropping pipette to spot a small amount of a solution onto some indicator paper, it will <u>change colour</u> depending on the pH of the solution.

<u>Litmus paper</u> turns <u>red</u> in acidic conditions and <u>blue</u> in basic conditions. <u>Universal indicator paper</u> can be used to <u>estimate</u> the pH based on its colour.

There's loads more about pH on page 73.

4) Indicator paper is useful when you <u>don't</u> want to change the colour of <u>all</u> of the substance, or if the substance is <u>already</u> coloured so might <u>obscure</u> the colour of the indicator. You can also hold a piece of <u>damp indicator paper</u> in a <u>gas sample</u> to test its pH.

5) <u>pH probes</u> are attached to pH meters which have a <u>digital display</u> that gives a <u>numerical</u> value for the pH of a solution. They're used to give an <u>accurate value</u> of pH.

Have your stopwatch ready before you try to time something

To make sure your results can be <u>trusted</u> by other scientists, you have to make sure all your measurements are <u>accurate</u>. So make sure you learn all the tips on these two pages for improving accuracy — e.g. using the right size of gas syringe for the measurement you're taking.

Safety and Heating Substances

Safety is really important when carrying out experiments. This is because experiments in chemistry can often involve using hazardous chemicals or heating substances. Read on to find out how to be safe in the lab.

Be Careful When You **Handle** or **Mix** Substances

1) There are lots of hazards in chemistry experiments, so before you start any experiment, you should read any safety precautions to do with your method or the chemicals you're using.

2) The substances used in chemical reactions are often hazardous. For example, they might catch fire easily (they're flammable), or they might irritate or burn your skin if you come into contact with them.

3) Whenever you're doing an experiment, you should wear a lab coat, safety goggles and gloves.

4) Always be careful that the chemicals you're using aren't flammable before you go lighting any Bunsen burners, and make sure you're working in an area that's well ventilated.

5) If you're doing an experiment that might produce nasty gases (such as chlorine), you should carry out the experiment in a fume hood so that the gas can't escape out into the room you're working in.

6) Never directly touch any chemicals (even if you're wearing gloves). Use a spatula to transfer solids between containers. Carefully pour liquids between different containers, using a funnel to avoid spills.

7) Be careful when you're mixing chemicals, as a reaction might occur. If you're diluting a liquid, add the concentrated substance to the water (not the other way around) or the mixture could get very hot.

The **Temperature** of **Water Baths** & **Electric Heaters** Can Be **Set**

1) A water bath is a container filled with water that can be heated to a specific temperature.

- Set the temperature on the water bath, and allow the water to heat up.
- Place the vessel containing your substance in the water bath using a pair of tongs. The level of the water outside the vessel should be just above the level of the substance inside the vessel.
- The substance will then be warmed to the same temperature as the water.

reaction vessel

temperature control

As the substance in the vessel is surrounded by water, the heating is very even. Water boils at 100 °C though, so you can't use a water bath to heat something to a higher temperature than this — the water won't get hot enough.

Handle any glassware you've heated with tongs until you're sure it's cooled down.

2) Electric heaters are often made up of a metal plate that can be heated to a certain temperature. The vessel containing the substance you want to heat is placed on top of the hot plate. You can heat substances to higher temperatures than you can in a water bath but, as the vessel is only heated from below, you'll usually have to stir the substance inside to make sure it's heated evenly.

Measure **Temperature** Accurately

You can use a thermometer to measure the temperature of a substance:

- Make sure the bulb of your thermometer is completely submerged in any mixture you're measuring.
- If you're taking an initial reading, you should wait for the temperature to stabilise first.
- Read your measurement off the scale on a thermometer at eye level to make sure it's correct.

Heating Substances

Sometimes water baths and electric heaters aren't <u>appropriate</u> for what you want to do — e.g. if you want to heat a sample of a compound to see what <u>colour</u> flame it produces, you should use a <u>Bunsen burner</u> instead.

Bunsen Burners Have a Naked **Flame**

1) Bunsen burners are good for heating things quickly. You can easily adjust how strongly they're heating.

2) But you need to be careful not to use them if you're heating <u>flammable</u> compounds as the flame means the substance would be at risk of <u>catching fire</u>.

3) Here's how to use a Bunsen burner:

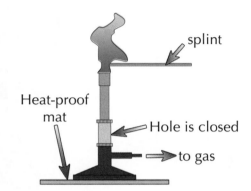

- Connect the Bunsen burner to a gas tap, and check that the hole is <u>closed</u>. Place it on a <u>heat-proof mat</u>.
- Light a <u>splint</u> and hold it over the Bunsen burner. Now, turn on the gas. The Bunsen burner should light with a <u>yellow flame</u>.
- The <u>more open</u> the hole is, the <u>more strongly</u> the Bunsen burner will heat your substance. Open the hole to the amount you want. As you open the hole more, the flame should turn more <u>blue</u>.

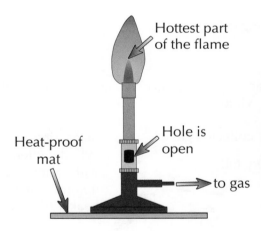

- The <u>hottest</u> part of the flame is just above the <u>blue cone</u>, so you should heat things here.
- If your Bunsen burner is alight but not heating anything, make sure you <u>close</u> the hole so that the flame becomes <u>yellow</u> and <u>clearly visible</u>.
- If you're heating something so that the container (e.g. a test tube) is <u>in</u> the flame, you should hold the vessel at the <u>top</u>, furthest away from the substance (and so the flame) using a pair of <u>tongs</u>.
- If you're heating something <u>over</u> the flame (e.g. an evaporating dish), you should put a <u>tripod and gauze</u> over the Bunsen burner before you light it, and place the vessel on this.

4) You'd use a Bunsen burner to carry out <u>flame tests</u> to identify metal ions in a compound (see page 169).

- A sample of the compound is placed on a <u>metal wire</u> that you hold just above the cone of a Bunsen burner with a blue flame.
- The flame should then <u>change colour</u> depending on what metal ion is in the sample.

You might not expect the blue flame to be hotter, but it is.

As you can see, it's not just when you're heating substances that you have to be safe — you should also be careful, for example, when you're using <u>hazardous chemicals</u> or if chemical reactions are likely to give off a lot of <u>heat</u>. Always <u>read through</u> any safety precautions you're given carefully <u>before</u> you start, otherwise you might do something dangerous.

Setting Up Equipment

Setting up the equipment for an experiment correctly is <u>important</u> if you want to take accurate measurements.

To Collect **Gases**, the System Needs to be **Sealed**

1) There are times when you might want to <u>collect</u> the gas produced by a reaction. For example, to investigate the <u>rate</u> of reaction.

2) The most accurate way to measure the volume of a gas that's been produced is to collect it in a <u>gas syringe</u> (see page 138).

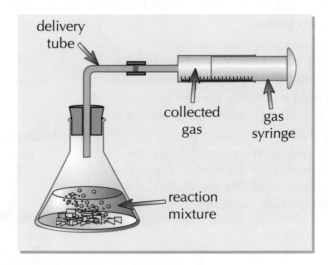

3) You could also collect it by <u>displacing water</u> from a measuring cylinder. Here's how you do it...

- Fill a <u>measuring cylinder</u> with <u>water</u>, and carefully place it <u>upside down</u> in a container of water. Record the <u>initial level</u> of the water in the measuring cylinder.

- Position a <u>delivery tube</u> coming <u>from</u> the reaction vessel so that it's <u>inside</u> the measuring cylinder, pointing upwards. Any gas that's produced will pass <u>through</u> the delivery tube and <u>into</u> the <u>measuring cylinder</u>. As the gas enters the measuring cylinder, the <u>water</u> is <u>pushed out</u>.

- Record the <u>level of water</u> in the measuring cylinder and use this value, along with your <u>initial value</u>, to calculate the <u>volume</u> of gas produced.

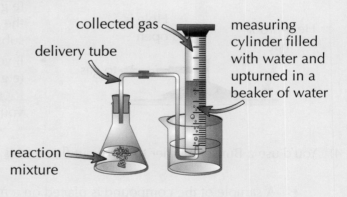

4) When you're measuring a gas, your equipment has to be sealed or some gas could escape and your results wouldn't be accurate.

5) If just want to <u>collect</u> a sample to test (and don't need to measure a volume), you can collect it over water as above using a <u>test tube</u>. Once the test tube is full of gas, you can stopper it and store the gas for later.

If the delivery tube is underneath the measuring cylinder rather than inside it then some of the gas might escape out into the air.

You can test the gas you've collected to find out what it is

EXAM TIP

Having a <u>good knowledge</u> of practical techniques won't just make your investigations more reliable, it might <u>come in handy</u> for questions in your exams. It's possible that you could be asked to comment on how equipment has been set up, e.g. suggest improvements.

Setting Up Equipment

Some experiments involve slightly more _complicated_ equipment that might be less familiar to you. For example, _electrolysis_ experiments use _electrodes_ — this page shows you how to set them up.

You May Have to **Identify** the **Products** of Electrolysis

There's more about electrolysis on p.82-86.

1) When you electrolyse an _aqueous solution_, the products of electrolysis will depend on how reactive the ions in the solution are compared to the H^+ and OH^- ions that come from water.

2) At the _cathode_ you'll either get a _pure metal_ coating the electrode or bubbles of _hydrogen gas_.

3) At the _anode_, you'll get bubbles of _oxygen gas_ unless a _halide ion_ is present, when you'll get the _halogen_.

4) You may have to predict and identify what's been made in an electrolysis experiment. To do this, you need to be able to _set up the equipment_ correctly so that you can _collect_ any gas that's produced. The easiest way to collect the gas is in a _test tube_.

5) Here's how to set up the equipment...

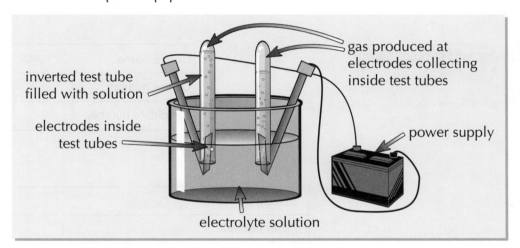

inverted test tube filled with solution

gas produced at electrodes collecting inside test tubes

electrodes inside test tubes

power supply

electrolyte solution

The tests for gases are described on pages 75, 129 and 162.

Make Sure You Can **Draw Diagrams** of Your Equipment

1) When you're writing out a _method_ for your experiment, it's always a good idea to draw a _labelled diagram_ showing how your apparatus will be _set up_.

2) The easiest way to do this is to use a scientific drawing, where each piece of apparatus is drawn as if you're looking at its _cross-section_. For example:

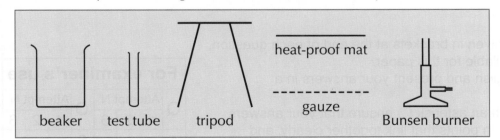

beaker   test tube   tripod   heat-proof mat   gauze   Bunsen burner

The pieces of glassware are drawn without tops so they aren't sealed. If you want to draw a closed system, remember to draw a bung in the top.

REVISION TIP

These simple diagrams are clear and easy to draw

Have a go at _drawing out_ some of the practical diagrams on these pages using a simplified cross-section drawing of each piece of equipment. It'll give you some practice at doing them and you can revise how to set up the experiments as well. Win-win.

Practice Exams

Once you've been through all the questions in this book, you should feel pretty confident about the exams. As final preparation, here is a set of **practice exams** to really get you set for the real thing. The time allowed for each paper is 1 hour 45 minutes. These papers are designed to give you the best possible preparation for your exams.

CGP   Practice Exam Paper
GCSE Chemistry

GCSE Chemistry

Paper 1

Higher Tier

In addition to this paper you should have:
• A ruler.
• A calculator.

Centre name				
Centre number				
Candidate number				

Time allowed:
• 1 hour 45 minutes

Surname	
Other names	
Candidate signature	

Instructions to candidates
• Write your name and other details in the spaces provided above.
• Answer **all** questions in the spaces provided.
• Do all rough work on the paper.
• Cross out any work you do not want to be marked.
• You are allowed to use a calculator.

Information for candidates
• The marks available are given in brackets at the end of each question.
• There are 100 marks available for this paper.
• You should use good English and present your answers in a clear and organised way.
• For questions marked with an asterisk (*) ensure that your answers have a logical structure with points that link together clearly, and include detailed, relevant information.

For examiner's use

Q	Attempt Nº			Q	Attempt Nº		
	1	2	3		1	2	3
1				6			
2				7			
3				8			
4				9			
5				10			
				Total			

Advice to candidates
• In calculations show clearly how you worked out your answers.
• Read each question carefully before answering it.
• Check your answers if you have time.

1   Atoms contain protons, neutrons and electrons.

(a) **Figure 1** shows the structure of an atom.
     Label a proton.

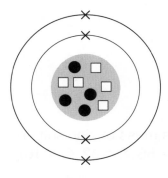

Figure 1

[1 mark]

(b) Where is most of the mass found in an atom?

☐ **A** in the neutrons

☐ **B** in the nucleus

☐ **C** in the electrons

☐ **D** in the electron shells

[1 mark]

Figure 2 shows the numbers of protons, neutrons and electrons in six different atoms.

Atom	Number of protons	Number of neutrons	Number of electrons
A	5	6	5
B	7	7	7
C	6	8	6
D	6	6	6
E	10	10	10
F	4	5	4

Figure 2

(c) Explain which **two** atoms in **Figure 2** are isotopes of the same element.

....

....

....

[2 marks]

Question 1 continues on the next page

Turn over ▶

(d) Zinc sulfate is an ionic compound with the formula $ZnSO_4$.

    (i) What is the charge on a sulfate ion?

       ☐ **A** +1

       ☐ **B** −1

       ☐ **C** +2

       ☐ **D** −2

[1 mark]

    (ii) Calculate the relative formula mass of zinc sulfate.
       (relative atomic masses: Zn = 65, S = 32, O = 16)

relative formula mass = ...

[2 marks]

    (iii) Calculate the number of oxygen atoms in 1.4 moles of zinc sulfate.

       Give your answer to two significant figures.

Number of oxygen atoms = ...

[3 marks]

[Total 10 marks]

2 Carbon dioxide is a simple molecular substance.

(a) Which one of the following is a typical size of a simple molecule such as carbon dioxide?

☐ **A** 10^{-10} m

☐ **B** 10^{-6} m

☐ **C** 10^{-12} m

☐ **D** 10^{-11} m

[1 mark]

(b) Explain why carbon dioxide does **not** conduct electricity.

Give your answer in terms of electrons.

....

....

[1 mark]

(c) Carbon dioxide is produced when a fuel reacts with oxygen in a combustion reaction.

Some data about the properties of oxygen is shown in **Figure 3**.

Melting point	Boiling point
−218 °C	−183 °C

Figure 3

(i) Predict the physical state of oxygen at −198 °C.

....

[1 mark]

(ii) Predict whether carbon dioxide would have a higher or lower boiling point than oxygen. Explain your answer.

....

....

....

[3 marks]

Question 2 continues on the next page

Turn over ▶

204

(d) Carbon dioxide can also be produced by heating zinc carbonate ($ZnCO_3$).

Zinc oxide (ZnO) is left behind.

The equation for the reaction is:

$$ZnCO_3 \rightarrow CO_2 + ZnO$$

1.32 kg of carbon dioxide is produced when a sample of zinc carbonate is heated.

Calculate the mass, in grams, of zinc carbonate that reacted.

(relative atomic masses: Zn = 65, C = 12, O = 16)

Mass of zinc carbonate = ... g

[4 marks]

[Total 10 marks]

3   A student wanted to find the concentration of a sodium hydroxide solution.

She decided to titrate 10 cm³ of the sodium hydroxide solution with
0.050 mol dm⁻³ sulfuric acid solution, using phenolphthalein indicator.

The student used phenolphthalein as an indicator rather than Universal indicator.

(a) Explain why Universal indicator should not be used for an acid-base titration.

....

....

[2 marks]

(b)   Complete and balance the equation for this reaction below.

H_2SO_4 + ... → .... + ...

[2 marks]

(c) (i) In the titration, 8.80 cm³ of sulfuric acid were needed to neutralise
10.0 cm³ of the sodium hydroxide solution.

How many moles of sulfuric acid reacted with the sodium hydroxide in the titration?

Number of moles = ...

[1 mark]

(ii) How many moles of sodium hydroxide reacted with the acid?

....

[1 mark]

(iii) Calculate the concentration of the sodium hydroxide solution in mol dm⁻³.
Show clearly how you work out your answer.

Concentration = ... mol dm⁻³

[2 marks]

[Total 8 marks]

Turn over for the next question

Turn over ▶

4 A student reacts four different metals with dilute sulfuric acid.

She controls all of the relevant variables to make sure that the test is fair.

She collects the gas given off by each reaction in a gas syringe.

Figure 4 shows all four reactions after 30 seconds.

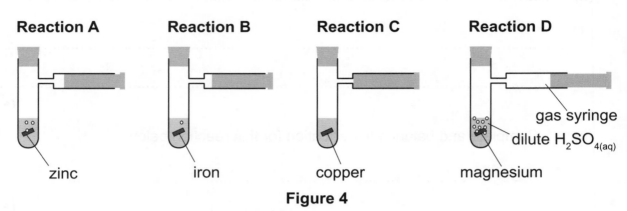

Figure 4

(a) State the dependent variable in this experiment.

....

[1 mark]

(b) (i) Name the gas that is being collected in the gas syringes.

....

[1 mark]

(ii) Describe a method that could be used to test for this gas,
and state the result you would expect to find.

....

....

....

[2 marks]

(c) Explain which reaction, **A**, **B**, **C**, or **D**, contains the **most reactive** metal.

....

....

....

[3 marks]

(d) In another experiment, the student placed pieces of different metals in metal salt solutions. She left them for 10 minutes. The student then recorded whether any reaction had occurred. The results of this experiment are shown in **Figure 5**.

	Did any reaction occur with the following metal salt solutions?		
	Iron sulfate	**Magnesium sulfate**	**Copper sulfate**
Iron	No	No	....
Magnesium	....	No	Yes
Copper	No	No	No

Figure 5

Complete **Figure 5** by filling in the gaps.

[2 marks]

(e) The equation for the reaction between magnesium and copper sulfate solution is:

$$Mg_{(s)} + CuSO_{4(aq)} \rightarrow MgSO_{4(aq)} + Cu_{(s)}$$

In this reaction, magnesium loses electrons.

What is the name given to this process?

☐ **A** electrolysis

☐ **B** reduction

☐ **C** neutralisation

☐ **D** oxidation

[1 mark]
[Total 10 marks]

Turn over for the next question

5 A company uses a process called the Contact process to make sulfuric acid.

The first step of the process is the exothermic reaction of sulfur dioxide with oxygen to form sulfur trioxide.

The equation for the reaction is shown below.

$$2SO_{2(g)} + O_{2(g)} \rightleftharpoons 2SO_{3(g)}$$

(a) This reaction can reach equilibrium.

Which of the following describes what happens when a reaction reaches equilibrium?

☐ **A** The forward reaction happens at a faster rate than the backward reaction.

☐ **B** The forward and backward reactions stop happening.

☐ **C** The forward and backward reactions happen at the same rate.

☐ **D** The backward reaction happens at a faster rate than the forward reaction.

[1 mark]

(b) State what will happen to the yield of sulfur trioxide in this reaction if the pressure inside the reaction vessel is decreased.

Explain your answer.

....

....

....

....

[3 marks]

(c) The company used 10 000 kg of sulfur dioxide to produce 7500 kg of sulfur trioxide each day.

The theoretical yield of sulfur trioxide is 12 500 kg when 10 000 kg of sulfur dioxide is reacted with oxygen.

(i) Calculate the percentage yield of the reaction.

Percentage yield = ... %

[1 mark]

(ii) The plant was modified to allow the sulfur trioxide to be removed from the reaction vessel as soon as it was made.

This allowed the yield of the plant to increase by 15%.

How many kilograms of sulfur trioxide could the modified plant make in five days?

mass made in five days = ... kg

[3 marks]

[Total 8 marks]

Turn over for the next question

6   A student is investigating how much calcium hydroxide is needed to neutralise 25 cm³ of 0.8 mol dm⁻³ hydrochloric acid.

The student used the following method:

1.   Measure out the hydrochloric acid into a conical flask.
2.   Measure out 0.1 g of solid calcium hydroxide using a mass balance.
3.   Add the calcium hydroxide to the hydrochloric acid.
4.   Wait for the calcium hydroxide to react completely.
5.   Record the pH of the solution.
6.   Repeat steps 2-5 until all of the hydrochloric acid has reacted.

(a) Suggest a piece of apparatus that the student could have used to measure out the hydrochloric acid.

....
[1 mark]

(b) Use the information above to calculate the mass of hydrochloric acid present in the 25 cm³ solution that the student used.
(relative formula mass of HCl = 36.5)

Mass of hydrochloric acid = ... g
[2 marks]

(c) (i) Describe what the student would have observed once all of the acid in the flask had reacted.

....

....
[1 mark]

(ii) Write the ionic equation for a neutralisation reaction.

Include state symbols in your answer.

....
[2 marks]

(d) (i) The student plotted a graph to show how the pH of the solution changed as the calcium hydroxide was added. The results are shown in **Figure 6**.

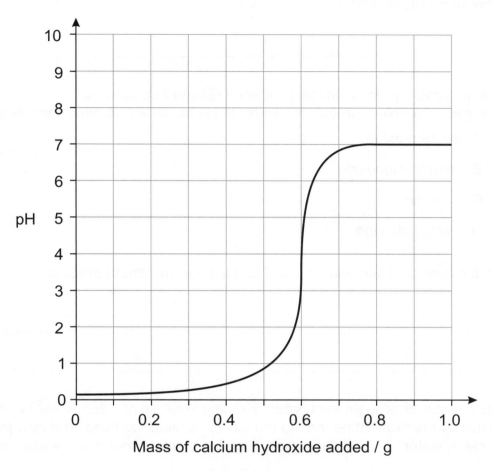

Figure 6

What mass of calcium hydroxide was required to completely neutralise the acid?

Mass of calcium hydroxide = ... g

[1 mark]

Another student is going to repeat the experiment. He plans to use Universal indicator to measure how the pH of the solution changes during the experiment.

(ii) Explain why this student would not be able to produce a graph like **Figure 6** using the results they gather.

....

....

[1 mark]

(iii) Suggest a piece of equipment that could be used to accurately record the pH value of the solution over the course of the experiment.

....

[1 mark]

[Total 9 marks]

Turn over for the next question

Turn over ▶

7 Water is made potable using several methods.

(a) Define the term potable water.

....

[1 mark]

(b) The water treatment process involves several different stages.
   (i) Which gas is bubbled through the water to kill bacteria and other microbes?

   ☐ **A** sulfur dioxide

   ☐ **B** carbon monoxide

   ☐ **C** chlorine

   ☐ **D** carbon dioxide

   [1 mark]

   (ii) Describe how sedimentation is used in the water treatment process.

   ....

   ....

   [2 marks]

(c) A city has a summer drought each year. Existing sources of clean water can't meet demand during the drought period, so the city is considering building a new plant to produce clean water. The city has good supplies of sea, ground and waste water.

	Sea water distillation plant	Water treatment plant
Energy usage	very high	moderate
Suitable water source/s	sea water	ground and waste water

Figure 7

Using the information from **Figure 7** and your own knowledge, evaluate whether the city should build a sea water distillation plant or a water treatment plant.

....

....

....

....

....

[4 marks]

[Total 8 marks]

8 A student carried out an experiment to investigate the electrolysis of copper sulfate solution, $CuSO_{4\ (aq)}$, using inert carbon electrodes. The diagram in **Figure 8** shows how his experiment was set up.

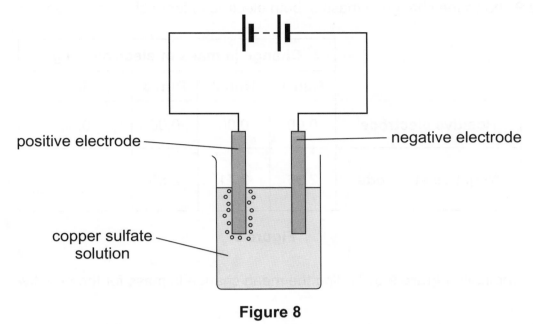

positive electrode — negative electrode

copper sulfate solution

Figure 8

(a) In electrolysis, what is the name given to the positive electrode?

▢ **A** cation

▢ **B** anode

▢ **C** anion

▢ **D** cathode

[1 mark]

(b) The experimental set-up in **Figure 8** involves the use of an electrolyte.

Explain what is meant by the term electrolyte.

....

....

....

[2 marks]

(c) Complete the half equation shown below for the reaction taking place at the positive electrode.

$$\text{.......}\ OH^- \rightarrow O_2 + \text{.......}\ H_2O + 4\ \text{............}$$

[1 mark]

Question 8 continues on the next page

Turn over ▶

The student repeated the experiment three times, running the electrolysis for exactly 30 minutes each time. He weighed the dry electrodes before starting each run. At the end of each run, he dried both electrodes and weighed them again.

Figure 9 shows the change in mass of both electrodes for each of the three runs.

	Change in mass of electrode in g			
	Run 1	Run 2	Run 3	Mean
Positive electrode	0.00	0.00	0.00	0.00
Negative electrode	2.36	2.71	2.55	....

Figure 9

(d) (i) Complete **Figure 9** by finding the mean change in mass for the negative electrode.

[1 mark]

(ii) Explain why the negative electrode increased in mass in this experiment.
Your answer should include the half equation for the reaction taking place at the negative electrode.

....

....

....

....

....

[4 marks]

(iii) The student decided to run the experiment for 60 minutes instead of 30 minutes.

Predict the effect that this would have on the change in mass of the negative electrode.

....

[1 mark]

[Total 10 marks]

9 Scientific models can help to explain complex scientific concepts.

(a) States of matter can be represented using the particle model.

How are particles represented in this model?

....

....
[1 mark]

(b) The particle model can be used to explain changes of state.

(i) Which state change occurs when a substance changes from a liquid to a gas?

☐ **A** condensing

☐ **B** evaporating

☐ **C** melting

☐ **D** subliming
[1 mark]

(ii) Using the particle model, explain how a substance changes from a liquid to a gas when it is heated.

....

....

....

....
[3 marks]

(c) Displayed formulae are another type of model.

The displayed formula of methane is shown in **Figure 10**.

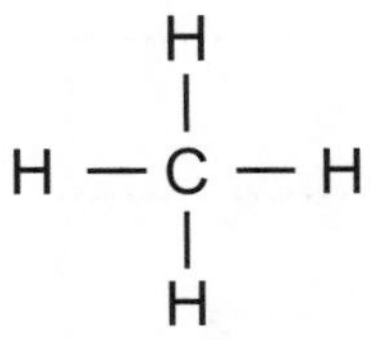

$$H - \underset{\displaystyle H}{\overset{\displaystyle H}{C}} - H$$

Figure 10

Explain the limitations of using displayed formulae to represent molecules.

....

....

....
[2 marks]

Question 9 continues on the next page

Turn over ▶

Two models of methane are shown in **Figure 11**.

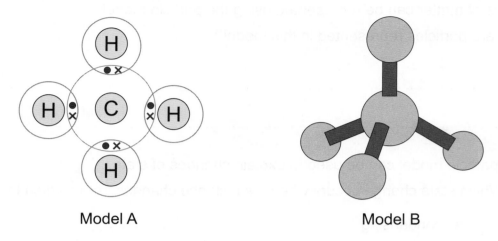

Model A   Model B

Figure 11

*(d) Compare the usefulness of these two models for representing methane.

....

....

....

....

....

....

....

....

....

....

....

[6 marks]

[Total 13 marks]

10 A student wanted to find out which of five dyes could be present in a particular black ink.

(a) The student was asked to suggest a method.

This is the method the student suggested:

- Take a piece of filter paper. Draw a pencil line near the bottom.
- Add spots of the dyes to the line at regular intervals.
- Put the paper into a beaker of water with the line just touching the water.
- Repeat these steps with a spot of the black ink on a second piece of filter paper, and put this paper into a beaker of ethanol.
- Place a lid on each beaker, and wait for the solvents to travel to the top of the paper.
- Compare the positions of the spots created by the black ink with those created by the dyes.

Identify **two** problems with this method. For each problem, suggest how you would alter the method to carry out the experiment correctly.

You can assume the student takes sensible safety precautions.

Problem 1 ....

....

....

Correction ....

....

....

Problem 2 ....

....

....

Correction ....

....

....

[4 marks]

Question 10 continues on the next page

Turn over ▶

(b) What property of the dyes makes them suitable for separation by chromatography?

☐ **A** They have different reactivities.

☐ **B** They have different melting points.

☐ **C** They have different solubilities.

☐ **D** They have different melting points.

[1 mark]

The student repeated the experiment using the correct method.
The results are shown in **Figure 12**.

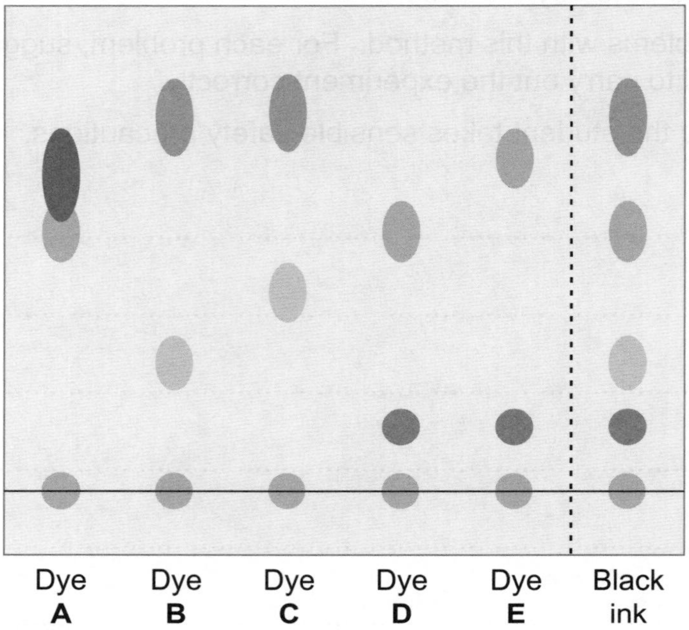

Diagram not to scale.

| Dye A | Dye B | Dye C | Dye D | Dye E | Black ink |

Figure 12

(c) Which dyes (**A-E**) could be present in the black ink? Explain your answer.

Dyes ....

Explanation ....

....

....

[2 marks]

(d) The student measured the distances moved by the solvent and one of the spots in the black ink. She found that the solvent had moved 6.4 cm from the baseline, and that the spot had moved 4.8 cm.

Calculate the R_f value of the spot in the black ink.

R_f value = ...

[1 mark]

*(e) The ink is a mixture of dyes that are dissolved in a solvent.
The solvent has a much lower boiling point than all of the dyes in the ink.

Describe how simple distillation could be used to separate the solvent from the rest of the ink mixture.

....

....

....

....

....

....

....

....

....

....

....

....

[6 marks]

[Total 14 marks]

END OF QUESTIONS

GCSE Chemistry

Paper 2

Higher Tier

In addition to this paper you should have:
- A ruler.
- A calculator.

Centre name				
Centre number				
Candidate number				

Time allowed:
- 1 hour 45 minutes

Surname	
Other names	
Candidate signature	

Instructions to candidates
- Write your name and other details in the spaces provided above.
- Answer **all** questions in the spaces provided.
- Do all rough work on the paper.
- Cross out any work you do not want to be marked.
- You are allowed to use a calculator.

Information for candidates
- The marks available are given in brackets at the end of each question.
- There are 100 marks available for this paper.
- You should use good English and present your answers in a clear and organised way.
- For questions marked with an asterisk (*) ensure that your answers have a logical structure with points that link together clearly, and include detailed, relevant information.

Advice to candidates
- In calculations show clearly how you worked out your answers.
- Read each question carefully before answering it.
- Check your answers if you have time.

	For examiner's use						
Q	Attempt Nº			Q	Attempt Nº		
	1	2	3		1	2	3
1				6			
2				7			
3				8			
4				9			
5				10			
	Total						

1 The halogens make up Group 7 of the periodic table.
Figure 1 shows some of the physical properties of the first four halogens.

Halogen	Atomic number	Melting Point / °C	Boiling Point / °C	Colour at room temperature
Fluorine	9	−220	−188	very pale yellow
Chlorine	17		−34	green
Bromine	35	−7	59	
Iodine	53	114	185	dark grey

Figure 1

(a) (i) Predict the melting point of chlorine, using the data in the table.

☐ **A** −231 °C

☐ **B** −216 °C

☐ **C** −101 °C

☐ **D** 107 °C

[1 mark]

(ii) Explain your answer to part (i).

....

....

[1 mark]

(b) Which of the following options best describes the appearance of bromine at room temperature.

☐ **A** a red-brown gas

☐ **B** a green-brown gas

☐ **C** a dark green liquid

☐ **D** a red-brown liquid

[1 mark]

(c) Write down the balanced equation for the reaction between bromine (Br_2) and potassium iodide (KI).

....

[2 marks]

Question 1 continues on the next page

Turn over ▶

(d) Chlorine is bubbled through sodium iodide solution.

Explain what will happen. Give your answer in terms of the relative positions of chlorine and iodine in the periodic table.

....

....

....

....

....

[3 marks]

(e) The halogens can react with hydrogen (H_2) to form hydrogen halides.
Write the balanced equation for the reaction between hydrogen and fluorine (F_2).

....

[2 marks]

[Total 10 marks]

2 A student is investigating how the rate of the reaction between marble chips (calcium carbonate) and hydrochloric acid is affected by the concentration of the acid.
The student compares different concentrations of acid by measuring how long it takes for the reaction to produce 20 cm³ of carbon dioxide gas.

The results of the experiment are shown in **Figure 2**.

Concentration of acid / mol dm⁻³	Time / s
0.2	58
0.4	29
0.6	18
0.8	15
1.0	12

Figure 2

(a) (i) Complete and balance the equation for the reaction between marble chips ($CaCO_3$) and hydrochloric acid (HCl).

.... + ... → $CaCl_2$ + ... + ...

[2 marks]

(ii) Plot the results shown in **Figure 2** on the axes below and draw a curve of best fit.

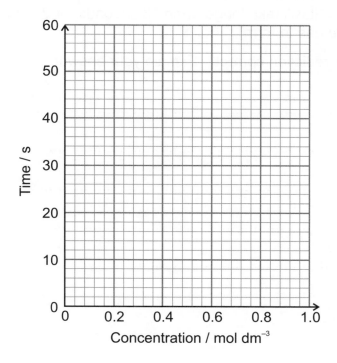

[2 marks]

Question 2 continues on the next page

Turn over ▶

(iii) Use your graph to predict the time that it would take for 20 cm³
of carbon dioxide gas to form with 0.5 mol dm⁻³ hydrochloric acid.

Time = ... s

[1 mark]

(b) Describe what the graph shows about the effect of concentration
on the rate of reaction.

....

....

[1 mark]

(c) Explain, in terms of collision theory, why concentration affects the rate of a reaction.

....

....

....

....

[2 marks]

(d) The student carries out the experiment again using 0.6 mol dm⁻³ hydrochloric acid.
This time powdered marble was used.

The student says "it will take longer than 18 seconds for 20 cm³
of carbon dioxide gas to form".

Is the student's prediction correct? Explain your answer.

....

....

....

....

....

[3 marks]

[Total 11 marks]

3 Ethanol (C_2H_5OH) is an alcohol. It can be made by the fermentation of glucose ($C_6H_{12}O_6$).

(a) (i) What is used in the fermentation process to convert glucose to ethanol?

    ☐ **A** yeast

    ☐ **B** ethanoic acid

    ☐ **C** an oxidising agent

    ☐ **D** oxygen

[1 mark]

(ii) Write a balanced symbol equation for the production of ethanol by fermentation.

....

[2 marks]

(iii) Fermentation is carried out at 30-40 °C.
Explain why the reaction isn't carried out at a higher temperature.

....

....

....

[2 marks]

(b) Fractional distillation is used to concentrate the dilute ethanol solution produced by fermentation. This involves heating up the fermentation mixture.

A student suggests that to speed up this process, the fermentation mixture should be heated to 100 °C. Explain why this won't lead to the collection of concentrated ethanol.

....

....

....

....

[3 marks]

(c) A 750 ml bottle of wine contains 69 g of ethanol.
Calculate the concentration of ethanol in $g\,dm^{-3}$.

Concentration = ... $g\,dm^{-3}$

[2 marks]

[Total 10 marks]

Turn over for the next question

Turn over ▶

4 Aqueous sodium thiosulfate and hydrochloric acid are clear, colourless solutions that react to form a yellow precipitate of sulfur.

An experiment is to be carried out to investigate the effect of temperature on the rate of this reaction.

25 cm³ of both reactants are used. Two different temperatures are investigated.

(a) Describe a method that could be used to carry out the experiment at each temperature being investigated.

....

....

....

....

....

....

....

....
[4 marks]

(b) Apart from the volumes of reactants, state **two** variables that need to be kept constant throughout the experiment.

1. ....

2. ....
[2 marks]

(c) In terms of collision theory, explain how carrying out the experiment at a higher temperature will affect the rate of a reaction.

....

....

....

....
[2 marks]

[Total 8 marks]

5 Heptane and triacontane are two molecules that are present in two of the fractions produced by the fractional distillation of crude oil.

Figure 3 shows the boiling points of these two molecules.

Hydrocarbon	Chemical formula	Boiling point / °C
Heptane	C_7H_{16}	98
Triacontane	$C_{30}H_{62}$	450

Figure 3

(a) Which of these two hydrocarbons would you expect to be collected further down the fractionating column?
Explain your answer, with reference to the boiling points of the hydrocarbons.

....

....

....

....
[2 marks]

(b) Cracking breaks down the products of fractional distillation into smaller molecules.

Figure 4 shows an example of cracking.

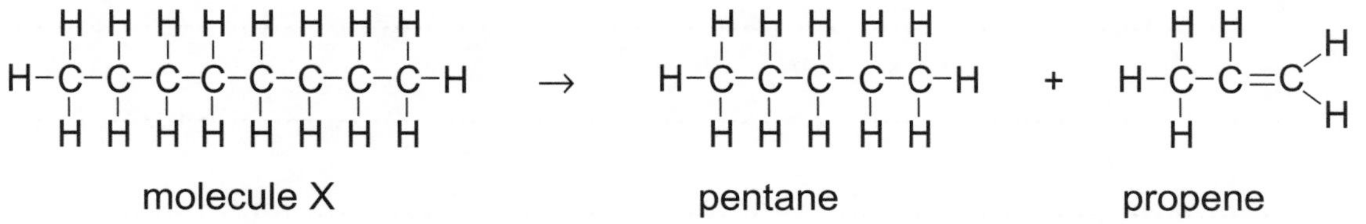

Figure 4

Which of the following is the chemical name given to molecule X?

☐ **A** ethanol

☐ **B** octane

☐ **C** decane

☐ **D** hept-1-ene

[1 mark]

Question 5 continues on the next page

Turn over ▶

(c) **Figure 5** shows the approximate supply and demand for some of the different fractions obtained from crude oil.

Fraction	Approximate % in crude oil	Approximate % demand
Gases	2	4
Petrol	16	27
Kerosene	13	
Diesel Oil	19	23
Fuel Oil and Bitumen	50	38

Figure 5

(i) Calculate the approximate percentage demand of kerosene.

.... %

[1 mark]

(ii) Using the data from **Figure 5**, suggest why fuel oil and bitumen, rather than diesel oil, are more likely to be cracked to provide petrol.

....

....

....

....

[2 marks]

[Total 6 marks]

6 Hydrogen can be burned in oxygen and used as a fuel.

$$2H_2 + O_2 \rightarrow 2H_2O$$

(a) Calculate the energy change for the reaction.
The bond energy values are given below.

Bond energy values ($kJ\ mol^{-1}$):

O=O   498

H–H   436

O–H   464

Energy change = ... $kJ\ mol^{-1}$

[4 marks]

(b) In another reaction, the energy change is exothermic.
Which of the following energy profiles shows the energy change of the reaction?

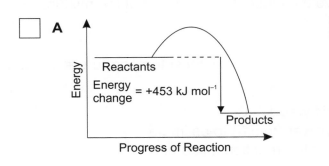

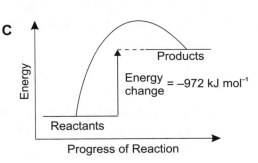

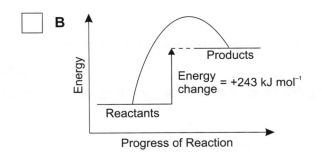

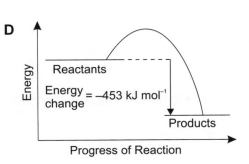

[1 mark]

Question 6 continues on the next page

Turn over ▶

(c) In another experiment, magnesium ribbon was reacted with dilute hydrochloric acid.

First, the initial temperature of the hydrochloric acid was recorded.

Magnesium was then added to the acid, and the temperature of the reaction mixture was measured at 10 second intervals.

The student's results are shown on the graph in **Figure 6**.

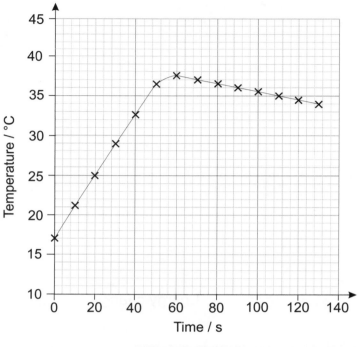

Figure 6

(i) Using the graph in **Figure 6**, give the highest temperature of the mixture that the student recorded.

Highest temperature = ... °C

[1 mark]

(ii) The initial temperature of the acid was 17 °C.
Use this information and your answer from (i) to estimate the total change in temperature of the reaction mixture.

Temperature change = ... °C

[2 marks]

(iii) State whether this reaction was exothermic or endothermic. Explain your answer.

....

....

[1 mark]

[Total 9 marks]

7 A student is investigating the properties of vinegar. Ethanoic acid is found in vinegar.

(a) Give the functional group of the homologous series that ethanoic acid belongs to.

....

[1 mark]

The student reacted some of the vinegar with solid sodium carbonate.
The apparatus that he used is shown in **Figure 7**.

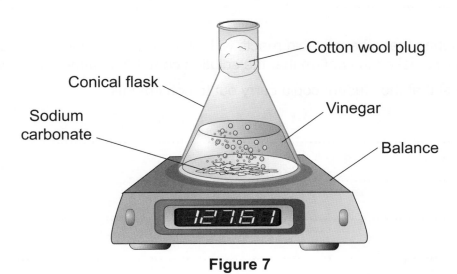

Cotton wool plug

Conical flask

Sodium carbonate

Vinegar

Balance

127.61

Figure 7

The student recorded the initial mass of the flask and then recorded it again after 60 s.
He repeated the experiment three times. His results are shown in **Figure 8**.

	Initial Mass / g	Final Mass / g	Loss of Mass / g
Run 1	128.00	127.61	0.39
Run 2	128.50	127.95	0.55
Run 3	128.35	127.90	0.45

Figure 8

(b) Calculate the mean loss of mass after 60 s.

mean mass lost = ... g

[2 marks]

(c) (i) Why would it be inappropriate to use a mass balance that has a resolution of 1 g for this experiment?

....

....

[1 mark]

Question 7 continues on the next page

Turn over ▶

(ii) The teacher asks the student to test the solid sodium carbonate that he was given to confirm that it contains sodium ions.

Suggest a simple test the student could perform and state what observation you would expect him to make.

....

....

[2 marks]

(d) The student found that ethanoic acid reacts with ammonia to produce a colourless solution. He was asked to confirm that the solution contained ammonium ions.

Describe a test that the student could carry out to confirm this.

....

....

....

....

[3 marks]

(e) The student also needed to identify the ions in two different metal halide solutions.

(i) Describe a test the student could use to distinguish between solutions of a metal iodide and a metal bromide. Say what you would observe in each case.

....

....

....

[2 marks]

(ii) The student did a flame test on the two solutions of the metal halides.
The flame appeared to turn red for both solutions.
What metal ion would you expect to be in both solutions?

☐ **A** sodium

☐ **B** lithium

☐ **C** copper

☐ **D** potassium

[1 mark]

(iii) A different ion gives an orange-red flame that could be mistaken for a red flame. Name a technique that could accurately distinguish between orange-red and red flame test results.

....

[1 mark]

[Total 13 marks]

8 Alkanes are hydrocarbon compounds found in crude oil. **Figure 9** shows how the boiling points of some alkanes change as the molecules get bigger.

Alkane	Molecular formula	Boiling point / °C
Propane	C_3H_8	−42
Butane	C_4H_{10}	−0.5
Pentane	C_5H_{12}	
Hexane	C_6H_{14}	69
Heptane	C_7H_{16}	98

Figure 9

(a) Using the data in **Figure 9**, plot a graph of the number of carbon atoms in an alkane molecule against boiling point on the axes below.
Draw a smooth curve through the points you have plotted.

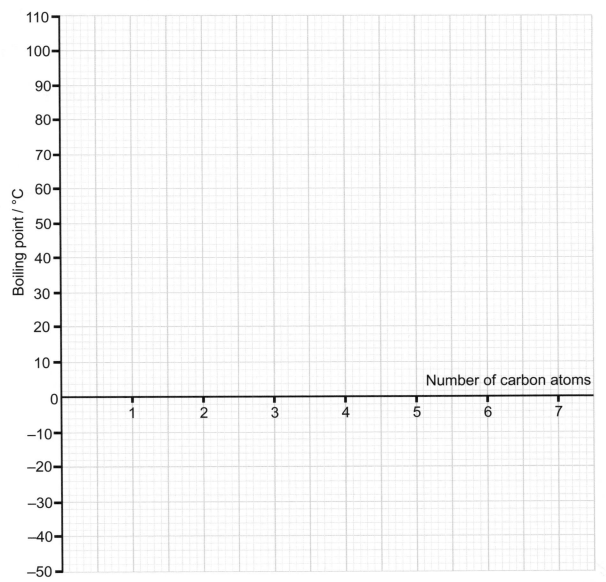

[2 marks]

Question 8 continues on the next page

Turn over ▶

(b) Use your graph to estimate the boiling point of pentane.

boiling point = ... °C

[1 mark]

(c) Which of the following is the general formula of the alkanes?

☐ **A** C_nH_{2n}

☐ **B** C_nH_{2n+1}

☐ **C** C_nH_{2n+2}

☐ **D** C_nH_{2n-1}

[1 mark]

(d) (i) Propane is an alkane with three carbon atoms.
Draw the displayed formula of propane.

[1 mark]

(ii) Propane burns in the presence of oxygen.
Complete and balance the equation for the complete combustion of propane.

C_3H_8 + ... → .... + ...

[2 marks]

[Total 7 marks]

9 **Figure 10** shows the electronic structures of a sodium atom and a chlorine atom.

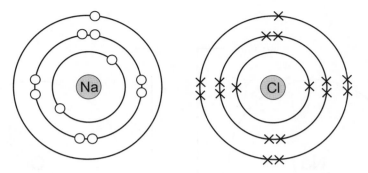

Figure 10

(a) Sodium is a group 1 metal.
Group 1 metals can react with non-metals to form ionic compounds.
Which of the following is the charge on a group 1 ion in an ionic compound?

☐ **A** +2

☐ **B** +3

☐ **C** −1

☐ **D** +1

[1 mark]

(b) Sodium and chlorine react to form the ionic compound sodium chloride.

(i) Which of the following is the correct balanced equation for the formation of sodium chloride?

☐ **A** $Na + Cl \rightarrow NaCl$

☐ **B** $2Na + Cl \rightarrow Na_2Cl$

☐ **C** $2Na + Cl_2 \rightarrow 2NaCl$

☐ **D** $4Na + Cl_2 \rightarrow 2Na_2Cl$

[1 mark]

Question 9 continues on the next page

Turn over ▶

(ii) Complete the dot and cross diagram of sodium chloride below. Show only the outer electrons.

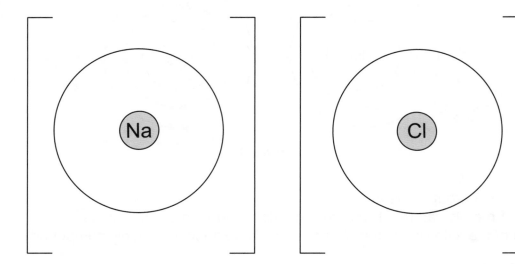

[4 marks]

(c) Chlorine has two major isotopes, ^{35}Cl and ^{37}Cl. ^{35}Cl has a relative abundance of 75%. Show that the relative atomic mass of chlorine is 35.5.

....

....

....

[2 marks]

(d) A student watched his teacher place small pieces of lithium, sodium and potassium into cold water. From his observations, the student decides that the order of reactivity of the three metals is:

- potassium (most reactive)
- sodium
- lithium (least reactive)

Explain the pattern of reactivity that the student has noticed in terms of the outer electrons of the atoms.

....

....

....

....

[3 marks]

*(e) The bonding between ions determines the properties of ionic structures. This is also true for the bonding between atoms in giant covalent structures such as diamond and graphite.

Figure 11 contains information about some of the properties of diamond and graphite.

	Hardness	**Melting point**	**Conducts electricity?**
Diamond	Hard	High	No
Graphite	Soft	High	Yes

Figure 11

Explain these properties of diamond and graphite in terms of their structure and bonding.

....

....

....

....

....

....

....

....

....

....

....

[6 marks]

[Total 17 marks]

Turn over for the next question

Turn over ▶

10 When a company is choosing what materials to use to make a particular product, they will consider the properties, availability and cost of the materials that they could use.

(a) **Figure 12** shows some properties of two different materials.

Material	Density / g cm^{-3}	Electrical conductivity	Flexibility	Corrosion resistance
PVC	1.3	Very Low	High	High
Glass	2.5	Very Low	Low	High

Figure 12

Use data from the table to explain why PVC is more suitable for covering electrical wiring than glass.

....

....

....

[2 marks]

(b) What kind of material is glass?

☐ **A** Polymer

☐ **B** Ceramic

☐ **C** Composite

☐ **D** Alloy

[1 mark]

*(c) A sports company is deciding on the best material to use for making the shaft of a professional, high performance golf club.

Look at **Figure 13**, below. Discuss which of the four materials shown in the table would be the most suitable choice for making the golf club shaft. Use the information in the table to justify your choice.

Material	Density / g cm⁻³	Strength / MPa	Corrosion resistance	Cost
Carbon fibre	1.5	4100	Good	High
Iron	7.8	200	Poor	Low
Stainless steel	7.8	780	Good	Low
Lead	11.3	12	Good	Low

Figure 13

....

....

....

....

....

....

....

....

....

....

....

[6 marks]

[Total 9 marks]

END OF QUESTIONS

Answers

Topic 1 — Key Concepts in Chemistry

Page 22

Warm-Up Questions

1     $2Fe + 3Cl_2 \rightarrow 2FeCl_3$

2   a)   water → hydrogen + oxygen

    b) $2H_2O \rightarrow 2H_2 + O_2$

3     $H^+_{(aq)} + OH^-_{(aq)} \rightarrow H_2O_{(l)}$

4   The student should wear gloves, a lab coat and goggles when handling chemical A / should only use low concentrations of chemical A. When handling chemical B, the student should take care to keep it away from naked flames.

Exam Questions

1   a)   sodium hydroxide + hydrochloric acid → sodium chloride + water *[1 mark]*

    b)   (aq) *[1 mark]*

2   a)   methane and oxygen *[1 mark]*

    b)   carbon dioxide and water *[1 mark]*

    c) $CH_4 + \mathbf{2O_2} \rightarrow CO_2 + \mathbf{2H_2O}$ *[1 mark for correct missing reactant, 1 mark for correctly balancing the equation]*

3   a) $H_2SO_4 + \mathbf{2NH_3} \rightarrow (NH_4)_2SO_4$ *[1 mark for correct missing reactant, 1 mark for correctly balancing the equation]*

    b)   15 *[1 mark]*
    There are eight atoms of hydrogen, one atom of sulfur, four atoms of oxygen, and two atoms of nitrogen.

    c)   8 *[1 mark]*
    There are 4 hydrogen atoms in NH_4 and there are two of these.

Page 26

Warm-Up Questions

1

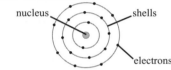

nucleus   shells   electrons

2   Relative charge of −1, relative mass of 0.0005.

3   The total number of protons and neutrons in the atom.

4   electrons = 19, protons = 19, neutrons = 39 − 19 = **20**

Exam Questions

1   a)   proton: **+1**, neutron: **0**
    [2 marks — 1 mark for each correct charge]

    b)   In the nucleus *[1 mark]*.

    c)   8 *[1 mark]*

    d)   1 *[1 mark]*

2   a)   7 *[1 mark]*

    b)   The number of protons is the same as the atomic number *[1 mark]*

3   How to grade your answer:

    Level 0:   No description is given. *[No marks]*

    Level 1:   Brief description of how the theory of atomic structure has changed. The points made do not link together. *[1 to 2 marks]*

    Level 2:   Some detail given of how the theory of atomic structure has changed. The answer has some structure. *[3 to 4 marks]*

    Level 3:   A clear and detailed description of how the theory of atomic structure has changed. The answer is well structured. *[5 to 6 marks]*

    Here are some points your answer may include:
    John Dalton described atoms as solid spheres that make up the different elements.
    J J Thomson concluded that atoms weren't solid spheres and that an atom must contain smaller, negatively charged particles (electrons). He called this the 'plum pudding model'.
    Ernest Rutherford conducted a gold foil experiment, firing positively charged particles at an extremely thin sheet of gold. Most of the particles went straight through, but a few were deflected more than expected and a small number were deflected backwards. This made him think that the plum pudding model of the atom couldn't be correct. He concluded that there was a positively charged nucleus at the centre, surrounded by a 'cloud' of negative electrons.
    Niels Bohr proposed a new model of the atom where all the electrons were contained in shells. He suggested that electrons can only exist in fixed orbits, or shells. This theory was supported by lots of evidence.
    The currently accepted model of the atom is a nucleus containing protons and neutrons, orbited by electrons in shells. The nucleus contains most of the mass of the atom, but is very small compared to the size of the atom.

Page 32

Warm-Up Questions

1   The average mass of one atom of an element, compared to $^1/_{12}$ the mass of one atom of carbon-12.

2   a)   by atomic mass and chemical properties

    b)   by atomic number

3   a)   2

    b)   8

    c)   8

4   2.8.7

Exam Questions

1   a)

    [1 mark]

    b)   Any one of: lithium / potassium / rubidium / caesium / francium *[1 mark]*

    c)   1 *[1 mark]*

2   a)   An isotope is a different atomic form of the same element *[1 mark]*, which has the same number of protons *[1 mark]* but a different number of neutrons *[1 mark]*.

    b)   Protons = 6 *[1 mark]*, neutrons = 7 *[1 mark]*, electrons = 6 *[1 mark]*

    c)   It has a different atomic number from carbon *[1 mark]*.

    d) $(13 \times 79) + (14 \times 21) = 1321$
    Relative atomic mass $= \dfrac{1321}{100} = 13.21 = \mathbf{13.2}$ (to 1 d.p.)

    [4 marks for correct answer to one decimal place, otherwise 1 mark for multiplying each relative isotopic mass by its percentage abundance and adding them together, 1 mark for dividing by 100, 1 mark for relative atomic mass to one decimal place.]

Page 38

Warm-Up Questions

1   A charged atom or group of atoms.

2   +2

3   Because the lattice is held together by a lot of strong ionic bonds, it takes a lot of energy to overcome these attractions and melt/boil the sodium chloride.

4   When ionic compounds are dissolved, the ions separate and are free to move in the solution. These free-moving charged particles allow the solution to carry electric current.

5     $Al(OH)_3$

Exam Questions

1   a)   Sodium will lose the electron from its outer shell to form a positive ion *[1 mark]*. Fluorine will gain an electron to form a negative ion *[1 mark]*.

    b)   Ionic compounds have a giant ionic lattice structure *[1 mark]*. The ions form a closely packed regular lattice arrangement *[1 mark]*, held together by strong electrostatic forces of attraction between oppositely charged ions *[1 mark]*.

2   a)   lithium oxide *[1 mark]*

    b)

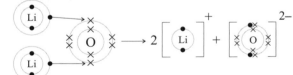

    [1 mark for arrows shown correctly, 1 mark for correct electron arrangement and charge on lithium ion, 1 mark for correct electron arrangement and charge on oxygen ion]

    c)   When molten, the Li^+ and O^{2-} ions are able to move *[1 mark]*. These ions are able to carry electric current *[1 mark]*.

    d)   The formula of the compound is **LiCl** *[1 mark]*. Lithium is in Group 1, so forms +1 ions. Chlorine is in Group 7, so forms −1 ions. Therefore there needs to be one lithium ion for every chloride ion for the compound to be neutral *[1 mark]*.

Page 41

Warm-Up Questions

1   A strong bond made by the sharing of a pair of electrons between two atoms.

2   2

3   10^{-10} m

4   gas or liquid

5   covalent bonds

6   intermolecular forces

Exam Questions

1

[1 mark for showing pairs of shared electrons between C and H. 1 mark for no other electrons shown.]

2 a)

[1 mark for showing a pair of shared electrons between H and Cl atoms. 1 mark for showing three non-bonding pairs of electrons on the chlorine atom]

   b)   2 *[1 mark]*
It makes two single bonds (one double bond).

3 a)   Hydrogen chloride doesn't contain any ions or free electrons to carry a current *[1 mark]*
   b)   Chlorine is a larger molecule than hydrogen chloride *[1 mark]* and therefore there are greater intermolecular forces between molecules *[1 mark]*. As the intermolecular forces are greater between chlorine molecules, its boiling point is higher than hydrogen chloride's *[1 mark]*.
Chlorine has three shells of electrons, whereas hydrogen only has one.
So Cl_2 is a bigger molecule than HCl.

Page 45

Warm-Up Questions

1   E.g. diamond is much harder than graphite. Diamond doesn't conduct electricity whereas graphite does.
2   Molecules of carbon, shaped like closed tubes or hollow balls.
3   A molecule made up of long chains of covalently bonded carbon atoms.
4   The electrostatic forces between the metal ions and the delocalised sea of electrons are very strong. To melt a metal, these forces need to be broken, and this requires lots of energy.

Exam Questions

1 a)   In a giant covalent structure, all of the atoms are bonded to each other with strong covalent bonds *[1 mark]*. It takes lots of energy to break these bonds and melt the solid *[1 mark]*.
   b)   E.g. diamond / graphite / graphene *[1 mark]*
2 a)   E.g. copper is a good electrical conductor as it contains delocalised electrons *[1 mark]* which are able to carry an electrical current *[1 mark]*.
   b)   The layers of atoms in copper are able to slide over each other *[1 mark]*.
3 a)   The layers of carbon atoms that make up graphite are held together weakly *[1 mark]*. The layers can easily slide over each other, making graphite soft and slippery *[1 mark]*.
   b)   E.g. each carbon atom has a delocalised electron/ an electron that is able to move *[1 mark]*.
The delocalised electrons can carry an electrical current through the material.
   c)   In diamond, each carbon atom forms four covalent bonds in a rigid lattice structure *[1 mark]*. This makes diamond very hard, so it would be good at cutting other substances *[1 mark]*.
   d) i)   graphene *[1 mark]*
      ii)   E.g. they have a very large surface area which catalyst molecules could be attached to *[1 mark]*.

Page 51

Warm-Up Questions

1   The sum of the relative atomic masses of all the atoms in a compound.
2   C_2H_4Cl
3   E.g. an amount of particles in a substance equal to Avogadro's constant (6.02×10^{23}).
4   moles = mass ÷ M_r = 90 ÷ 18 = **5.0 moles**
5   M_r = mass ÷ moles = 87.0 ÷ 0.500 = **174**
6   200 cm³ = (200 ÷ 1000) dm³ = 0.2 dm³
   mass = concentration × volume = 55 × 0.2 = **11 g**

Exam Questions

1   C *[1 mark]*
M_r of $CaCl_2$ = 40 + (2 × 35.5) = 111
2 a) M_r(MgCO$_3$) = 24 + 12 + (3 × 16) = **84** *[1 mark]*
   b)   The mass of the reaction vessel and its contents is likely to decrease over the course of the reaction *[1 mark]* as one of the products is a gas *[1 mark]*. Since the reaction vessel isn't sealed, the gas will escape from the reaction vessel and so its mass won't be measured *[1 mark]*.
3 a) M_r of KOH = (39 + 16 + 1) = 56
   Mass of 4 moles of KOH = 4 × 56 = 224 g
   Extra mass needed = 224 – 140 = **84 g**
   [3 marks for correct answer, otherwise 1 mark for Mr of KOH and 1 mark for mass of 4 moles of KOH]
   b) M_r of K_2SO_4 = (2 × 39) + 32 + (4 × 16) = 174
   mass of K_2SO_4 = moles × M_r = 1.25 × 174 = 217.5 = **218 g**
   [2 marks for correct answer, otherwise 1 mark for M_r of K_2SO_4]

c)   volume = 1500 ml = 1.5 dm³
   mass of copper ions = concentration × volume = 12 × 1.5 = 18 g
   moles of copper ions = mass ÷ M_r = 18 ÷ 63.5 = 0.28346... moles
   no. of copper ions = moles × Avogadro's constant
   $= 0.28346... \times 6.02 \times 10^{23}$
   $= 1.70645... \times 10^{23} = \mathbf{1.7 \times 10^{23}}$ (2 s.f.)
   [4 marks for correct answer, otherwise 1 mark for mass of copper ions, 1 mark for number of moles of copper ions and 1 mark for correct working used to calculate the number of copper ions]

Page 56

Warm-Up Questions

1   mass of oxygen = 45.6 – 13.9 = 31.7 g
   moles = mass ÷ M_r
   moles of oxygen = 31.7 ÷ 16 = 1.98125
   moles of nitrogen = 13.9 ÷ 14 = 0.99...
   Divide by the smallest number (0.99...).
   oxygen = 1.98125 ÷ 0.99... = 1.99... = 2
   nitrogen = 0.99... ÷ 0.99... = 1
   Ratio of O : N = 2 : 1.
   So empirical formula = NO_2
2   The reactant that gets used up in a reaction and therefore limits the amount of product formed.
3   It halves.

Exam Questions

1 a)   moles of metal X = mass ÷ A_r = 3.5 ÷ 7 = **0.5 mol**
   moles of oxygen = mass ÷ M_r = 4.0 ÷ 32 = **0.125 mol**
   moles of metal oxide = mass ÷ M_r = 7.5 ÷ 30 = **0.25 mol**
   [2 marks for all three correct answers, otherwise 1 mark for two correct answers]
   b)   Divide by the smallest number of moles (0.125):
   X: $\frac{0.5}{0.125} = 4$ O$_2$: $\frac{0.125}{0.125} = 1$ Oxide: $\frac{0.25}{0.125} = 2$ *[1 mark]*
   The balanced symbol equation is:
   $4X + O_2 \rightarrow 2X_2O$ *[1 mark]*
Even if your answer to (a) was wrong, you'd still gets the marks for part (b) if you used the correct method.
2 a) i) M_r of $NaHCO_3$ = 23 + 1 + 12 + (3 × 16) = 84
   Moles of $NaHCO_3$ = 6.0 ÷ 84 = 0.0714... mol
   1 mole of Na_2SO_4 is made for every 2 moles of $NaHCO_3$ that reacts, so moles of Na_2SO_4 = 0.0714... ÷ 2
   = 0.0357... = **0.036 mol**
   [3 marks for correct answer, otherwise 1 mark for M_r of $NaHCO_3$ and 1 mark for moles of $NaHCO_3$]
      ii) M_r of Na_2SO_4 = (2 × 23) + 32 + (4 × 16) = 142
   Mass of Na_2SO_4 = 142 × 0.036 = 5.112 = **5.1 g** (2 s.f.)
   [2 marks for correct answer, otherwise 1 mark for M_r of Na_2SO_4]
Even if your answer to (i) was wrong, you'd still gets the marks for part (ii) if you used the correct method.
   b) H_2SO_4 is in excess/$NaHCO_3$ is the limiting reactant *[1 mark]*.
3 a) M_r (Fe_2O_3) = (2 × 56) + (3 × 16) = 160
   A_r (C) = 12 *[1 mark]*
   Moles = mass ÷ M_r (or A_r)
   Moles of Fe_2O_3 = 2.4 ÷ 160 = 0.015 mol
   Moles of C = 0.36 ÷ 12 = 0.03 mol *[1 mark]*
   Dividing by the smallest number of moles (0.015): Fe_2O_3 = 1, C = 2
   In the balanced equation, Fe_2O_3 and C react in a ratio of 2 : 3.
   Using the masses, there is a 1 : 2 ratio of Fe_2O_3 to C
   (which is the same as 2 : 4) *[1 mark]*, so Fe_2O_3 is the reactant that is not in excess *[1 mark]*.
   [4 marks for correct answer, otherwise 1 mark for each stage of the working as shown in the answer above]
   b)   mass of element Y present = 52.00 – 17.92 = 34.08 g *[1 mark]*
   moles = mass ÷ M_r (or A_r)
   moles of Fe = 17.92 ÷ 56 = 0.32 moles
   moles of product = 52.00 ÷ 162.5 = 0.32 moles
   moles of Y_2 = 34.08 ÷ 71 = 0.48 *[1 mark]*
   So ratio of Fe : Y_2 : product = 0.32 : 0.48 : 0.32.
   Divide them all by the smallest number of moles, which is 0.32:
   Ratio of Fe : Y_2 : product = 1 : 1.5 : 1.
   Multiply by 2 to make everything a whole number:
   Ratio of Fe : Y_2 : product = 2 : 3 : 2 *[1 mark]*
   So balanced equation: $2Fe + 3Y_2 \rightarrow 2$(product). To make the equation balance, the product must contain 1 atom of Fe and 3 atoms of Y.
   So the balanced equation is:
   $2Fe + 3Y_2 \rightarrow 2FeY_3$ *[1 mark]*
   [4 marks for the correct balanced equation, otherwise 1 mark for each stage of the working as shown in the answer above]

Topic 2 — States of Matter and Mixtures

Page 61
Warm-Up Questions
1   gas, liquid, solid
2   The particles move faster.
3   a)   freezing
    b)   condensing
    c)   melting
    d)   subliming

Exam Questions
1   a)   Particles are held in fixed positions in a regular lattice arrangement *[1 mark]*.
    b)   The particles gain energy, so they move faster *[1 mark]*. The intermolecular bonds are weakened and, when the particles have enough energy, the bonds break *[1 mark]*. This means the particles are free to move far apart from each other and the liquid becomes a gas *[1 mark]*.
2   a)   liquid *[1 mark]*
    b)   gas *[1 mark]*
3   a)   The particles are free to move about / have virtually no forces of attraction between them *[1 mark]*, so they move randomly, spreading out to fill the container *[1 mark]*.
    b)   Liquids can flow because the particles in a liquid are free to move past each other but tend to stick together *[1 mark]*. Solids cannot flow because the particles in a solid are held in fixed positions *[1 mark]*.

Page 66
Warm-Up Questions
1   A pure substance is a substance that only contains one compound or one element.
2   Impurities in a substance will result in it boiling over a wider temperature range.
3   fractional distillation
4   crystallisation

Exam Questions
1   Methanol will be collected in the first fraction *[1 mark]*, because it has the lowest boiling point of the three compounds in the mixture *[1 mark]*.
2   a)   E.g. mix the lawn sand with water to dissolve the ammonium sulfate *[1 mark]*. Filter the mixture using filter paper to remove the sharp sand and leave it to dry in a warm place/desiccator/drying oven *[1 mark]*. Pour the remaining solution into an evaporating dish and slowly heat it to evaporate the water and crystallise the ammonium sulfate until you have a dry product *[1 mark]*.
    b)   E.g. the products were not completely dry *[1 mark]*.
3   a)   The boiling points of water and methanoic acid are too close together to allow them to be separated by simple distillation *[1 mark]*.
    b)

Temperature on thermometer	Contents of the flask	Contents of the beaker
30 °C	both liquids	no liquid
65 °C	water	propanone
110 °C	no liquid	both liquids

[3 marks for whole table correct otherwise 1 mark for each correct row]

Page 71
Warm-Up Questions
1   a piece of filter paper
2   Pencil marks are insoluble, so the baseline won't dissolve into the solvent and separate along with the substance being analysed.
3   Chemical A will end up closer to the solvent front than B.
4   The water is first filtered through a wire mesh to filter out large objects, and then through gravel and sand to filter out smaller solid objects. Then, a sedimentation process is used. This involves adding aluminium sulfate/iron sulfate to the water, causing fine particles to clump together and settle at the bottom. Finally, chlorine gas is bubbled through the water to kill harmful bacteria and other microbes.
5   distillation

Exam Questions
1   Tap water could contain other ions that might interfere with the reaction *[1 mark]*. He should use deionised water instead *[1 mark]*.
2   a)   All of the inks in Figure 1 have separated into at least two different substances, so none of them can be pure *[1 mark]*.
    b)   A *[1 mark]*
    c)   C *[1 mark]* because the spots in the chromatogram for C match those in sunrise yellow *[1 mark]*.
    d) R_f = distance travelled by substance in sunrise yellow ÷ distance travelled by solvent
R_f = 9.0 ÷ 12.0 = **0.75**
[2 marks for correct answer, otherwise 1 mark for using the correct formula to calculate R_f]
    e)   distillation *[1 mark]*

Topic 3 — Chemical Changes

Page 77
Warm-Up Questions
1   A substance that reacts with an acid to produce a salt and water.
2   0 to 14
3   neutral
4   a)   Strong acids ionise almost completely in water, so a large proportion of the acid molecules dissociate to release H^+ ions. Weak acids do not fully ionise, so only a small proportion of the acid molecules dissociate to release H^+ ions.
    b)   A concentrated acid has a much larger number of acid molecules per litre of water than a dilute acid.
5   sodium chloride and hydrogen
6      $H_2SO_4 + CaCO_3 \rightarrow CaSO_4 + H_2O + CO_2$
7   Carbon dioxide turns limewater cloudy.

Exam Questions
1   a) H^+ ions/hydrogen ions *[1 mark]*
    b)   neutralisation *[1 mark]*
2   a) $2HCl + Ca(OH)_2 \rightarrow$ **$CaCl_2 + 2H_2O$**
[1 mark for formulas of both products correct, 1 mark for putting a 2 in front of H_2O to balance the equation]
    b)   From red *[1 mark]* through orange/yellow to green *[1 mark]*.
    c)   Difference in pH = 5 − 2 = 3
So the H^+ concentration decreased by a factor of 10^3 / 1000 *[1 mark]*.
    d)   Because a lot of the H^+ ions will react with OH^- ions to form water during the reaction *[1 mark]*.
    e)   alkali *[1 mark]*

Page 81
Warm-Up Questions
1   a)   soluble
    b)   insoluble
    c)   insoluble
    d)   soluble
2   E.g. barium nitrate/barium chloride and copper sulfate.
Any soluble barium salt and any soluble sulfate would be correct.
3   Because if you don't use a titration, you can't tell when the reaction is complete. Also you can't add an excess of alkali/acid, because alkalis/acids are soluble and would contaminate the soluble salt produced.

Exam Questions
1   lead chloride — insoluble *[1 mark]*
potassium nitrate — soluble *[1 mark]*
2   Filter the product mixture through some filter paper *[1 mark]*. Rinse the solid/calcium sulfate left behind on the filter paper with deionised water *[1 mark]*. Scrape the solid/calcium sulfate onto fresh filter paper and leave it to dry in an oven/desiccator *[1 mark]*.
3   a)   The excess copper oxide will sink to the bottom of the flask and stay there *[1 mark]*.
    b)   filtration *[1 mark]*
    c)   Heat the copper sulfate solution gently using a Bunsen burner to evaporate some of the water *[1 mark]*. Leave the solution to cool until crystals form *[1 mark]*. Filter out the crystals and dry them *[1 mark]*.
4   How to grade your answer:
Level 0:   There is no relevant information. *[No marks]*
Level 1:   There is a brief explanation of how to prepare the salt, but it has limited detail and little technical equipment is mentioned. The points made are basic and not linked together. *[1 to 2 marks]*
Level 2:   There is an explanation of how to prepare a pure sample of the salt and some of the equipment required is named, but there are limited details. Some of the points made are linked together. *[3 to 4 marks]*
Level 3:   There is a clear and detailed explanation of how to prepare a pure, dry sample of the salt and all the equipment needed is clearly named. The points made are well-linked and the answer has a clear and logical structure. *[5 to 6 marks]*
Here are some points your answer may include:
Measure out a set amount of hydrochloric acid into a conical flask using a pipette.
Add a few drops of indicator, e.g. methyl orange or phenolphthalein.
Slowly add the sodium hydroxide solution to the acid in the flask using a burette, until the acid has been exactly neutralised and the indicator changes colour.
This is the volume of sodium hydroxide solution needed to neutralise this volume of acid.
Carry out the reaction again using exactly the same volumes of hydrochloric acid and sodium hydroxide solution but with no indicator.
Slowly evaporate off some of the water from the solution in the flask, then leave the solution to cool and crystallise.
Filter off the solid and dry it.
You'll be left with a pure, dry sample of sodium chloride.

Page 87
Warm-Up Questions
1 a) Oxidation is a loss of electrons.
  b) the anode
2 E.g. clean the surfaces of two inert electrodes with emery paper/ sandpaper. Place both electrodes into a beaker filled with the electrolyte solution. Connect the electrodes to a power supply using crocodile clips and wires. Turn the power supply on.
3 zinc and chlorine
4 oxygen
5 copper

Exam Questions
1 a) $Al^{3+} + 3e^- \rightarrow Al$ *[1 mark]*
  b) $2O^{2-} \rightarrow O_2 + 4e^-$ *[1 mark]*
  c) The oxygen made at the positive electrode reacts with the carbon (to make carbon dioxide) *[1 mark]*, wearing the electrode away *[1 mark]*.
2 a) hydrogen *[1 mark]*
  b) $2H^+ + 2e^- \rightarrow H_2$ *[1 mark]*
  c) chlorine *[1 mark]*
  d) $2Cl^- \rightarrow Cl_2 + 2e^- / 2Cl^- - 2e^- \rightarrow Cl_2$ *[1 mark]*
  e) Sodium is more reactive than hydrogen, so the sodium ions from the sodium chloride stay in solution *[1 mark]*. Hydroxide ions are also left in solution when hydrogen is produced from water *[1 mark]*.
  f) Copper is less reactive than hydrogen *[1 mark]*.

Topic 4 — Extracting Metals and Equilibria

Page 94
Warm-Up Questions
1 How easily it loses electrons to form positive ions/cations.
2 Gold is less easily oxidised.
3 metal + water → metal hydroxide + hydrogen
4 A gain of electrons.
5 zinc/Zn

Exam Questions
1 a) any one from: potassium/sodium/calcium *[1 mark]*
  b) copper *[1 mark]*
  c) i) hydrogen *[1 mark]*
    ii) Bubbles of hydrogen gas would be produced *[1 mark]* more slowly than zinc and dilute acid / very slowly *[1 mark]*.
You don't need to use these exact words — the two points you need to cover are that it would still produce hydrogen gas, but at a slower rate than the zinc.
2 In tube A there will be no change *[1 mark]*. In tube B the solution will have changed from blue to green *[1 mark]*. Iron is more reactive than copper, so in tube A the copper cannot displace the iron from iron sulfate *[1 mark]*, but in tube B the iron does displace the copper from copper sulfate, forming green iron sulfate *[1 mark]*.

Page 101
Warm-Up Questions
1 Carbon can only take away the oxygen from metals which are less reactive than carbon itself.
2 Plants are grown in soil that contains metal compounds. The plants are harvested, dried and burned in a furnace. The ash contains metal compounds from which the metal can be extracted by electrolysis or displacement reactions.
3 E.g. it saves money (compared to extracting new metals) and creates jobs.
4 Choice of material used to make the product / obtaining the raw materials, how the product is manufactured, product use and product disposal.

Exam Questions
1 a) $2Fe_2O_3 + 3C \rightarrow 4Fe + 3CO_2$ *[1 mark for all reactants and products correct, 1 mark for correctly balancing the equation]*
  b) Oxygen is being lost from iron oxide *[1 mark]*.
2 a) To lower the melting point of the aluminium oxide *[1 mark]*.
  b) $Al^{3+} + 3e^- \rightarrow Al$ *[1 mark]*
3 a) Bacteria get energy from the bonds between atoms in the ore and separate copper from its ore in the process *[1 mark]*. A solution called a leachate is produced which contains copper ions *[1 mark]*. Copper ions are extracted from the leachate using electrolysis/displacement with a more reactive metal *[1 mark]*.
  b) Advantage: e.g. they have a smaller impact on the environment *[1 mark]*. Disadvantage: e.g. they are slower *[1 mark]*.
4 How to grade your answer:
  Level 0: There is no relevant information. *[No marks]*
  Level 1: There is a brief discussion of some environmental impacts of each type of bag. The points made are basic, don't link together and don't cover all of the information given in Figure 1. If a conclusion is present it may not link to points made. *[1 to 2 marks]*

Level 2: There is a logical discussion of possible environmental impacts of each type of bag, but there is limited detail. There is a good coverage of the information given in Figure 1 and the answer has some structure. A clear conclusion is given. *[3 to 4 marks]*
Level 3: There is a clear and detailed discussion of the possible environmental impacts of each type of bag. The answer has a logical structure and makes good use of the information given in Figure 1. A conclusion is present that fits with the points given in the answer. *[5 to 6 marks]*
Here are some points your answer may include:
The raw materials used to make plastic bags come from crude oil, which is a non-renewable resource.
Obtaining crude oil from the ground and refining it requires a lot of energy and generates air pollution due to the release of greenhouse gases.
The raw materials used to make paper bags come from trees.
Trees are a renewable resource, although they take up land that could be used for other uses e.g. growing crops.
Cutting down trees and processing the raw timber requires power.
This power is often generated by burning fossil fuels, which releases harmful greenhouse gases into the atmosphere.
Cutting down trees to make paper also reduces the amount of carbon dioxide that can be absorbed by trees, which contributes to climate change.
The manufacture of plastic bags involves fractional distillation, cracking and polymerisation, which all require large amounts of energy.
As this energy often comes from burning fossil fuels, the manufacture causes the release of pollution (e.g. greenhouse gases) into the atmosphere.
Manufacturing paper bags also requires lots of energy. This could come from burning fossil fuels and so would generate pollution, such as greenhouses gases, which have a negative impact on the environment.
In addition, the manufacture of paper bags also creates lots of waste, which has to be disposed of and may cause pollution (e.g. if sent to landfill).
Plastic bags are reusable, which could reduce the amount of waste sent to landfill.
Paper bags are usually single-use, which could increase the amount of waste sent to landfill.
Plastic bags are not biodegradable so will stay in the environment for a long time if disposed of in landfill sites.
Plastic bags can be recycled, which would reduce the need to extract raw materials to make new bags.
Paper bags are biodegradable so will break down more easily than plastic bags if sent to landfill sites, reducing the impact on the environment.
Paper bags are also non-toxic, so won't releases poisonous/toxic substances into the environment after being disposed of.
Paper bags can be recycled, which would reduce the need to gather raw materials to make new bags.

Page 105
Warm-Up Questions
1 They are the same.
2 A system in which none of the reactants or products can escape.
3 It would have no effect (because there are equal numbers of gas molecules on both sides).
4 The equilibrium will move to the left/towards reactants and the amount of reactants will increase.

Exam Questions
1 a) The reaction is reversible *[1 mark]*.
  b) Both (the forward and reverse) reactions are taking place at exactly the same time and rate *[1 mark]*.
2 a) Less $NO_{2(g)}$ will be produced *[1 mark]*, because there are more moles of gas on the right hand side of the equation *[1 mark]*.
  b) It will have no effect *[1 mark]*, because there are the same number of moles of gas on both sides of the equation *[1 mark]*.
3 a) It gives out energy *[1 mark]*, because it's exothermic *[1 mark]*.
As the forward reaction is endothermic, you know that the reverse reaction is exothermic and therefore gives out energy.
  b) A reversible reaction is always exothermic in one direction and endothermic in the other direction *[1 mark]*, so a change in temperature will always favour one reaction more than the other *[1 mark]*.
  c) It would move to the right *[1 mark]*.

Topic 5 — Separate Chemistry 1

Page 112
Warm-Up Questions
1 Any two from: e.g. high melting point / high density / form coloured compounds / have catalytic activity
2 copper and zinc
3 The metal loses electrons and is oxidised. The oxygen gains electrons and is reduced.

Exam Questions

1 a) B *[1 mark]*
   b) i) aluminium *[1 mark]* and magnesium *[1 mark]*
      ii) E.g. magnalium is used to make parts for cars/aeroplanes *[1 mark]* as it is stronger/lighter/corrodes less easily than aluminium *[1 mark]*. / Magnalium is used in fireworks *[1 mark]* as it's reactive and burns brightly, but is more stable than pure magnesium *[1 mark]*.

2 a) A *[1 mark]*
   b) The nail in tube D would not rust whereas the nail in tube B would *[1 mark]*. The paint covering the nail in tube D creates a barrier that keeps out water and oxygen and so prevents rust from forming *[1 mark]*.
   c) E.g. zinc is a more reactive metal than iron *[1 mark]*, so water and oxygen will react with this before iron *[1 mark]*. Also, the coating of zinc acts as a barrier that keeps out water and oxygen *[1 mark]*.

Page 116
Warm-Up Questions

1 E.g. to find out exactly how much of an alkali is needed to neutralise an acid. / To find out exactly how much of an acid is needed to neutralise an alkali. / To determine the concentration of an acid/alkali.
2 number of moles = concentration × volume
   = 0.1 × (25 ÷ 1000) = **0.0025 mol**
3 molar volume = gas volume ÷ number of moles
   = 45 ÷ 2 = **22.5 dm³ mol⁻¹**

Exam Questions

1 a) number of moles = concentration × volume
      number of moles = 1.00 × (30.4 ÷ 1000) = **0.0304 mol** *[1 mark]*
   b) H_2SO_4 and NaOH react in a 1:2 ratio, so number of moles of H_2SO_4
      = 0.0304 ÷ 2 = **0.0152 mol** *[1 mark]*
   c) concentration = number of moles ÷ volume *[1 mark]*
      volume = 25 ÷ 1000 = 0.025
      concentration = 0.0152 ÷ 0.025 = **0.608 mol dm⁻³** *[1 mark]*
2 M_r($CaCO_3$) = 40 + 12 + (3 × 16) = 100 *[1 mark]*
   no. of moles of $CaCO_3$ = 25 ÷ 100 = 0.25 mol *[1 mark]*
   1 mole of CO_2 is formed for every mole of $CaCO_3$ that reacts.
   So 0.25 moles of $CaCO_3$ reacts to form 0.25 moles of CO_2.
   Volume of CO_2 = 0.25 × 24 dm³ *[1 mark]* = 6.0 dm³ *[1 mark]*
3 Moles of NaOH = concentration × volume
   = 0.10 × (9.0 ÷ 1000) = 0.00090 mol *[1 mark]*
   HA and NaOH react in a 1:1 ratio, so moles of HA = 0.00090 moles *[1 mark]*
   Concentration of HA = number of moles ÷ volume *[1 mark]*
   volume = 25 ÷ 1000 = 0.025
   Concentration of HA = 0.00090 ÷ 0.025 = **0.036 mol dm⁻³** *[1 mark]*

Page 120
Warm-Up Questions

1 100%
All reactions with one product will have 100% atom economy.
2 Reactions with low atom economies use lots of raw materials and produce lots of waste. Raw materials are expensive to buy and waste products can be expensive to remove and dispose of responsibly.
3 percentage yield = (actual yield ÷ theoretical yield) × 100
4 percentage yield = (4 ÷ 5) × 100 = **80%**

Exam Questions

1 A *[1 mark]*
2 M_r of ethanol = (12 × 2) + 6 + 16 = 46,
   M_r of ethene = (12 × 2) + 4 = 28 *[1 mark]*
   Atom economy = (28 ÷ 46) × 100 *[1 mark]* = **61 %** (2 s.f.) *[1 mark]*
3 How to grade your answer:
   Level 0: There is no relevant information. *[No marks]*
   Level 1: Brief description of one reason why yields are less than 100% is given. The points made do not link together. *[1 to 2 marks]*
   Level 2: Two reasons why yields are always less than 100% are described clearly. The answer has some structure. *[3 to 4 marks]*
   Level 3: Three reasons why yields are always less than 100% are described clearly. The answer is well structured. *[5 to 6 marks]*
   Here are some points your answer may include:
   If not all of the reactants are converted to product, the reaction is incomplete and the yield will be lower than expected.
   Losses may occur during practical procedures.
   For example, transferring solutions from one container to another often leaves behind traces on the containers.
   There may be unexpected reactions happening, resulting in extra products forming other than the ones you wanted.

4 a) M_r(CuO) = 63.5 + 16 = 79.5 *[1 mark]*
      So moles of CuO = 4.0 ÷ 79.5 = 0.0503... mol
      From the equation, 1 mole of Cu is produced for every 1 mol of CuO that reacts. So 0.0503... mol CuO reacts to form 0.0503... mol Cu *[1 mark]*
      So theoretical yield of Cu = number of moles × M_r
      = 0.0503... × 63.5 = **3.2 g** (2 s.f.) *[1 mark]*
   b) Percentage yield = (2.8 ÷ 3.2) × 100 *[1 mark]* = **88%** (2 s.f.) *[1 mark]*
Even if you got the answer to part (a) wrong, you'd still get the marks for part (b) if you used the correct method.

Page 125
Warm-Up Questions

1 a) Haber process
   b) iron
2 NH_4NO_3
3 An electrical cell that's supplied with a fuel and oxygen and uses energy from the reaction between them to produce electrical energy efficiently.

Exam Questions

1 a) phosphorus *[1 mark]*, potassium *[1 mark]*
   b) E.g. fertilisers provide/replace missing elements in the soil that are essential for plant growth *[1 mark]*. This helps to increase crop yield *[1 mark]*.
2 a) $2H_2 + O_2 \rightarrow 2H_2O$ *[1 mark for the correct reactants and products, 1 mark for correct balancing]*
   b) Advantage: e.g. fuel cells contain no moving parts, so energy isn't lost through friction. / Fuel cells don't produce any conventional pollutants. / There aren't lots of stages to the process of generating electricity in fuel cells, so there aren't many places for energy to be lost as heat *[1 mark]*. Disadvantage: e.g. hydrogen requires a lot of storage space. / Hydrogen is explosive to store safely *[1 mark]*.
3 a) $3H_2 + N_2 \rightleftharpoons 2NH_3$ *[1 mark for the correct molecules on the left side of the equation, 1 mark for correct balancing.]*
   b) It would increase *[1 mark]*. Lowering the temperature moves the position of equilibrium towards the products *[1 mark]*.
   c) E.g. if the pressure was higher the plant may become too expensive to build/dangerous to operate *[1 mark]*.
4 How to grade your answer:
   Level 0: There is no relevant information. *[No marks]*
   Level 1: There is a brief explanation of how to prepare crystals of ammonium sulfate in the laboratory but some major details are missing. The points made do not link together. *[1 to 2 marks]*
   Level 2: There is a good explanation of how to prepare pure crystals of ammonium sulfate in the laboratory. Some minor details may be missing. The answer has some structure. *[3 to 4 marks]*
   Level 3: There is a clear and detailed explanation of how to prepare pure crystals of ammonium sulfate in the laboratory. The answer is well structured. *[5 to 6 marks]*
   Here are some points your answer may include:
   Use a pipette (and pipette filler) to measure out a set volume of ammonia solution into a conical flask.
   Add two or three drops of an indicator/methyl orange to the ammonia solution.
   Use a funnel to fill a burette with dilute sulfuric acid.
   Record the initial volume of the acid in the burette.
   Use the burette to add the acid to the ammonia solution a bit at a time.
   Swirl the contents of the flask whilst adding the acid.
   Go especially slowly as you approach the endpoint/colour change. Take a note of how much sulfuric acid it took to neutralise the ammonia solution.
   To get a pure sample of ammonium sulfate, repeat the titration using the volume of sulfuric acid needed to neutralise the volume of ammonia solution used, but do not add any indicator.
   Then gently evaporate the solution (using a steam bath) until only a small amount is remaining.
   Leave this to crystallise/form ammonium sulfate crystals and then filter out these crystals and leave them to dry.

Topic 6 — Groups in the Periodic Table

Pages 134-135
Warm-Up Questions

1 1
2 more reactive
3 It increases.
4 sodium chloride/NaCl
5 A reaction where a more reactive element displaces a less reactive element from a compound.
6 negative
7 Group 0

Exam Questions

1 a) Highest (X): fluorine *[1 mark]*
    Lowest (Y): iodine *[1 mark]*
Halogens at the top of Group 7 are more reactive than those at the bottom of the group.
  b) iodine *[1 mark]*
2 a) Group 1 *[1 mark]*
  b) *[2 marks — 1 mark for correct number of electrons in correct shells, 1 mark for square brackets and charge]*

3 a) Hold a piece of damp blue litmus paper in the gas *[1 mark]*. If the litmus paper turns from blue to white, chlorine is present *[1 mark]*.
  b) E.g. displacement reaction *[1 mark]*
  c) Iodine/I_2 *[1 mark]* as it is displaced from potassium iodide *[1 mark]*.
A more reactive halogen will displace a less reactive halogen from a compound.
  d) The products of the reaction will be aqueous potassium chloride/$KCl_{(aq)}$ *[1 mark]* and bromine gas/$Br_{2(g)}$ *[1 mark]*. Chlorine is more reactive than bromine as its outer shell is closer to the nucleus *[1 mark]*. This results in chlorine displacing bromine from potassium bromide *[1 mark]*.
  e) Group 0 elements are generally inert *[1 mark]*. This is because they don't need to lose or gain electrons to have a full outer shell *[1 mark]*.
4 a) They have a single outer electron which is easily lost, so they are very reactive *[1 mark]*.
  b) As you go down Group 1, the outer electron is further from the nucleus *[1 mark]*. So the attraction between the nucleus and the electron decreases *[1 mark]*. This means the outer electron is more easily lost and the metal is more reactive *[1 mark]*.
  c) i) hydrogen *[1 mark]* and potassium hydroxide *[1 mark]*
    ii) $2K + 2H_2O \rightarrow 2KOH + H_2$ *[1 mark for correct products and reactants, 1 mark for correct balancing]*

Topic 7 — Rates of Reaction and Energy Changes

Pages 143-144
Warm-Up Questions
1 E.g. how quickly a reaction happens.
2 Reaction A
3 It increases the rate of the reaction.
4 gradient = change in y ÷ change in x

Exam Questions
1 a) stopwatch/stopclock/timer *[1 mark]*
  b) gas syringe *[1 mark]*
  c) E.g. place a conical flask on a mass balance *[1 mark]* and record the change in mass at regular intervals as the gas leaves the flask *[1 mark]*.
2 a) Any two from: e.g. the concentration of sodium thiosulfate/hydrochloric acid / the depth of liquid / the person judging when the black cross is obscured / the black cross used (size, darkness etc.) *[2 marks — 1 mark for each correct answer]*.
Judging when a cross is completely obscured is quite subjective — two people might not agree on exactly when it happens. You can try to limit this problem by using the same person each time, but you can't remove the problem completely. The person might have changed their mind slightly by the time they do the next experiment — or be looking at it from a different angle, be a bit more bored, etc.
  b)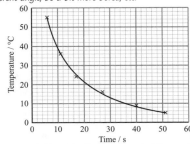
[1 mark for correctly drawn axes with a sensible scale, 2 marks for all points plotted correctly, otherwise 1 mark if 5 of 6 points plotted correctly, 1 mark for a suitable line of best fit]
  c) As the temperature decreases, the time taken for the mark to disappear decreases *[1 mark]*.
  d) At each temperature it would take longer for the reaction to complete *[1 mark]*.
  e) E.g. by repeating the experiment *[1 mark]*. If the results gained are similar then the experiment is repeatable *[1 mark]*.
3 a) A *[1 mark]*
  b) The temperature needed to be controlled so that the teacher could tell if the variable she changed/the independent variable/the change in HCl concentration caused the change in rate *[1 mark]*.

c) 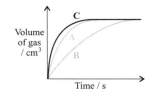 *[1 mark]*
Curve C should be to the left of the curves A and B — this shows that curve C has a steeper gradient than curves A and B. It should also finish with the same volume of gas produced as curves A and B.
4 a) Rate = amount of product formed ÷ time
    = 40 ÷ 60 = **0.67 cm^3 s^{-1}** *[1 mark]*
  b) E.g.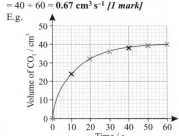
[1 mark for correctly plotting the two missing points, 1 mark for a suitable line of best fit.]
  c) E.g.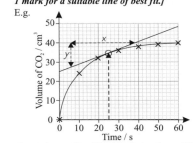
change in y = 40 − 27 = 13, change in x = 38 − 6 = 32,
rate = change in y ÷ change in x = 13 ÷ 32 = 0.4 cm^3 s^{-1}
[1 mark for drawing a tangent at 25 s, 1 mark for correctly calculating a change in y from the tangent, 1 mark for correctly calculating a change in x from the tangent and 1 mark for a rate between 0.3 cm^3 s^{-1} and 0.5 cm^3 s^{-1}]

Page 148
Warm-Up Questions
1 They must collide with at least the activation energy.
2 Breaking a reactant into smaller pieces increases its surface area to volume ratio. This means there is a greater surface area available for collisions to occur on, so the rate of reaction is increased.
3 True
4 Enzymes help to speed up chemical reactions in living cells.

Exam Questions
1 a) Any two from: e.g. volume of acid / mass of calcium carbonate / size of solid particles / temperature *[2 marks — 1 mark for each correct answer]*
  b) 140 − 87.5 = **52.5 cm^3** *[1 mark]*
  c) The gradient of the graph at the start of the reaction is steeper for 0.4 mol dm^{-3} / the curve for the 0.4 mol dm^{-3} reaction finishes/flattens out first, so the rate of reaction is faster than when 0.2 mol dm^{-3} HCl was used *[1 mark]*.
This is because increasing the concentration of a reactant increases the number of particles of that substance in the reaction mixture *[1 mark]*. This increases the frequency of collisions between particles of the reactants, increasing the rate of the reaction *[1 mark]*.

2   How to grade your answer:

Level 0:   There is no relevant information. *[No marks]*

Level 1:   One or two ways of increasing the rate are described and there's reference to collision theory. The points made do not link together. *[1 to 2 marks]*

Level 2:   At least two ways of increasing the rate are given with appropriate reference to collision theory. The answer has some structure. *[3 to 4 marks]*

Level 3:   There is a clear and detailed discussion of three ways by which the rate can be increased, which includes relevant references to collision theory. The answer is well structured. *[5 to 6 marks]*

Here are some points your answer may include:

Collision theory says that the rate of reaction depends on how often the particles collide and how much energy is transferred during a collision. If the particles collide with at least the activation energy they will react. Increasing the temperature makes particles move faster, so they collide more often and with greater energy. This will increase the rate of reaction.

If the surface area of the nickel catalyst is increased then the particles around it will have more area to work on. This increases the frequency of successful collisions and will increase the rate of reaction.

Increasing the pressure of the hydrogen will mean the particles are more crowded. This will increase the frequency of the collisions and increase the rate of reaction.

Page 153

Warm-Up Questions

1   An exothermic reaction is one which gives out energy to the surroundings.
2   An endothermic reaction is one which takes in energy from the surroundings.
3   The activation energy is the minimum amount of energy the reactants need to collide in order to react.
4   An increase in the temperature of the surroundings.
5   When bonds are formed.

Exam Questions

1   B *[1 mark]*
2 a)   Exothermic, because the temperature of the mixture has increased *[1 mark]*, therefore the particles have transferred energy to the reaction mixture *[1 mark]*.
  b)   A lid was placed on the cup to reduce energy lost to the surroundings (by evaporation) *[1 mark]*.
3 a)   C – H and O = O *[1 mark]*
  b) $(4 \times 414) + (2 \times 494) = 2644$ kJ mol^{-1}
This is the amount of energy required to break the bonds in CH_4 and $2O_2$.
    $(2 \times 800) + (4 \times 459) = 3436$ kJ mol^{-1}
This is the amount of energy released by forming the bonds in CO_2 and $2H_2O$.
    $2644 - 3436 = $ **−792 kJ mol^{-1}**
    [4 marks for correct answer, otherwise 1 mark for finding the energy needed to break the bonds in the reactants, 1 mark for finding the energy released by forming bonds in the products, 1 mark for subtracting the energy released by forming bonds from the energy required to break bonds.]

Topic 8 — Fuels and Earth Science

Page 159

Warm-Up Questions

1 a)   e.g. aircraft fuel
  b)   e.g. as fuel in some cars / trains
  c)   e.g. surfacing roads and roofs
2   water and carbon dioxide
3   e.g. alkanes / alkenes
4   E.g. the longer the hydrocarbon molecules, the less easily it ignites. / The shorter the hydrocarbon molecules, the more easily it ignites.

Exam Question

1 a)   A *[1 mark]*
  b)   F *[1 mark]*
  c)   Inside the fractionating column there is a temperature gradient with the hottest part at the bottom and coolest at the top *[1 mark]*. Crude oil that is gaseous moves up the column and when hydrocarbons in the gas reach a part of the column where the temperature is lower than their boiling point they condense and drain out of the column *[1 mark]*. Hydrocarbons with longer chain lengths have higher boiling points so condense lower down the column whereas hydrocarbons with shorter chain lengths have lower boiling points so condense higher up the column *[1 mark]*.
  d)   Because shorter-chain hydrocarbons generated by cracking tend to be more useful than longer ones *[1 mark]*.
  e) $C_8H_{18} \rightarrow $ **C_2H_6** + 2C_3H_6 *[1 mark]*

Page 163

Warm-Up Questions

1   Burning hydrocarbons without enough oxygen for all of the hydrogen and carbon atoms to be converted to carbon dioxide and water.
2 a)   carbon monoxide and soot
  b)   Carbon monoxide: stops the blood from carrying oxygen around the body / causes fainting/comas/death.
       Soot: causes/worsens respiratory problems.
3   Advantage: e.g. hydrogen gas is a very clean fuel / hydrogen can be obtained from a renewable resource.
    Disadvantage: e.g. hydrogen gas needs an expensive engine to be used as fuel / hydrogen needs to be manufactured, which can be expensive/ require another energy source that might not be clean or renewable / hydrogen is hard to store / hydrogen is not widely available.

Exam Questions

1   B *[1 mark]*
2 a)   Fossil fuels contain sulfur impurities *[1 mark]*.
  b)   When sulfur dioxide mixes with water in clouds *[1 mark]* it forms dilute sulfuric acid, which falls as acid rain *[1 mark]*.
  c)   E.g. it kills plants/animals / damages buildings and statues / makes metals corrode *[1 mark]*.
3   How to grade your answer:

Level 0:   There is no relevant information. *[No marks]*

Level 1:   There is a brief description of the Earth's early atmosphere and how the atmospheric composition has changed over time, but no explanation for the changes has been given. The points made are basic and not linked together. *[1 to 2 marks]*

Level 2:   There is a description of the Earth's early atmosphere and how atmospheric composition has changed over time. Some explanation for the changes has been given, but some details are missing. The answer has some structure. *[3 to 4 marks]*

Level 3:   There is a detailed description of the composition of Earth's early atmosphere. There is a clear explanation of how and why the atmospheric composition has changed over time. The points made are well-linked and the answer has a clear and logical structure. *[5 to 6 marks]*

Here are some points your answer may include:

The early atmosphere was mostly made up of carbon dioxide and water vapour, with very little oxygen.

Most of the early water vapour condensed to form the oceans, so the amount of water vapour in the atmosphere has decreased over time to just 0.25%.

A lot of the early carbon dioxide dissolved in the oceans.

Green plants then evolved. These removed more carbon dioxide from the atmosphere during photosynthesis.

Much of this carbon dioxide became locked up in fossil fuels and sedimentary rocks.

So the amount of atmospheric carbon dioxide has decreased significantly over time, to just 0.04%.

Photosynthesis also produced oxygen.

This increased the level of oxygen to the present day concentration of 21%.

Page 167

Warm-Up Questions

1   e.g. water vapour, methane
2   The process by which gases in the atmosphere act like an insulating layer, keeping Earth warm.
3 a)   E.g. plants take carbon dioxide out of the atmosphere, so removing trees causes carbon dioxide levels to rise.
  b)   E.g. an increase in energy consumption means more fossil fuels are burnt. Burning fossil fuels releases carbon dioxide into the atmosphere, so it would increase atmospheric CO_2.
  c)   E.g. methane is a greenhouse gas that is produced from the digestive processes of certain livestock. An increase in livestock farming will cause an increase in methane emissions to the atmosphere.
4   The increase in the average temperature of the Earth's surface.

Exam Questions

1 a)   Any one from: e.g. less data was collected / data was collected at fewer locations / the methods used to collect the data were less accurate *[1 mark]*.
  b)   E.g. $317 + ((317 \times 22.7) \div 100) = 388.959 = $ **389 ppm** (to 3 s.f.)
    [2 marks for correct answer to three significant figures, otherwise 1 mark for 388.959 ppm.]
  c)   E.g. the temperature at the Earth's surface is correlated to the concentration of carbon dioxide in the atmosphere *[1 mark]*.
2 a)   Carbon dioxide absorbs long wavelength radiation emitted from the Earth *[1 mark]*. It is then re-radiated back towards the Earth, warming the Earth's surface *[1 mark]*.
  b)   Any two from: e.g. flooding / melting of the polar ice caps / changes in rainfall patterns *[2 marks]*.

c) i) E.g. walking/cycling instead of driving / turning down their central heating *[1 mark]*.

ii) E.g. they could create financial incentives that encourage people to cut their own personal carbon dioxide emissions / they could encourage an increase in research into new/renewable energy sources *[1 mark]*.

Topic 9 — Separate Chemistry 2

Page 174
Warm-Up Questions

1   potassium (ions)
2 a) blue
  b) $Cu^{2+}_{(aq)} + 2OH^-_{(aq)} \rightarrow Cu(OH)_{2(s)}$
3   white
4   Any two from: e.g. instrumental methods are very sensitive/fast/accurate.

Exam Questions

1

Flame colour	Metal ion
blue-green	**Cu²⁺**
red	Li⁺
yellow	**Na⁺**
orange-red	Ca²⁺

[4 marks — 1 mark for each correct answer.]

2   Compare the spectrum produced by the experiment against reference spectra *[1 mark]*. The spectrum produced from the experiment will be a combination of reference spectra, allowing A and B to be identified *[1 mark]*.

3 a) iron(II) iodide *[1 mark for iron(II), 1 mark for iodide]*
  b) No, the student is not correct. The sample produced a white precipitate with hydrochloric acid and barium chloride solution, so he can be sure that it contains sulfate ions *[1 mark]*. Calcium does produce a white precipitate with sodium hydroxide *[1 mark]*, but so does aluminium, so he cannot be sure that it contains calcium ions *[1 mark]*.

Page 181
Warm-Up Questions

1   Alkanes are a homologous series of hydrocarbons with the general formula C_nH_{2n+2}.
2   Because they can make more bonds with other atoms.
3

4   amino acids

Exam Questions

1

Name of alkene	Formula	Displayed formula
ethene	C_2H_4	
propene	C_3H_6	

[4 marks — 1 mark for each correct answer.]

2 a) water *[1 mark]*
  b) E.g. dicarboxylic acids *[1 mark]* and diols *[1 mark]*
3 a)

[1 mark for all bonds drawn correctly]

  b) poly(propene) *[1 mark]*
4   How to grade your answer:
  Level 0:   There is no relevant information. *[No marks]*
  Level 1:   There is a brief description of some of the advantages OR disadvantages of recycling polymers compared to disposing of them in landfill or by combustion. Answer demonstrates some chemical understanding, but points are not fully developed and include errors. The points made do not link together. *[1 to 2 marks]*
  Level 2:   There is a description of the advantages AND disadvantages of recycling polymers compared to disposing of them in landfill or by combustion. Answer demonstrates chemical understanding, but points may not be fully developed and may include minor errors. The answer has some structure. *[3 to 4 marks]*

  Level 3:   There is a detailed description of the advantages AND disadvantages of recycling polymers compared to disposing of them in landfill or by combustion. Answer demonstrates a clear, chemical understanding. All points are relevant and fully developed. The answer is well structured. *[5 to 6 marks]*

Here are some points your answer may include:
Advantages:
E.g. recycling polymers reduces the amount of non-biodegradable waste filling up landfill sites. The land can instead be used for other purposes.
Recycling reduces emissions of greenhouse and toxic gases that are released when polymers are disposed of by combustion.
Recycling reduces the need to produce new polymers.
Crude oil is used to make polymers, so less crude oil is used as a result. This is important because crude oil is a finite resource so will eventually run out.
Recycling also uses up less water and energy resources than when making new polymers.
Recycling generally saves money and creates jobs.
Disadvantages:
E.g. polymers must be separated by type before they can be recycled, which can be difficult/expensive.
If polymers aren't properly separated, the quality of the final recycled polymer product could be reduced.
Polymers can only be recycled a finite number of times, as over time the strength of the polymer can decrease.
Melting down polymers can release dangerous gases into the atmosphere. These can be harmful to plants and animals.

Page 186
Warm-Up Questions

1    $C_nH_{2n+1}OH$
2 a) yeast
  b) E.g. the temperature must be between 30 °C and 40 °C, and no oxygen can be present/conditions must be anaerobic.
3    $C_6H_{12}O_6 \rightarrow 2C_2H_5OH + 2CO_2$
4   methanoic acid, ethanoic acid, propanoic acid, butanoic acid

Exam Questions

1   C *[1 mark]*
2 a)

[1 mark]

  b) i) propanol *[1 mark]*
   ii) an oxidising agent *[1 mark]*
3 a) methanol *[1 mark]*
  b) $C_2H_5OH + 3O_2 \rightarrow 2CO_2 + 3H_2O$
    [1 mark for correctly balanced equation]
  c) How to grade your answer:
    Level 0:   There is no relevant information. *[No marks]*
    Level 1:   There is a brief description of the method. Answer demonstrates some chemical understanding, but steps are missing to the method and it include errors. The points made do not link together. *[1 to 2 marks]*
    Level 2:   There is a description of the method. Answer demonstrates chemical understanding, but steps may be missing from the method and may include small errors. The answer has some structure. *[3 to 4 marks]*
    Level 3:   There is a detailed description of the method. Answer demonstrates a clear, chemical understanding. A complete practical method is described with only very minor errors present if at all. The answer is well structured. *[5 to 6 marks]*

Here are some points your answer may include:
E.g. put some ethanol into a spirit burner and measure the mass of the burner and fuel using a mass balance.
Measure a set volume of distilled water into a copper calorimeter.
Insulate the calorimeter with a draught excluder and insulating lid.
Measure the initial temperature of the water inside the calorimeter using a thermometer.
Place the burner below the calorimeter and light the wick.
Stir the water constantly.
When the temperature of the water has increased by 20 °C, blow out the spirit burner.
Immediately reweigh the burner and ethanol.
Calculate the mass of ethanol used to increase the water temperature by 20 °C.
Repeat the experiment using pentanol.
The fuel that uses less mass to heat the water by 20 °C will be the more efficient one.

Page 192

Warm-Up Questions

1   It increases.
2   Any two from: e.g. catalysts/cosmetics/drug delivery/lubricant coatings/ electric circuits/sports equipment/surgical masks/wound dressings.
3   They are brittle, stiff materials made by baking substances such as clay.
4   e.g. fibreglass / concrete
5   Any two from: e.g. polymers are flexible/easily moulded/less dense than most metals or ceramics/thermal insulators/electrical insulators.

Exam Questions

1   E.g. some people are concerned about the use of nanoparticles as not enough is known about their effects on the body following long-term use *[1 mark]*. Thorough testing could be carried out before products containing nanoparticles are used by humans to help minimise the risk *[1 mark]*.

2 a) Polypropene plastic *[1 mark]*. Then any two from: e.g. it is much cheaper than the other materials in Figure 1, which could allow the chair to be sold at a lower price / polypropene has a lower density than the other materials, so it would make a lightweight chair that can be easily moved around the garden / polypropene is flexible, so the chair will be comfortable to sit on / polypropene is resistant to corrosion, so it would make a chair that won't be damaged by being exposed to outdoor conditions *[2 marks]*.
   b) i) Aluminium alloys are far less dense than steel (3 g cm⁻³ compared to 7.8 g cm⁻³), so the parts are much lighter *[1 mark]*. They are also more resistant to corrosion *[1 mark]*.
      ii) E.g. carbon-fibre composite is a more expensive material than aluminium alloy *[1 mark]*.

Practice Paper 1
Pages 200-219

1 a) E.g.

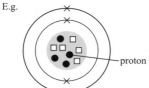

proton

[1 mark]

Remember that atoms have the same number of electrons and protons.
   b) B *[1 mark]*
   c) C and D *[1 mark]* — they are the only pair with the same number of protons *[1 mark]*.
   d) i) D *[1 mark]*
      ii) $M_r = 65 + 32 + (4 \times 16) = \textbf{161}$
         [2 marks for the correct answer, otherwise 1 mark for correct working]
      iii) moles of oxygen atoms = $1.4 \times 4 = 5.6$ moles *[1 mark]*
This is because there are 4 moles of oxygen atoms for every 1 mole of $ZnSO_4$.
         atoms of oxygen = moles of oxygen × Avogadro's constant
              = $5.6 \times 6.02 \times 10^{23}$ *[1 mark]*
              = $3.3712 \times 10^{24} = \textbf{3.4} \times \textbf{10}^{\textbf{24}}$ **atoms** *[1 mark]*
         [3 marks for correct answer given to 2 significant figures without working, otherwise 1 mark for correct number of moles of oxygen atoms, 1 mark for multiplying number of moles of oxygen atoms by Avogadro's constant]
Make sure you give your final answer to the number of significant figures stated in the question. If you don't do this you won't get full marks.
2 a) A *[1 mark]*
   b) It has no free electrons *[1 mark]*.
   c) i) liquid *[1 mark]*
      ii) Carbon dioxide would have a higher boiling point than oxygen. Because carbon dioxide is a larger molecule *[1 mark]*, the intermolecular forces would be stronger *[1 mark]* so would require more energy to break *[1 mark]*.
   d) mass of CO_2 = 1.32 kg = 1320 g
       M_r of $CO_2 = 12 + (2 \times 16) = 44$ *[1 mark]*
       moles of CO_2 = mass ÷ M_r = 1320 ÷ 44 = 30 moles *[1 mark]*
       moles of $ZnCO_3$ = 30 moles
This is because one mole of $ZnCO_3$ reacts to produce one mole of CO_2.
       M_r of $ZnCO_3 = 65 + 12 + (16 \times 3) = 125$ *[1 mark]*
       mass of $ZnCO_3$ = moles × M_r = 30 × 125 = **3750 g** *[1 mark]*
       [4 marks for correct answer without working]
3 a) During an acid-base titration you want to see a sudden colour change at the endpoint *[1 mark]*. Universal indicator changes colour gradually over a pH range, so it is not suitable for acid-base titrations *[1 mark]*.
   b) $H_2SO_4 + 2NaOH \rightarrow Na_2SO_4 + 2H_2O$
      [1 mark for the correct reactant and products, 1 mark for correctly balancing the equation]
   c) i) $(8.80 \div 1000) \times 0.050 = \textbf{0.00044}$ **moles** *[1 mark]*
      ii) 0.00044 moles × 2 = **0.00088** *[1 mark]*
From the equation you can see that one mole of H_2SO_4 reacts with two moles of NaOH so the number of moles of NaOH will be double that of H_2SO_4.

      iii) $10 \text{ cm}^3 \div 1000 = 0.01 \text{ dm}^3$
         concentration = moles ÷ volume
         $0.00088 \div 0.01 = \textbf{0.088 mol dm}^{-3}$
         [2 marks for correct answer, otherwise 1 mark for dividing the moles of NaOH by the volume]
4 a) The volume of gas produced *[1 mark]*.
   b) i) hydrogen/H_2 *[1 mark]*
      ii) Place a lighted splint in the gas *[1 mark]* and it will make a squeaky pop sound *[1 mark]*.
   c) Reaction D *[1 mark]*. The most reactive metal will react fastest with the acid *[1 mark]*. In reaction D the largest volume of gas has been collected in the syringe / the most bubbles are being given off *[1 mark]*.
   d) Reaction of copper sulfate with iron: yes *[1 mark]*
      Reaction of iron sulfate with magnesium: yes *[1 mark]*
   e) D *[1 mark]*
A more reactive metal will displace a less reactive metal in a salt.
5 a) C *[1 mark]*
   b) The yield of sulfur trioxide will decrease *[1 mark]*. When pressure is decreased the position of equilibrium moves towards the side with more gas molecules *[1 mark]*. There are two molecules of gas on the right, compared to three on the left, so the position of equilibrium will move to the left *[1 mark]*.
   c) i) percentage yield = (actual yield ÷ theoretical yield) × 100
         = (7500 ÷ 12 500) × 100 = **60%** *[1 mark]*
      ii) E.g. 15% of 7500 kg = 7500 × 0.15 = 1125 kg
         new mass made in a day = 7500 + 1125 = 8625 kg
         new mass made in 5 days = 8625 × 5 = **43 125 kg**
         [3 marks for correct answer, otherwise 1 mark for calculating the new mass made in a day and 1 mark for calculating the new mass made in five days]
6 a) E.g. a pipette / measuring cylinder *[1 mark]*
   b) volume of HCl = 25 cm³ = 0.025 dm³
      moles of HCl = concentration × volume
           = 0.8 × 0.025 = 0.02 moles
      mass of HCl = moles × M_r
           = 0.02 × 36.5 = **0.73 g**
      [2 marks for correct answer, otherwise 1 mark for correct number of moles of HCl]
   c) i) There would be unreacted calcium hydroxide/ solid at the bottom of the flask *[1 mark]*.
      ii) $H^+_{(aq)} + OH^-_{(aq)} \rightarrow H_2O_{(l)}$
         [1 mark for correct ionic equation, 1 mark for correct state symbols]
   d) i) 0.75 g *[1 mark — accept any answer between 0.72 g and 0.78 g]*
      ii) E.g. monitoring pH using Universal indicator doesn't provide accurate data for the value of pH as the reaction progresses *[1 mark]*.
      iii) a pH meter/probe *[1 mark]*
7 a) Potable water is water that is fit to drink *[1 mark]*.
   b) i) C *[1 mark]*
      ii) Iron sulfate/aluminium sulfate is added to the water *[1 mark]*, which makes fine particles clump together and settle at the bottom *[1 mark]*.
   c) E.g. the sources of water available to the city mean that either plant is possible to use *[1 mark]*. The sea water distillation plant would be more costly to run since it uses more energy than a water treatment plant *[1 mark]*. The higher energy usage of sea water distillation means that this type of plant is likely to have a larger environmental impact due to greenhouse gas emissions linked to power generation *[1 mark]*. In conclusion, a water treatment plant is likely to have lower costs and less environmental impact, which suggests that this may be a better option that sea water distillation *[1 mark]*.
In questions that ask you to evaluate you need to include a conclusion that supports what you've talked about in the rest of your answer — that's what the last mark is for in the example answer shown above.
8 a) B *[1 mark]*
   b) A molten or dissolved ionic compound *[1 mark]* that decomposes when an electrical current is passed through it *[1 mark]*.
   c) $4OH^- \rightarrow O_2 + 2H_2O + 4e^-$ *[1 mark]*
   d) i) 2.54 *[1 mark]*
      ii) E.g. at the negative electrode, copper ions/Cu^{2+} ions are being reduced to copper metal/Cu *[1 mark]*. The half equation for this reaction is: $Cu^{2+} + 2e^- \rightarrow Cu$ *[2 marks for the correct half equation, otherwise 1 mark for correct reactants and product, 1 mark for correct balancing]*. So a layer of copper metal forms on the negative electrode during the electrolysis *[1 mark]*.
      iii) The negative electrode would change in mass by twice as much *[1 mark]*.
9 a) Each particle is represented by a solid sphere *[1 mark]*.
   b) i) B *[1 mark]*
      ii) When a liquid is heated, the particles gain energy *[1 mark]*. The energy makes the particles move faster, which weakens the bonds holding the liquid together *[1 mark]*. At a certain temperature the particles have enough energy to break their bonds and the liquid becomes a gas *[1 mark]*.
   c) Displayed formulae don't show the shape of the substance *[1 mark]* or the size of the atoms *[1 mark]*.

d) How to grade your answer:

Level 0: There is no relevant information. *[No marks]*

Level 1: There is a brief description of one or both of the models but no comparisons are made. The points made do not link together. *[1 to 2 marks]*

Level 2: There is a description of both models and a limited attempt to compare their strengths and weaknesses. The answer has some structure. *[3 to 4 marks]*

Level 3: There is a clear and detailed comparison between the two models, including the strengths and weaknesses of each one. The answer is well structured. *[5 to 6 marks]*

Here are some points your answer may include: e.g.

Model A is a dot and cross diagram.

Model B is a 3D model.

The dot and cross diagram is useful for showing the detail of the bonding in methane.

The electrons drawn in the overlap between the outer shells of the atoms are shared between those atoms.

The dot and cross diagram is useful for showing which atoms the electrons in the covalent bonds come from.

However, dot and cross diagrams don't show the relative sizes of the atoms, or how the atoms are arranged in space.

The 3D model is useful for representing the spatial arrangement of the atoms in a molecule of methane.

The covalent bonds between the atoms are represented by lines.

However, it doesn't show where the electrons in the bonds have come from, or give any other information about the electronic structure of the atoms.

10 a) Any two from: Problem — the spots of dye/ink are touching the solvent *[1 mark]*. Correction — the student should put the filter paper in a beaker of solvent with the pencil line above the level of the solvent *[1 mark]*. / Problem — the ink and dyes are compared using different solvents *[1 mark]*. Correction — the student should use the same solvent for the black ink and the dyes so that it's a fair test *[1 mark]*. / Problem — the ink and dyes are compared on different pieces of filter paper which could make it difficult to directly compare them *[1 mark]*. Correction — the student should put the spots of the dyes and the ink on the same piece of filter paper *[1 mark]*.

b) C *[1 mark]*

c) Dyes B and D *[1 mark]*
Explanation — all of the spots from these two dyes are in the same positions as the spots from the black ink *[1 mark]*.

d) R_f = distance travelled by solute ÷ distance travelled by solvent = 4.8 ÷ 6.4 = **0.75** *[1 mark]*

e) How to grade your answer:

Level 0: There is no relevant information. *[No marks]*

Level 1: There is a brief explanation of how to carry out simple distillation but it has limited detail and is incomplete. Several errors are present. There is no clear explanation of how the solvent is separated from the ink mixture. The points made do not link together. *[1 to 2 marks]*

Level 2: There is an explanation of how to carry out simple distillation that contains correctly named pieces of equipment. The explanation may miss small details and contain a few small errors. An attempt is made to explain how the solvent is separated from the ink mixture, but it may contain small errors. The answer has some structure. *[3 to 4 marks]*

Level 3: There is a clear and detailed explanation of how to carry out simple distillation with all equipment correctly named. The answer explains accurately how distillation could separate the solvent from the ink mixture. The answer is well structured. *[5 to 6 marks]*

Here are some points your answer may include: e.g.

Attach a distillation flask to a condenser.

Place the end of the condenser over a beaker/conical flask.

Connect the bottom end of the condenser to a cold tap using rubber tubing.

Run cold water through the condenser to keep it cool.

Pour the ink into a distillation flask.

Place a thermometer and a bung in the top of the distillation flask.

Gradually heat the distillation flask using a Bunsen burner.

The solvent will evaporate, as it has the lowest boiling point, whilst the rest of the ink mixture will stay in liquid form.

The gaseous solvent will then pass into the condenser.

In the condenser, the gaseous solvent will cool and condense.

It will then flow into the beaker/conical flask, where it is collected separately from the rest of the ink mixture.

Practice Paper 2
Pages 220-239

1 a) i) C *[1 mark]*
Melting point increases down the group, so chlorine will have a melting point about halfway between the melting points of fluorine and bromine.

ii) It is around halfway between the melting points of bromine and fluorine *[1 mark]*.

b) D *[1 mark]*

c) $Br_2 + 2KI \rightarrow I_2 + 2KBr$
[1 mark for correct products, 1 mark for correct balancing]

d) Chlorine is higher up group 7 than iodine, which means that chlorine is more reactive than iodine *[1 mark]*. This is because chlorine can attract an electron to its outer shell more easily than iodine, because the nucleus is closer to the outermost shell *[1 mark]*. This means that chlorine will displace iodine in the solution *[1 mark]*.

e) $H_2 + F_2 \rightarrow 2HF$
[1 mark for correct reactants and products, 1 mark for correct balancing]

2 a) i) $CaCO_3 + 2HCl \rightarrow CaCl_2 + CO_2 + H_2O$
[1 mark for correct reactants and products, 1 mark for correct balancing]

ii)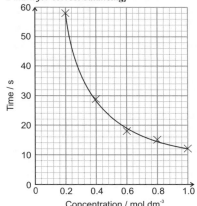

[1 mark for plotting points correctly, 1 mark for sensible curve of best fit]

iii) E.g. 23 s (accept 22-24 s) *[1 mark]*

b) The rate increases as the concentration increases *[1 mark]*.

c) At higher concentration there are more particles of reactant in a certain volume *[1 mark]*. This means that collisions between particles are more likely, so the reaction rate increases *[1 mark]*.

d) No. The powdered marble has a larger surface area *[1 mark]*. This will increase the rate of the reaction *[1 mark]*, so it will take less than 18 seconds for 20 cm³ of carbon dioxide to form *[1 mark]*.

3 a) i) A *[1 mark]*

ii) $C_6H_{12}O_6 \rightarrow 2C_2H_5OH + 2CO_2$
[1 mark for correct reactants and products, 1 mark for correct balancing]

iii) Yeast contains an enzyme that speeds up/catalyses the fermentation reaction *[1 mark]*. Above 40 °C, the yeast enzyme would be denatured/destroyed and the reaction would stop *[1 mark]*.

b) E.g. 100 °C is the boiling point of water and is higher than that of ethanol *[1 mark]*. Heating the fermentation mixture to 100 °C would evaporate all the ethanol and some/all of the water, so they wouldn't separate out *[1 mark]*. The collected vapours would be an ethanol solution that was the same or only slightly more concentrated than the fermentation mixture *[1 mark]*.

c) volume = 750 ÷ 1000 = 0.75 dm³
concentration = mass ÷ volume = 69 ÷ 0.75 = **92 g dm⁻³**
[2 marks for correct answer, otherwise 1 mark for writing a correct expression for calculating the concentration]

4 a) E.g. measure out 25 cm³ of sodium thiosulfate solution and 25 cm³ of hydrochloric acid using measuring cylinders *[1 mark]*. Use a water bath to gently heat the separate solutions to the required temperature *[1 mark]*. Place a flask over a black mark on a piece of paper, and add both solutions to the flask *[1 mark]*. Use a stopwatch to time how long it takes for the black mark to disappear due to the formation of the yellow sulfur precipitate *[1 mark]*.

b) E.g. the concentrations of reactants *[1 mark]* and the depth of liquid in the flask *[1 mark]*. *[Accept any other valid answer]*

c) E.g. at higher temperatures, particles move faster, so they collide more often and with more energy *[1 mark]*. This means more particles collide with enough energy to react, so the reaction rate is faster at a higher temperature *[1 mark]*.

5 a) Triacontane has a higher boiling point than heptane because it is a larger hydrocarbon *[1 mark]*. This means that triacontane will turn to liquid and drain out / be collected lower down the column where the temperature is higher *[1 mark]*.

250

b) B *[1 mark]*
c) i) 8% *[1 mark]*
ii) E.g. the supply of fuel oil and bitumen (50%) is larger than the demand (38%), so there is plenty of unused fuel oil and bitumen that can be cracked to provide petrol *[1 mark]*. However, the demand for diesel oil (23%) is already greater than the amount in crude oil (19%), so there isn't any spare for cracking *[1 mark]*.

6 a) Bonds broken $(2 \times 436) + 498 = 1370$
Bonds formed $(4 \times 464) = 1856$
Energy change = $1370 - 1856 = \textbf{-486 kJ mol}^{-1}$
[4 marks for the correct answer, otherwise 3 marks for the correct answer with the wrong sign, 1 mark for calculating the correct amount of energy needed to break the bonds and 1 mark for calculating the correct amount of energy released in bond formation]

b) D *[1 mark]*
c) i) 37.5 °C *[1 mark]*
ii) Temperature change = final temperature – initial temperature
= $37.5 - 17 = \textbf{20.5 °C}$
[2 marks for correct answer, otherwise 1 mark for writing a correct expression for calculating the temperature change]

If your answer to i) was wrong, you can still have both marks for correctly subtracting 17 from it to find the temperature change.

iii) The reaction was exothermic as the temperature of the surroundings increased during the reaction *[1 mark]*.

7 a) –COOH *[1 mark]*
b) $(0.39 + 0.55 + 0.45) \div 3 = \textbf{0.46 g}$ (2 s.f.)
[2 marks for correct answer, otherwise 1 mark for writing a correct expression that could be used to find the mean]
c) i) The loss of mass for each run is less than 1 g *[1 mark]*.
ii) A flame test *[1 mark]*. If sodium ions are present the substance would burn with a yellow flame *[1 mark]*.
d) Add some sodium hydroxide to the solution and gently heat it *[1 mark]*. Hold a piece of damp red litmus paper over the solution *[1 mark]*. If the paper turns blue, ammonium ions are present in the original solution *[1 mark]*.
e) i) Add dilute nitric acid, followed by a few drops of silver nitrate solution to the metal halide solutions *[1 mark]*. The metal bromide would produce a cream precipitate, and the metal iodide would produce a yellow precipitate *[1 mark]*.
ii) B *[1 mark]*
iii) flame photometry *[1 mark]*

8 a)
[1 mark for all four points correctly plotted, 1 mark for a smooth curve that passes through all the points]
b) 36 °C *[1 mark for any answer in the range 34-38 °C]*
c) C *[1 mark]*
d) i)
[1 mark]
ii) $C_3H_8 + 5O_2 \rightarrow 3CO_2 + 4H_2O$
[1 mark for correct reactants and products, 1 mark for correct balancing]

9 a) D *[1 mark]*
b) i) C *[1 mark]*
ii) E.g.
[1 mark for 8 electrons in sodium, 1 mark for 8 electrons in chlorine, 1 mark for each correct charge]

c) Cl is 25% ^{37}Cl and 75% ^{35}Cl *[1 mark]*
To find the relative atomic mass of chlorine these abundances need to be taken into account using the calculation:
$A_r = ((37 \times 25) + (35 \times 75)) \div 100 = 35.5$ *[1 mark]*
d) E.g. as you go down group 1 the outer electron gets further from the nucleus *[1 mark]*. This means that the outer electron is more easily lost because it feels less attraction from the nucleus *[1 mark]*. The more readily a metal loses its outer electrons, the more reactive it is, so reactivity increases as you go down group 1/from lithium to sodium to potassium *[1 mark]*.
e) How to grade your answer:
Level 0: There is no relevant information. *[No marks]*
Level 1: A brief attempt is made to explain one or two of these properties in terms of structure and bonding. The points made do not link together. *[1 to 2 marks]*
Level 2: Some explanation of three or four of the properties, in terms of their structure and bonding, is given. The answer has some structure. *[3 to 4 marks]*
Level 3: Clear and detailed explanation of five or all of the properties, in terms of their structure and bonding, is given. The answer is well structured. *[5 to 6 marks]*
Here are some points your answer may include:
Diamond
Each carbon atom in diamond forms four covalent bonds in a rigid giant covalent/lattice structure, making it very hard.
Because it is made up of lots of covalent bonds, which take a lot of energy to break, diamond has a very high melting point.
There are no free electrons or ions in the structure of diamond, so it can't conduct electricity.
Graphite
Each carbon atom in graphite forms three covalent bonds, creating sheets of carbon atoms that can slide over each other. The carbon layers are only held together weakly, which is what makes graphite soft and slippery.
The covalent bonds between the carbon atoms take a lot of energy to break, giving graphite a very high melting point.
Only three out of each carbon's four outer electrons are used in bonds, so graphite has lots of free/delocalised electrons and can conduct electricity.

10 a) E.g. PVC is more flexible than glass, so wires that are coated in it can bend more easily *[1 mark]*. PVC is lighter/has a lower density than glass, so it won't weigh down the wires as much *[1 mark]*.
b) B *[1 mark]*
c) How to grade your answer:
Level 0: There is no relevant information. *[No marks]*
Level 1: A sensible material has been chosen. An attempt has been made to justify the choice by referring to one of the properties in the table. The points made do not link together. *[1 to 2 marks]*
Level 2: A sensible material has been chosen, and there is a good justification of the choice that refers to two or three of the properties shown in the table. The answer has some structure. *[3 to 4 marks]*
Level 3: A sensible material has been chosen, and there is a clear and detailed justification of the choice that refers to all four of the properties given in the table. The answer is well structured. *[5 to 6 marks]*
Here are some points your answer may include:
The golf club shaft needs to be strong to withstand forces applied when the ball is hit.
Carbon fibre and steel have the greatest strength (4100 MPa and 780 MPa, respectively). Neither iron (200 MPa) or lead (12 MPa) would be strong enough.
The shaft needs to be as lightweight as possible, since the club will be both carried around and lifted into the air. Carbon fibre has the lowest density of all the materials (1.5 g cm^{-3}), so would make the lightest club. Stainless steel and iron are both denser than carbon fibre, but with a density of 7.8 g cm^{-3} they would make lighter clubs than lead.
The club will be used outdoors in all weather, so it should be corrosion resistant.
Carbon fibre, stainless steel and lead are all corrosion resistant, but iron is not, so would not be suitable.
The cost of carbon fibre is very high. Any of the other materials shown would be cheaper.
E.g. though carbon fibre is expensive, because the golf club is a professional golf club, the cost of the club can be high, so carbon fibre would be the best choice.

Make sure that you remember to say what you think is the best choice of material in questions like this. It would have been OK to pick stainless steel here too (as long as you justified your choice clearly), because it would still be a suitable material. It wouldn't be OK to pick lead or iron because they are unsuitable (neither of them is strong enough, iron is not corrosion resistant and lead is very dense).

Answers

Index

Index